COLD CASE KENNEDY

FLIP DE MEY

COLD CASE
KENNEDY

LANNOO

For Martine, my dear wife,
who made this book possible
with her dedication, humor and unconditional support.

The very word 'secrecy' is repugnant in a free and open society; and we are as
a people inherently and historically opposed to secret societies, to secret oaths
and to secret proceedings. We decided long ago that the dangers of excessive and
unwarranted concealment of pertinent facts far outweighed the dangers which
are cited to justify it.

President John F. Kennedy
Address before the American Newspaper Publishers Association (April 27, 1961)

TABLE OF CONTENTS

INTRODUCTION

US President John Fitzgerald Kennedy was assassinated in Dallas, Texas on Friday November 22, 1963. Thousands of books have since been published on the case. Fifty years later however, the core questions still remain unanswered: was it really Lee Harvey Oswald who assassinated the president, and did he act alone? What really happened on November 22? There is no simple, watertight answer. In 2007, after 21 years of study, Vincente Bugliosi undertook the most ambitious attempt to write the definitive book on the assassination. His *Reclaiming History* became a monster with more than 1,600 pages. Strangely enough, the enormous effort made by this eminent expert only increased the controversy. In a murder investigation, volume indicates the inherent weakness of the dossier, not its strength. If you need a book the size of the Bible forty years after the facts, something is fundamentally wrong. Could the final answers not be found in the 27 volumes that were produced by the Warren Commission? Or in the much more profound report of the parliamentary inquiry, the *House Select Committee on Assassinations* (HSCA), which re-examined the case fifteen years later?

Initially, however, there was a great deal of certainty. The presidential commission chaired by Earl Warren, the highest magistrate in the country, decreed the official truth in 1964: Oswald was the killer and he acted alone. Any discussion was nipped in the bud. But two totally irreconcilable camps very quickly arose: the *Warren-believers*, who stubbornly stick to the official version, and, diametrically opposite, those who consider the official version as a pure falsification of history and a cover-up operation. From here on, we will refer to them as the *believers* and the *conspiracists* respectively. The believers 'believe' that Oswald acted on his own, and that he killed President Kennedy and police officer Tippit. The conspiracists are willing to believe anything as long as it does *not* agree with the content of the Warren report. Their theories endlessly mutate from one strange tale to another. Bugliosi inventorizes the crop of conspiracy literature into 44 groups and 214 individuals who are said to have been accomplices in the attack, and mentions 82 alleged marksmen by name.* The breed of conspiracists is thereby ineradicable.

The believers have been carrying on this hopeless and unjust fight for fifty years. It is tragicomical that they are so absolutely convinced of being intellectually in the right, but, at the same time, are completely unable to settle their cause once and for all. The believers are, moreover, also losing ground. The figures speak for themselves: of the 68.4 percent of Americans who accepted the decisions of the Warren Commission in 1964, only about 19 percent still believed that Lee Harvey Oswald was the sole perpetrator forty years later.** The reason is obvious: the critics have been crying out for years that the official version is shaky – and it is indeed. As long as the believers are not willing to recognize this simple fact, and are not prepared to meet serious investigators from the conspiracy camp halfway, they will continue to lose ground.

If so much ink has already flowed on the assassination of Kennedy, what is the point of yet another book? *Cold Case Kennedy* places the emphasis on what the whole thing is supposed to be: a murder investigation. The emphasis is on what the evidence says, not on what *believers* or *conspiracists* claim.

In the end, the fragments of truth that we can rescue from the debris after all these years finally fit into a story that was originally consistent and complete. This must be the case, because the fact remains that Kennedy was indeed assassinated in Dallas on November 22, 1963. But how do the pieces fit together? The only certainty that we currently have is the observation that if we keep the strong items in both views, we are faced with a puzzle that is beyond any solution. The official story requires a lot of highly improbable happenings. But chances that Oswald did not do it are even more at odds. The puzzle of the lone madman fits together, but many puzzle pieces that fit nowhere are then left over. And if you pick one of the endless conspiracy puzzles, you are left with even more pieces that don't fit. The Kennedy file resembles a Rorschach test in which everyone recognizes an image of his own. Sometimes it seems more like a Sudoku puzzle with too few numbers.

---

* Bugliosi, 2007, p. 1489.
** Gallup New Service, Nov. 21, 2003, www.gallup.com/poll/9751/americans-kennedy-assassination-conspiracy.aspx.

The best we can do is to sort the mess out again, eliminate everything that is nonsense, think logically, eliminate critically once again and then think logically again. My aspiration is to use this approach to reconstruct the murder investigation step by step as far as is possible. We constantly remain close to the original information: the original witness statements, the concrete facts, the actual documents. We examine the entire file again, not just the pieces that fit into one particular puzzle. We gradually uncover whatever can still be found in terms of truth and facts. We could call such a process 'forensic archeology'. If we work accurately, we may perhaps come to a picture of what really happened on November 22, 1963 that is maybe incomplete, but is reasonably reliable.

A murder investigation looks at every link in the chain of evidence between the victim on the one hand and the suspect(s) on the other. *Cold Case Kennedy* also follows this structure. We look broadly into what happened and into who qualify as suspects. We then examine the bullets and the weapon. Next, we scrutinize the scene of the crime and investigate the injuries of the victims. This will enable us to determine when and from where the shooting took place. Ultimately, we should be able to prove that the accused was indeed at the scene of the murder. Only when this investigation is complete can we provide reasoned answers to the four key questions: did Oswald commit the murder, did he act on his own, would he have been convicted by a court and was there a cover-up operation? There are also several ancillary questions that we should be able to answer during this investigation. We need these answers in order to reach valid conclusions regarding the key questions, and, for this reason, a great deal of attention is also paid to them. This relates to the following questions:

- Did Lee Harvey Oswald know his killer Jack Ruby, who shot him after his arrest in the police station?
- Could one bullet – the so-called *magic bullet* – have caused seven consecutive injuries in two victims? This is the only possible explanation for an attack that does not involve a conspiracy.
- Although the official report only refers to three bullets, Jim Tague, a spectator at Dealey Plaza, was injured by a flying fragment of concrete. Does this mean there was a fourth bullet after all, and does this therefore point towards a conspiracy?
- Could Oswald find himself four floors below the *sniper's nest*, the place from where the shooting took place, only ninety seconds after the assassination without having met any witnesses?

Cold Case Kennedy is not a compilation of existing books about the assassination of Kennedy, but a new investigation of the basic material. I therefore constantly indicate where the evidence and the witness statements can be found. Many of these documents can be consulted online on the website of the Mary Ferrell Foundation (www.maryferrell.org). Most witness testimonies can be found on jfkassassination.net/russ/wit.htm. The reader can always revert to the original source in the course of the investigation. But the file is still extremely complex, and choices must sometimes inevitably be made. It is clear, however, that nothing beats the original material when it comes to establishing one's own opinion.

Finally, my answer to the classic question as to where I was when I heard about the assassination of President Kennedy. Everyone in my immediate environment also experienced the characteristic 'flashlight memory' that was triggered worldwide by the shock. I was seven at the time, almost eight. We had a TV at home, a heavy piece of furniture that stood in our lounge on a small metal table with castors – quite modern for those days. I stood a few feet away from the TV, level with the screen, and mouthed the long, recurring name, quite unfamiliar for a Belgian boy: 'prezident-khennedi'. The series of sounds was almost magical, like Nebuchadnezzar or abracadabra, but was much more realistic because of the picture of the recognizable family, a small girl and a brave little boy. The strange name was repeated so often in those days that it became permanently etched in my database, together with the shock to which all the adults seemed to have fallen prey. For the first time, terrible things that happened far away had consequences in our living room. Just like the first picture of Earthrise on the moon changed our view of Mother Earth forever, the assassination of 'prezidentkhennedi' definitely opened up my little world.

PART 1

INITIAL ORIENTATION

1. CHRONOLOGY OF EVENTS

The people involved

THE PRIME SUSPECT: LEE HARVEY OSWALD

Lee Harvey Oswald was 24 years old in 1963. The skinny, balding young man had a curious background. His father died before he was born, and Oswald's education was therefore subject to the whims of his eccentric and quarrelsome mother Marguerite. The family moved 22 times. As a small boy, Lee attended twelve different schools, and quit his studies altogether at the age of sixteen, without any qualifications. But with an IQ of 119, he was certainly not stupid. One week after his seventeenth birthday, he managed to escape the suffocating family situation by enlisting in the Navy. Thanks to the military, he traveled to California, Japan, Taiwan and the Philippines. That's a pretty broad horizon for a boy who was only nineteen at the time.

Oswald also learned Russian. The circumstances under which this happened have never been clarified. Maybe his outspoken communist sympathies – he himself referred to 'Marxist sympathies' – were the reason he became interested in the language. His fellow recruits scornfully called him *Comrade Oswaldskovich*. But the story of a marine with overt communist sympathies in the middle of the Cold War, who had also learned Russian on his own, caused many eyebrows to be raised after the attack on Kennedy. Oswald even went one step further than simply communist sympathies. In 1959, he took the drastic decision to defect to the Soviet Union. An American who defected to the Russians was, of course, highly unusual, so unusual that even the Russians were not quite sure how to handle it. In the end, Oswald managed to enforce a residence permit with a half-hearted suicide attempt. Things went smoothly after this. He found a job in a lamp factory in Minsk, and, by Soviet standards, was able to lead a life of relative luxury. He also met the young and pretty Marina Prusakova soon after a previous failed romance. The couple married almost immediately, and their first baby, June, was born in the Soviet Union.

But the fitful Oswald was not the kind of person who settles down somewhere. He soon wanted to return to the United States, and this was how the young family ended up in New Orleans in 1962, and later on in Dallas. In March 1963, Oswald purchased an Italian army surplus rifle and a pistol by mail order. That in itself is an everyday occurrence in Louisiana or Texas; more disturbing, however, is that he is suspected of having carried out an attack on the retired, ultra-right general Edwin Walker with that weapon on April 13. From the darkness of the garden, someone took a shot at the general, who was sitting in his lit office. The bullet missed Walker's head by a hair. The case remained unsolved, but it turned out that – precisely on that day – Oswald left Marina a letter with instructions of what to do should he not return, and where the prison was situated.

Meanwhile, Oswald's marriage was on the rocks. He was unpredictable and sometimes violent. Marina was sullen and felt neglected. She loathed the shabby rooms – a pigsty in her eyes – where Oswald had to spray disinfectant to keep the cockroaches away from their bed. Oswald's income was just enough to survive, poised on the edge of poverty. Oswald's political behavior during his New Orleans period was also enigmatic. He stood out as a pro Fidel Castro militant, but, on the other hand, was also seen as a provocateur who opposed Fidel Castro. He appeared on both radio and TV due to his striking views, and even ended up spending a night in jail after a skirmish. For an uneducated 22-year-old laborer, Oswald certainly didn't give the impression that he was stupid in the televised debate. The argument that nobody would have wanted to enter into a conspiracy with him is not as obvious as it is often claimed. In September 1963, Oswald sent Marina to Dallas with baby June. He himself made a strange bus trip to Mexico around that time, where he visited the Cuban embassy to try and obtain a visa for the communist island. Cuba seemed to be the new Promised Land, but, in the end, Oswald had to return to the US empty-handed, with yet another illusion destroyed. He then settled down in Dallas as well, but not under the same roof as Marina.

Marina, who was heavily pregnant at that time with a second daughter, moved in with Ruth Paine, a woman who was also separated from her husband. Ruth Paine was happy to welcome Marina to her sunny and comfortable house in Irving, a suburb of Dallas, and wanted to improve her Russian by inviting Marina to live with her. Marina was in need of rest and welcomed the offer, although it was mainly a calculated move on her part. Her new accommodation was certainly much better than what she had been used to with Lee in Russia and later in the USA. After the assassination of Kennedy, she thanked Ruth for her hospitality by calling her 'not too smart' in front of the gathered public opinion.[1] She also accused Ruth of seeking publicity. As soon as benevolent Americans started sending Marina money,[2] she dropped Ruth like a brick, and the long series of letters from her former benefactress pleading for her friendship all remained unanswered.[3] Ruth Paine never understood what caused such rejection. She assumed that Marina had been taken in by her new surroundings, but Marina was perhaps simply young, capricious and selfish in her need for self-preservation and the preservation of her children.

Oswald was only welcome in Irving at the weekends. During the week, he stayed in Dallas in bare, unadorned rented rooms. His last address in a series of moves, from October 15 onwards, was at Beckley Avenue, 1026, St. Oak Cliff, a room he rented for eight dollars a week under the alias O.H. Lee.[4] The tiny house where the landlady lived with fourteen tenants and the two owners is still there now – as if time had stood still for fifty years. When I rang the bell there in 2012, Patricia Hall opened the door. The sympathetic middle-aged woman turned out to be the granddaughter of the former owner, Gladys Johnson. Mrs. Hall did not at all agree with the stories that describe Oswald's rented room as a 'den'. It was a pleasant room with plenty of light. For the eight dollars Oswald paid, his room was also cleaned twice a week, and linen and towels were provided. It wasn't a luxury hotel, of course, but it was no den.

THE VICTIM: JOHN FITZGERALD KENNEDY

Kennedy was narrowly elected as 35th president of the United States in 1960. It was the dream of his ambitious and immensely rich father Joe Kennedy that his eldest son, Joe Jr., would one day become president, but when he was killed in World War II, it was up to John to take up the gauntlet. John was not really predestined for politics. He was more the *golden boy*, with an abundance of natural charm. He was, moreover, brilliant, well-read, glib, and was always the first to have a *wisecrack* ready. In addition, the young man also possessed a sharp pen, and seemed to have more of a future as a writer or passionate journalist than as a banker or a cynical power politician. But when tragedy struck, John was ready to continue the political family ambitions. He did what could be expected of a politician, such as personally introducing himself to thousands of voters door-to-door, and cashing in on his status as a war hero at tea parties. He was elected to the House of Representatives, pushed on to the prestigious Senate after six years, and married the attractive and stylish Jacqueline Bouvier. He also wasted no opportunity to raise his profile and gain national prominence. Yet, despite this acknowledged track record, he remained somewhat of an outsider in the political establishment. He belonged to one clan only – that of the Kennedys. He didn't lick anybody's boots and didn't stand in line while pursuing his way to the top. Moreover, thanks to the family fortune, he could afford to build up his career without becoming indebted to anyone. His courage, his intelligence and his dislike of hypocrites earned him a host of admirers and supporters who would do anything for him, but there was also much gnashing of teeth. The hyper-competitive Kennedys seemed to delight in making their opponents bite the dust. John Kennedy prospered, except for one aspect: he suffered from poor health. It was not only his war injuries that haunted him, there was far more. At one point, he was so ill that he four times received the last rites. Kennedy passed through the eye of a needle and recovered.

In 1959, his father considered that the time was right to make a bid for the ultimate prize. Joe Kennedy made a few deals that were intended to secure his son's election, but it was by no means certain that he would win. John's opponent was the ambitious Republican Nixon, the young vice-president of incumbent president, Dwight Eisenhower. The very first televised debate ever between the two presidential candidates played a major role in the final election result. Nixon was ill that day, and his poor make-up gave him a real mugshot appearance on the black-and-white TV screen. The bright lighting also made him sweat profusely. With his tanned complexion, Kennedy came across on the television as very relaxed and friendly. The final difference in the vote was so small that a different outcome in the televised debate could also have changed the election result[5]. But John F. Kennedy made it in the end, and all those who had made deals with his father rubbed their hands. A narrow election victory was ideal for those who helped, because each helper could boast that it was precisely his support that brought Kennedy into the *Oval Office*.

As a 43-year-old, Kennedy was the youngest elected president ever, and the first to have been born in the twentieth century. He had never tasted executive power as a governor or as a member of cabinet, and had to learn the tricks of the trade by doing. This resulted in several nasty slips. He lost face in front of the Russian President Khrushchev, and the Bay of Pigs Operation in Cuba turned into an unmitigated nightmare. Even though this attempt to overturn the Castro regime was a legacy of the Eisenhower administration, the new president bravely took the responsibility himself. It would not happen to him again. He gradually found his own style and approach. Those who had thought they would be able to control the incorrigible playboy had to think again. Step by step, a progressive agenda appeared: an agenda that paid attention to civil rights, that aimed at a more open society and at more direct contact via the media. Everything breathed change, progress, increased well-being and justice. With his elegant and attractive wife Jacky and their two young children, Kennedy offered Americans something they had perhaps secretly dreamed of: their own, glamorous 'royal family'.

The campaign for the 1964 elections was to be launched in the fall of 1963. Kennedy was very worried about Texas. In those days, the state of Texas was still a real 'swing state', where a presidential candidate could never really win a clear majority. Vice-presidential candidate Lyndon Johnson had still had Texas in his grasp in 1960, and the Democrats had won by a narrow margin. But Johnson's political power was waning – he was in a tight spot due to legal issues relating to a series of fraud scandals – and Kennedy's proactive approach with regard to the civil rights issue had not exactly endeared him to the southern states. Something had to be done about Texas. Governor John Connally, who had previously been part of Kennedy's administration as Secretary of the Navy, was now the man in charge there. The local elite also had 'deep pockets' and Kennedy certainly wanted to visit Dallas in order to build up his campaign funds. Kennedy and Connally set the dates of November 21, 22 and 23 for the trip to Texas. It was symptomatic of Johnson's waning power that he was not even involved in the discussions regarding the campaign in Texas. For the first time in years, and for the first time after she had lost a baby, Jackie also came along. Kennedy was well aware of the huge political value of his wife, and was thrilled about her decision to join in the full campaign. One could never be sure about Texas, but all seemed to be starting well for the trip scheduled for late November.

The events

In October, Oswald received a tip about a job opening at the *Texas School Book Depository*[6] (TSBD) from the brother of a neighbor of Mrs. Paine. It was a cushy job that earned him barely 1.25 dollar an hour, but Oswald could live with it. His application form is dated October 15, 1963.[7] Roy Truly, the superintendent of the book depository, considered Oswald a decent man, and gave him the open position. He could start immediately, the day after his application. This commonplace decision would soon become part of global history. On November 22, 1963, Oswald had therefore been working at the TSBD for about five weeks. There is no criminal link whatsoever between the recruitment and the subsequent attack. On October 15, nobody could predict the route the president would take during his visit to Dallas in late November.

Every Friday night, Oswald was given a lift to the town of Irving by Wesley Frazier, a workmate, so that he could spent his weekend with his wife and children. He phoned his wife twice a day during the week. Despite his poor record as a husband, he was unhappy with the separation and the arrangements. There is no doubt that, as a father, he tried the best he could in his own way. During the weekend of November 16 and 17, the weekend prior to the attack, however, Marina did not want to see her husband. After yet another quarrel by phone, she had crashed the handset down onto the hook.

On Thursday, November 21, the day before the assassination, Oswald arrived in Irving completely unannounced during mid-week. Marina was moody and refused to say a word to Lee, who did his best to soften her up, looking after the new baby and playing with June in the garden. Oswald wanted to reunite his family in an apartment in Dallas, but the stubborn Marina rejected him.[8] She argued that she wanted a washing machine, but when Oswald offered to buy her one, she refused his offer and said she could take care of herself. The rest of the evening, the couple watched television in silence. Lee went to bed at 9 p.m. He was up early on Friday, November 22. Ruth Paine shook her head afterwards when she found he had once again forgotten to switch off the light in the garage. Oswald's Italian rifle, the old Mannlicher Carcano, was allegedly stored in this garage, wrapped in a blanket. When Oswald joined his workmate Frazier in the car, he had an elongated package wrapped in brown paper with him. When asked what the package contained, Oswald replied: 'curtain rods.'

After an initial light rain shower, the weather was unexpectedly clear and pleasant on November 22. Everything went according to plan in Forth Worth, the first stop on the campaign trip. On Friday morning, Air Force One, the majestic plane with the presidential seal, landed at Love Field, an airport just outside Dallas. After a 15 kilometer drive to downtown Dallas, the President was to attend a lunch with 2,500 guests at the Trade Mart.

John Kennedy was sitting in the back of a specially converted Ford Lincoln open limousine, on the right-hand side. The President wore a linen corset to keep the pain of a war injury to his lower back under control. Because of the good weather, the 'bubbletop', the transparent hood of the limo, was removed and the President was driven through downtown Dallas in an open car. The motorcycle police officers who were escorting the limousine were instructed to keep driving behind the car, no matter what happened.[9] Kennedy considered it very important to maximize his visibility for the public. According to Mrs. Connally, he asked Jacqueline to take off her sunglasses up to three times during the trip, so that people would be able to see her properly. Governor John Connally sat in front of Kennedy, on a jump seat, slightly lower and a little more to the center of the limousine. Their respective spouses sat to the left of the two men. *Secret Service* agent William Greer, who had the longest service record, was given the honor of driving the car. Secret agents are basically trained to remain focused at all times. If necessary, they must form a living shield to protect the president. But seven of the officers on duty that day had been out on the town the night before, and had been drinking heavily in *The Cellar Door*.[10] They had joked about the safety of the president now being solely in the hands of the Dallas' fire department.[11] Paul Landis was even said to have still been hanging about at *The Cellar Door* at 5 a.m.[12] It is not known whether William Greer was among the night revelers, and it is also not sure whether this behavior could truly be considered as a breach of duty. Clint Hill, the agent responsible for Jackie, had a reasonable explanation for the nocturnal escapade: the Kennedys had only arrived in their suite after midnight, and the Secret Service agents hadn't had a chance to eat all day. When it turned out that the hotel kitchen had already closed, they had ended up in the bar in search of a quick bite to eat. They were out of luck there as well, and had to fill their stomachs with cocktail nuts. The late hour was simply the inevitable result of the overloaded agenda of the previous day.[13] But whether due to an overloaded agenda, poor organization or neglect of duty, the security staff had had too short a night in any case.

For now, however, everything was running according to plan. The reception in Dallas was enthusiastic. In several places, the waving spectators along the road stood many rows deep. The president halted the motorcade several times. He greeted children who were holding a sign saying 'Please stop, Mr. President', and, a little later, he also stopped near a group of nuns. This caused the presidential procession to be slightly behind schedule.

DEALEY PLAZA

The motorcade approached Dealey Plaza at 12:29. They should, in fact, have already been at the Trade Mart at that time, where the organist was practicing *Hail to the Chief* one more time. Dealey Plaza is a funnel-shaped square: Houston Street forms the top of the funnel, and the funnel neck is a railway bridge. Three avenues pass underneath this railway bridge (Figure 1). Main Street is situated in the center, with Elm Street on the left and Commerce Street on the right: three major, broad avenues in downtown Dallas. Because the three avenues pass underneath the railway bridge in the shape of a funnel, the bridge is known as the *Triple Underpass*. The TSBD, a six-storey, robust, tatty, red-brick building, is situated on the corner of Elm and Houston Street.

Figure 1 - Dealey Plaza is a funnel-shaped square. Three avenues pass underneath the railway bridge in the shape of a funnel, the bridge is known as the Triple Underpass.

Oswald was last seen by his colleagues in the TSBD in the lunchroom on the first floor between 11:45 and 12:00. A little later, colored worker Bonnie Ray Williams was eating his lunch on the sixth floor. Around 12:20, he went looking for his friends, who were one floor lower. The meanwhile infamous 6th floor had more the gloomy appearance of a giant lumber room rather than an efficient book depository. This is the reason why the barricade of book boxes that shielded the window in the northeastern corner from view was not noticed at all. Williams didn't see or hear anyone on the sixth floor.

The weather was excellent. Tailor Abraham Zapruder decided to try out his new movie camera to film the passage of the president. He took up a position on a concrete platform that was part of a decorative colonnade, about halfway along Elm Street. It was the ideal spot: Zapruder would have the president perfectly in the picture from the bend onwards. The limousine finally appeared around the corner of Main Street at 12:29. Once on Dealey Plaza, the car drove in northwestern direction up to the end of Houston Street. There it had to take a 120 degree turn, driving past the TSBD, continuing slightly downhill along Elm Street and finally driving in the direction of the Triple Underpass.

THE ATTACK

Zapruder's Bell & Howell camera was continually focused on Elm Street during the fatal seconds. Because the whole sequence was captured on this amateur film, the frames were used throughout the investigation as a universal Dealey Plaza timeline. Moments in time are referred to as 'Z' for Zapruder, supplemented with the number of the corresponding frame. 18.3 frames passed by Zapruder's camera lens every second. At the latest around Zapruder frame Z-220, when the president, as seen from Zapruder's position, was hidden behind the Stemmons Freeway sign, the limousine suddenly came under fire. Kennedy was thereby severely injured by at least one bullet, to the left of his right shoulder blade. According to the official version, the bullet left his body through an exit wound at the level of the knot in his tie. Governor Connally, in the jump seat in front of Kennedy, was also seriously injured. The doctors in the Parkland Hospital later counted five bullet wounds on him.

As soon as he heard the first shot, Marion Baker, a motorcycle officer of the *Dallas Police Corps*, immediately raced towards the TSBD, because he saw pigeons flying off the roof of the building. Driver William Greer was less alert, and hesitated endless seconds after his passengers had been seriously injured. He even looked back twice. There was another shot, and the head of the president exploded. Blood, brains and human tissue scattered about the car. Jacqueline Kennedy climbed onto the trunk to recover a piece of her husband's skull. Secret agent Hill had to push her back into the limousine, and clung to the handles of the trunk cover. Only then, around Z381,[14] 3.7 seconds after the fatal shot, did Greer finally give full throttle for a wild drive to Parkland Hospital.

Vickie Adams, a young office clerk, worked at the TSBD on the fourth floor. She was standing by the window when the president drove by, and walked down the stairs with her friend immediately after the limousine disappeared under the railway bridge.[15] She did not see or hear Oswald on the staircase.

Meanwhile, motorcycle officer Baker had parked his Harley and met Roy Truly, the superintendent of the book depository at the entrance of the TSBD. Baker wanted to get to the flat roof as quickly as possible because he suspected that the sniper (or snipers) was situated there. This brave, one-man action was an admirable move on his part. Viewed rationally, there was a reasonable chance that he would not have survived a direct confrontation with the presidential assassin(s). Because the elevator on the first floor did not seem to be available, Baker and Truly rushed up the stairs after some delay. They heard or saw nobody on the staircase, but the officer saw somebody move on the second floor through a window in a door. He entered the room with his gun drawn. The man he met responded in a calm and collected manner. Truly confirmed that he was an employee, a certain Oswald. In itself, this was not enough to exclude Oswald as a suspect. But due to his calm demeanor and his location seconds after the shooting – far away from the roof – Baker and Truly decided that Oswald was not the man they were looking for. They continued up the stairs, only to establish that there was no sniper, and that a shot from the roof was virtually impossible because of the broad eaves.

The general reaction from the spectators in the square also points towards the fact that the shots originated from a direction other than the TSBD. Everyone ran towards a small sloping hill with some greenery in the vicinity of the pergola, where Zapruder was also situated. From then onwards, this grassy hill and the wooden fence behind it would become known as the *Grassy Knoll* and the *Picket Fence*. The spectators and police officers who ran to the knoll found nothing special, and saw no suspicious persons.

At 12:33, Gordon Shankley, Head of the Dallas FBI, called his boss J. Edgar Hoover to report that President Kennedy had been the victim of an attack. Hoover immediately informed Robert Kennedy, brother of the president and Attorney General, at 12:35 with the words 'The president has been shot, I think it's serious' and put down the phone without further ceremony.[16]

Oswald left the TSBD at 12:33, three minutes after the assassination and, outwardly calm, walked for approximately seven minutes[17] east along Elm Street before boarding a bus in the opposite direction at the intersection with Murphy Street[18]. This means that, in fact, he returned towards Dealey Plaza. Moreover, if he had intended to return to his rented room he also took the wrong bus, as he boarded a bus in the direction of Marsalis Street, instead of a bus to Beckley Street.

The police did not seal off the School Book Depository to any extent until 12:40, but then also allowed normal traffic onto Dealey Plaza again almost immediately. Cars, trucks and buses were driving across the evidence of the assassination. Meanwhile, Oswald's bus became stuck in the traffic jams caused by the event. He got off the bus[19] at 12:44, after first asking the driver for a transfer ticket – which, at the very least, is a strange reaction for an assassin on the run. He then took a taxi, which he first offered to give up to a middle-aged lady.[20] She refused the offer, and Oswald then drove in the direction of 1026 North Beckley Street, his boarding house.

James Tague, a spectator who had been standing near the central tunnel of the railway bridge, told a police officer that he had seen something splash up near the place where he was standing. The officer pointed out to him that his chin was bleeding. Damage to a concrete curb was indeed found at the place Tague indicated, and a concrete shard had probably hit Tague. Journalists noted this information. Brennan, another spectator who had been sitting on a wall directly in front of the school book depository during the attack, reported to a police officer that he had seen the shooter. He said that he had seen the barrel of a rifle protruding from the window, referring to the corner window on the sixth floor. It is not quite clear how the police handled this information, because the *sniper's nest* was only found three quarters of an hour later.

At 12:45[21], the police radio broadcast the following, very vague description of the suspect: 'white male, approximately 30, slender built, height five feet ten inches, weight 165 pounds'. Oswald was 5 foot 9 tall, but, according to his death certificate, his weight was 140 pounds[22], an important difference of 25 pounds. He was also only 24 years old, quite a bit younger, but his balding head made him look somewhat older. The clothing of the wanted man was not mentioned in the APB, and this made it so hopelessly vague that thousands of men in Dallas met the description.

In the meantime, Oswald let the taxi driver drive more than 500 yards past the address of his rented room, to No. 500, Beckley Street. This seems to be a very large safety margin if he wanted to make sure there were no police at his door. It was a short trip of just under three miles, but the taxi had to drive past the traffic chaos at Dealey Plaza[23], so we can assume that the trip took a few minutes longer. The meter stood at 95 cents.[24] According to the driver, Oswald headed south after he left the taxi, even further away from his rented room. In view of the fact that, after having turned back again, Oswald had to walk at least 500 yards in the opposite direction, he couldn't have arrived at his boarding house before 13:00 at the earliest. Walking all the way back took at least as much time as the taxi ride itself. Oswald clearly seemed to have literally lost his bearings. Mrs. Earlene Roberts, Oswald's obese and half-blind landlady, saw her tenant, who she knew under the name of O.H. Lee, enter the house around 13:00, gruff and in a hurry. In his room, Oswald changed his clothes[25] and put his loaded pistol in his pocket. He was in an unusual hurry, according to his landlady. Oswald is said to have left the premises at 13:04, or at least about four minutes after he had come in. Mrs. Roberts was not quite sure about the exact time, because she was busy with her poor television picture. She wanted to hear more news about the attack on the President. The landlady was sure, however, that a police car had driven past and given a short, double horn signal in the short period that Oswald was in the house. But the house with number 1026 is located in the immediate vicinity of a traffic light, and, according to Mrs. Hall, the granddaughter of the then proprietor, it was quite possible that, by blowing its horn, the police car was only urging a dawdling driver to drive on after the lights had turned green. This is a logical and acceptable explanation for a detail around which conspiracists love to weave an entire plot. Landlady Roberts then saw Oswald waiting for a while at a bus stop to the right of the house and on the same side of the street. Perhaps the ever-stingy Oswald hoped to be able to use his transfer ticket. But the bus that he was waiting for would again have taken him in the opposite direction, in the direction of Dealey Plaza. No bus showed up, and, in the end, Oswald walked away, once again in the other direction.[26] His behavior clearly did not point towards a specific plan or a concrete appointment. And what should we think of a person who hurriedly changes his clothes in the middle of the day, pockets a gun, and then leaves without knowing whether to turn left or right? Was Oswald, like everyone else, just surprised and shocked by the assassination he had nothing to do with? But why did he then feel the need to change his clothes as quickly as possible and to arm himself? Why did he not stay at the TSBD, like other direct witnesses? Why, like so many others, did he not phone up people he knew to talk about the shocking events he had witnessed? Why did he not eagerly wait to hear more news, like everybody else? Oswald took so little interest in the televised news about the president that he preferred to wait around aimlessly at a bus stop.

PARKLAND HOSPITAL

Kennedy was rushed to the nearest hospital, the Parkland Hospital. At 12:52[27], the doctors in *Trauma Room* 1 determined that the president no longer had a pulse, and made a final desperate attempt with cardiac massage. Eventually, Dr. Clark told his colleague Perry that it was too late, and Perry stopped the cardiac compressions. Dr. Clark placed a sheet over the president's face and addressed the wife of the president: 'Your husband has sustained a fatal wound.' 'I know', the brave widow replied.[28] At 12:58, Father Huber arrived on the spot to administer the last rites. At 13:00, the medical confirmation of what everyone who had seen the injured president already knew followed: the 35th President of the United States of America was dead. The reason why the official time of death was determined as 13:00[29] had to do with the fact that the administering of the Roman Catholic last rites for the forgiveness of sins is only carried out if the recipient of the sacrament is alive, and is therefore able to sincerely repent. Father Huber was the first to confirm the death of the president to the outside world when he left the hospital.

OSWALD'S WANDERINGS

At the bus stop at 13:05, Oswald was still a good distance away from the spot where police officer Tippit would be murdered. Using Google Maps, we can visualize the scene as follows (Figure 2):

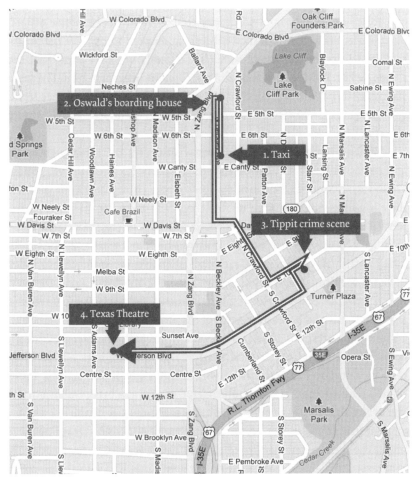

Figure 2 – The route from Oswald's boarding house to the place where police officer Tippit was murdered and from there to the Texas Theatre. Could Oswald have been at the place where Tippit was killed before 13:15?

The distance from his rented room to East Tenth Street 410, where the patrol car of police officer Tippit was situated, was 0.88 *miles*. Witnesses saw the police officer speaking to this killer-to-be through the open window on the passenger side of the car. When Tippit stepped out of the car, the man killed him mercilessly with four gunshots. Tippit's service weapon was later found underneath his body. He had presumably opened his holster and reached for his gun while getting out of the car. The killer removed the empty shells from his gun during his flight and threw them away.

When the coast seemed clear again, witnesses appeared from several places. T.F. Bowley did not witness the murder himself. He was driving into the street and saw the stationary police car and the police officer lying on the ground beside it. His primary concern was for the police officer. Meanwhile, Benavides, another witness, attempted to operate the police radio to report the murder of the police officer, but didn't know how the radio worked. Bowley then took the microphone over from him. The message reporting the murder of officer Tippit was received at the police headquarters at 13:16.[30] Bowley had then been on the spot for at least one minute already.

If Bowley arrived at 13:15, and several witnesses had already gathered at the spot by that time, the killing must have occurred at the very latest around 13:14. Since the killer had a conversation with the officer through the car window beforehand, he must logically have already been on the scene of the crime at 13:13. Oswald could only have left the bus stop at 13:04 or 13:05. If he was the perpetrator, and we give him 8.5 minutes, he would have covered the distance of 1,440 yards at an average speed of 5.10 miles an hour. Moreover, he would have walked back and forth along the way, which seems consistent with all his movements since the attack. Oswald is also said to have urinated at the side of the road.[31] If he thereby lost one and a half minutes, and his conversation with Tippit took a further 30 seconds, he must have been walking at a speed of 7.90 miles an hour already. It is clear that covering this distance in 8.5 minutes is very fast indeed. I personally covered the distance in fourteen minutes at a brisk walking pace. You need to run to score anything below eleven minutes, or above 4.6 miles an hour over this distance. Not a single witness saw Oswald running by. If he left the scene where he allegedly killed Tippit at 13.13, he then suddenly progressed at a snail's pace. Oswald apparently took 22 minutes to cover the shorter distance of 960 yards to the *Texas Theatre*. This represents a speed of 1.9 miles an hour.

DISCOVERY OF THE SNIPER'S NEST

Meanwhile, after searching the floors above and below, the police were finally concentrating on the sixth floor of the TSBD. At 13.15, in the southeast corner, they found a barricade constructed with cardboard boxes approximately 1.5 feet from the windows on the street side: the *Sniper's Nest*. Soon afterwards, they also found a rifle, hidden among stacks of boxes filled with books. The Head of the Homicide and Robbery Bureau, Captain Fritz, opened the magazine, and an unused bullet fell from the rifle. The shooter had apparently reloaded the rifle after the last shot.

Oswald's trail re-emerged in the vicinity of an old cinema, the *Texas Theatre*, on Jefferson Boulevard. Johnny Calvin Brewer, manager of a shoe store, observed Oswald hiding in a doorway with his back turned to a passing police car at 13:35. Brewer followed Oswald and observed how he entered the *Texas Theatre* without paying. He informed the lady at the counter who, in turn, alerted the police at 13:45. The police, who had raided a library nearby just before,[32] arrived at the *Texas Theatre* quickly and with great show of power. Oswald was arrested ten minutes later. He resisted, tried to pull his gun and received several blows. He finally surrendered, shouting that 'it was all over now'. One of the police officers snapped 'Kill the president, ya!', even though the arrest officially had nothing to do with the assassination of the president. The police failed to record the identity of the other people present in the cinema.

At the time of his arrest, Oswald was wearing a rust-brown shirt, without a jacket. A jacket was later found in a parking lot.[33] Conspiracists quibble and carp about the color, but Oswald had been wearing a jacket when he left Beckley Street, and arrived at the *Texas Theatre* without one. A hidden jacket was found on the route between these two points. That was evidence enough. When witnesses mention different colors of Oswald's clothing, this does not point to a mysterious doppelganger. It is enough to be aware of the fact that witnesses often make mistakes when it comes to details they believe to have seen in a brief moment and while under emotional stress.

Oswald was led into the police station at 14:15, and was interrogated practically non-stop from then onwards. He arrogantly denied any involvement in the attack at Dealey Plaza and the murder of Officer Tippit. His interrogation took place without the assistance of a lawyer and without a police record being made. The Dallas police didn't even possess a tape recorder. Between interrogations, Oswald was submitted to a number of haphazardly organized identification lineups. At 20:55, the police conducted a paraffin test on his hands and his right cheek, to determine any presence of gunpowder residues. The test was positive for his hands, but negative for his cheek, which could indicate that he had fired a pistol, but not a rifle. The test was relatively unreliable. The traces of nitrate on his hands, for example, could also have originated from urine.

BACK TO WASHINGTON

Using military force, the Secret Service left the Parkland Hospital at 14:04, with the body of the president in a heavy bronze casket. By law, a murder committed in Texas is a matter for the jurisdiction of the State of Texas, even if it involves the president. The medical examiner therefore insisted that the autopsy should take place in Texas, but the Secret Service agents roughly brushed him aside. One of them indifferently accepted a bullet that a hospital worker had found somewhere on a gurney.

On board the presidential plane, Vice President Lyndon Johnson took the oath as 36th President of the United States of America at 14:38. This was a purely symbolic act, because Johnson had already taken the oath at the inauguration, and had only been a 'heartbeat away' from the presidency since then. But the oath was an important signal to the outside world: there was still a president, still continuity, and law and order. Upon his arrival in Washington, the new president charged his neighbor and old friend J. Edgar Hoover and the FBI with the full further investigation. At 15:01 (Dallas time; it was then 16:01 in Washington), FBI Director Hoover wrote in a memorandum that he believed the perpetrator had been captured. One hour and forty-five minutes after Oswald's arrival at the police station, Hoover had already concluded the case!

THE ZAPRUDER FILM

Abraham Zapruder, in the meantime, had his unique film developed by Kodak. The presence of mind of the little tailor would be one of the few windfalls in the search for the truth. He didn't move a yard away from his film while it was being developed. He then immediately had three copies made at another address, the Jamieson Film Company. Here also, he never lost sight of the film for one second. He even demanded that the Kodak production supervisor and the owner of Jamieson sign a written statement that there were no more than three copies.[34]

Although he was clearly shocked by what he had captured on his camera, Zapruder nevertheless seemed well aware of the great value of his footage. Now that fate was (financially) on his side, he didn't rush decisions and he regularly phoned his son, who was an attorney, for legal advice. But he was also a man of principle, who would only surrender the film under certain conditions. He wanted to absolutely avoid inappropriate sensational use of the images, even if this would cost him money. He was still thinking about this on Friday night. He provisionally declined all offers and deposited the film in his safe in the meantime. This sensible man had, however, first let the world know about his prized possession via the television. The Zapruder film could no longer be removed from the assassination investigation.

On Saturday morning, Time Life Inc. became the happy owner of the film for the price of 150,000 dollars – this would be equivalent to more than one million dollars today. Very soon afterwards, *Life* magazine published some spectacular photographs on the basis of the still frames from the film. But no one outside the FBI got to see the footage itself. New Orleans District Attorney Garrison was able to subpoena the film in 1969 as evidence in his case against businessman Clay Shaw. But the general public was only able to see the terrible images for the first time in 1975, during the *ABC Late Night Show* with Geraldo Rivera. That screening led to a dispute between *Life* and the Zapruder family, after which *Life* returned the film to Zapruder's heirs for 1 dollar. The final agreement to definitely regulate the film rights cost the American state more than 16 million dollars in 2009. In 2013, the 8.5 relevant seconds of amateur film had earned approximately 2 million dollars per second.

The investigation

A POOR START

The autopsy started in the Bethesda Naval Hospital near Washington at 21:15 (Dallas time, 20:15 EST). The body of the victim normally provides the 'best evidence', but they managed to make a mess of it in Washington. In the end, the autopsy would raise more questions than it answered.

The Dallas police had meanwhile deemed it useful to talk to the journalists during a midnight press conference. Oswald also had to be placed in the spotlight. When a reporter asked whether Oswald was a member of the *Free Cuba Committee*, a balding, middle-aged man corrected him. 'That's the *Fair Play for Cuba Committee!*' the man shouted out to the public. He was not a journalist, but Jack Ruby or Rubinstein, the owner of a striptease bar. Around midnight, the Dallas police had to transfer all the evidence to the FBI. They did so reluctantly and, either consciously or subconsciously, forgot to include several crucial items. From then on, November 22, 1963 would be definitely included in the history books.

On Sunday, November 24, at 11 a.m., nightclub operator Jack Ruby shot the only suspect in the assassination case, Lee Harvey Oswald, while the authorities were preparing to transfer him to prison. The murder in the basement of the police headquarters was broadcast live on television, *coast to coast*. The omens at the start of the investigation were anything but good.

THREE INVESTIGATION COMMISSIONS

Warren Commission

On November 29, President Johnson established a commission that would be chaired by Earl Warren, Chief Justice of the Supreme Court, together with a number of politicians without specific police or forensic experience. The notable commission members, who all already had their own busy personal agendas, were told that their task was mainly to confirm the FBI reports. In September 1964, just in time for the upcoming presidential elections, the commission presented its voluminous report of 296,000 words to the president. Later, another 26 volumes, totaling 17,000 pages with annexes, were to follow. Chairman Warren was not in favor of also making these annexes public. He believed this was superfluous. Nobody would really read the report, and the word of the FBI and the presidential commission would sufficiently reassure the public. These predictions did not come true. Vigilant citizens started digging into the evidence, and found flagrant contradictions and gaps in the dossier. The controversy was born, never to cease.

House Select Committee on Assassinations (HSCA)

In 1978, under the pressure of the public opinion, the House of Representatives set up a new commission. This *House Select Committee on Assassinations* (HSCA) was not only to re-investigate the assassination of President Kennedy, but also the assassination of his brother Robert Kennedy and the Reverend Martin Luther King. The HSCA went through the Warren homework again. The parliamentary inquiry was thorough, appointed competent experts and spent nearly six million dollars (current value[35] approximately 20 million dollars) on the investigations, but even then the bickering did not end.

Assassinations Records Review Board (ARRB)

After the release of the controversial film *JFK* by Oliver Stone in 1991, the authorities finally relented to the pressure to release the as yet undisclosed parts of the dossier. Because state interests and national security could be jeopardized, yet another new commission, the *Assassination Records Review Board* (ARRB), would review the tons of evidence that had been declared top secret. The ARRB was to make as much material public as possible, in dribs and drabs. Wherever necessary, thick, black stripes were used to cross out the passages that could constitute a state hazard. In this way, the dossier was slowly released for the public. New contradictions with the documents that were already known fanned the flames of the conspiracists even more. The believers, on the other hand, pointed out with increasing zeal that, despite the release of thousands of pages of new material, not a single hard piece of evidence for a conspiracy had emerged.

On the fiftieth anniversary of the attack, the debate is still as fierce as on November 22, 1963, and it does not look like it will finish soon.

2. INHERENT FLAWS IN THE ORIGINAL INVESTIGATION

If the offense occurs in the pouring rain, the evidence will be wet. Any evidence that is washed away by the rain will never be found. This does not point towards a sinister plot, but to the occurrence of a downpour. The circumstances under which a murder investigation starts off are often decisive for its overall further progress. The Kennedy investigation is no exception to this. The only difference is that the circumstances in this case were very special due to the unique and exceptional nature of the assassination of a head of state. Moreover, a wide range of exceptional elements had an impact on the investigation:

- Very premature conclusions, up to the top layers of the hierarchy;
- The general confusion that had everyone in its grip;
- The presence of Attorney General Robert Kennedy, brother of the assassinated president, in the administration;
- The absence of a unified action and command hierarchy in the investigation;
- The murder of the sole suspect;
- The political power shifts caused by the assassination;
- The bureaucratic cover-up operation;
- FBI Director J. Edgar Hoover;
- The geopolitical context of the assassination in the middle of the Cold War.

Many of the issues in the Kennedy dossier are associated with this exceptional situation at the start of the investigation, and a number of subsequent problems also find their origin there.

Very premature conclusions

As soon as the initial data is known, every murder investigation develops a working hypothesis. This is an efficient approach: it helps to establish an initial idea of how the murder could have been carried out. This, in turn, helps to give direction to the investigation. The working hypothesis in the assassination of John Kennedy was: *Oswald did it.* A series of factors supported this working hypothesis. Oswald had been arrested. His workplace was the place from where the President had presumably been shot. He had ordered the weapon that was found there and had it delivered to his mailbox. He allegedly had shot Officer Tippit because he was on the run from the police. He also had an excellent background for a suspect: he was a truant and had left school without qualification, was a jack-of-all-trades and master of none, was a Soviet defector, a down-and-outer, a failed and violent husband, a Castro provocateur... He had to be the killer. The second assumption was: *He did it alone.* He acted on his own. This assumption also made sense. Oswald certainly did not appear to be the prototype of a gangster on the payroll of organized crime, or of a secret agent of the CIA or the military – and even less that of a professional assassin.

The hypothesis that Oswald was 'a lone nut' quickly found supporters. A great many people convinced themselves that this was what must have happened. Random coincidence and nobody's fault. It seems highly unlikely that Oswald could eliminate the most powerful man on Earth with a dilapidated piece of old iron all by himself, but, if you think about it, the assumption is less crazy than it sounds. The chance of a meteorite falling on your head is also minute, but if you are lying dead in your garden with a boulder in your skull, then the chances that you have been hit by a meteorite are suddenly quite high. On November 21, 1963, the day before the assassination, the probability that the President would be shot by a nobody was very small. But on November 23, a day after the attack, the probability calculation had completely changed. For Oswald, nothing was going his way, and then, suddenly, JFK drove by completely unprotected. John Kennedy was his complete antithesis, a man who seemed to be successful in everything he undertook. The presidential limousine drove downhill past Oswald's workplace and perfectly parallel with the barrel of an aimed gun. The direction it was driving and the slight slope just about allowed for three shots with barely any time to aim. *Bang, bang, bang* – the highly improbable event had occurred after all. And, as the icing on the cake, it was nobody's fault. President Kennedy himself had assured his security guards that nobody would be able to prevent an attack by a madman wielding a gun, and then he had smiled his reassuring, irresistible smile.

Soon after the handcuffed Oswald had been brought into the police headquarters and the initial information became known, the consensus began to grow: the perpetrator was *a lone nut*. This view provided a quick solution to which all the bodies concerned could immediately and definitively subscribe. As soon as Oswald had been arrested, the top police officer in the nation, FBI Director J. Edgar Hoover, dictated a memo that the perpetrator had been caught[36]. As early as the afternoon of the assassination, Hoover simply rejected applications from his agents to investigate other trails. He wrote on the applications in his own hand: 'Not necessary to cover as true subject located' (Figure 3).[37] With only one negotiable option, there could be no question of an objective, let alone full investigation.

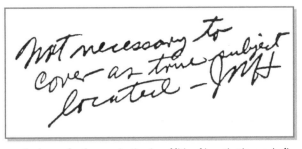

Figure 3 – Hoover, a few hours after the assassination: 'no additional investigation required'

General confusion

In assessing the first days of the investigation, we also must show some understanding for the extremely exceptional situation. The entire government apparatus was, understandably, in shock. There was also no ideal approach. If Texas had carried out the investigation, this could have led to claims of interference in the local legislation by Lyndon Johnson, a Texan. This would not have been his first offense in this field. If the federal administration had investigated the assassination, Hoover, who was as powerful as he was unreliable and also happened to be Johnson's best friend, would have been pulling all the strings. If the Secret Service had been in charge, the investigation of the murder would have been exclusively in the hands of the new president, who was also the main beneficiary. The ultimate mix of all these official bodies, with everyone improvising, proved to be the least satisfactory of all options, however.

In retrospect, dysfunctional, chaotic improvisation was probably the most obvious reaction after the crushing blow to the government machinery. A similar pattern could also be observed after the attacks of September 11, 2001. The element of surprise and the magnitude of such a disaster determine the extent of the chaos and the duration of the initial inertia. Extreme stress and high emotions are not the ideal state of mind for logical thinking, strict compliance with procedures and flawless action and communication. Inability to immediately respond efficiently to a new constellation that one is unable to fully grasp, is actually the normal reaction. The fact that President George W. Bush continued to read the children's book *The Pet Goat* for several minutes in the primary school class he was visiting when he learned of the attack on the WTC towers shows that this attack came as a complete surprise to him. In the case of a 'stage-managed incident', the president would have immediately emerged in the right context and in the role of the decisive leader. The conspirators would have been mad to put him in a kid's class at the time of their attack, unprepared and with several cameras pointing at him, reading a children's book with a silly grin on his face.

In situations like this, you find yourself in a twilight zone. Conspiracy theorists find evidence of dark conspiracies in errors and contradictions. But if you think this through for a moment, you may find that perhaps the opposite is more likely. Real conspirators would probably have done a much better job during those initial, defining moments. On the basis of this simple principle, half the conspiracy literature in the Kennedy library can already be classified under the heading 'fiction'. Yes, driver William Greer looked back twice, and only responded adequately after the fatal bullet had splattered the president's brain all over the car. But only a very stupid conspirator would have taken the wheel of a car that he knew would come under heavy gunfire. The delayed reaction of the driver was very unfortunate, and perhaps cost the president his life, but it is undoubtedly the response that best fits the situation of complete surprise, and it could just as well have also cost Greer's life.

To start an investigation in complete chaos is never a good beginning, and the evidence bears the indelible scars of those adverse conditions.

Robert Kennedy

Robert (Bobby) Kennedy had a very close relationship with his brother John (Jack). The two had grown even closer during the Cuban Missile Crisis in 1962. Some claim that Robert Kennedy neglected his demanding duties as Attorney General in favor of his time-consuming role as chief confidant of the president. In 1961, Bobby was 35 years old, had no practical experience as a lawyer and suddenly found himself at the head of the Justice Department with 30,000 officials under him and an annual budget of 130 million dollars (current value: about one billion dollars). This relatively young man's tasks included keeping FBI Director Hoover in check, a man who already held the position of FBI Director before Bobby was born. When Jack presented his administration to the press, he had to urge his brother to at least comb his hair and not to giggle during his official presentation as Attorney General. Bobby's personal involvement and political responsibility led to a highly schizophrenic situation in the assassination investigation. Obviously, Bobby, in his function of Attorney General, could not take the investigation of his brother's assassination into his own hands. Jack's death was a devastating blow for him. In addition to the excruciating pain, he was burdened by his sense of responsibility, and even feelings of guilt. If the mafia was behind the assassination, it would have been Bobby's political decision to crack down hard on organized crime that had killed his brother. Robert Kennedy also lost his actual political power when his nemesis Johnson became president. Without Jack, Bobby was fair game in the political arena.

The figure of Bobby Kennedy also seems to have played a role in the poorly performed autopsy on the murdered president. Jack had heroically rescued the crew of the patrol torpedo boat he was commanding in the Pacific during World War II. But this heroic adventure had left him with a broken back. As a result, he would be on painkillers for the rest of his life in order to get through the day. This fact was concealed during the campaign for the presidency. Moreover, JFK was an Addison patient. Addison's disease is a serious disorder affecting the adrenal cortex, causing insufficient production of the hormones cortisol and aldosterone. It was already possible to reduce the progression of the disease through medication in 1963, but, a decade earlier, this serious condition was still fatal in the long run. Especially stressful situations could lead to an Addisonian crisis and a state of shock in a patient. This is not a very good recommendation for someone who is applying for the position of president of the United States, and this information had also been withheld from the voters. In a normal autopsy, the forensic experts can immediately determine that the victim was an Addison patient with a single glance at the adrenal cortex. But the autopsy was *abnormal* in the case of John Kennedy. To complicate the picture, Jack also suffered from chronic enteritis and diarrhea, and also took medication for this. In addition, he was taking antibiotics for a urine infection (scandalmongers would later claim that it was a venereal disease).[38] Is there a link between the precarious health condition of the assassinated president and the selective autopsy? Did the Kennedy family arrange it like this? In any case, the autopsy was minimal and was carried out poorly. It took place in the secure atmosphere of the Bethesda Naval Hospital – where a court-marital was guaranteed for those who talked too much. The incomplete and inaccurate autopsy was arranged by Admiral Burkley at the request of the Kennedys, who more than likely also decided on Bethesda. The errors in the autopsy were largely due to the lack of experience of the pathologists who carried out the autopsy. This, again, was a consequence of the Kennedys' interference in the procedure.

But this was not the end of Robert Kennedy's suffering. He was also aware of JFK's extramarital escapades. The ladies involved were very discreet, but things got seriously out of hand with movie star Marilyn Monroe. In such a delicate matter, only Bobby was able to do the president's firefighting. Bobby had dutifully done everything he could to soothe the overwrought diva. But this had not gone unnoticed. In the nineties, a CIA document appeared[39] with the contents of the wiretapped telephone conversations about Kennedy's relationship with Monroe. The CIA wrote the following about her:

- Subject repeatedly called the Attorney General and complained about the way she was being ignored by the President and his brother.
- Subject threatened to hold a press conference and said she would tell all.
- Subject made reference to 'bases' in Cuba and knew of the President's plan to kill Castro.
- Subject made reference to her 'diary of secrets' and what the newspapers would do with such disclosures.

On August 5, 1962, barely three days after this CIA memorandum was prepared, Marilyn Monroe was found dead in her beach house in Los Angeles. She was naked and lying on her stomach. The official cause of death was an overdose of sleeping pills. After divorcing Kennedy's sister Patricia, Peter Lawford would spread the nasty rumor that Bobby was involved in the death of Marilyn Monroe. The 'suicide' was certainly remarkable, to say the least. Monroe must have taken a large dose of sleeping pills, yet her stomach was empty. This led to the suspicion that she could have been murdered with an injection of barbiturates in her anus. This would eliminate the possibility of her throwing up an overdose that was administered to her against her will. The 'diary of secrets' mentioned in the CIA memorandum had vanished. The motive for the murder should be sought in the world of the mafia, who, according to the rumors, intended to compromise Robert Kennedy through the 'suicide'. The mafia was aware that Bobby often spoke with the overwrought and depressive Marilyn on the phone, and allegedly lured Bobby to the beach house with a desperate and very disturbing call from Marilyn. The plan was to greet him with the flashlights of the paparazzi while Marilyn was lying naked – and dead – on her bed inside. There are two things that are certain to kill a political career: to be caught in bed with a live boy or with a dead woman. Robert Kennedy was tipped off just in time, however. He did not show up at the beach house, but had to urgently exercise some damage-control. For the first time, Bobby had to ask Hoover for a favor: to erase all telephone conversations between him and Marilyn during the weeks preceding her death.[40] Hoover was still striving for his lifetime appointment in 1962, and so the phone traffic between Bobby and Marilyn was discreetly overlooked during the investigation into her death. However, Robert Kennedy knew Hoover well enough to be sure that the phone records would only remain 'untraceable' as long as this would benefit Hoover. On November 22, 1963, for the first time, Bobby stood completely on his own, without presidential protection, against two mighty enemies who hated him and who would stop at nothing: Lyndon Johnson and J. Edgar Hoover. With the snap of a finger, both men could destroy JFK's reputation as a family man and as a physically able man suitable for the demanding office of president, as well as Bobby's marriage and future political career. When Hoover and Johnson stuck to the lone nut theory, and were not prepared to investigate any other trails, Robert Kennedy was left facing an extremely difficult choice.

There were other factors that kept Bobby from having further investigations carried out into the murder of his brother. JFK had also placed his flamboyant brother at the helm of secret commissions, such as the

Cuban Coordinating Committee (CCC) and *Covert Operations Cuba* (COC). These commissions were actively involved in the destabilization of the Castro regime, which included acts of sabotage on Cuban oil plants, sugar refineries and power plants. People were killed in these activities, including civilians. The top-secret Operation Mongoose was also under Robert Kennedy's direct authority. Among other things, Operation Mongoose contrived half-baked plans to assassinate the Cuban President: a stab with a poisoned pen, an exploding cigar, a potion that would make Fidel's beard fall out... Not exactly the heroic deeds with which Bobby wanted to be associated. Moreover, master manipulator Johnson insinuated, rightly or wrongly, that the two Kennedys had been involved in the assassination of the Vietnamese President Diem and his brother. Before Robert Kennedy could point an accusing finger at anybody in the case of the presidential murder, he had better carefully weigh the pros and cons.

Who's in charge?

Hoover's decision to take the whole case into his hands and to define the final conclusion in advance soon clashed with both the law and practical concerns. Much to everyone's amazement, the assassination of the President was not a federal crime, and the *Dallas Police Department* (DPD) was, without question, responsible for the investigation of the century. The initial acts of the DPD with regard to the investigation could provide enough inspiration to fill a full season of the *Police Academy*. But there are also counter arguments. In a number of matters, the Dallas Police Department performed better than the federal investigators who abruptly cut them off. As it happens, the Dallas police knew a lot more about bullet injuries and murder investigations than Washington did.[41] Once the initial shock was over, the Dallas police would certainly have gradually recovered their normal routine, and would probably have finalized the case relatively quickly and conclusively. In Dallas in 1963, this would more than likely have meant that Oswald, without much ado, would have been sentenced to death for the assassination of the president and - even worse according to some - for the murder of a police officer.

But no-one in the north-east of the USA really trusted *Texas justice*, or 'southern cowboy justice', as they regarded it. There was an immediate tacit consensus that this was not solemn or discreet enough for the President. The quick local solution did not meet public relations concerns, and even less the desired and appropriate national and international credibility. The Kennedy entourage had instinctively sensed this, and acted accordingly. The Secret Service therefore took control of the body of the deceased – contrary to the law[42] (and deliberately contrary to the law)[43] – with guns drawn. The Texan judge and the autopsy doctor were absolutely correct, but were aggressively pushed aside.[44] Johnson, the new president, did not hesitate for one second to ratify this state of affairs. The Kennedy dossier was snatched from the hands of the rightful judiciary from day one. On the evening of the assassination, Johnson officially subjugated the dossier to an exceptional regime: the FBI, headed by his best friend Hoover, was to conduct the investigation. This had immediate, tangible effects.

The FBI took the evidence back with them to Washington on the day of the murder, while the police in Dallas were still in the middle of their investigations. Police Chief Curry publicly expressed his frustration about this during a press conference. This was the start of a conflict between the Dallas police and the FBI, which quickly escalated: the initial skirmishes soon turned into a major conflict.[45] *Morning News* police reporter Jim Ewell wrote: '... and the wrath of J. Edgar Hoover came down in a hurry.'[46] The vindictive Hoover banned all Dallas police officers from entry to the *National FBI Police Academy* in Quantico Virginia, with immediate effect. This unreasonable attitude continued until 1968, when, tired of the constant provocations, Curry was forced to resign. Both his career and his health were shattered.

The CIA and the Secret Service were also still involved in the investigation. The CIA had photographed anyone entering or leaving the Cuban Embassy in Mexico City from three secret locations. Oswald had been there three times at the end of September 1963. Yet, for reasons unknown, the CIA was unable to produce a single picture of Oswald. The CIA left absolutely no doubt as to what their priorities were with regard to the Kennedy dossier, and reasons of state clearly ranked above uncovering the truth. The Secret Service also continued to meddle in some aspects of the investigation, despite the fact that they had no authority whatsoever in this respect.

One of the major murder investigations of the twentieth century clearly started without the presence of a central authority, command lines or strategy, and this had a very adverse impact on the quality of the work that was being done. The blunders in the investigation are sometimes so massive that it is hard to believe that they were not intentional. But the sobering fact is that, from an organizational perspective, the investigation got off to a very poor start, resulting in many avoidable errors.

Oswald's murder

The number of irreversible procedural errors had become overwhelming due to the unfavorable circumstances. This would have come to light in a painfully harsh way in any courtroom. But nightclub operator and friend of the police Jack Ruby then appeared on the scene – a godsend, and another lone nut without a motive. It took no more than one shot in the stomach to kill Lee Harvey Oswald. In one fell swoop, Oswald's death eliminated all the procedural problems, including the sole suspect. There would never be a contradictory trial before a jury in Dallas – in any case not against Oswald, and not in his presence.[47]

We will never learn Oswald's version of the facts, and that is a major impediment in any investigation seeking to uncover the truth. It also makes sense to assume that many of the initial errors would have been corrected thanks to further and better investigation if Oswald had remained alive. In the eyes of the FBI, there was now no longer any reason for such an investigation and, without the prospect of a court trial, the role of the Dallas Police Department also came to an end. Inspector Day, Chief of the Dallas Police Crime Lab, immediately stopped his investigation when he heard about Oswald's death: 'I looked at the others and said: "Well, damn it, we might as well stop and go home." We simply put our hands up in the air and stopped what we were doing.'[48] This provided the FBI with an opportunity to monopolize the dossier even more, which did not serve the interest of the investigation or historic truth. If the FBI wanted to avoid prying eyes, their main reason was that they wanted *less* truth.

Political pressure

Oswald's death and the absence of a public trial for the murder paved the way for a more politically manageable alternative to come to the official truth. Washington had already announced parliamentary inquiry commissions, and a special commission had also been planned to take up the issue in Texas, but brand-new President Johnson firmly put a stop to this guaranteed political disaster. He did this in his own inimitable style – dubbed 'the treatment' in Washington – by blocking all ongoing investigations by one stroke of his pen and then appointing the Warren Commission. Only the seven members of this Commission would determine the 'official truth' about the murder. From the very beginning, the emphasis was on 'official' and not on 'truth'. Nicholas Katzenbach, who replaced Robert Kennedy as Attorney General, summarized it as follows in an official statement dated November 25, the first working day after the assassination:

> The public must be satisfied that Oswald was the assassin; that he did not have confederates who are still at large, and that the evidence was such that he would have been convicted at trial.

During the first two executive sessions of the Warren Commission, on December 5, 1963[49] and January 22, 1964[50], the commission members expressed their astonishment[51] about the fact that the FBI consistently leaked its version of the facts to the press. If the FBI was the gold standard in police matters, why was someone from their ranks blazoning out that Oswald had been the sole perpetrator, long before the inquiry could have come to any conclusions? Commission member Dulles, former head of the CIA, only had one explanation for this: 'They [the FBI] would like to have us fold up and quit.' Counsel Rankin, the *General Counsel* of the Warren Commission, could only agree that the role of the Commission had apparently been curtailed from the very start:

> There is nothing more to do. The Commission supports their conclusions, and we can go home and that is the end of it.

The commission members did not sound particularly indignant about the notion that they were to carry out the investigation on a mere pro-forma basis. They didn't blame Hoover for using Oswald's death to finalize the case as quickly as possible. Authorities don't make trouble for themselves unnecessarily. Trust in the administration in general and in the FBI in particular was still enormous in 1963. If Hoover said it, the public would buy it. Commission members Russell and Dulles both agreed:

> There is no man in the employ of the Federal Government who stands higher in the opinion of the American people than J. Edgar Hoover.[52]

That was the spirit of the age. There is no point moralizing about this now, but there were consequences. Because this climate created the context in which the headstrong FBI Director, who fancied himself all-powerful, and the 'serfs' of the commission were allowed to continue as they pleased, with disastrous results for the investigation. They knew nothing better than that no one would ever have the guts, the time or the energy to question the official version. The death of Oswald had eliminated a number of important inherent protections against legal error or manipulation of the procedure. The presumption of innocence, on which Oswald could normally have relied, no longer applied, and the errors of the initial hours and days could remain hidden forever. There was no problem in selecting biased evidence. The FBI, the Secret Service and the CIA were allowed to run the investigation into their own failures themselves. Contradiction was not expected and, if any questions sporadically surfaced, they were firmly silenced. To play it even safer, the file was declared 'top secret' for all eternity. But this clumsy attempt at firefighting only managed to fuel the smoldering fire of those who were asking questions.

The eminent members of the commission were merely there as a PR stunt, and they apparently soon became aware of this. Meanwhile, the law-abiding members of the press also marched in step behind the Warren Commission and the FBI. The members of the commission presumably had the intention to render an honest account of the facts, although they were very biased against Oswald[53], just like the vast majority of the population at the time. But there is no reason to believe that the commission would be part of a criminal cover-up operation, let alone a conspiracy. Nonetheless, the fact remains that the FBI leaked the conclusion of the commission before this conclusion was reached. The politically appointed commission of humble servants could not really afford to make a stand against the men who had officially installed them, and yet another circuit in the protection of the truth failed.

The bureaucratic cover-up operation

As a politically appointed commission had the final word, the administration could firmly keep the lid on the bureaucratic Pandora's Box. A whole range of unsavory side issues would undoubtedly have surfaced if a full investigation had been conducted, a situation that obviously nobody wanted. It goes without saying that the military, the Secret Service, the CIA and the FBI destroyed any information that was damaging to them.[54] We will never know with certainty the contents of the note that Oswald gave to FBI agent Hosty immediately before he was attacked. Hosty flushed that document down the toilet on the order of the overwrought Dallas FBI Chief Shanklin. We will never know what was in Oswald's military file, because it was destroyed in a routine clean-up of army archives. We will never find out who was working for the CIA in those days. Commissioner Dulles admitted that he was obviously prepared to lie, even under oath, if he could thereby protect the cover of one of his secret agents.[55] If the conspiracists spin yarns on the basis of this information, the authorities concerned only have themselves to blame. The list of 'self-inflicted injuries' in the file is endless, but the organizations involved would certainly do the same again today. If the danger of potentially being caught destroying information is less damaging than the damage the – destroyed – information could have caused, the choice is easy.

The necessary cooperation between the FBI, the CIA, the Secret Service and similar institutions was therefore established in circumstances in which uncovering the truth was not a priority – to put it gently. For each of these gargantuan bureaucracies, more investigation always entailed more risk. It seemed better to err on the side of caution and to keep the investigation as superficial as possible, and, if necessary, to revert to sabotage or deception. Anyone who had to know this, knew. Johnson and Hoover were not idealistic white knights, but cynical power mongers. The signal that the files could be adapted to suit the needs with complete impunity was clear. Those involved even responded with indignation when conspiracists later had the audacity to suggest that the destruction of evidence was equivalent to involvement in the assassination.

Bureaucracies have their own logic, which transcends individual files. They have a thousand reasons to falsify documents, destroy records or tell blatant lies. Files that will be browsed through by a competing bureaucracy will be purified of any information that is harmful to the organization. In a sense, this is even one of the principles of good governance. It really is that simple. Everyone loves the whole naked truth, until someone else puts their nose into their business, then the love of truth could suddenly find itself significantly reduced. But America is an admirable nation when it comes to granting its citizens the right of initiative. The *Freedom of Information Act* (FOIA) grants every individual the opportunity to demand that the administration should release information from official dossiers. In a bureaucracy, it is very difficult to remove everything that is not for publication with surgical precision, while at the same time retaining everything that is desired. In the long term – and that's where we now are after fifty years – we did learn a lot that was originally not intended for our eyes and ears. But it is still necessary to carefully consider every item in the light of whether we are just dealing with a bureaucratic white lie, or with a criminal cover-up pointing towards a dark conspiracy. The first possibility is much more likely than the second.

J. Edgar Hoover

FBI Director Hoover was already discussed when we considered the negative impact that the FBI and the rushed decision for one specific solution had on the case, and when we hinted at the silence on the part of the Kennedy clan, which was unexplainable except through reasons of blackmail. His personality and state of mind undoubtedly constituted an additional, heavy mortgage on the investigation. Donald A. Adams was an *FBI Special Agent* recruit in 1963. In 2012, he wrote the following about the Kennedy investigation: 'I have come to believe that the FBI's investigation was compromised from the top down, beginning with FBI Director J. Edgar Hoover. His authority at that time was unquestioned, and his prerogative to direct the focus of any investigation was sacrosanct.'[56] Adams also described the ceremonial presentation of FBI diplomas that he had witnessed. At the head of a room full of graduate FBI agents, President Kennedy, Attorney General Robert Kennedy and J. Edgar Hoover were sitting side by side on a dais. Hoover's companion and Associate Director, Clyde Tolson, was sitting behind him. Behind Tolson, another four FBI officials were sitting one behind the other. When Hoover stood up, the five FBI acolytes behind him devoutly stood up as well, as if it was some kind of worship service. When Hoover sat down again, they did as well. During this ridiculous pantomime, Hoover protégé Cartha DeLoach brought in a note. He handed this over to the hindmost sub-director, who read the note and handed it over to the man in front of him, over his shoulder. This continued until Hoover received the note. Hoover read it, turned round to Tolson and whispered something to him. Tolson then turned round and whispered something to the man behind him - and so on, until DeLoach received the Director's reply and left the dais.[57] The message to the graduating agents was clear: there is a hierarchy, everyone in the entire line of command above you knows *everything* and keeps an eye on you, and – above all – Hoover is the only boss.

Hoover was an unreasonable potentate, who had never been contradicted by a single subordinate for decades. He was without exaggeration a power-hungry tyrant, an unpredictable Roman emperor who controlled the powerful administration of the FBI as his personal palace guard. Without a hint of shame, he referred to his own office in the internal FBI memos as *SOG*, which stood for *seat of government*. He had four armored limousines in the garage for his own use. When he fancied a steak from Colorado, it was delivered to him by aircraft at the cost of the public purse. He even had the FBI laboratory design a special, customized, heated toilet seat for his personal use.[58] Hoover didn't have a cultural background or a single intellectual interest. Never in his life had he done anything to broaden his horizon or adapt his view of the world to reality. He was completely unscrupulous, and his only concern was to protect his own power and dark secrets. Only after Hoover's death in 1975 was the impeccable image he enjoyed in the public eye adjusted to match the less appealing reality. *Time Magazine* broke the taboo in 1975, and wrote in no uncertain terms:[59]

> *As an administrator, he was an erratic, unchallengeable czar, banishing agents to Siberian posts on a whim, terrorizing them with torrents of implausible rules, insisting on conformity of thought as well as dress.*
>
> *The fact that such a man could acquire and keep that kind of power raises disturbing questions not merely about the role of a national police in a democracy, but also about the political system that tolerated him for so long.*

The reign of terror that Hoover imposed on the FBI decimated the formidable forensic strength of this corps when it came to the most significant dossier they ever had to deal with.

The geopolitical context

There was another important reason for scooping up the official 'Oswald soup' – with a pinched nose if necessary – a reason of a geopolitical nature, the acceptability of which is hard to assess in today's context. The Cold War, Cuba and the Missile Crisis had brought the world to the brink of a nuclear war the year before. If the Soviet Union had been involved in the assassination, no matter how marginally, Johnson had good reason to conceal this under absolute state secrecy.

Kennedy was dead, and a nuclear war was madness. The first fact didn't change anything about the reality of the second. The Cuba crisis had made it sufficiently clear that not everyone in Washington was equally convinced of the absurdity of a nuclear war. High-ranking military personnel, including General Curtis LeMay, claimed that the United States could win a nuclear war if they were the first to strike a devastating blow. These saber-rattlers had no qualms about sabotaging Kennedy's attempts to reach a diplomatic solution for the Cuban Missile Crisis, for instance by stepping up the state of alert of the military to *DEFCON* 2, one step away from nuclear war, without Kennedy's permission. They also conducted an unsolicited test with a hydrogen bomb in the middle of the already extremely tense international crisis.

One year earlier, Kennedy had been able to ward off the danger of a nuclear war at the very last minute. Whatever the role of the Soviet Union in the Kennedy assassination, any retaliation, accusation or even the merest suspicion of the complicity of the Soviet Union was unthinkable. Johnson urged Earl Warren to ensure that, in its considerations, the Commission took into account the fact that millions of American lives were at stake. Johnson told future Commissioner Russell:

> We've got to take this out of the arena where they're testifying that Khrushchev and Castro did this and did that and kicking us into a war that can kill 40 million Americans in an hour...

No doubt Johnson laid it on rather thick, to make it quite clear to the future commissioners what the country needed from them. Who could deny the President anything in an affair that could potentially escalate into a nuclear war? But this was certainly a genuine concern for Johnson, and we should be grateful to him for his correct judgment. In such cases, it is better to err on the safe side.

The DNA of the investigation

This tangle of inherent and mutually reinforcing problems is irrevocably woven into the DNA of the entire further investigation. It is disconcerting for this investigation, but, at the same time, there is also a positive side. A lot of the conspiracy nonsense creates stories around peculiarities that are a demonstrable consequence of the aforementioned adverse factors.

In an investigation with one adverse factor, one error is made. In the case of two adverse factors, this quickly becomes three errors. These matters evolve exponentially. One error inevitably leads to the next. One destroyed piece of evidence leads to a mystery in a completely different area of the case. But not every flaw in the investigation is proof of a conspiracy. We know that the above adverse factors place a heavy burden on the investigation. If it is possible to explain a flaw without the additional assumption that there was a conspiracy, then the explanation based on the known adverse factors, excluding the conspiracy, is adequate. Whenever a possible clue emerges that points towards a conspiracy, we must therefore first examine whether there are any other possible explanations. The inherent weaknesses that we have referred to are at the top of the checklist. If there is another adequate explanation, this option should be given priority over the less likely explanation that presupposes a sinister conspiracy.

3. CHALK AND CHEESE

In the previous chapter, we have considerably curtailed the conspiracists in their tendency to suspect a conspiracy behind everything that went wrong. Before starting our own investigation, I would also like to reflect on some of the classic truisms on the side of the believers. It's also time to dismiss some of the frequently used arguments on this side.

A clue is not the same as evidence

According to the believers, the investigation proved Oswald's guilt beyond doubt. It is a mantra they don't seem to be able to repeat often enough, but it is a myth. If there was one definitive piece of proof of Oswald's guilt, the file would have been conclusively closed decades ago, which is not the case. Vincent Bugliosi, the author of the voluminous standard work *Reclaiming History*, implicitly admits this by empathically referring to the number of '*things*' that point towards Oswald's guilt. He deems Oswald's guilt proven because, in his opinion, 'more than fifty pieces [of evidence] *point* irresistibly to his guilt'.[60]

There is, of course, a logical relationship between clues and evidence. The more clues there are without any evidence showing up anywhere, the stranger the case. The Kennedy case has held the unchallenged record in this context for more than fifty years: there are clues in abundance, yet there is not one single piece of conclusive evidence, whatever the believers may claim.

'Cherry Picking': Selective picking of evidence

The believers assume that they can simply pick the evidence that suits them. The other information, which they consider less useful, doesn't need to be taken into account. That's a very strange reasoning. Imagine that you would like to prove that a bag only contains red marbles. You reach into the bag once and bring out only red marbles. You again produce only red marbles a second time, and you are becoming quite sure of your case. But when you reach into the bag a third time, one white marble appears, together with red ones. As far as you are concerned, however, that's no problem: the white marble doesn't count. Your final conclusion therefore is: there are only red marbles in the bag.

It sounds crazy, but Vincent Bugliosi, leaseholder of all wisdom in the matter of the Kennedy case, frequently solves the problem of diametrically contradictory information in exactly this way. If several elements in the file all point in one direction, he believes that any clue that it could have been different can be brushed aside.[61] This is true in many cases. If Oswald was sitting in a local bus nine minutes after the assassination, he could not have been stepping into a green station wagon at the same time. This is just basic logic. This decision is not based on Bugliosi's unique understanding, but on the certainty that Oswald could not have been in two different places at the same time. Event A and event B are mutually exclusive. One of the two testimonies is incorrect, and the strongest evidence then prevails, which is the bus ticket in this case. The other testimony about the green station wagon can be ignored. But this reasoning does not always apply.

Bugliosi claims that 'once you prove the positive or negative of a matter in dispute, all other questions about the correctness of the conclusion become irrelevant.' In other words, once it had been established that Oswald was guilty, all the unsolved riddles were no longer important. In a footnote, Bugliosi lists a number of amazing examples of questions that, in his opinion, are no longer relevant.

His first example relates to a peculiar object that is visible on the autopsy photographs of the back of Kennedy's head, and which looks very much like a bullet fragment (Figure 4). Bugliosi is annoyed with Dr. David Mantik, who seems 'obsessed' by this. Oswald was guilty, so what does it matter what those photos and X-ray pictures show?

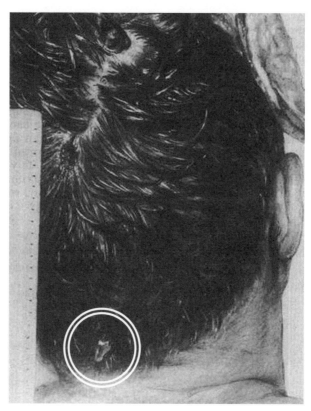

Figure 4 – An unexplained flake of metal on the back of Kennedy's head

This is certainly a very remarkable statement in the context of an objective investigation. The object, whatever it is, is obviously relevant, as it could indicate that Kennedy was hit three times, and not twice as the Warren Commission maintains. The possibility of an additional shot should *never* have been ignored, even if it had been proven that Oswald was the killer. And why is there not a word of this phenomenon in the autopsy report? Moreover, Mantik can hardly be accused of being a fantasist who is dreaming up crazy conspiracy theories. The metal object is definitely visible on Kennedy's skull, nobody is disputing this today, yet, at the same time, no explanation whatsoever can be found as to what it is, how it got there and why it was not examined. Bugliosi's second example of an irrelevant question relates to a number of autopsy photographs whose existence was registered, but that seem to have disappeared without leaving a trace. This should also not be a problem, because, since Oswald was guilty, there is certainly an innocent explanation for the mysterious disappearance of the photographs. It also does not matter whether Oswald was a good marksman, according to Bugliosi. We can follow this reasoning to some extent. A poor shot may also hit the jackpot once in a while at the shooting stall of the annual fair. But there is a limit: if the shot appears impossible from a technical or ballistic point of view, or highly unlikely for a particular shooter or a specific gun, then this is very relevant from a forensic perspective. And from a historic point of view, it is certainly also significant to know whether Oswald hit the target with one chance in a thousand, or with one in two.

Bugliosi uses the vanishing trick whenever it suits his argument. A flagrant example: a witness sees Oswald still on the 1st floor of the TSBD at 12:15. According to Bugliosi, this is impossible: '... because a mountain of evidence conclusively shows that Oswald shot Kennedy at 12:30.'[62] The white marble doesn't count. I refer to Bugliosi because he is undoubtedly the principal author among the defenders of the Warren Commission, but all believers are suffering from the same disease. They only see and hear the evidence they want to see and hear. A murder file is a whole, however, and a solution must take all the evidence into account if it is to be credible.

Who seeks shall find?

Bugliosi has yet another argument he is very proud of. He boasted that he could prove an entire room full of conspiracists wrong in one minute by simply asking them who had read the entire Warren report, including the 26 volumes of annexes. Anyone who had not done this could not reasonably claim that the report was wrong! To deny someone the right to contest a report because he has not first read 18,000 pages from a to z is nonsense. The question whether a person has learned the facts directly or indirectly is quite irrelevant. You know that the Earth is round without having to travel around it yourself. But Bugliosi also suggests something else with his reasoning. He implies that if you read the 27 volumes, as well as the tens of thousands of pages that are included in the annexes, the solution to any contradiction would certainly emerge *somewhere*. Meanwhile, it has become quite clear that no adequate answer can be found *anywhere* in the dossier for many of the relevant bones of contention.

Many of the most ardent critics, in fact, became relentless critics *after* they had thoroughly read and re-read the report, after they had studied and re-studied thousands of documents, after they had searched for years on end for the answer to a specific question. Ray Marcus, Vince Salandria, Harold Weisberg, Shirley Martin, Penn Jones, Mary Ferrell and many other conspiracists read and re-read the dossier again and again over several years. They only became more convinced that the official truth is teeming with errors, manifest lies and omissions. Based on my own experience, I can agree with these passionate critics. Reading the volumes and the many underlying, unpublished documents does *not* bring clarification. Quite the opposite: instead of finding answers, you go from one surprise to another. Gaps, distortions, contradictions, nonsensical window-dressing, legal trickery, deception of witnesses, ambiguous wording... there's no end to it. In short, the argument that everything can be found in the Warren report is not true.

The authority argument

There is apparently an unwritten law that is applicable to this assassination case: those who stick to the official theory are exempt from providing evidence or from studying the file; those who shout that Oswald is the sole perpetrator can continue to talk the most extreme nonsense: they will get away with it. Let us take the book *Voodoo Histories. How conspiracy theory has shaped modern history* by David Aaronovitch[63] as an example. With his book, the author aims to rid the world of conspiracy theories. The Kennedy case is, of course, a classic example of the genre. Aaronovitch uses the grand total of 73 words to summarize what, according to him, is irrefutable evidence that conspiracists are unwilling to acknowledge:

> [Oswald] He worked at the Texas Schoolbook Depository where, on the sixth floor, after the shooting, his rifle was <u>discovered inside an improvised sniper's nest</u>. People had seen a man at the sixth-floor window, had seen the rifle barrel, and had heard the shots. Oswald was the only employee unaccounted for after the shooting, and was picked up shortly afterwards in a cinema having just shot a policeman <u>looking for someone of his description.</u>

'*Slam dunk!*'* concludes the author. But the sentence that precedes his version of the hard facts is the following: 'If one reads the Warren Report, the circumstantial evidence that Oswald was the lone killer seems overwhelming.' That's a poor start. If you read Collodi's *Pinocchio* in the firm conviction that the story is based on undisputed facts, then the viability of wooden dolls is also proven, and with it the nose-lengthening effect of telling lies. This quote is found in a book emphasizing the necessity of critically holding on to the facts whenever a conspiracy theory emerges. But the quote that is intended to illustrate this claim is teeming with demonstrable errors, very questionable assumptions and inadmissible concealments. We list some of the most striking ones here:

- The rifle was not found in the sniper's nest, but at the opposite end of the building;
- The motive behind the meeting between Oswald and Tippit is not known. The assumption that the police officer would have recognized Oswald from the very vague description that was broadcast over the police radio is pure speculation;
- Oswald was not the only employee who was missing from the roll call. Givens was also missing;
- Assuming Oswald was guilty obviously does not prove that he acted *alone*.

The problem is not that the author fails to demonstrate the 'overwhelming' evidence of Oswald's guilt in 73 words – Bugliosi could not do this in thousands of pages – but rather that he feels compelled to charge the critics of the Warren report with a lack of seriousness, and gets away with it unpunished, despite his appalling lack of knowledge of the dossier, purely and simply because he adheres to the official version. That is unacceptable. Every hypothesis, including the official one, is subject to the same burden of proof. Believers who just copy each other by saying that there is an abundance of evidence against Oswald are in no way better than the most woolly-headed conspiracy author.

---

* A slam dunk is a basketball term that refers to the point that a player scores by jumping high enough to cling to the ring of the basket.

Shooting the pianist

The classic counter-arguments brought forward by believers are also often quite monotonous: bad faith in terms of the selective use of information, lack of knowledge of the files, psychosomatic needs, paranoia, greed... Another classic truism is the remark that the conspiracists have the tendency to give retrospective meaning to what are, in fact, coincidences. If you look hard enough, and especially if you are able to look from the opposite direction, in other words starting from the coincidence and working your way to the link to the assassination, relationships can be found everywhere.

Coincidentally or not, these arguments are exactly the arguments that, in its memorandum *Countering criticism of the Warren Report*[64], the CIA advised its confidants to spread among media people, politicians and elite acquaintances every time books by conspiracists were being discussed:

> *Our ploy should point out, as applicable, that the critics are (I) wedded to theories adopted before the evidence was in, (II) politically interested, (III) financially interested, (IV) hasty and inaccurate in their research, or (V) infatuated with their own theories.*

The memorandum then continues with a list of specific answers to classic arguments used by the critics. One final tip from the CIA is 'the idea that, checking back with the report itself, they found it far superior to the work of its critics'. The unedifying nature of the memo is also reflected in the final instruction: 'Destroy when no longer needed'.

The CIA manipulation of the debate is disturbing, but the objections stated against the conspiracists are therefore not necessarily unjustified. Conspiracy theories certainly make selective use of the evidence, they often reflect a distressing lack of basic awareness of the facts, are often purely sensationalist, see far-fetched connections everywhere, or ultimately tell more about the personal disorders of the creator than about the assassination. But these are shortcomings that apply to the conspiracy authors involved, and these reproaches cannot be transferred to the actual facts.

Reversal of the burden of proof

The final argument that is invariably cited by the believers is that not a single conclusive hypothesis has come forward from all the tons of paper that have been wasted on conspiracies. There has been no Darwinian selection, where the next generation of conspiracists synthesized the best from the books of their predecessors into a new and better explanation. Instead, the conspiracy theories tend to exhibit a centrifugal force: they are becoming even crazier, claim the believers.

Again, this is true, but every hypothesis must provide its own proof. It cannot be accepted that Oswald is automatically the only perpetrator until someone proves otherwise.

4. NO *SLAM DUNK*

The best way to solve a homicide case is to make a fundamental breakthrough. An investigation sometimes only needs one windfall: like catching the perpetrator in the act, or coming across an autistic witness who never forgets a car license plate. You can sometimes get lucky. This is not the case for the Kennedy dossier. The file is what it is, and that is what we have to work with. But before starting on this arduous journey, it may perhaps be useful to pause and consider the remarkable fact that this case is still so very topical, as well as undecided. Most homicides quickly fall into a definitive pattern. One strong witness may be sufficient, footprints, fingerprints, a detail the perpetrator overlooked, DNA, a key motive that fits one particular perpetrator...

Dealey Plaza and the TSBD were teeming with witnesses, quite a few with cameras. An agent met the alleged killer less than ninety seconds after the assassination. According to the official version, the suspect also murdered a police officer, again with a series of witnesses. One hour and fifteen minutes[65] after the attack, he was well and truly arrested. As a further example, Oswald could have made a confession on his deathbed. A gigantic investigation with unlimited resources was carried out, yet no final proof turned up. Fifteen years later, another investigation followed with even more means, and, yet again, no conclusive evidence was found.

Of course, believers empathically emphasize that the case was most certainly resolved. Bugliosi argues that Oswald's guilt has not only been proven beyond reasonable doubt, but even beyond *all* doubt.[66] He claims: 'With the mountain of evidence that was against Oswald, it is simply not possible that he could be innocent.' But one solid, decisive piece of evidence would still be infinitely better than Bugliosi's mountain. Such a piece of ultimate proof, however, either in favor of or against a conspiracy, some evidence that took away everyone's doubt, has never surfaced. Both camps have now been flinging reproaches back and forth at each other for fifty years, which does not bring the case one step forward. We must therefore accept once and for all that there is no single element that solves the case at one blow. This is not necessarily a disaster. We can switch our attention to finding solutions for sub-areas. This may be somewhat more difficult and labor-intensive, but that's the only option we have. Conclusive evidence of the elements and the logical link between these elements will ultimately also prove the whole hypothesis.

PART 2

THE SUSPECTS

5. NOT THE TINIEST SPARK
OF EVIDENCE?

Three issues of guilt arise with regard to Oswald:

- Did he shoot on Dealey Plaza?
- Did he murder Tippit?
- Did he act alone?

From the perspective of the process procedure, the third question should be asked first, because if Oswald acted alone, all three questions are answered at once, because we know with certainty that the shooting did take place at Dealey Plaza, and that Tippit was murdered. But how could we provide conclusive proof that there was no conspiracy? Proving with complete certainty that something does not exist is by definition impossible, this will always remain a matter of probability. It is therefore appropriate that we rephrase the third question: to what degree of certainty can the existence of a conspiracy be excluded?

J. Edgar Hoover knew the answer. He reported to the Commission on May 14, 1964:

I have been unable to find any scintilla of evidence showing any foreign conspiracy or any domestic conspiracy that culminated in the assassination of President Kennedy.[67]

Two or three minutes before this statement, he had sworn to say the truth, and nothing but the truth.

Scintilla is Latin for 'spark'. *Not a scintilla of evidence* is commonly used in courts of law to argue that there is really not the smallest, tiniest trace of evidence in support of a plaintiff's claim. This is completely different from saying, for example: 'Ultimately no real conclusive evidence was found.' Not a shred of evidence, Hoover said.

The believers fully agree with this. In the ABC-documentary on the occasion of the fortieth anniversary of the assassination, presenter Peter Jennings said it solemnly and sonorously: 'After all these years there has not been a single piece of credible evidence to prove a conspiracy.' In his memoirs, Chief Justice Warren still maintains that his Commission had found 'no facts upon which to hypothesize a conspiracy', and that the FBI, CIA, Secret Service and government departments in question '[could not find] any evidence of conspiracy'[68]. In the preamble of his major opus, Bugliosi claims that 'Not the smallest speck of evidence has ever surfaced that any of the conspiracy community's favorite groups (CIA, Mob, etc.) was involved, in any way, in the assassination.' Absolute statements such as 'not a scintilla' may sound tough, but they are very vulnerable. It suffices to give one counterexample to refute them.

As a possible counterargument, let us have a close look at Ruby and his entourage. If there was no conspiracy, Ruby murdered Oswald without motive. Then we are stuck with a second 'lone nut' within a time frame of 48 hours. But what if we assume that Oswald had been killed to silence him? In this case, Ruby was commissioned, which by definition implies a conspiracy. Jack Ruby is therefore a key figure in the question of whether or not there was a conspiracy.

6. DECLINE OF A SHOW-OFF

Ruby's motive

On Sunday morning, November 24, at 11:21, Jack Ruby shot Lee Harvey Oswald in the basement garage of the Dallas police station. Ruby did not have the slightest motive.[69] On the advice of his shady lawyer Tom Howard, he stated that he had wished to save Jacqueline Kennedy the trauma of an Oswald trial, but that turned out to be completely fabricated.[70] This lack of a motive is an important observation, as it is typical for a contract killing. The assassin has no personal motive – it's his client who has the motive.

The approach of the Warren Commission

Was Ruby hired as a hitman? The Warren Commission invested no energy in solving this question, quite the contrary. Any connection between Ruby and the criminal underworld was brushed away. Fifteen years later, in 1978, the U.S. Congress established the new commission, the *House Select Committee on Assassinations*, to review the case. The HSCA did investigate the real Ruby and his entourage. One of the points of attention in this context was Ruby's phone traffic in the weeks prior to the assassination of Kennedy.[71] Ruby apparently spoke to a bunch of notorious underworld figures during October and November 1963. This should not be surprising for a nightclub manager who had moved over from Chicago. But how could the Warren Commission possibly have come to the following conclusion?

Based on its evaluation of the record, however, the Commission believes that the evidence does not establish a significant link between Ruby and organized crime. Both State and Federal officials have indicated that Ruby was not affiliated with organized criminal activity. And numerous persons have reported that Ruby was not connected with such activity.

What strikes us first and foremost here is the Warren Commission's excessive use of legalistic language. 'Based on its evaluation of the record' sounds good, but, on reflection, the record in question turned out to be far from complete, and the specified evaluation was extremely concise. It also states: the Commission 'believes'. The report therefore does not state that Ruby had no connections with organized crime, only that the Commission 'believes' that he hadn't, or rather that the 'evidence' did not establish 'significant' links. The HSCA made no secret of its opinion about the Warren investigation into Ruby:

While the Warren Commission and the FBI did obtain some of the records, an extensive effort to collect them was not carried out. Griffin stated that Commission general counsel J. Lee Rankin vetoed their full request because the effort would have been too burdensome and was too far-reaching. The Commission and the FBI failed to analyze systematically and to develop the data in those records which were obtained.[72]

The Warren Commission had the authority to decide for itself how to apply its power and what priorities to set, but, if they had not investigated this, they were not entitled to claim with great certainty in their final report that Ruby had no ties with organized crime. The fact that Rankin, the operational head of the Warren Commission, explicitly vetoed the investigation into Ruby's contacts with the underworld is very strange indeed. He claimed this would be 'too burdensome and too far-reaching'.

Ruby is not a marginal figure in this account. He was a killer, and there are good reasons to assume that he had been hired as a hit man. The commission investigated some utter nonsense extensively. They knew about Ruby being a bed-wetter 45 years earlier, but an examination of his telephone contacts with the mob was too burdensome and too far-reaching!

Who was Ruby?

Jack Ruby turned 52 in 1963. He was, in fact, a failure, with little hope for improvement. The *Carousel Club*, which he co-owned and managed, was a shabby striptease joint on one of the floors of a house on the main Commerce Street, not much more than half a mile from Dealey Plaza. The Carousel was not a house of prostitution. The acts that were performed did not to exceed Ruby's views on obscenity.[73] The police were regular customers, and more than once turned a blind eye in exchange for free drinks. Ruby occasionally coupled his girls with a police officer.[74] Ruby never drank himself.[75] He regularly visited the synagogue, was generally well-mannered and did not curse. He shared a grubby apartment with a man, George Senator, but was definitely not a homosexual. Ruby had sporadic relationships with women, one of which lasted for more than ten years. Most women did not want to be involved with him due to his 'uncouth manners and untidy dress'.[76] A bizarre detail is that Ruby – half seriously – referred to Sheba, one of his seven dachshunds, as his 'wife'; the other six he called 'his kids'. Ruby displayed violent behavior from time to time, and liked to boast about this. But after an outburst of anger, he usually expressed his regret – often in tears – and made every effort to befriend the victim again.[77] Professionally, he was a small business owner in the nightlife sector; a poser who left a trail of either blood or slime, depending on what suited him. The FBI had once made an attempt to use Ruby as an informant, but, sensibly, had soon renounced the use of his services. It is also clear that Ruby in no way had a profile that might have been of interest to the CIA.

Ruby was up to his neck in tax arrears in 1963. He could just about pay the staff and bills of the Carousel,[78] but that was as far as it went. Ruby owed the IRS, the Internal Revenue Service, more than 20,000 dollars in outstanding tax payments,[79] an amount that can be multiplied by seven today. This was a very acute problem for Ruby.[80] His prospects were bleak, and at the end of 1963, he was really at his wit's end. In September, he placed an advertisement in which he offered The Carousel for sale,[81] but no buyers showed up. Conspiracists claim that Ruby suddenly had plenty of cash immediately before the assassination of Kennedy; that he was planning a cruise, mentioned the prospect of paying an installment on his outstanding tax payments for the first time, etc. There is no single proof of this, but his police file in the county archives states that 3,109.11 dollars was found in cash in Ruby's pockets, car and apartment.[82] Everything was paid cash in The Carousel, however, so this amount is therefore not an indication of sudden prosperity. At the end of 1963, Ruby only seems to be going one way: downhill.

In 1963, Ruby was a show-off in a state of decline. Despite his frantic efforts to survive financially, physically and mentally, he gradually could not even manage to keep up appearances. Despite his tough demeanor, he appeared emotionally instable and almost naively impressionable, especially with regard to people he looked up to,[83] if they seemed to have prestige, power and money.[84] When it suited him, he was an arms smuggler, illegal gambler, pimp and rowdy, but up to November 23, 1963 he was not a murderer, and because of his emotional instability, certainly not a stereotypical, cold assassin.[85]

According to conspiracist Sylvia Meagher, the Commission undertook a suspiciously intensive *effort to remodel* Ruby in their report.[86] Why was the 'real' Ruby such a major threat? The major differences between the nice Ruby, as displayed by the Warren Commission, and the Ruby of the HSCA relate to gunrunning, Cuba and the mafia.

Ruby, gunrunning and Cuba

A well-documented account on the contacts Ruby had with a Castro gun runner in 1959 is available. Ruby, who was always looking for deals with which he could earn a quick dime, tried to flog some rusting army jeeps and a batch of old slot machines to Castro. Fifteen years later, the HSCA found that the FBI and the Commission 'failed to investigate in this matter adequately.'[87] This is an *understatement*. The 27 volumes of the Warren Commission made no mention whatsoever of this. In a letter to the Commission,[88] Hoover even flatly denied the existence of any contact between Ruby and the arms smuggler. His own FBI agents had, however, established this contact, and both parties, Ruby and the arms smuggler, had confirmed it themselves. What could have been so dangerous about a meeting in 1959 that came to nothing? Why did cannon of the caliber of a Hoover need to be used on a mouse like Ruby? Presumably this was because the Cuba involvement in this affair had to be kept out of the file at whatever cost.

But the Commission could not escape this one. Ruby did indeed appear in Havana in this summer of 1959. According to the Commission, this happened only once, and Ruby went as a tourist. The HSCA refers to at least three trips[89] and does not exclude that it could have been six in the end. All this is of little importance, however. The gun-running circuit shows Ruby in his role of criminal grocer, but, in truth, there is no link whatsoever with the assassination of Kennedy.

Mafia connections

Ruby's telephone traffic was also problematic. It turned out to be fraught with possible mafia connections: Al Gruber, Lewis McWillie, Michael Shore, who was considered to be part of the Giancana clan, Pete Marcello, Frank Carracci, Nofio Pecora, connected to Carlos Marcello, Joe Glaser, a Costello contact, Dusty Miller, Irwin Weiner, Barney Baker from Hoffa's entourage, Russell Matthews, who falls under Santos Trafficante, and Frank Goldstein. All this was also quickly swept under the carpet by the FBI and the Commission. The HSCA did pay a reasonable amount of attention to this. Today, we know at least with whom Ruby had telephone contact on his traceable phone lines, although, as the HSCA reported[90] , we are not aware of how many and what phone conversations were held over non-traceable lines. But we also need not worry too much here. The telephone conversations are not important. Why should frantic telephones calls be made about the urgent liquidation of Oswald before Kennedy was shot and before Oswald fell into the hands of the police alive? Imagine the mafia discussing its potential hits months in advance over dozens of phone calls with twelve contact persons... We may at least assume a minimum of professionalism among professional criminals. If Ruby was part of a conspiracy, this was certainly not what the telephone discussions in October were about.

AGVA

But what was the reason for all these phone calls? According to the official version, they were the subject of a feud between Ruby and his hated rivals, the Weinstein brothers. The argument was about a striptease contest for upcoming talent in the sector.[91] During this type of talent show, amateurs stripped free-of-charge, and Ruby, who was working with professionals, considered this unfair competition.[92] He involved the *American Guild of Variety Artists* (AGVA), a kind of strippers' trade union. The job of the AGVA was to stop those who spoilt the trade on behalf of the 'artists', but the AGVA dragged its feet and Ruby was trying to plead and accelerate his case by telephone. In hindsight, this appears rather suspicious, because the AGVA was not simply a stripper's union. It was also, and perhaps above all, a kind of subsidiary of the mafia organization La Cosa Nostra.[93] But the telephone calls' common denominator was the stripper's union, according to the official version, and not the mafia.

In any case, whatever the reason for the phone calls, they provided a number of people from the criminal milieu a good insight into Ruby's mind. This could have been an important element when an emergency operation in the police station unexpectedly imposed itself. On November 23, the organized crime environment was aware of Ruby's unique access to the Dallas Police Station, his readiness to resort to violence, his naïve and patriotic ideas, and the fact that he was in these areas highly susceptible to manipulation. His significant financial problems can be added to this. Ruby was not exactly a person who discreetly kept his problems to himself. The mafia was aware that Ruby could be persuaded to carry out a criminal job.[94] But, as the problem of Oswald's arrest had not yet arisen, this could certainly not have been the subject of the above-mentioned telephone calls.

Ruby's activities after the assassination of Kennedy

As a result, everything Ruby did before the attack on Kennedy is irrelevant. It proves that Ruby was a peripheral figure in the Dallas underworld, and that the FBI and the Commission were lying in this respect, but neither issue implies that Ruby was involved in a conspiracy. The relevant factor is what Ruby did *after* the arrest of Oswald.

Ruby had a conclusive alibi for the time Kennedy was shot; he was not at Dealey Plaza. (Sylvia Meagher raises the pertinent question as to why, on Friday, his alleged love for the Kennedys was not strong enough to walk a couple of blocks, while he was willing to risk the death penalty for it on Sunday?[95]). According to star reporter Seth Kantor, after the assassination Ruby was hanging around at the Parkland Hospital, where the fatally injured Kennedy had been taken,[96] until about 13:30. That could well be: Ruby was a notorious disaster tourist, who also closely followed any events in the police environment.[97] When nothing exciting was happening anymore, Ruby returned to his Carousel club. There, in a highly emotional state of mind, he – like a maniac – phoned several people for about one hour. His first long-distance telephone call took place at 14:37. Ruby phoned Al Gruber in California. Gruber was a vague acquaintance of Ruby. Twenty years earlier, he had shared accommodation with him in Chicago.[98] They had lost sight of each other afterwards but, in mid-November 1963, Gruber had suddenly emerged at the Carousel to visit his old buddy Jack for a few days.[99] On November 22, Gruber was back at home already in Los Angeles. He was the first person Ruby phoned after he had heard that Oswald had been arrested. Gruber claims that the conversation, barely two hours after Kennedy had been assassinated, was about 'a number of things including the car wash business', and about Ruby's plan to send him a dog. Only then had the attack that had taken place at half a mile from the Carousel been discussed. Gruber's statement is very shaky, and is moreover inconsistent with Ruby's version of the facts. Overcome with emotion towards the end of the conversation, Ruby was unable to continue talking.[100] This did not prevent him from being engaged in another intensive telephone talk with someone else two minutes later.[101] The impression Ruby makes in these initial hours after the assassination is that of an unstable, slightly demented comedian.

According to the believers, there is nothing behind the telephone call with Gruber. Surely Gruber made a mistake when he claims to have chatted about the carwash and dogs. Gruber has firm mafia connections, but where is there no chaff among the wheat? His unexpected visit to Dallas at a crucial time could be a coincidence, and Ruby was simply confused and emotional during his telephone chat with Gruber.[102] But there must have been plenty of such telephone calls made that day.

An uninteresting death threat

Another problem, however, emerged in Gruber's statement. The FBI questioned him on Monday, November 25, the day after Ruby had shot Oswald.[103] On that day, at 12:54, an anonymous caller had asked for Gruber. When he was told that Gruber was not at home, the anonymous caller said: 'Ask him if he likes living' and put the phone down. The FBI dryly recorded the reported crime, a death threat, and did nothing more about the information. We can reasonably assume that the death threat was not a figment of Gruber's imagination. Why would he invent a death threat while being questioned by the FBI, who were conducting an investigation into the murder of the president? The lack of interest from the side of the FBI is incomprehensible. The threat should have been thoroughly investigated, if only because making death threats happens to be a criminal offence and citizens deserve protection. But this death threat was also relevant in the investigation into the assassination of Kennedy. What did Gruber have to shut up about? Who was the anonymous caller? The FBI and the Commission didn't want to know.

Mysterious deaths

This is not an isolated case. According to the conspiracists, the Kennedy dossier harbors even more victims of threats, shootings, bizarre car crashes on deserted roads, unexpected suicides and sudden heart attacks at the wrong time. The believers minimize all this, and the conspiracists undoubtedly exaggerate. Obviously people die every day, and if one is to follow up everyone who is in one way or another somehow involved in the boundless file over a number of years, one will doubtlessly come across a number of strange deaths. Nut Ruby is our test case for checking whether there is not the slightest indication of a conspiracy. Let us therefore delve a little deeper into this issue.

The *Times Herald* of November 25, 1963 published an article about C.A. Droby, the lawyer who had been contacted by Ruby. The article mentioned two threatening phone calls that were received by Droby's wife. 'They would be next' if her husband would defend Ruby. Some time later, an anonymous phone was received at Droby's office announcing that his car would be blown up. Droby refrained from representing Ruby any further.[104] This may have been just an empty threat or a sick joke. There were no victims.

Jim Koethe and Bill Hunter were less lucky. The two journalists, who were working for the *Dallas Times Herald* and *Long Beach Press Telegram* respectively, had had a hectic day on November 24, 1963. Ruby had killed Oswald that morning. When they had finished their work, they went for a drink together in the only bar where they could get something stronger. They met Ruby's roommate George Senator and his lawyer Tom Howard there. The four subsequently ended up in Ruby's apartment, where the reporters nosed around for a while, but apparently didn't find anything of interest. Five months later, on April 23, 1964, a police officer shot Bill Hunter in Long Beach. The policeman had accidentally dropped his gun and it went off. When it transpired during the investigation that this was technically impossible, the police officer remembered: he had played a game of 'quick draw', and the gun had fired accidentally. His colleague officer had not seen it happening, as he had been looking the other way. Court reporter Bill Hunter, in any case, was dead. A stupid accident. Five months after his colleague, Jim Koethe was also killed. On September 21, 1964, a stranger broke into his apartment and killed Koethe with a karate blow. The culprit was never caught. Another six months later, in March 1964, lawyer Tom

Howard died unexpectedly of a heart attack at the age of 48. The man, however, did not have a particularly healthy lifestyle.

Eight months after Howard, it was Dorothy Kilgallen's turn. Kilgallen was a reporter, columnist and well-known TV personality. She claimed to have interviewed Ruby in prison for eight minutes in 1964. Bugliosi disputed that, quoting Bill Alexander: 'Whatever Dorothy Kilgallen said, she said through the bottom of a bottle of booze.'[105] Apart from the fact whether or not an interview with Ruby exists, it is certain that Kilgallen had a source within the Warren Commission. She managed to obtain, before the publication of the annexes to the Warren Report, 102 until then unpublished pages of documents relating to Ruby. The FBI investigated the case, but was unable to identify the source of the leak. On November 8, 1965, the 52-year-old famous scandal reporter died of an accidental overdose of sleeping pills and alcohol. Her hairdresser found her in a bed in a bedroom she hadn't used for years. She was holding a book she had finished two weeks before, and which she had discussed in detail with her hairdresser. Moreover, Kilgallen could not read without her reading glasses, and these were nowhere to be found in the room. On investigation, the overdose turned out to consist of three different barbiturates, only one of which could be found in Kilgallen's home pharmacy. According to this version, Kilgallen seems to have been murdered. Bugliosi, who only paid attention to this one apparently mysterious case of death, considers a violent death impossible, however, because Kilgallen's husband and son were in the house at the time. Alcohol and sleeping pills are and remain a dangerous combination.

In less than two years, at least six persons who had been in direct contact with Jack Ruby with regard to the Kennedy file had either received death threats or had died. To complete the list, we may also add Jack Ruby himself. He died of lung cancer on January 3, 1967, after having announced several times that he feared for his life.

We will not spend further attention to the mysterious deaths listed in this book. But there is no doubt that these death threats and deaths are *facts*. Whether those facts corresponded with the official position that there was not a single indication that pointed towards a conspiracy could only be determined on the basis of a thorough investigation, but the FBI preferred not to take such a risk.

Ruby's unique feature

The FBI did spend plenty of time on investigating the existence of a possible link between Ruby and Oswald. Paradoxically, that indicates that they were probably well aware that there was no such link. Everyone who had come even near to Carousel was questioned by the FBI. Nobody had ever seen Oswald there.[106] Whether or not the two knew each other ultimately means little or nothing. It proves at the most that Ruby and Oswald were not actively involved together in a conspiracy. Of course it is possible that a client behind the scenes asks B to kill A, also if A and B do not know each other. Ruby was not exactly a person on which a conspirator wanted the fate of a complex conspiracy to depend.[107] But, highlighting this is again beside the point. If the mafia was involved in the murder of Oswald, then Ruby was no more than a tool for them, a lever which they operated.

Ruby certainly was not a professional killer, not at the service of the mob, not an ideal conspirator - quite the contrary. His indiscretion was a major obstacle for anyone who wanted to settle important affairs in the underworld.[108] But he did know almost every police officer in the Dallas police force, and had free access to the basement of the police building. *That's* the essence.

7. MARCELLO AND CO

A major problem the Commission could not avoid, is Ruby's lack of a motive to kill Oswald. On the one hand, Ruby was certainly very impulsive and some consider him able to have grabbed his chance to play an important supporting role in a tragedy [109]– as a compensation for his minority complex. On the other hand, the absence of a personal motive for Ruby increases the suspicion of a hit contract and a conspiracy. Bugliosi claims that any group with a motive 'also had an even greater motive not to do it, namely, that if they did it and got caught, they could be tried, convicted and sentenced to death.'[110] That's utter nonsense, insinuating that a suspect *with* a motive would shrink back from the risk, while a suspect *without* a motive would not. Having a motive is obviously not proof of any involvement, but it is a good reason to further investigate the track.

Who benefited from the death of John Kennedy? The mafia should certainly be considered. Organized crime certainly had significant motives to first assassinate the president and then Oswald, who, against all odds, was taken into custody alive. The HSCA report, which contrary to the Warren Report mentioned the elephant in the room, contains a revealing graph regarding the prosecution of the mafia[111] (Figure 5). John and Robert Kennedy came to power in January 1961, and their empire ended in 1963. The graph shows a clear correlation between this period, the increase in the fight against the mafia and its abrupt end on November 22, 1963. This fight was not merely a cosmetic operation, where the small fish were hunted and the big sharks got away scot-free. Robert Kennedy was serious. He went for Carlos Marcello, among others, the godfather in New Orleans. Marcello had risen in the ranks of organized crime for thirty years. In the early sixties, he was the untouchable organized crime ruler in the Gulf States. The *New Orleans Crime Commission* reported that Marcello's organization was sometimes called *The Wall Street of Cosa Nostra*. A parliamentary commission estimated organized crime annual income in New Orleans at 1.114 billion dollar: 500 million from illegal gambling activities, 400 million from legal income in the transport sector, finance, real estate and services, 100 million from illegal activities in the more than 1,500 bars that were connected with the syndicate, 100 million from fiscal fraud, finally 8 million from burglaries and robberies, and finally 6 million from prostitution.[112] Former Attorney General Ramsey Clark estimated organized crime profit – the most conservative estimate – comparable with the accumulated profits of the ten largest industrial organizations (General Motors, Standard Oil, Ford, General Electric, Chrysler, IBM, Mobile Oil, Texaco, Gulf and U.S. Steel).[113] Needless to mention that Marcello tended to disagree with this, insisting that he was a tomato seller who earned approximately 1,600 dollars per month. It was still safer to cross the street for a moment, however, if your path was about to cross Carlos Marcello's path. One cannot but highlight the courage and moral fiber of Robert Kennedy in his determination to combat this cancer in society.

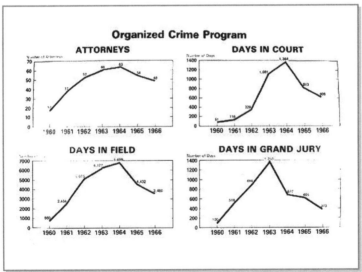

Figure 5 – *The rising graphs indicating the intensity of the mafia prosecution drop rapidly from the first day after Kennedy's assassination.*

Robert Kennedy could not count on the support of J. Edgar Hoover and the FBI in this battle. Hoover, who had already proved himself a great fan of placing microphones under creaking hotel beds, had no tapping activities on Marcello in place in the early sixties. In 1963 and 1964, the FBI undertook two attempts that failed.[114] It is clear that Carlos Marcello was so powerful that he would always manage to get his affairs sorted, and he was certainly not used to encounter any resistance in the pursuit of his criminal activities. But Robert Kennedy was not the kind of man to evade danger, and hence these two natural forces stormed head-on towards each other, whereby neither even considered the possibility of having to bend his head. With the entire state machinery behind him, Robert Kennedy easily won the first rounds. Marcello suddenly found himself into trouble with criminal and tax laws. In September 1963, Robert Kennedy, in his function of Attorney General, once again explicitly confirmed to the *McClellan Committee* that he intended to even step up the war on organized crime. He mentioned Hoffa, Giancana and Marcello by name as the main targets of his legal battle.

Carlos Marcello's plan

In 1978, the HSCA also investigated the information included in *The Grim Reapers*, a book on organized crime that was published by Ed Reid in 1969. Reid spent a voluminous chapter on the account of a man who claimed to have been present when Marcello uttered a death threat aimed at President Kennedy in 1962.[115] The witness on whom Reid based his story was private investigator Edward Becker, who fully endorsed the account Reid had related in his book in his statement to the HSCA.

According to this account, Becker met, on September 11, 1962, several men at Churchill Farm, Carlos Marcello's pied-a-terre of 2,400 hectares – the reader may keep this location in the back of his mind, we will come back to it later. The men were drinking heavily. When someone mentioned Robert Kennedy, Marcello became very angry and 'clearly stated that he was going to arrange to have President Kennedy murdered in some way.' According to Marcello, Bobby was but the tail of the dog. If you only cut off its tail, the dog will keep biting you, he said, but if the dog's head were cut off, the dog would die. Marcello had a clear plan:

Marcello 'clearly indicated' that his own lieutenants must not be identified as the assassins, and that there would thus be a necessity to have them use or manipulate someone else to carry out the actual crime.[116]

Reid never doubted the seriousness of Marcello's death threat. It had become a matter of honor:

Marcello did not joke about such things. In any case, the matter had gone beyond mere 'business'; it had become an affair of honor, a Sicilian vendetta. Moreover, the conversation at Churchill Farm also made clear that Marcello had begun to plan a move. He had, for example, already thought of using a 'nut' to do the job.[117]

Marcello, the honest tomato retailer who owned a 2,400 hectares estate, naturally denied that he had ever intended to have John Kennedy killed in order to eliminate Robert Kennedy, and to have the assassination carried out by a *patsy*, a fall guy. According to the HSCA, the FBI completely focused its attention on discrediting Becker, who was an informant, instead of establishing whether the story could be confirmed or disproved.[118]

Carlos Marcello and Lee Harvey Oswald

There is also a connection between Oswald and Carlos Marcello. Oswald had an uncle who showed some concern about him after the death of his father. Charles (Dutz) Murret was married to Lillian, the sister of Oswald's mother Marguerite. In his youth, and again for a short time after his return from the Soviet Union in 1962, Oswald lived with this uncle and considered him basically as a surrogate father. The Warren Commission claims that Uncle Charles was an ordinary ship's clerk. The HSCA dug a little deeper also here, and found Murret to be an illegal bookmaker, associated with Sam Saia, one of the major bookmakers in New Orleans.[119] Murret is even said to have been Marcello's driver at some point in time.[120] Not at all a gray clerk as the Warren Commission claimed.

Marguerite Oswald confirmed the connection between her brother in law and Marcello, but insisted:

Just because Mr. Murret worked for those people, and may have known Marcello, that doesn't mean anything about Lee.[121]

That is, of course, true, but it does not erase the fact that there was a surprisingly direct link also between Marcello and Lee Harvey Oswald. Another of Murret's associates was Nofio Pecora.[122] When we look through the list of Ruby's long-distance calls during the crucial time before the assassination, we see the same Nofio Pecora emerging. It's a small world after all.

8. DAVID FERRIE AND CO

David Ferrie and Carlos Marcello

In the weekends preceding the assassination, a weird character settled down on Churchill Farm: David Ferrie. He was, to say the least, an oddball, an intelligent – brilliant according to some – eccentric.[123] At the time, Carlos Marcello was being prosecuted on the suspicion of have forged his birth certificate and was risking another deportation from the U.S., which was, of course, a nasty hitch when it came to preserving his criminal empire. David Ferrie came to support Marcello. According to the FBI report, he assisted in devising a 'strategy for Marcello's trial.'[124] The FBI did not find it strange that billionaire Marcello called upon the strategic advice of the raving mad David Ferrie regarding a legal battle with a very important outcome for him. The FBI never even questioned Ferrie. Yet, with the exception of Oswald, Ferrie was the only person who was actively tracked as a suspect immediately after the assassination of Kennedy. Still, his name is not even mentioned in the Warren Report, and he wasn't called up as a witness. Conspiracists have an alternative explanation for the presence of Ferrie at the time Marcello was facing deportation from the U.S. As a stunt pilot, Ferrie had smuggled Marcello back into the U.S. after his first deportation to Guatemala.[125] It does not seem illogical to look for a link between both men in the field of Ferrie's ability as a pilot, rather than as a strategic legal advisor. But who was this mysterious Ferrie actually?

David Ferrie was born in 1918. He studied for the priesthood at a seminary for a while, but his vocation was abruptly interrupted when his sexual orientation came to light. Ferrie was a practicing homosexual, with a penchant for young boys. He obtained his pilot's license and was employed as an aeronautics instructor at a high school, but was dismissed for reasons of 'overattachment to his young male students.' He suffered from a rare skin condition, *alopecia areata,* which caused him to lose all his body hair. His attempts to hide this with a wig and fake eyebrows were not quite successful. He pretended to be a doctor, psychologist and hypnotist. Journalist James Phelan even wrote that Ferrie – unsuccessfully – tried to build his own submarine.[126] He also experimented with chemicals, in search of a cure for cancer, although he only had a diploma he had purchased by mail order.[127] In between, Ferrie was an insurance inspector, and even climbed to the rank of 'bishop' within a movement of the American Orthodox Catholic Church at one point in time.[128] Ferrie was initially also supporting the risky military operations of pro-rebel leader Fidel Castro. Once in power, however, Castro sided with Russia, and Ferrie, a rabid anti-communist, became in many adventurous ways actively involved in the counter-revolutionary movement in Cuba, which may have been on behalf of the CIA. In the sixties, things went quickly downhill for Ferrie. He had persistent legal, financial, psychological and medical problems. He took more pills than was good for him, and, increasingly often, his dynamism and temperament dominated his mental capacity. When he was therefore arrested as a suspect in the Kennedy assassination, he had to admit that he, in a fit of anger about the lack of American air support in the Bay of Pigs' operation, had publicly said that Kennedy should have been shot[129].

Ferrie's overexcited brain sparked with short circuits, but as a pilot he was and remained exceptionally talented. He was 'a natural as an aviator'.[130] Ferrie always had to do with airplanes. In 1944 as a fighter pilot, in the fifties as an airline pilot for Eastern Airlines, and in between as *Civil Air Patrol* flight instructor for cadet groups. By another bizarre coincidence, a photograph of a Civil Air Patrol campfire dating back to 1955 exists, on which both Ferrie and a fifteen-year old Oswald can be seen. Ferries career as a pilot ended when Eastern Airlines dismissed him, again because of sex offences. In the aftermath of the trial in this context, he became an assistant of private detective Guy Banister, a former FBI agent who was, just like Ferrie, a staunch anti-Castro activist of an ultra-right persuasion. Detective Banister's office was situated in the *Newman Building,* a corner building with a double address: 544 Camp Street / 531 Lafayette Street, New Orleans. As it happens, this is also the address Oswald used on the pro-Cuba pamphlets he was distributing! This links Oswald and Ferrie to the same building in New Orleans. According to the believers, Oswald had stamped any address, which just happened to be Camp Street 544, on his pamphlets to create the impression that there really was a *Fair Play For Cuba* organization. It's easy to create links afterwards, they claim. Oswald put a random address on the pamphlet, and, naturally, it is possible to find a link with maybe ten other addresses in one way or another. And each of these ten addresses can be linked to at least ten people who had ever been there, or lived or worked there. These hundred people, in turn, no doubt knew someone who could be linked to the JFK file as a suspect.

But the chain is perhaps not quite so coincidental. Let's follow the links:

1. Oswald, who claimed to be only a fall guy in the assassination of Kennedy;
2. He states a random address on a pro-Cuba pamphlet: New Orleans Camp Street 544;
3. That was the same building as Lafayette Street 531;
4. Which is where the detective agency of Guy Banister was established;
5. Banister worked together with David Ferrie;
6. Ferrie advised Carlos Marcello in proceedings concerning his extradition to Guatemala;
7. Marcello was a mafia godfather who, in 1962, had plans to have Kennedy murdered by... a fall guy.

The chain is brittle at the start and at the end. The link between Banister and Oswald is only proven at the level of a joint address. From Banister, over Ferrie, to Carlos Marcello, the chain is strong: Ferrie worked for Banister and provided Carlos Marcello with strategic advice in proceedings regarding falsified birth certificates. So much we already know. But this is not punishable. The last link – from Marcello to the actual assassination – is obviously also unproven. A vendetta tirade by a seething temperamental Sicilian mobster is something else than evidence of involvement in a murder. The central figure in the chain is Ferrie. He knew, beyond any doubt, both Banister and Carlos Marcello.[131] The fact that Marcello would have liked to see Kennedy 6 feet deep, also speaks for itself. The evidential value of the entire chain therefore revolves around the link between Ferrie and Oswald. The fact that these two are together on a photograph of 1955, is – obviously – pure coincidence again, according to the believers. But it forms a first reinforcement of the crucial link in the chain.

Another nuance is that the chain is not so 'accidental' and created by far-fetched interlinking. The Oswald/Ferrie connection is not a figment of the imagination of a conspiracy buff, quite the contrary, it is one of the first links the police made immediately after the assassination of Kennedy.

David Ferrie and Jack Martin

Besides Ferrie, detective Banister also employed the alcoholic Jack Martin as cheap labor in a part-time job. Martin had once been a highly intelligent man, in fact a former CIA detective,[132] but in 1963 he was only a shadow of his former self. Banister and he apparently had no reason to grieve on November 22, and they went down to the *Katz & Jammer* bar after work. But the drinking bout ended in a violent argument. Martin was hit several times with the butt of a heavy colt .357 Magnum by his employer. The police interfered, but Martin refused twice to lodge a complained against Banister. After treatment in the hospital, he managed to get home on his own accord[133] to sleep it off.

The next day, the Kennedy tragedy was constantly covered on TV, and the subject of many heated discussions everywhere. On Saturday night, Martin was speculating about Ferrie's possible involvement in the assassination with his friend W. Hardy Davis. Ferrie was een weapon freak, and allegedly possessed a similar weapon to the one that was shown on TV. His public statements about murdering the president were common knowledge. Several assumptions were reviewed before Davis went home. But moments later, Martin phoned him again. He was in quite a state, because on television he had heard a former classmate of Oswald state that the latter had been a member of the *Civil Air Patrol*. Martin 'flipped' (to quote his own words afterwards[134]), because who had been instructor at the very same Civil Air Patrol? Indeed: Ferrie! Meanwhile, Martin also heard that Ferrie 'was not in town'[135], and was presumably on his way to Texas. Martin suddenly felt himself at the center of the action, and, *en passant*, saw his chance to settle an old account with Ferrie, whom he hated. He trumpeted the around to whoever cared to listen: the rifle, the personal contact between Oswald and Ferrie at the CAP, and then the trip to Texas which – in Martin's view – could only serve to smuggle Kennedy's assassin out of the country by plane! This spectacular news naturally caused a stir, and attracted new rumors which, in turn, thickened the plot even more. Other people who heard Martin's rumors deemed it their civic duty to also report the matter, and this quickly created the impression that several witnesses brought David Ferrie in connection with the assassination and with Oswald.

At first sight, all indications point towards Jack Martin's speculation being unreliable, and the legal action that followed it, unjustified. We cannot afford to simply rule it out, though, because whatever way you look at it, Ferrie indeed was instructor at the Civil Air Patrol when Oswald was a cadet there, and he was in Texas on Saturday night. He also had to publicly admit that he had propagated the assassination of Kennedy. Let us therefore stick to the assumption that Martin's tip to the police, which was to persecute Ferrie for the rest of his brief further life, was – at best – a stroke of luck.

Something that stands out as odd in Martin's statement is the absence of one specific piece of information. His statement contained four specific items of information: (1) Ferrie was in Texas, at least on Saturday night; (2) as a pilot, Ferrie was not easily put off by anything, and he had already carried out rescue missions in the past; (3) Ferrie knew Oswald from his time with the Civil Air Patrol; and (4) Ferrie allegedly gave Oswald shooting lessons.[136] But something is missing. Martin and Ferrie both worked for Banister in the building Oswald had indicated as the address of the fake organization FPCC. Why did Martin omit to mention that Ferrie and Oswald actually had some business in the same building? Martin hated Ferrie ('A completely degenerated person'[137]). The fact that Ferrie and Oswald were connected to the same building should obviously have been the concluding piece of Martin's allegation, but Martin did not mention this. There can only be one explanation for this: Martin had never met Oswald in the building at any time, or even had the suspicion that Oswald could have been so close to his and Ferrie's vicinity.

Even though Martin did not know about the connection via the address, we now know that this link certainly existed. Even if Martin only guessed when he linked Oswald and Ferrie through their mutual CAP membership, again we now know that a photograph on which they are both seen together exists. Martin's blind guess accidentally hit a major target, and, even though it was not quite clear what exactly he had hit, the police were feverishly looking for Ferrie within 48 hours of the assassination, thanks to Martin. This means that there was a second suspect after all, and this suspect was being actively searched for on November 22. Perhaps we should have a closer look at David Ferrie.

Ferrie's activities November 22

Despite his lack of any legal training, David Ferrie was working for attorney G. Wray Gill[138]. Gill was Marcello's attorney in the deportation trial.[139] In an issue that was of vital importance for his immensely rich client, this lawyer was supported by a crazy queer, a dismissed pilot with a squeaky voice and fake eyebrows. From a legal point of view, as the issue related to a deportation, the counterparty was the Department of Justice, or, in other words, Robert Kennedy. The decision in the case *Marcello versus the Department of Justice* would fall precisely on November 22, 1963. The news that Kennedy had been assassinated, in fact, reached those present in the courtroom in New Orleans just before the verdict in the Marcello case.[140] For Ferrie, as a suspect in the Kennedy assassination, this was obviously very fortunate. His presence in court, together with Gill and their client Marcello provided him with a perfect alibi for the time of the murder. Yet, up to today it is still unclear where exactly Ferrie was on November 22. For at least three reasons, this is incomprehensible. The first reason is that even during the weekend of the murder, Ferrie was already frantically searched for in New Orleans. According to Jack Martin, Ferrie was in Dallas. Ferrie himself claimed he was in New Orleans. One would expect that he would have produced his iron-clad court alibi while being questioned on Monday, November 25, yet that was not the case. A second reason is that he was in a public area, a courthouse, more precisely. David Ferrie was an easily recognizable person because of his unique appearance, and it should therefore not have been a problem to find witnesses who saw Ferrie on this day and at that time in the courthouse, but, again, this does not appear to be the case. The third reason is that most people who were old enough at the time remember for the rest of their days exactly where they were when they heard the news of Kennedy's assassination. For Marcello and Ferrie, this must have been even more so, as both had expressed their approval of killing the president loud and clear in the months prior to the shooting. But Ferrie seemed to have found it difficult to remember where exactly he was when he heard about the assassination on Monday morning already.

The file regarding Ferrie's presence in court is hopelessly contradictory. Yet, whether he was in court, or in Gill's office or anywhere else in New Orleans, Ferrie was in any case not in Dallas, not even in Texas. On Friday afternoon and evening, he was hanging around in New Orleans for a while before he left for Texas.

For Marcello, November 22 quickly turned into a day never to forget. The court pleaded in his favor in his deportation case. In 1978, the HSCA report would mention that two members of the jury had been bribed, but the verdict must still have been a relief for the accused. At the time Marcello and Gill heard the favorable verdict, they were also informed about the death of Kennedy. Marcello must have pinched his arm to make sure he was not dreaming. His two major problems had been definitively solved in one hour's time. However, if he had been involved in the assassination plans, no matter how remotely, his first concern must undoubtedly have been to delete all traces of this thoroughly. It is therefore interesting to have a look at Marcello's whereabouts on Friday afternoon. And, interestingly: Marcello gives Ferrie a nice little bonus of 7,000 dollars[141] (current value: 52,000 dollars)[142], as a fee for his efforts in the deportation trial. But Marcello stated afterwards that he only knew Ferrie very vaguely, and that Ferrie did not work for him, but for Gill. Ferrie was already paid 300 dollars a month by the lawyer. Why then did Marcello pay him an additional amount corresponding to two years salary?

What's going on here? What is the key? As with Ruby, we must also ask ourselves what makes Ferrie unique in the context of this murder investigation. His strategic insight into a legal procedure regarding a birth certificate? Or rather the fact that he was an exceptionally skilled pilot? The further course of event will quickly make this clear. If Ferrie the 7,000 dollars for his legal assistance, this means that, on Friday afternoon, his job was finished. If he received the money to fly conspirators out of the country, he had another job to do that weekend. It is therefore important to know what Ferrie did, after having continuously worked for a full month on Marcello's strategy, and after having received a glorious fee. Did he have a night on the town, or did he stay quietly at home? Or did the news that the president had been shot perhaps restrain the merrymaking after all? The entire country was in shock and grieving. Should Ferrie, an ardent Irish Catholic, not have been sitting in front of the tube on that particular Friday, mourning the death of the Irish Catholic president? No. He was not staring hollow-eyed at the television screen. He decided for a modest party[143] at the Royal Orleans.[144] The first stage ended around 6 p.m. Ferrie then picked up two young men with his car, Melvin Coffey and Al Beauboeuf, and left without really knowing where to drive to or what to do. 'Hunting, drinking or driving'[145] was the rather vague action plan of the three men. Contrary to this statement, Ferrie also claimed to have phoned Chuck Rolland, the owner of a skating rink whom he did not know himself, from the apartment of Melvin Coffey. The *Winterland Skating Rink* was situated in Houston, about 375 miles from the place where Ferrie was at the time of his alleged phone call. Beauboeuf apparently was an excellent roller skater, and he wanted to see what he was worth on ice. Ferrie wanted to start a business with his 7,000 dollars, and operating a skating rink together with Beauboeuf suddenly seemed an excellent idea on this Friday evening.

At least, that is the official version. The relationship between Beauboeuf and Ferrie is not clear, but for the sake of the story, it can be reported that the young man was Ferrie's sole heir after his death. The entrepreneurial trio first had a bite to eat at *Jean Paul's Restaurant* and left there around 9 p.m. for a 375 mile journey through a stormy night from Louisiana to Texas, where they arrived at 4.30 a.m. The purpose of that hellish trip was to visit a skating rink, which only opened eleven hours later, and 3.30 in the afternoon. Beauboeuf didn't see any problem in this: 'The weather was terrible, so what?' He and Ferrie ware accustomed to flying through storms and 'driving through one was no big deal.'[146]

A weekend in Texas

The company therefore arrived in the early hours of Saturday in Houston, and descended on the Alamotel, a motel owned by Carlos Marcello.[147] The receptionist incorrectly entered November 22 as the date of arrival. That played right into the hands of the conspiracists, but there's no need to find anything sinister behind this: for the porter it simply still was the night from Friday to Saturday, hence the incorrect date. It was Saturday afternoon by the time the trio woke up. Ferrie phoned his boss G. Wray Gill to tell him that he took a little holiday.[148] Then the men made a few purchases in a Sears Department Store and by its opening time, at 3:30 p.m., they made their way to the Winterland Skating Rink. Ferrie claimed that he had a long conversation with the manager about the costs and benefits of running an ice rink, and he was able to submit a local folder to the FBI. But Chuck Rolland, the manager of the *Winterland Skating Rink*, said that Ferrie had only spent his time on the pay phone in the vicinity of the ice rink with incoming and outgoing phone calls.[149] Ferrie had said nothing with regard to the alleged acquisition plans[150] and the skating rink was actually not for sale. Rolland had no reason whatsoever to lie about this, and we must therefore conclude that Ferrie was the one who was lying. This all strongly resembles a rather construed alibi for the trip to Houston. Because Ferrie used a pay phone at the skating rink, it is no longer possible to establish with whom he was so busy on the phone that Saturday afternoon. The strange group returned from the skating rink to the Alamotel, where Ferrie phoned the *Town and Country Motel* in New Orleans, Carlos Marcello's headquarters.[151] Then the men visited a second ice rink, the *Belaire Skating Rink*, where they found that the manager was absent, so this time no interesting conversations about an unsolicited takeover were conducted. The men hung around for one and a half hours, and then went away to have something to eat. Finally, shortly after 9 p.m. on Saturday night, they decided to drive 45 miles further, to the coastal town of Galveston, in 1963 an island town with 67,000 inhabitants. The company arrived between 10:30 and 11:00[152] in the *Driftwood Motel*[153] on Saturday evening. Galveston did not have an ice rink, and hunting was also not possible. The city is situated on the Gulf of Mexico, however, and therefore an ideal departure point for an escape to Mexico. Incidentally, the tiny city of Galveston did have an airport, the *Scholes International Airport*.[154]

In 1968, Raymond Broshears, a former roommate of Ferrie, stated that the latter confessed to him to have waited with an airplane in Houston, Texas to fly the Kennedy assassins to South America.[155] Unfortunately, Broshears is a source of dubious quality. Even public prosecutor Jim Garrison, who was desperately searching for evidence against Ferrie, refrained from calling Broshears as a witness in his trial against Clay Shaw. We therefore give you Broshears' account for what it's worth: a possible, but never proven, scenario of why Ferrie could have been in Galveston.

Home again

On Sunday morning, the murder of Oswald was broadcast live on television. Ferrie and his companions started their return trip to New Orleans immediately afterwards, even though they still had the whole of Sunday for their trip. What it comes down to is that they drove over 800 miles to and fro to do some shopping at a Sears Department Store, visit two ice rinks without any apparent reason, to stay overnight at a seaside resort and to make plenty of phone calls. Weird. On the way home, they also stopped in Alexandria, where, again, Ferrie did not get off the phone. This is how he learned, much to his surprise, that he was sought as a suspect in the Kennedy assassination case. Jack Martin's story had raised hell in New Orleans. That was the end of the fun for the three men, and they drove back to New Orleans, arriving there around 9:30 p.m. on Sunday night. Ferrie, now well aware that he was wanted, drove past his own apartment so that he 'could check to see if anyone was waiting'[156] and phoned his own number from a pay phone. Someone he didn't know – 'some dumb ox' – answered, and Ferrie immediately put the phone down. He sent Beauboeuf in on his own, and the eventful weekend promptly ended with his friend being arrested.

Ferrie could not return to his own house. As there was nowhere else for him to go, he decided to report to public prosecutor Garrison in the morning. But if this whole fuss was based purely on Martin's nonsense and he had an iron-clad alibi, what was Ferrie afraid of, and why did he flee and lie? Garrison turned Ferrie over to the FBI after questioning him, assuming that they would pursue the matter further. But the FBI did not appear to be very interested in this trail. Garrison only started a new investigation into Ferrie's involvement in the assassination of Kennedy in 1967. But just before he could arrest him, Ferrie died, completely unexpectedly. According to the pathologist, it was a perfectly natural death. Ferrie had a congenital structural weakness in an artery to the brain, a cerebral aneurysm that ruptured at the wrong time.[157] An unfortunate coincidence. But this is not the last of the coincidences. This is the Kennedy file – never believe that you have come to the bottom of your amazement.

Return to Galveston

The New Orleans-Dallas-Galveston triangle is comparable to the position of the European cities Brussels, Copenhagen and Berlin. Galveston is situated at about 400 miles from New Orleans, roughly the distance between Brussels and Berlin. The seaside town is situated at 270 miles from Dallas, roughly the distance from Copenhagen to Berlin. Dallas and New Orleans are 500 miles apart, the distance from Brussels to Copenhagen. Yet, despite these distances, it's really a small world. This became apparent again when a certain Breck Wall, traveling from Dallas, arrived in Galveston just before midnight on November 23. Wall was the stage name of Billy Ray Wilson, a revue artist or entertainer who, after the events, kept himself afloat for many years in the Las Vegas casino circuit with his burlesque show *Bottom's up*. Wall had performed in Ruby's club a few weeks, but this had ended, once more, in a blazing row.[158] After some time, Wall and Ruby had just about made up, but working together was out of the question. Meanwhile, however, Wall had also become chairman of the dubious artists' guild AGVA. Wall and his friend Joe left for Galveston[159], a trip of 270 miles, around 5:30 on Saturday afternoon, and arrived there around 11:43 p.m. Barely three and a half minutes after Wall had arrived at the house of a family friend in Galveston,[160] his friend's phone rang. It was Ruby. The reason for the call was allegedly again the argument concerning the non-syndicated amateur strippers.

This doesn't make sense. Why would Ruby suddenly devote his full attention to a trivial stripper problem? Did he for a moment forget the deep grief that would compel him to commit murder a few hours later? When Ruby learned that Breck Wall had unexpectedly left town, he didn't let it go. He got hold of the phone number of Wall's family friends, and called the AGVA chairman in the middle of the night, as if the latter would be willing and able, at midnight, to do something to help Ruby in his feud with the Weinstein brothers, and from Galveston. Jack Ruby then hung up and, as if by magic, was immediately overwhelmed by nationalist feelings again. The next morning, at 11:21 a.m., he was to shoot Oswald.

At the very same time, however, Ferrie was also driving head over heels towards the very same town of Galveston, 440 miles away, while the whole police force in New Orleans was hectically searching for him as a suspect in the Kennedy case. The Commission only reported that 'the check of the long-distance telephone records reveals no conspiratorial implications.'[161] Life is indeed made up of coincidences; we have a few more in store.

9. BRADEN AND CO

Cabana Motel

Lawrence Meyers was a traveling businessman who had been visiting the *Carousel* occasionally for several years. He had more or less befriended Ruby, and they met several times a year. On November 21, the day before the assassination, 53-year-old Meyers was in town again, with 27-year-old Jean West or Jean Aase, as she called herself, in tow.[162] Aase was a semi-professional prostitute and, to quote Meyers, 'a rather dumb but accommodating broad'.[163] He added discreetly that his family and business associates had no knowledge of his 'association' with the lady. After Meyers' undoubtedly busy day, the couple ended up at the *Carousel Club*. Ruby treated Mrs. Aase to two champagne cocktails. After about an hour, Meyers and Aase called it a day, and returned to their hotel, the *Dallas Cabana Motel*. They invited Ruby to join them there for a drink in the *Bon Vivant Room*. Around midnight, Ruby indeed turned up at the hotel, but he didn't stay long. He had to close down his own establishment and empty the till.[164]

So far, all is clear. At precisely the same day, however, Eugene Hale Brading, aka Jim Braden, had also booked into the *Dallas Cabana Motel*, which, by coincidence, was also owned by no one else but Carlos Marcello. Braden was a tough guy with an impressive criminal record. He had been convicted 35 times, and, in the course of just a few years, had married twice – each time a wealthy woman – once before and once after the Kennedy assassination. Braden had traditionally been a minion of Carlos Marcello, but he had meanwhile converted to the oil business, and this was the reason for the business meeting he had on November 21 with Lamar Hunt, son of oil billionaire Haroldson L. Hunt, presumably the richest man in the world. Lamar would inherit five billion dollars after his father's death in 1974. But the son of the wealthiest man in the world apparently enjoyed doing business in private with a repeatedly convicted criminal.

Lamar Hunt

This may have been quite normal for Lamar Hunt, though, because on the same day he had another meeting with some quite ordinary people. On November 21, he also met the unemployed Ms Connie Trammel, who turned out to be also known as Mrs. Penny. None other than Jack Ruby gave her a lift to Hunt's office. In a recent past, Connie Trammel had been a *senior at the University of Texas*, and had one fine day visited Dallas. Now what would any self-respecting student in this situation do but to visit a strip joint? Perhaps her sociology studies needed a boost, or some additional tuition on the subject of anatomy would do her good. Trammel's eye fell on the *Carousel Club*. Then, when she was in the Carousel and went to the bathroom, Ruby followed her with the stale excuse: 'Do I know you from somewhere?' How would any student respond but to give a clammy little man, who was thirty years her senior, her telephone number and name – which was Connie Trammel at the time. Jack Ruby then stalked her for a while: 'he made several calls to Mrs. Penny at the University attempting to get Mrs. Penny to go to work at the Carousel Club as a stripper'. He called her several times at the university, offering her a job as striptease artist at the *Carousel*. But Ms Trammel/Mrs. Penny did not give in. Her telephone number also did not appear anywhere in Ruby's diary or in his telephone bills, which were thoroughly examined afterwards. When she had graduated, Mrs. Penny again ended up in Dallas. As a university graduate, she suddenly did see the splendid perspectives the professional night live had to offer. She asked Ruby, who was always ready to rescue a lonely, stranded girl, for a job as cloakroom lady in the Carousel. Ruby may then have been all but a chivalrous helper in need, his business nose still told him that Mrs. Penny was more suitable for the better work on stage. She was not too keen on stripping, but Ruby was not someone who gave up quickly, and he continued to insist by phone – all be it without having her number down in his diary and without connections being charged on his phone bill – but these are mere details.

One of these ghost phone calls occurred by mere coincidence on the morning of November 21, 1963. Mrs. Penny told Ruby 'that she had talked with Lamar Hunt regarding employment.' She had an appointment for an application interview on the same day with Lamar in person. Unfortunately, she did not have a car, so it was difficult for her to go and meet Hunt. Fortunately, Jack Ruby happened to call her just then and he was willing to drive the sweet young thing to her appointment with Lamar Hunt.

This happened in the morning of November 21. Mrs. Penny could not remember the correct time and the correct suite where the interview took place. It would appear that also Lamar had made a mistake, because on reflection, the job for which he had Ms. Penny and her driver Jack Ruby turn up no longer existed.[165] No matter how implausible this story may sound, it is used as an important piece of evidence by the Warren Commission. Below is an excerpt from the official document:

> The A.M. of November 21, 1963, exact time she could not recall, Ruby picked up Mrs. PENNY at the apartment and inquired as to how Mrs. PENNY had made the appointment with LAMAR HUNT, at which time RUBY stated that he would like to meet HUNT. Mrs. PENNY exeplained she had made a personal call to LAMAR HUNT's residence, at which time a maid in the LAMAR HUNT home gave her the telephone number of a straight line into LAMAR HUNT's office. Mrs. PENNY called LAMAR HUNT and made the appointment to talk to LAMAR HUNT in his office in the Mercantila Bank Building. Mrs. PENNY could not recall the suite number where she was interviewed by LAMAR HUNT.

The fact that Hunt was no ordinary American is also clear from the personal attention Kennedy paid to his father Haroldson Lafayette Hunt, owner of the *Hunt Oil Company*. Kennedy was annoyed about the fact that oil billionaires paid hardly any taxes. Two of them he mentioned explicitly by name: J. Paul Getty and H.L. Hunt. 'These men', the president said, 'use various forms of tax exemption and special tax allowances to subsidize the ultra right on television, radio and in print.'[166] The so-called super PACs (Political Action Committee) of today, whereby a billionaire such as Sheldon Adelson invested 100 million dollars (about 0.4 percent of his wealth) in an attempt to stop President Barack Obama from winning a second term in 2012, are nothing new under the sun. Already in 1963, extreme right-wing billionaires financed ongoing campaigns against the United Nations, against progressive tax scales, against development aid, health support and other traditional pet areas of wealthy reactionary forces. Hunt's support included the ultra-right-wing John Birch Society, communist-hunter McCarthy, neo-Nazi fanatics, anti-Castro guerillas, right-wing General Walker, who was allegedly shot at by Oswald. Moreover, he is said to have been friends with Carlos Marcello. There are witnesses confirming the almost irrational hatred Haroldson Hunt had against the Kennedy administration.[167] In 1961, he openly stated that things had reached the point where there seemed to be no way left 'to get those traitors out of our government' except by 'by shooting them out'.

This hatred was irrational, because the oil industry really had no cause to complain about the minor contribution the community dared to claim from its monstrous profits. The tax loophole the oil barons were using was the *Oil Depletion Allowance*, a tax reduction of no less than 27.5 percent, which was deemed necessary in 1913 when increasing oil drilling was a must for the economy. In 1964, with a turnover of 50 billion dollars (current value: 350 billion dollars) oil was the largest industry, larger than steel, cars and chemicals combined.[168] Moreover, the ample tax reduction inevitably applied to any profits the concerns channeled through their oil companies. The mechanism of the *Oil Depletion Allowance* was downright perverse. In his book *Cronies: Oil, the Bushes, and the Rise of Texas, America's Superstate*, Robert Bryce describes how the system works: costs for drilling an oil well amount to 100,000 dollars. If this oil well yields one million dollars worth of oil for ten years, the owner can claim ten times 275,000 dollars tax exemption. At a tax rate of, roughly estimated, 25 percent, final tax savings amount to approximately 700,000 dollars, which is not bad for an investment of 100,000 dollars. It makes you think, though: you drill a hole in the ground at a cost of 100,000 dollars. Whether or not any oil comes out of it, is irrelevant. Then you channel the profits of other business activities through the company who owns the hole in the ground, and you save 700,000 dollars in taxes.

Tax exemptions therefore involved astronomical amounts and huge interests. Whoever aimed to touch the *Oil Depletion Allowance* could be sure of the worst imaginable opposition. The latest president who had undertaken an attempt to curb the oil industry had been F. D. Roosevelt. Sam Rayburn, the Texan *Majority leader* of the House of Representatives, made quite sure that the law was not accepted, and that everything remained as it was. President Eisenhower received ample political sponsoring from the oil industry, and he consequently kept his hands off their favorable tax regime. During his presidential campaign against Eisenhower's Vice President Richard Nixon, Kennedy had wisely pleaded in favor of preserving the tax exemption. But on October 16, 1962, Kennedy pushed a law through Congress that would cost the oil barons fifteen to thirty percent yield loss on their foreign investments with immediate effect. They did not consider this a laughing matter. On January 17, 1963, Kennedy, now well and truly at cruising speed, proposed a tax reform aiming to reduce the tax burden on low incomes and pensions. He also announced that he would finance the tax cut by closing loopholes and by cancelling preferential regimes, such as the *Oil Depletion Allowance*. For the Texan oil industry, the abolition of the preferential measure was estimated at an annual cost of 300 million dollars (current value: 2.1 billion dollars), spread over a very select group of just a few oil magnates. If Kennedy meant business, the gauntlets would be thrown, and he would have a war on his hands. Precisely at this point in time, Kennedy was shot by a lone madman without a motive, performing a truly miraculous shot with an ancient, poorly adjusted rifle. Suddenly, Lyndon Johnson – Texan and trusted friend of the oil barons – was president. Clearly, the abolition of the *Oil Depletion Allowance* disappeared from the agenda after November 22, 1963. Nixon, Johnson's successor, did not touch the issue either. It would take another twenty years nearly before Jimmy Carter was able to abolish the profoundly unjust exemption at the end of the seventies.[169] Carter was not reelected.

The name Haroldson L. Hunt is therefore very high on the list of those who had in interest in the death of John Kennedy, and by extension, this also includes his son Lamar. John Currington, Hunt's lawyer, would later claim that he was commissioned by his client Haroldson Hunt to go and observe the situation at the Dallas Police Station on the spot on Saturday, November 23. Currington had no trouble in entering and leaving the police station not just once, but three times, and he had even found himself in the elevator together with Oswald and several police officers at some point.[170] Why was Haroldson Hunt so interested in the security of the police station the day before Oswald was to be shot there?

Jack Ruby and Haroldson Hunt

There are also indications that Ruby knew Haroldson Hunt personally. One of Ruby's partners in crime was Harry Hall, who was questioned by the FBI while in prison on November 30, 1963. The modus operandi of Handy Harry and Ruby consisted of seeking out wealthy gamblers, and to entice them to bet on horse races and other sports events. If Hall lost, he paid with a fake check and fled the city. If he won, he split the spoils with Ruby, who was in it for forty percent. Ruby was indispensable 'because he was supposed to have influence with the police, so that he [Hall] would have no worry about any gambling arrest.'[171] One of the Texan millionaires who became a victim of the 'gambling trick' was none less than H. L. Hunt, according to Harry Hall: 'He and Ruby bet Hunt on the Cotton Bowl and Rose Bowl games, winning a large sum of money from Hunt, which they split.'[172] As Ruby's role in the attempted scams was primarily damage control when the scam failed, it is not sure that Hunt and Ruby actually came into contact with each other in this context. But the entire setup, whereby Ruby also was to supply the potential victims, points towards some proximity.

The fact that Ruby had few scruples was also confirmed by another joint adventure Hall reported. Ruby knew that Bill Byers, a Texan millionaire, always had large amounts of cash on him. Ruby asked Hall to keep an eye on where and when Byers was on his own. He would then have some of his men grab hold of Byers 'without injuring him', and the spoil would be split. Hall can hardly be expected to admit to a crime for which he was not arrested, so he claimed that he did not rise to the attractive bait. But the fact remains that Byers had been robbed exactly according to this scenario. Another story was circulating about Bill Byers: the oil millionaire is said to have been a personal friend of Hoover and, even more interestingly, the only person Hoover phoned after the assassination that Friday afternoon, besides Robert Kennedy and the head of the Secret Service. What did Hoover have to discuss so urgently with an oil baron at the time the nation was in a state of absolute crisis?[173]

Hall, who was now running warm in his statements as a witness against Ruby, also told the FBI that he could not imagine that Ruby would do something out of patriotism. According to him, Ruby was 'the type who was interested in any way of making money and he had good contacts with the police.'

Although Ruby's contact with Hunt seems rather anecdotal, Hall's testimony reveals another Ruby than the groomed version that was presented in the Warren Report. Hall's statement shows Ruby in a role he was good at: *damage control* on the basis of his good contacts with the Dallas Police. This aspect does not seem to be without any weight in our considerations as to whether Ruby was a second lonely nutcase that weekend, or whether he was used as an instrument in the hands of conspirators.

Lee Harvey Oswald and Haroldson Hunt

A scribbled note in Oswald's handwriting dated November 8, 1963 (Figure 6) emerged in the course of the HSCA investigation. The recipient is a certain 'Dear Mr. Hunt'. The note reads as follows: 'I would like information concerning my position. I am only asking for information. I am suggesting that we discuss the matter fully before any steps are taken by me or anyone else'. Conspiracists assume that the note is genuine, that the recipient was either Hunt senior or junior, and that 'the matter' related to the assassination of the president.

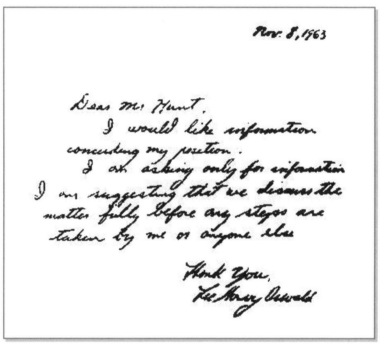

Figure 6 – To which 'Dear Mr. Hunt' did Oswald write this note? Or is the document a fake?

The HSCA was unable to confirm or disprove the authenticity of the note, as they only had a copy of the document in their possession. If it is a forgery, it is certainly not a bad imitation of Oswald's handwriting and style. Some claim that the KGB, the secret police of the Soviet Union, produced the forgery on the basis of letters they intercepted during Oswald's stay in the communist state. But what was the point of this forgery then? What could possibly be the benefit of the Soviet Union in producing a fake note from Oswald to Hunt? The identity of Mr. Hunt is a second item for discussion. The question sometimes arises whether the recipient may not have been Howard Hunt, a CIA employee who later became a 'plumber' in the White House during Nixon's presidential term. Howard Hunt certainly played a prominent role in Nixon's infamous White House tapes. Political advisor Chuck Colson said the following about Howard Hunt to Nixon on July 1, 1972: 'Well, he's certainly done a lot of hot stuff... Oh Jesus. He pulled a lot of very fancy stuff in the sixties'. A section is then missing from the transcription of the tape: 'Withdrawn Item. National Security.' is written there. When the transcription resumes, Nixon is speaking. He says: 'Well, I don't agree. If anything ever happens to him, be sure that he blows the whistle, the whole Bay of Pigs.' The president of the United States was worried enough to let himself be blackmailed. 'Bay of Pigs' was the code language for the assassination of Kennedy. The following was written by none other than Bob Haldeman, Nixon's Chief of Staff at the White House, in his memoires The Ends of Power: 'It seems that in all of those Nixon references to the Bay of Pigs, he was actually referring to the Kennedy assassination.' If the note was forged, then what reasons did the forger have? If the note is genuine, was it addressed to Lamar or to Howard Hunt? One is more of a clue towards a conspiracy than the other. We are also completely in the dark as to exactly what Oswald and Hunt had to discuss before anyone took further steps. The Hunt note was simultaneously and anonymously sent from Mexico to three researchers on August 18, 1975. After 1963, Haroldson Hunt lived at his big ranch in Mexico. He died nine months before the note emerged. Could that be the link?[174]

On the one hand, the conspiracists cannot be deterred from being convinced that one of the Hunts had something to do with the assassination. No other person called Hunt is known with whom Oswald had to discuss whatever on November 8, two weeks before the assassination. The conspiracy theory is that either Hunt senior or Hunt junior had put a price on Kennedy's head, and that Oswald wanted to go through the small print of the contract with his client once again. On the other hand, the believers can also not be deterred from claiming that the mysterious note signifies nothing. It's a fake, because everything that is contrary to the official version is a forgery by definition. This certainly seems to be a law of nature for the believers.

To come to the conclusion that a conspiracy is a possibility, only one item must be conclusive. Oswald's note will presumably not be that decisive item, and, besides the note, there are still plenty of other arguments we can consider.

Jim Braden

700,000 people were living in Dallas in 1963. Jack Ruby went for a drink at the Cabana Motel on November 21, and, by coincidence, met Jim Braden at the hotel. On the following day, this very same Jim Braden had to make an urgent phone call in the building across the street from the TSBD, precisely at the time that Oswald shot Kennedy – a second coincidence. Ruby and Braden, who allegedly did not know each other at all, again found themselves both visiting another place on November 21, the same building – another coincidence. They both wanted to meet Lamar Hunt, son of the wealthiest man in the world. For us, this is reason enough to have a closer look at Braden's account (or Brading, his other name). The Warren Commission and the FBI were clearly of another opinion.

Braden was at Dealey Plaza around noon on November 22. According to Braden, the reason for this was that he had to report to his probation officer, Roger Caroll, in the courthouse. Later, the probation officer did not remember anything about this appointment, and firmly denied having met Braden that day. The Warren Commission took Braden, a criminal who was present at the exact site of a murder, at his word. The commission simply brushed aside a public officer with an impeccable track record and no reason to say anything other than the truth. Warren logic. Braden claims that he bought a sandwich after his appointment and was looking for a taxi when screaming people ran towards him shouting that the president had been shot. He continued his account as follows:

> So I figured, well Jesus, I'll call my family... So I proceeded around and asked a girl 'Is there a telephone around anywhere?' She said 'Upstairs, where I work [in the Dal-Tex Building]. Come on in here with me.' We went through a passageway and into an elevator, a freight elevator... So we proceeded to the third floor. I got out. I go over there, and there's a telephone hanging on the wall. A woman was trying to use it. I said 'Does that telephone work?' 'No. I tried it, it didn't work.'

In brief, a big-time criminal returning from an appointment no-one else could remember anything about bought a sandwich and was looking for a taxi. Because he was buying the sandwich, and despite the spectators all around, he missed the fact that he president could drive by any moment, or, in any case, he was more interested in buying a sandwich than in seeing the president. When he learned that he was at the exact place where the president was assassinated, he did not stay at the plaza talking with other people, like the rest of the crowd, nor did he take a look at the *Grassy Knoll*. Our friend was not at all curious by nature, and so he went to the nearest building, the Dal-Tex building, and immediately found his way to the third floor. Incidentally, this building is just opposite the Texas School Book Depository. Braden claimed he entered the building at the suggestion of yet another person without a name or a face. As a result, nobody could confirm Braden's version of the facts. Braden was not walking about the Plaza – curious, perhaps, or surprised – because he immediately wanted to report to his family what the screaming women had said, even before he had collected more concrete information, or had a chance to experience the historic moment for himself. He then entered a building; picked a random floor to find a telephone, but then the blasted thing didn't work. This means that, unfortunately, Braden's relatives also could not confirm his story. As the phone didn't work, Braden returned to the elevator. Afterwards, he stated the following:

> So I get in there, and I'm going down. Now he [the elevator operator] begins to look at me. He had a little radio, and the voices are coming over that, screaming and yelling that the president has been shot and that whole business. Now he looks at me, and he's scared to death. He said, 'You're a stranger. I shouldn't have let you up in this building.' And with this, he takes off and runs for the cop.[175]

C.L. Lewis, a local deputy sheriff, took Braden to police headquarters because of his suspicious behavior. There, Braden's records were checked, but nobody realized that he had simply changed his name two months before, on September 10, 1963. As there was no criminal record in the name of Braden, Jim Hale Brading could go, free to continue his path in the oil industry or in crime unabated.[176] Life can be sweet, sometimes.

Another man was, in fact, also briefly detained for his suspicious presence in the Dal-Tex building, but, as far as we know, his name and identity have not been recorded anywhere. According to Officer Vaughn[177], he was a very well-dressed man who had no explanation for his presence in the Dal-Tex building, and who had a wallet with more credit cards than Vaughn had ever seen ('a dozen or more'). Vaughn handed the man over to other officers, who took him to the sheriff's office. A few minutes later, the man was free to go again, but his identity remained unknown in the subsequent investigation.

As coincidence is rapidly becoming the leitmotif in this account, we briefly mention here that Jim Braden was also present in the *Ambassador Hotel* in Los Angeles on June 4, 1968,[178] the place and time of Robert Kennedy's assassination. Dallas' Dealey Plaza and the Los Angeles Ambassador Hotel are at a distance of 1,400 miles from each other, and four and a half years passed by between November 22, 1963 and June 4, 1968. Yet Jim Braden was the only person on the planet who – purely by coincidence – was present at the assassinations of both John and Robert Kennedy. Ready for another coincidence? In *Legacy of doubt*[179], CBS producer Peter Noyes revealed that Braden was working in the office of Vernon Main Jr. during the fall of 1963, on the same floor of the Pere Marquette building where Gill had his law firm.[180] Braden, Gill and Ferrie all accidentally found themselves in the same building and on the same floor, six doors apart. For the proper understanding of this fact, please note that New Orleans is not a village with only one office building.

Let's throw another block of wood onto our fire of coincidences, and briefly return to November 21. We have already mentioned that, the night before the assassination of John Kennedy, Jack Ruby was present in the bar of the hotel where also Braden was staying, a hotel that was known as a mob hangout. He raised his glass to his old friend Meyers, who was accompanied by Mrs. Aase, a 'semi-professional', a rather dumb but accommodating lady of half his age; a lady Mrs. Meyers did not know about.

Jean Aase

In 1967, District Attorney Jim Garrison prosecuted businessman Clay Shaw for complicity in the assassination of Kennedy. Garrison's case against Shaw was appallingly weak. Actually, Ferrie should have been sitting in the dock, but, just before his arrest, the latter had suddenly died through 'natural causes'. Garrison had investigated with whom Ferrie had been on the phone from the office of his boss, Attorney G. Wray Gill.[181] Garrison was particularly interested in the phone traffic of September 24, 1963, because that was the day before Oswald left New Orleans and departed for Mexico. Garrison made a note of an outgoing phone call from the law firm to a number in Chicago (WH 4-4970), but he was initially not able to figure out who this number belonged to. But then the same number emerged somewhere else in the Kennedy file. Mary Ferrell, a passionate Kennedy researcher who noted *everything* she found on separate cards and filed them carefully, had already seen this number WH 4-4970 somewhere in her archives. It also appeared in a list of telephone numbers of the *Ero Manufacturing Company*, the company that belonged to Lawrence Meyers.[182] In fact, the telephone number turned out to belong to the 'rather dumb but accommodating' Mrs. Jean Aase.

Let's have another look at the chain.

1. Lawrence Meyers was a friend of Ruby;
2. Meyers brought along his sweetheart of the moment, Mrs. Aase;
3. Ruby, Meyers and Mrs. Aase happened to be in the same hotel as Jim Braden on November 21;
4. The hotel is the property of Carlos Marcello;
5. Neither Ruby nor Meyers know Ferrie or Marcello's lawyer Gill;
6. By pure coincidence, Mrs. Aase received a phone call from Gill's office, presumably from Ferrie, two months before.

Isn't this amazing? The believers insist that it is not proven that it was Ferrie who phoned from Gill's office. Obviously, in the end it is not possible to prove who was actually using the phone in the law firm. But, whether it was Ferrie or not, the fact remains that *someone* called Jean Aase from the office where Ferrie was employed. The same Aase also met Ruby on the eve of the assassination, in the same hotel as Jim Braden. Both Braden and Ruby visited Hunt on November 21. They were in the same hotel in the evening. Ruby was there in the presence of Mrs. Aase. Braden's office in New Orleans was situated on the same floor as Gill's law firm, where Ferrie was employed, and Ferrie phoned Mrs. Aase from that office. But you can take the believers at their word: Ruby, Ferrie, Braden and Lamar Hunt had nothing, absolutely nothing at all to do with each other. All this was pure coincidence.

Jack Ruby and James Dolan

We will add one more man to this tangle: James Dolan, a former boxing champion who was AGVA representative for the Dallas region from 1958 to 1961. Dolan apparently had a suitable CV for the Agva, because, at that particular time, he had been released from prison with probation measures. According to the HSCA, Dolan was one of the two top gangsters in Dallas. He was allegedly the strong arm of mafia boss Santo Trafficante.

His specialties included armed robbery or robbery of bookmakers, gamblers, and houses of prostitution, confidence swindlers and shakedown rackets.[183]

The list of crimes in which Dolan was involved went on for three full pages. Dolan's son said the following about his father's job as AGVA representative:

I believe my father was either recruited by, or himself approached Marcello, and took the contract to turn over rackets in Dallas to the New Orleans don and his organization. In carrying out this contract, my father was naturally put in contact with the downtown strip club owners.[184]

Still according to his son, Dolan was the intermediary between Ruby and the mafia 'because of my father's attempts to forcibly represent their interests in the Dallas underworld of the late 50s, early 60s.' Apparently, the offices of the AGVA were regularly used for playing poker, and during his office hours for the union, Dolan also participated in the preparations for robbing a bank. The informant of the HSCA also claimed that Dolan blackmailed the members of the union he represented.[185] Dolan's son, who eventually accepted that his father would never change, described him as 'a career con, always playing his scams in the grifter underworld, never preying, to my knowledge, on the 'straight citizens' of the world.' This tumultuous AGVA period was, moreover, a relatively quiet period in his father's career.

The FBI questioned Dolan at the time of the Kennedy investigation as an acquaintance of Ruby.[186] Dolan did not paint a very pretty picture of Ruby, but he did not remember specific names and facts. He had not seen Ruby in the three months preceding the assassination. The FBI did not consider asking Dolan about his connections with the underworld or the mafia. For those who read the 27 volumes of the Warren Report, Dolan seems merely to be a quiet trade union representative who interfered in a couple of Carousel incidents. The Commission never even questioned Dolan. Fifteen years later, the HSCA reported that 'there is no indication that the Warren Commission was aware of the extent of Dolan's criminal activities.' The three full pages of criminal facts listed by the HSCA was something the FBI had overlooked in 1963.

When the HSCA did what the Warren Commission should have done, namely mapping out Ruby's entourage, they had to question Dolan in a state prison. Some of Ruby's good acquaintances were reviewed in Dolan's statement: Carlos Marcello and his henchman Nofio Pecora; James Bradlee Lee, aka Eugene Hale Brading or James Braden; Haroldson Lamar Hunt in the capacity of a notorious gambler and Breck Wall. Dolan's son said the following about Brading: 'Brading was one of the people known to have contacted my father during his time there in the early 50s.' So Braden had known Dolan ten years already. Moreover, Braden was closely linked to the Agva and all Ruby's long-distance telephone calls were in connection with the Agva. This is an observation, nothing more.

10. LIKE KNOWS LIKE

We started this component of our investigation with a bold assertion of J. Edgar Hoover and Earl Warren, the two major bigwigs in the first investigation into the assassination of Kennedy. Both were formal in saying that there was not the slightest scintilla of evidence pointing towards a conspiracy. Authorities such as Peter Jennings and Bugliosi were still endorsing this vision decades later. In order to determine whether a conspiracy could indeed radically and entirely be excluded, we picked the figure of Jack Ruby, and the question whether he could have been working on a contract when he shot Oswald.

The official account emphasizes that there is no direct connection between Ruby and Oswald, and, strictly speaking, this appears correct. There is no solid proof whatsoever of any contact between both protagonists. But when is there a mutual connection between several people in the context of a crime? Let us think about six people with mutual connections according to the diagram below (Figure 7). We will not try to confirm the experiment of behavioral scientist Milgram who attempted to demonstrate that, with 'six degrees of separation', two random individuals are almost certainly linked in one way or another to one another. Milgram relates to a chain whereby A is connected to B, B to C and finally E to F. In our mind experiment, all six people have a connection with the other five, except for two people who don't have a connection with one another, but with each of the four others. Could we then insist that there is no connection whatsoever between those two? The answer is not a clear 'yes' or 'no', because this depends on what those connections are. How strong are they, how real, how recent? How relevant are they for the envisaged end connection between A and B?

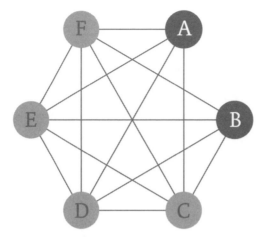

Figure 7 – Is there a connection between A and B in this diagram?

It is possible that A and B indeed have nothing to do with each other, despite all the other connections. Many marriages, in fact, started like this. But the fact that A and B do not know each other does not mean it can be claimed that there is no indication whatsoever of a connection between A and B. Assume that colleague A is retiring from a department with five staff members. The company then recruits B to replace A. Sometime later, A invites his former colleagues out for a meal, and the new staff member is also welcome. Everyone around the table knows everybody, except for A and B, who have never met each other. There is certainly a connection between A and B, even if they do not know one another. In this case, B has replaced A in the company.

Let us now concretely apply this to our story. After the weekend of November 22-23, the investigation focused on four people:

1. Oswald was arrested for the murder of Tippit and Kennedy;
2. Braden had been detained and released in connection with the assassination of Kennedy;
3. Ferrie was feverishly sought in New Orleans for his possible involvement in the Kennedy assassination;
4. Ruby was arrested for the murder of Oswald.

Two more people who had a strong motive to get rid of Kennedy entered the scene:

5. Marcello, a mafia boss from New Orleans who hated the Kennedys because Attorney General Robert Kennedy made life a misery for anyone involved in organized crime.

6. Hunt, who hated Kennedy because his announced tax reforms were about to end the erratic preferential regime of the oil business.

Between a limited number of subjects (n), only a maximum number of connections (x) is possible. This can be calculated on the basis of a formula $x = \frac{n.(n-1)}{2}$. There can therefore be maximum fifteen connections between the six suspects in our investigation. One of those is the connection between Ruby and Oswald. If that single link is missing there is no evidence that points to the existence of a conspiracy. Is that really so? Let us first review the fourteen remaining connections (Figure 8).

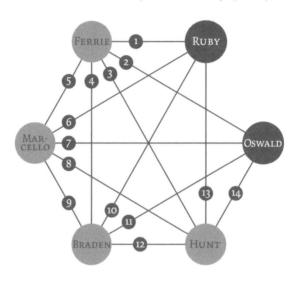

Figure 8 – There are fourteen possible connections between six people of which two do not know each other at all.

1. **Ferrie – Ruby:** *three connections*

1.1 On November 22, 1963, Ferrie made a journey of about 430 miles, which ended in the unsightly town of Galveston. At the time of Ferries arrival there, Ruby called a direct acquaintance, Breck Wall, who also happened to be in Galveston. Wall had also driven almost 270 miles to get to Galveston on Saturday, November 23.

1.2 The notorious gangster Dolan was a mutual acquaintance of Ferrie and Ruby.

1.3 Mrs. Aase is the third connection. Ruby was sitting with her in a bar on November 21. A staff member of a law firm in New Orleans, presumably Ferrie, called her at an earlier point in time.

2. Ferrie – Oswald: *two connections*

2.1 Oswald attended a CAP training camp where a photograph showing him with Ferrie was made.

2.2 For his pro-Cuba activities, Oswald used the address of a building in which also Ferrie was working in a detective agency.

3. Ferrie – Hunt: *one connection*

Both stated openly that Kennedy should be killed.

4. Ferrie – Marcello: *three connections*

4.1 In his capacity of pilot, Ferrie allegedly flew Marcello back to the United States after his deportation.

4.2 Ferrie provided Marcello with 'legal advice' just before the assassination, something he did not particularly excel in.

4.3 Marcello paid Ferrie 7,000 dollars in cash on the day of the assassination for no apparent reason.

5. Ferrie – Braden: *one connection*

In New Orleans, Braden worked in an office in the same building, at the same floor and even in the same corridor of the law firm where Ferrie was employed.

6. Marcello – Ruby: *three connections*

6.1 In the weeks preceding the assassination, Ruby had telephone contacts with at least three of Marcello's minions.

6.2 Ruby phoned the Agva Chairman in Galveston. Agva was an affiliate of Marcello's criminal network.

6.3 The gangster Dolan was a mutual acquaintance of Marcello and Ruby.

7. Marcello – Oswald: *one connection*

Oswald's uncle, his stepfather in a sense, was part of the illegal gambling circuit that was controlled by Marcello, and allegedly even worked for Marcello as a driver.

8. Marcello – Hunt: *four connections*

8.1 Billionaire Haroldson Hunt, father of Lamar Hunt, was a personal friend of Carlos Marcello.

8.2 Hunt and Marcello both verbally expressed their desire to have Kennedy killed.

8.3 Both men were billionaires. This may not be a direct connection, but two billionaires emerging in a random group of six people is statistically improbable, to say the least. It is even more unlikely that the two billionaires would not have known each other.

8.4 The gangster Dolan was a mutual acquaintance of Marcello and Hunt.

9. Marcello – Braden: *three connections*

9.1 Jim Braden stayed at the Cabana Hotel, which was owned by Marcello.

9.2 Braden was regarded as a Marcello minion.

9.3 The gangster Dolan was a mutual acquaintance of Marcello and Braden.

10. Braden – Ruby: *three connections*

10.1 Braden and Ruby were twice simultaneously in the same place on the day preceding the assassination. The first time they were in the office of Lamar Hunt, where Braden, free on probation, was discussing business matters with Lamar Hunt. Ruby was there at the same time, because he had given a job applicant who also had an appointment with Lamar Hunt a lift.

10.2 The second time, Ruby and Braden were in the same bar in the Cabana Hotel on the night preceding the assassination.

10.3 The gangster Dolan was a mutual acquaintance of Braden and Ruby.

11. Braden – Oswald: *one connection*

Just before Oswald was about to shoot Kennedy from the TSBD, Braden was at Dealey Plaza purely by accident and accessed the building immediately opposite the TSBD.

12. Braden – Hunt: *two connections*

12.1 Braden and Hunt had a meeting to discuss oil business on the day before the assassination.

12.2 The gangster Dolan was a mutual acquaintance of Braden and Hunt.

13. Hunt – Ruby: *four connections*

13.1 On November 21, Ruby gave a job applicant a lift to her appointment with Lamar Hunt.

13.2 Ruby appeared to know Haroldson Hunt as a gambler, and had even swindled him.

13.3 The gangster Dolan was a mutual acquaintance of Braden and Hunt.

13.4 Hunt had lawyer John Currington check out the security situation at the police station on Saturday, November 23, where Ruby shot Oswald on the following day. It remained unclear how he was able to enter the police station.

14. Hunt – Oswald: *one connection*

Two weeks before the assassination, Oswald wrote a mysterious note – if it is not a forgery – to a certain Mr. Hunt.

We can assume that Ruby and Oswald did not know each other personally because in the fifty years that have elapsed since the event, not a single piece of hard evidence to the contrary has surfaced. But there was apparently a whole circle of people who all knew each other, and at the same time they all individually also knew Ruby and Oswald. This entourage was a strange mixture of billionaires and losers, criminals, businessmen and hangers-on, of successful hard guys and failed Nancy Boys. Four major groups with a strong motive to get rid of Kennedy were represented in it: the extreme right, *big oil*, anti-Castro supporters and the mafia. Both through Marcello and through Hunt to Murchison and Byers, there was also a direct link to Hoover. The contacts were all reasonably fresh, to a large extent only a few days or hours old when Oswald was killed. It must be admitted that this is a strange and highly explosive mix. To cap it all, Braden was in a place where he was not supposed to have been at the time of the assassination, but where he had the president perfectly in sight. Let us not forget that Braden also turned up at the place where Robert Kennedy was assassinated in 1968.

The picture that emerges can also be explained as follows: there was a criminal group that could have deployed both Oswald and Ruby. This is possible without these two knowing each other (or perhaps even because they did not know each other). Shooting someone you know represents a larger risk. Suppose Oswald had shouted 'Damn, Ruby!', then the potential conspirators would have had another problem on their hands.

It is also interesting to add the incorrigible criminal Dolan to the network. Dolan knew four of the five people in this network. The only one he didn't know – except for Oswald – was Ferrie. But the connection between Ferrie and Marcello is very strong. If Dolan knew Marcello very well, he must have been very close to a contact with Ferrie. Moreover, Dolan had known Braden for more than ten years, and the latter was working in an office on the same floor as Ferrie. Nobody actually asked Dolan the question whether he knew Ferrie. Dolan was, in addition to his criminal main activity, also 'representative' of Agva, which means there is an undeniable connection between this network and Ruby's telephone traffic.

The FBI clearly filtered the evidence, and the Warren Commission wrote down its conclusions as dictated by Hoover. But, if the filter is removed, which is what the HSCA attempted to do, the brew is a lot less clear – or, if you change the perspective, rather enlightening. Claiming that there is no connection whatsoever between Ruby and the mafia requires a very large pair of blinkers. If we map the connections we have established, the following diagram emerges (Figure 9):

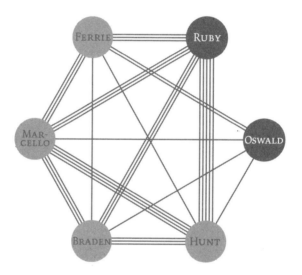

Figure 9 – Is there no connection whatsoever between Ruby and Oswald in this diagram?

Can we claim that there is not a single connection between Ruby and Oswald on the basis of the hard facts outlined above?

11. POPPY SPEAKS

The not-a-scintilla-of-proof argument has another remarkable, prominent defender. George H. W. Bush stated when he was President of the United States in 1991, following the release of Oliver Stone's JFK movie:

Nobody has come into this [oval] office with serious – with any – questions about the findings of the, what was it, the Warren Commission? So I don't spend any time thinking about it.[187]

That sounds like a perfect echo of the not-a-scintilla-of-proof argument. Not a single president entered the Oval Office with questions or doubts regarding the Kennedy assassination. Can this be true? Let us briefly review the presidents who succeeded Kennedy.

Lyndon Johnson

On September 18, 1964, Lyndon Johnson had a telephone conversation with Commissioner Russell about the conclusions of the Warren Commission[188]. Russell said openly that he did not believe the conclusions of the commission of which he was a member. Johnson replied: 'Neither do I.' The assassination would weigh heavily on Johnson's mind to his dying day. To claim that Johnson never had any doubts regarding the findings of the Warren Commission is absolute nonsense. Johnson undoubtedly spent many hours in the Oval Office pondering the assassination of Kennedy.

Richard Nixon

Richard Nixon was in Dallas on November 22, 1963. He departed from the Love Field airport shortly after Kennedy had landed there. Nixon was in Dallas to attend a Pepsi Cola congress, one of the key accounts of his law firm. Madeleine Brown, Lyndon Johnson's extramarital girlfriend, said in an interview for the TV show *A Current Affair* that a meeting took place on November 21, 1963, at the home of Texan oil billionaire Murchison. According to her, the following people were present: oil billionaire Haroldson L. Hunt; J. Edgar Hoover and his deputy and consort Clyde Tolson, who had been good friends of Murchison since the forties; John J. McCloy, later a member of the Warren Commission; and Richard Nixon. Towards the end of the evening, also Johnson arrived. The men then withdrew behind closed doors for a meeting. According to Brown, when the meeting was finished, Johnson snapped to her: 'After tomorrow those goddamn Kennedys will never embarrass me again - that's no threat - that's a promise.' It cannot be proven that Brown was speaking the truth. But there is evidence that Nixon knew, or at least suspected, more about the assassination of Kennedy.

Haldeman, Nixon's Chief of Staff, was intrigued by the Kennedy assassination and would have liked to re-open the investigation when he became chief at the White House. Nixon quickly made him change his mind. This was an issue he apparently firmly preferred to keep under lock and key. We already mentioned the Howard Hunt connection, where Nixon cryptically referred to the 'Bay of Pigs issue' which Hunt could cause to burst open. At a specific point in time during the Watergate scandal, Haldeman had to put pressure on CIA Director Richard Helms. Nixon instructed Haldeman to *literally* give Helms the following message: 'The president asked me to tell you this entire (Watergate) affair may be connected to the Bay of Pigs, and if it opens up, the Bay of Pigs may be blown'. In his memoires, The Ends of Power, Haldeman wrote the following on this: 'This prompted an explosive reaction from the spymaster: Turmoil in the room, Helms gripping the arms of his chair leaning forward and shouting, 'The Bay of Pigs had nothing to do with this. I have no concern about the Bay of Pigs.' Haldeman, former Chief of Staff of the White House, claims that 'Bay of Pigs' was code language for the assassination of Kennedy. The blackmail worked, and Haldeman was able to report to Nixon that, on second thoughts, the CIA Director was 'very happy to be helpful'.[189]

The conspiracists often claim that Nixon allegedly called the Warren Report 'the greatest hoax that has ever been perpetuated'. That is not the case, though, because the quote is used out of context.[190] But the argument that Nixon entered the Oval Office without any doubts with regard to the Warren Commission is, to put it mildly, quite wrong.

Gerald Ford

Gerald Ford succeeded Nixon as president. He had been on the Commission himself. Later in this book, we will demonstrate how Ford had deemed it necessary to personally tamper with the final report of the Warren Commission with regard to the location of Kennedy's back wound; this is how certain he was that the Warren Report had told the truth and nothing but the truth. From the minutes of the Commission's executive sessions it is as plain as day that the Commissioners, including Ford, were aware that the FBI lied to them. Ford also had his doubts about the information that had been provided by the CIA. In a preface for the final edition of the Warren Report, entitled *A Presidential Legacy and The Warren Commission*, Gerald Ford wrote that the CIA had withheld 'critical secrets connected to the 1963 assassination of President John F. Kennedy' from the examiners, or had destroyed them.[192] Ford was an intelligent man. He had attended the debates relatively intensively, compared to his fellow Commissioners. He cannot have been ignorant about the huge discrepancies between the final report and the underlying documents.

Jimmy Carter

Jimmy Carter allegedly told his UNO Ambassador Andrew Young that he was convinced that the assassination of Kennedy was a conspiracy. At least, that is what researcher Donald Freed claims in his book *Death in Washington*. Carter intended to appoint Ted Sorenson as Director of the CIA, giving the latter the opportunity to launch a thorough new investigation.[191] Carter met with so much opposition against the appointment of Ted Sorensen that he had to withdraw his candidacy. Subsequently, no new investigation was ever envisaged.

Ronald Reagan

Before Ronald Reagan was president, he was involved in radio talks – roughly in the period from 1975 to 1979 – in which he voiced his opinion on a wide range of subjects. One of the talks focused on the assassination of Kennedy.[193] Being a communist hunter in those days, he naturally primarily suspected the Russians:

> *Have we hesitated to investigate that Oswald might have been carrying out a plot engineered by a foreign agency? Even the original investigation by the Warren Commission seems to have ignored some obvious clues and has been rather in haste to settle for Oswald as a lone killer.*

Reagan was convinced that Johnson had prevented the truth from coming to light for fear of an international conflict:

> *It has been reported by more than one source that President Johnson and the Commission were fearful that evidence of a communist conspiracy involving as it would the Soviet Union and or Cuba would angry the American people and lead to a confrontation possibly even to war.*

Reagan also did not have any doubts regarding the cover-up operation:

> *It is also reported that the FBI files indicate there might have been a Communist conspiracy involving Oswald but that the Commission was unwilling to pursue this. The files further show that the Justice Department and the Warren Commission wanted to establish Oswald as alone in the case and get this conclusion to the American people as quickly as possible.*

Perhaps one day a new investigation would be able to prove this, concluded Reagan.

George H.W. Bush

Reagan's successor George H.W. Bush, aka Poppy Bush, was involved in the Texan oil business at the time of the assassination. He was also a CIA informant and preparing for a political career. In the year following the assassination, he was to challenge democratic Senator Yarborough for his seat in the Senate.

In his campaign, Bush criticized Yarborough for having supported JFK in his attempt to grant Afro-Americans equal rights. Given his political ambitions, home state and philosophy, George Bush could not possibly have been indifferent to the assassination. Yet President Bush could not remember the name of the Warren Commission ('… what was it, the Warren Commission?'). The statement that he doesn't spend any time thinking about it is also quite strange. How can a president possibly claim that he was not interested as to why and by whom one of his direct predecessors had been assassinated? Yet the fact that he doesn't waste any time on it doesn't prevent Bush from exuding absolute certainty: the findings of the 'what-was-it-again Commission' were all perfectly excellent. Bush was a true believer. He knew nothing about it, and wasn't in the least interested, but he was in no doubt whatsoever that the Warren Commission was absolutely right.

But Bush lied. The documents that were eventually declassified include an FBI memorandum[194] dated November 22 (Figure 10), the day of the assassination. This document states that Bush on that day reported 'hearsay in recent weeks' regarding a planned assassination of Kennedy. Why would Poppy Bush have reported rumors about an impending attempt on the president's life after the facts, when the assassination had already taken place? The memorandum further also discloses that Bush was in Dallas on November 22. Another spicy little detail in the light of the fact that, once president, he didn't waste any time thinking about the events of that day.

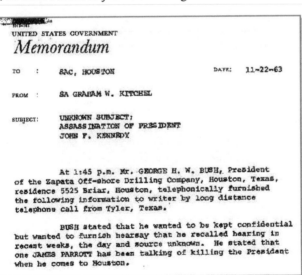

Figure 10 - George H.W. Bush denounced a man who was planning to assassinate JFK in Houston only after the assassination. Bush denied that he was the informant George H.W. Bush.

A second memorandum was found; not the dregs of yet another wild rumor, but a report prepared by Hoover on November 29, on the subject of a meeting held on November 23 (Figure 11). The day after the assassination, a meeting took place between the FBI and the CIA. They discussed that 'some misguided anti-Castro group might capitalize on the present situation and undertake an unauthorized raid against Cuba, believing that the assassination of President John F. Kennedy might herald a change in U.S. Policy, which is not true.' Hoover himself wrote this memorandum, so it must have been a serious matter. In the last paragraph, we learn that the information was provided by a certain 'George Bush of the Central Intelligence Agency'. When Bush was confronted with this, he lied again and said that this must have related to another George Bush. But there was only one CIA informant by the name of George Bush, and that was the later CIA Director and President of the United States George H. W. Bush.

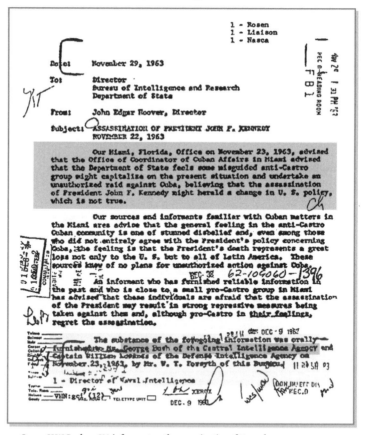

Figure 11 – George H.W. Bush as CIA informant on the assassination of Kennedy.

Why did this man lie? The man who was in Dallas on November 22, and provided information regarding the attack twice on the same day; who was CIA informant, opponent of the Kennedy policies; who later became CIA Director and even president; who uttered statements such as '… what was it, the Warren Commission?' and 'I never spend any time thinking about the assassination of Kennedy' and 'Not a single president has ever doubted the findings of the Warren Commission'? Why did he deny that it was his name that occurred in the FBI memoranda, although the first memorandum even states the name of his company Zapata and his address?

Bill Clinton

Bill Clinton finally, the democratic successor of Republican George Bush, had personally had the opportunity of shaking Kennedy's hand when he was sixteen. Kennedy was his idol. The assassination must have shaken his very soul. It is unthinkable that he would never have considered it while he was in the Oval Office. According to an anecdote, the first thing Clinton said when he entered the Oval Office, with a smile on his face, was: 'So where are the Kennedy files here?'

The truth is that all presidents, from Johnson to Clinton and including Bush, can be considered as honorary members of the club of conspiracists. It goes without saying that they all reflected on what had happened to their illustrious predecessor while they occupied the Oval Office, and what could be learned from it. Bush recites the not-a-scintilla-of- evidence argument as some kind of incantation: 'Vade retro, conspiratori!' It can easily be demonstrated, however, that this is no more than a hollow phrase that does not stand up against reality.

For the sake of completeness we may add that the three passengers in the limousine with Kennedy were *conspiracists*. When she decided not to take off her bloodied Chanel suit, Jacqueline Kennedy said: 'Let them see what they have done.' John Connally and his wife remained convinced that the Governor had not been hit by the same bullet as Kennedy. Two bullets between Z211 and Z237 would be inevitable proof that there were two snipers.

12. THE USUAL SUSPECTS

We can wave aside the not-a-scintilla-of-evidence argument as wishful thinking. The next question is where we should look if we wanted to uncover a possible conspiracy. Who would qualify as suspects in this context? Virtually all conspiracy scenarios that are put forward by the conspiracists focus on one or several of the following potential perpetrators.

The anti-Castro movement

Every single one of the financiers and pacesetters of the anti-Castro movement is also a rabid Kennedy hater. Did they use Oswald, with his ostentatious communist and pro-Castro sympathies as a fall guy? Did they make Oswald believe that he would be greeted as a hero in Cuba, or did they promise him a lot of money? The anti-Castro movement certainly had a motive. They were furious with Kennedy for the Bay of Pigs debacle. The assassination of Kennedy provided them with a unique opportunity to push their agenda through, i.e. the invasion of Cuba as an essential retaliation campaign – killing two birds with one stone, as it were.

George Bush lied in 1991 when he claimed not to have been the informant at the time. It seems that Bush was a tattletale, happy with an opportunity to repeat an interesting scrap of information. There is no reason whatsoever to doubt the content of his report: on the day of the assassination, the anti-Castro movement was ready to use the opportunity to provoke the US to invade Cuba. Kennedy was gone, and Oswald was the perfect excuse to finally push the American invasion of the island through. When you're wielding a hammer, everything looks like a nail. But President Johnson did not take the bait that was offered.

Lyndon Johnson was a strange guy. That Friday night, while Kennedy was still lying on the autopsy table, he had – in his pajamas – outlined his policy plans for an ambitious presidency to his exhausted staff, until 4 o'clock in the morning. Johnson had been in Washington for thirty years, and had been elected to the House of Representatives six times, and twice to the Senate. He had, moreover, been both opposition and majority leader. As Vice-President, however, he had wasted away like a dog on a chain. 'Lyndon who?' the members of the Kennedy clan mockingly asked when this name was mentioned. After the assassination, though, this political primal force suddenly found itself at the helm of the entire state machinery. Johnson was ready to amaze everyone with his progressive agenda. His aim was to completely abolish all poverty in America, nothing less would do.[195] The Kennedys were good at campaigning, was his analysis, but they didn't have a clue about pushing through a law. All this would quickly change now. But Johnson, raring to leap into political action, did not fancy a war with Cuba at all, and the military arsonists once again drew a blank. Pearl Harbor and 9/11 prove, however, that history could easily have been quite different.

Everything in the Kennedy dossier seems in one way or another to have links with Cuba, yet it is unlikely that the marginal anti-Castro movement had the means to carry out the assassination, and their ability to prevent the prosecution of the perpetrators afterwards is even less likely.

The CIA

The name of George H. W. Bush, the man who had stepped into the Oval Office without any questions on the Kennedy assassination, comes up once again in the file in another context. He appears to have been a personal friend of George de Mohrenschildt, a baron who was operating in the international oil business, besides also being a geologist and professor. The baron spoke six languages (English, Russian, German, French, Spanish and Polish) and had 'a smattering of a number of other languages'.[196] He also was a CIA informant, and had personally known Jacqueline Kennedy when she was young. It can certainly be said that de Mohrenschildt was at home in high places.[197] Conspiracist Gaeton Fonzi came across Bush's name in de Mohrenschildt's address book: 'Bush, George H. W. (Poppy), 1412 W. Ohio also Zapata Petroleum, Midland.'[198] George H. W. Bush had been a personal friend of the nobleman-geologist since 1940.[199] In 1976, de Mohrenschildt was suffering from psychological problems. He thought that he was being followed and stalked wherever he went. He wrote a letter about this to Bush, who was at the time Director of the CIA. The two knew each other well enough for Bush to reply to him personally, addressing the baron by his first name.[200] But is it not strange that precisely this aristocratic gentleman became the only friend of the unskilled, destitute laborer Oswald, holding a 1.25 dollars an hour job? Or could this improbable friendship perhaps imply that the baron was Oswald's 'babysitter' for the CIA?

Edward Epstein, academic and crime writer, interviewed de Mohrenschildt in the morning of March 29, 1977. The baron stated that he would not have contacted Oswald in a million years in Dallas in 1962, if he would not have received the green light to do so from J. Walton Moore, the CIA man in Dallas.[201] On the same day of the interview, the HSCA let the baron know that they wished to question him. When the baron received this message, he committed suicide with a shotgun at 3:45 p.m. There were no witnesses around. The young reporter Bill O'Reilly, now TV anchor of The O'Reilly Factor talk show on Fox TV, arrived on the spot shortly after he heard the gunshot.[202] No suicide note was found, and also de Mohrenschildt's address book apparently disappeared without a trace, despite intensive searches. Epstein made a note that he had been asked six times whether he had seen the black address book anywhere.

And so we can add another fatality, precisely at the moment the HSCA, who was tackling witnesses a little bolder than the Warren Commission, had been close to learning more about Oswald from him. For the conspiracists, de Mohrenschildt provides clear evidence that the CIA was all too aware of who Oswald was. We cannot but agree with this. As is befitting for self-respecting conspiracists, they take the issue still a step further and grant the CIA honorary membership in the conspirators' club. The conspiracists especially question Oswald's defection to the Soviet Union, and the fact that Oswald was involved in the flight coordination of the top secret U2 spy plane at the Atsugi Basis in Japan. Before Oswald was employed at the TSBD, he had a job at the company Jaggars-Chiles-Stovall, a company that handled photo material on behalf of the government, including top secret classified material, such as the photographs of the U2 flights over Cuba.

The conspiracists refer to many other irregularities in Oswald's curriculum, for example with regard to his trip to Mexico. Apparently, Oswald also had a 'babysitter' when he traveled to Mexico. Oswald obtained tourist visa no. 24085 at the Mexican Consulate in New Orleans. The FBI made a list of everyone who had also applied for a visa on the same day.[203] Visa 24084 was granted to William Gaudet, who had been a CIA informant[204] for more than twenty years, a detail the FBI failed to notice. Gaudet was, however, questioned by the HSCA. He knew Oswald, although not personally, and he stated to the HSCA that he had seen Oswald together with Guy Banister,[205] the same private detective for whom Ferrie was working. Unfortunately, the CIA had already completely destroyed William Gaudet's file in 1969.[206] The fact that he and Oswald had applied for a tourist visa at the Mexican Consulate at the same time was pure coincidence, Gaudet claims. Oswald visited the Russian Embassy several times while he was in Mexico. The CIA took photographs of the embassy 24 hours a day from three secret locations, but nowhere in its files could any photograph showing Oswald be found. The photographs that are supposed to show him are, again purely by coincidence, always the photographs of a completely different man. Despite the constant observation of everyone who entered or left the embassy, and the use of associated electronic listening equipment, the identity of the man on the photographs could not be ascertained.

The fact is that there is no hard evidence to be found anywhere for a connection between Oswald and the CIA, but it is quite clear that the CIA's interest in Oswald was beyond normal. This is in itself interesting enough. According to Marina Oswald, de Mohrenschildt knew about the failed attempt on General Walker's life that Oswald had allegedly carried out. If this is true, it is disturbing, to say the least. If de Mohrenschildt had indeed been Oswald's CIA watchdog, he undoubtedly must have alerted his organization of the major fact that Oswald had allegedly committed an assassination attempt on the general, and that he now, being employed in a building along the route of the parade, constituted a security risk. In this hypothesis, the CIA would have been aware that Oswald was working at the TSBD, and that he moreover was 'potentially deployable' for an act of violence.

It is not all that illogical to suspect the CIA of complicity in a coup d'état and a covert operation. This was, in fact, one of the major reasons of its existence. The *Central Intelligence Agency* was founded in 1947, and was inevitably an institute that escaped all standard forms of control. To be able to compete on an equal footing with the KGB, the Russian Committee for State Security, the CIA could virtually act as it pleased. Everything to do with the CIA was state secret: its activities, the methods they used and the personnel who worked for them. Moreover, the CIA had ample expertise with regard to coups d'état and assassination plots. In 1953, the organization had brought the Shah to power in Iran, they had overthrown the government in Guatemala in 1954, and had assisted in the assassinations of the Head of State of the Dominican Republic Rafael Trujillo, and of Patrice Lumumba in Congo, in 1961. It goes without saying that the CIA was also actively involved in the attempts to oust Castro, in which they collaborated with the mafia,[207] a criminal organization that, according to the FBI, did not actually exist. The CIA was also occupied with secret projects like MK/ULTRA, which entailed dangerous experiments with drugs and hypnosis. That's all it needs to capture the imagination of the conspiracists. They believe that Oswald may have been brainwashed.

All this belongs to the realm of speculation. What is certain, however, is that the CIA had a major motive to participate in a conspiracy against Kennedy. Kennedy had sworn to 'splinter the CIA into a thousand pieces and scatter it into the winds.'[208] The president was convinced that the CIA had tried to force him into an invasion of Cuba by means of the failed Bay of Pigs operation. Kennedy disliked liars and warmongers, but what he disliked even more was being manipulated into decisions he disagreed with, in state affairs that in his opinion fell exclusively under his jurisdiction.

On December 22, 1963, former President Harry Truman, who had personally established the CIA in 1947, published a remarkable article in the Washington Post:

> For some time I have been disturbed by the way the CIA has been diverted from its original assignment. It has become an operational and at times a policy-making arm of Government. This has led to trouble and may have compounded our difficulties in several explosive areas. [...] There is something about the way the CIA has been functioning that is casting a shadow over our historic position and I feel that we need to correct it.[209]

To make it quite clear what he meant, it was no accident that this opinion was published exactly one month to the day after the assassination.

Six months later, in response to an article in *Look* on the subject of the CIA, the former president wrote the following to the Editor-in-Chief of this magazine:

> The CIA was set up by me for the sole purpose of getting all available information to the president. It was not intended to operate as an international agency engaged in strange activities.[210]

The Warren Commission was not particularly inclined to find out what 'strange activities' exactly President Truman was referring to.

The military-industrial complex

On January 17, 1961, President Dwight Eisenhower took his leave from the nation with a very remarkable speech. As former general – he was certainly not a notorious pacifist – he warned his fellow countrymen about the increasing power of the military-industrial complex. War is *big business*. There was no need to convince his successor Kennedy of this fact. The latter obstinately refused to respond to the provocations of the defense top. On two occasions, the Chiefs of Staff maneuvered him into a position where he had hardly any other option but to proceed with military force. The first time this had been the case with the Bay of Pigs operation, and the second time was during the missile crisis, but the Chiefs of Staff had each time drawn a blank. This president, whom they had initially down as an inexperienced playboy who wouldn't stand a chance against their power machinations, kept his cool.

In 1963, Kennedy realized that the USA had no business in Vietnam. Following the peaceful resolution of the missile crisis, Kennedy's popularity rose, and with it the acceptance of his policies. The large majority of the population was hardly in favor of the overthrowing of a Communist regime just about 90 miles beyond the national borders, let alone in Vietnam, which was 9,000 miles away. On October 11, Kennedy approved *National Security Memo 263*, stating the following (underlining added by the author):

> The President approved the military recommendations contained in Section I B (1-3) of the report, but directed that no formal announcement be made of the implementation of plans to <u>withdraw 1,000 U.S. military personnel by the end of 1963</u>.[211]

The withdrawal from Vietnam had therefore already tacitly started on October 11, 1963. But on November 26, 1963, Johnson's second day in office, *National Security Memo 263* was revoked and replaced by number 273:

> 1. *It remains the central object of the United States in South Vietnam to assist the people and Government of that country to win their contest against the externally directed and supported Communist conspiracy. The test of all U. S. decisions and actions in this area should be the effectiveness of their contribution to this purpose.*
> 2. *The objectives of the United States with respect to the withdrawal of U. S. military personnel remain as stated in the White House statement of October 2, 1963.*

With respect to the withdrawal of military personnel, *National Security Action Memo* of October 2 became applicable again. This implied that the statement of October 11 regarding the initial withdrawal of the troops was declared as being unwritten. An innocent explanation could of course be the assassination on November 2 of South Vietnamese president Diem. But was this drastic reversal in the Vietnam policy so urgent that the new president was required to sign this statement on his second day in office? Stranger still is the draft of memo 273 that surfaced in 1991. Apparently, this draft had been prepared on November 21, 1963, the day preceding the assassination (Figure 12). Could it be that, on November 21, Kennedy himself had drastically changed his mind regarding the withdrawal from Vietnam? Or did *someone* expect, after Kennedy's departure for Texas on November 21, that there would be another president in the White House 24 hours later?

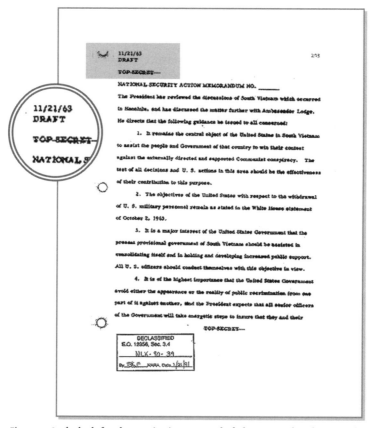

Figure 12 – On the day before the assassination, someone drafted a memorandum that reversed Kennedy's decision of October 11 to withdraw from Vietnam.

FBI Director Hoover

In 1962, the appointment of an FBI Director had never been an item on the agenda. The position of Hoover had been untouchable for 38 years. Somehow, the power of dismissing or appointing an FBI Director had never been bestowed on the president, and also the Senate had never obtained the usual advice and consent responsibility. Hoover had simply occupied the Director's chair since time immemorial. All presidents since Hoover had taken office in 1924 apparently had their reasons to maintain this situation as it was, be it with varying degrees of enthusiasm, with the exception of Hoover's friend Johnson. Hoover was soon to turn seventy. *Governing Statute 5 USC 2255-Sec.5 (a)* provided that an employment relationship in the public service ended automatically when an official reached the age of seventy and had a service record of fifteen years. This law applied even to Hoover. Only the president could grant an exception, if "the public interest so required".[212]

The first advance warning came from the Senate on July 10, 1962. The implementation of *Senate Bill 3526* would, in the future, place the appointment of the FBI Director entirely in the hands of the president, and the Senate would be granted the right of 'advice and consent'.[213] Hoover hit back three days later with a radio speech during the NBC program *Monitor*, in which he equated communism with moral decay. Patriotism and conservatism were the only values that could save the country from doom. He finished his speech with a very clear message: 'I can meet this problem, because I'm not going to give up.' The emphasis on moral decay was a clear hint in the direction of Kennedy. And, in passing, Hoover also managed to enhance his reputation with the general public. He continued his campaign in the written press. On July 16, 1962, the *St. Louis Globe Democrat* asked the question: 'Who Will Fill Hoover's Shoes?' According to the article, the FBI was effectively the protector of national security, and this for two reasons: 'One it has kept above politics. Two its able Director is also a vigilant anti-communist...'[214] Robert Kennedy responded to Hoover a few weeks later, also on the radio program *Monitor*. He ridiculed Hoover's rabid anticommunism: there was not really a communist lurking behind every bush.[215]

Communication via the media became a habit between Hoover and the Kennedys. On October 9, 1962, Hoover addressed the national convention of the American Legion in Las Vegas. He pulled out all the stops on the tragic consequences of immorality. In his overwrought rant, he also referred to the brutality of communism and the Berlin wall.[216]

President Kennedy gave him tit for tat the very next day. With a relaxed smile, he professed to the *New York Times*:

> *One Las Vegas gambler is supposed to have said he hoped we'd be as tough on Berlin as we have been on Las Vegas. Well we intend to be... From January through June this year there were 83 convictions.*[217]

Hoover didn't have a sense of humor, and Kennedy was well aware of that. To call Hoover 'one Las Vegas gambler' in public was a sophisticated insult that hit home on several levels, and the 83 convictions of organized crime cronies were just the cherry on the cake. Hoover could certainly forget an exception with regard to his mandatory retirement now. Kennedy had openly expressed his contempt and Hoover, who had been surrounded by bootlickers and admirers throughout his career, was not too pleased with this turn of events. When his own interests were at stake, Hoover never had any scruples. In his logic, it was merely a matter of survival. For Hoover, the reelection of Kennedy would have spelled disaster, while his death kept all this trouble at bay. Was it a surprise that Hoover could not detect the minutest, slightest trace of a conspiracy after the assassination?

Vice-President Johnson

Lyndon Johnson also often tops the list of suspects for an obvious reason: his personal ambition to become president. On his way to the top, he had spared nothing and nobody. Johnson had grown up in very poor conditions after the bankruptcy of his father's ranch. This situation, together with the modest degree he obtained from San Marcos, a 'crappy' university in his own eyes, left him with a massive inferiority complex, yet at the same time fuelled a burning ambition and a huge ego to compensate for his feelings of inferiority. Johnson's major talent was that he could see through his political opponents. He was a genius in this field, according to all those who had personally experienced it. He started to work his way up from a very young age, initially as the secretary of a rich man's son who had made it to congressman. In this capacity, he handled all the correspondence on behalf of his boss, and worked day and night. Soon he employed some young, academically-trained staff to assist him, added them to the payroll of a public institution, and required them to work for him free-of-charge after hours. One of these young staff members was the later Governor Connally.

When a seat in the House of Representatives became available due to the death of one of the congressmen, the then 28-year-old Johnson didn't hesitate one moment to register as one of the eight candidate successors. He was a complete outsider, who, at first sight, never had a chance in a million. But Johnson was not an ordinary candidate. He was the only one to realize that the seven other candidates were fighting each other over the densely populated urban areas. Johnson, however, took to the country and concentrated on the rural areas, where he canvassed almost from door to door. He didn't need to share the available votes with anybody, and consequently won the seat. Once elected as Representative, Johnson's dark political talents blossomed. At some point, he even managed to be awarded a totally undeserved Silver Star Medal, normally reserved for war heroes.

After twelve years in the House of Representatives, Johnson took another step towards the White House. He won a Senate seat in an election that is considered to feature among the darkest chapters in American's democratic history. Johnson stole thousands of votes. In the Duval County district, the discrepancy was so striking that questions arose, but then the electoral lists were either stolen or accidentally burned by the diligent wife of the head of the polling station. Despite the manifest fraud, Johnson was eventually still 113 votes short of winning. At this point, a forgotten ballot box turned up out of nowhere in precinct 13 of the small town of Alice. The ballot box contained 202 additional Johnson votes. The 202 voters had come to cast their votes in alphabetical order, and had all placed the same signature on the electoral list, using the same green ink. Strangely enough, also this list disappeared without a trace.

Johnson's opponent Stevenson started legal proceedings to fight the stolen election, but Johnson called upon his cunning lawyer Abe Fortas. The latter used some legal trickery to bypass the local procedure, and catapulted the case straight to the Supreme Court. There, the dossier was handled by a befriended judge, who ruled in favor of Johnson. All ongoing investigations into the electoral fraud were blocked. Johnson's biographer Robert Caro wrote the following about this election: 'even in terms of a most elastic political morality – the political morality of 1940s Texas – his methods were immoral.'[218] Later in his career, Johnson laughed heartily about this matter.

This is how Johnson, at the age of forty, entered the powerful Senate. It was here that he further honed his talent for power politics. Johnson mixed without scruples in everything he or his friends could benefit from on the home front as well. It would take us too far to list all the murders and fraud scandals in which he is said to have been involved. Here again, there are usually plenty of indications, but little or no evidence. But it is certainly a fact that Johnson, on his relatively modest income as parliamentarian, became very rich in a very short period of time. Brutal intimidation became his trademark. He forced his staff to take dictation while he was sitting unashamedly on the toilet. He liked to shout at people with his nose barely 2 inches away from his victim's nose. Johnson boasted that he knew every Senator's weak spot – an achievement in which he was presumably aided by his good friend Hoover with his notorious secret files. No, it was not always a pretty sight, but extremely efficient in politics. As leader of the majority, Johnson knew exactly how to push his agenda through, and how to secure the occasional interesting deal for himself or his friends.

But the nomination as democratic presidential candidate – the culmination of his ambition, and the only prize that matched his ego – he saw being snatched away from him by John F. Kennedy. Kennedy needed Texas to win the presidential election, and he was well aware that an envious Johnson as majority leader in the Senate could be a considerable pain in the neck. The next step was that Johnson appeared on the scene completely unexpectedly as candidate Vice-President. This happened in the midst of a tumultuous convention, and very much against the opinion of Robert Kennedy, who had a visceral dislike of the Texan giant. From 1961 onwards, Johnson was just one heartbeat away from his lifelong dream, but the Vice-Presidency seemed to be his end station. The position did not provide him with any real power or freedom of movement, and the many scandals he had been able to keep the lid on throughout his career now started to crop up dangerously. It was also quite certain that Kennedy would dump him in 1964, and opt for a candidate Vice-President who was less of a political risk. In the fall of 1963, the huge agricultural subsidy fraud in which Johnson's friend Billie Sol Estes was involved and the corruption files of his political secretary Bobby Baker were festering boils that were about to burst open. And Attorney General Robert Kennedy did not lift a finger to help Johnson, quite the contrary.

According to some, Johnson not only had the greatest interest in the assassination of Kennedy, he also had the least to lose. His political career, his sole purpose in life, was over, and chances were that he would end up in jail rather than in the White House. But the fact that Johnson benefited from Kennedy's death does not automatically imply that he committed a crime. Johnson was an eccentric personality, and there are strong suspicions that he was manic-depressive. He also suffered from extreme paranoia.

He proved time and time again that he could lash out mercilessly to elimi-nate a political opponent, but there is no evidence whatsoever of any direct involvement in the assassination of Kennedy.

Not a scintilla of evidence?

For the sake of good understanding, and before we continue our investiga-tion, I would like to point out clearly that we do not yet have a claim that Kennedy was the victim of a conspiracy. Yet to say that there was not even the semblance of evidence that there was a plot is something quite differ-ent. Can we really state that there was not the least, minutest indication, not a *scintilla of evidence* that points towards a conspiracy? 'Too often we enjoy the comfort of opinion without the discomfort of thought', could have been JFK's answer to his successor Bush in the Oval Room.

Oswald and Ruby did not know each other, and yet we find strong pointers towards a network they both had close contact with. This net-work incorporates organizations and figures with strong motives for both murders, the assassination of both Kennedy and Oswald. We can therefore not a priori exclude the existence of a conspiracy. This means that in our further investigation we must take into account that there could have been other perpetrators or accomplices, besides Oswald. In this context, the in-vestigation of the Warren Commission, which was only interested in find-ing incriminating evidence against Oswald, was not a valid investigation. We must therefore, step-by-step, re-construct the whole investigation.

PART 3

THE BULLETS

13. EVIDENCE LAW

In order to convict Oswald, evidence must be provided for every necessary component of the accusation. If there is any reasonable doubt about even a single essential component of the crime, there will also be reasonable doubt about the whole. The Supreme Court of the United States clearly stressed this principle once again in 1970 in the Winship case (397 US 358 at 364): '[...] Due Process Clause protects the accused against conviction except upon proof beyond a reasonable doubt of *every* fact necessary to constitute the crime with which he is charged.'[219] Another basic rule with regard to evidence law is the requirement of the authenticity of the evidence. To satisfy the requirement of authentication or identifying an item of evidence, the proponent must produce evidence sufficient to support a finding that the item is what the proponent claims it is.[220]

To give an example: the police find a knife and claim that it belongs to the accused. The prosecution must then not only prove that the knife really does belong to the accused, but that the knife in the evidence is also still the same knife that was found at the scene of the crime. There are two accepted techniques for this. Some items can gain and maintain the requirement of authenticity through their unique characteristics. The knife in our example could have an antique, beautifully carved ivory handle. This would be established at the scene of the crime and this data remains intact, whatever else happens to the knife. But how do you deal with items that have no specific and/or unique characteristics? In this case, the chain of custody of the piece of evidence is absolutely essential. Three criteria must be met for every link in the chain of custody: the receipt from the previous link, the safe keeping and the handover to the following link. If even one link fails in one of these three criteria, the evidence is simply inacceptable.

It then no longer matters whether the evidence is credible or how much weight it carries in considering whether the accused is guilty or not: this evidence is simply excluded from the discussions.

Summarizing briefly, this comes down to the following:

1. Evidence must be provided for every essential part of the crime.
2. This evidence must be beyond all reasonable doubt.
3. This evidence must be authentic. You must prove that it is what you claim it is. If a piece of evidence is not unique and specific, its authenticity must be proven on the basis of a complete, unbroken *chain of custody*.
4. If there is any doubt that the evidence is authentic, it will be declared inadmissible, and be radically excluded from the discussions. The jury must then assess the case as if the inadmissible evidence was totally non-existent and as if they had no knowledge of it.

Bullets obviously form an essential part of the evidence in the case of an assault with a firearm. Bullets are normally always found when there is a victim, and the bullet-victim link is not usually a problem. The problem with the evidence mostly occurs in the first two steps: the perpetrator has disposed of the weapon or the user of the weapon is unknown. But if the weapon is found, it is also usually possible to undeniably prove that the bullet was fired from it. The trajectory through the barrel leaves traces on the bullet, and these are unique for every weapon.

The chain of evidence in the case of a murder using a firearm therefore has four basic links:

How far does that bring us in the Kennedy case on the basis of the bullets as material evidence?

14. THE VERY FIRST PIECE OF EVIDENCE

The first piece of evidence that arrived at the FBI in Washington was the *magic bullet*. The bullet was given FBI number C1 (and Q1 for the FBI laboratory). We will start our investigation with this first item of evidence.

Officially, the magic bullet was labeled 'CE399' in the Commission file (Figure 13). It caused seven injuries: Kennedy's back (in), Kennedy's throat (out), Connally's armpit (in), Connally's chest (out), Connally's wrist (in), Connally's palm (out) and Connally's thigh (in). On its way, the bullet also broke Connally's fifth rib and his wrist. It then found its way, under mysterious circumstances, under the mattress of a gurney in the Parkland Hospital. What's more, it also emerged from the entire adventure virtually intact. It's immediately clear how CE399 earned its nickname. The authorities realized only too well that such an exceptional bullet would not be beneficial to the credibility of the story. It also took a long time before the Warren Commission dared to move in the direction of the magic bullet, but they ultimately had no choice. The Zapruder film left no doubt: there were either two shooters with one victim each, or one shot with two victims. It is clear which possibility was the only acceptable option for the Commission. The magic bullet turned out to have been fired with the Mannlicher Carcano[221] that was found in the TSBD, thereby excluding of all other possible weapons. That is just about the only good news for the progress of the investigation.

The link between the bullet and the victim

Normally, the bullet should have been found by the nurses who undressed Connally or by the doctors who treated him, which would have established the link between the bullet and the victim. But things went a little differently in this case. Half an hour after the mortally wounded president was brought into Parkland Hospital, hospital technician Tomlinson pushed an empty gurney out of the hospital elevator on the first floor. According to his statement, he placed it behind a bed that was already in the corridor. Tomlinson then carried out a number of other tasks. When he returned, he pushed the foremost bed – the bed that had already been there, not the bed from the elevator – against the wall. He heard a metallic sound and saw a bullet lying on the edge of the bed.[222] Tomlinson called O.P. Wright from the Personnel Department, and showed him the bullet.[223] They wanted to inform the responsible authorities about their discovery, but that wasn't too easy. The FBI did not consider themselves authorized to take any action, as the murder investigation was still in the hands of the Dallas police at that time. The police were nowhere to be found, however.[224] Due to the fact that the president and the vice-president were both present in the building, a team of Secret Service personnel were in the area. The Secret Service had already enough to do, and didn't listen to Tomlinson's story.[225] Together with Wright, Tomlinson then removed the bullet from its original position himself and handed it over to Secret Agent Johnsen. The latter was clearly already busy planning the departure of Jacqueline Kennedy and the casket to the presidential plane, and put the bullet in his pocket without any more ado.

The statements of Tomlinson and Wright are the only ones that record anything about the discovery of the bullet. The Secret Service recapitulated the events in which the service was involved in a memo dated March 19, 1964[226]. The memo makes no mention of the receipt of the bullet. The Secret Service had simply acted as the postman. They passed on the package to the FBI, and preferred to have nothing more to do with it.

The start of the chain of evidence

If the official version is correct, the bullet came from Connally's thigh, the last injury that it allegedly caused. But Secret Agent Johnsen, who passed the bullet on to his boss in Washington, stated that the bullet had been found on the bed on which Kennedy 'could' have been laid.[227] The FBI memorandum of November 23[228] then also (incorrectly) situated the location at which the bullet was found as being in the *emergency room*. Where the bullet was really found, and on whose gurney, apparently did not matter to the investigators.

Little data is therefore available regarding the discovery of the bullet, and the little that is quoted is wrong. The bullet is also not directly linked to Connally. At best, it is linked to Connally's bed. We therefore find ourselves with a hell of a problem from the very start. The start of the *chain of custody* is not documented at all: there are no photographs of where it was found, no findings on the spot, no marks on the bullet, no fingerprints, no statements from the finders... all this had to be sorted out subsequently, but that also went fundamentally wrong.

Kennedy's gurney

It soon became clear that the bullet did not come from Kennedy's bed. The president remained lying on his gurney the whole time, and was never even laid on an operating table. The four nurses who were present[229] were unanimous about this, and nurses in an emergency department are very reliable, no-nonsense witnesses. Dr. Baxter also replied 'No', short and sweet, to the question whether the President had been removed from the emergency gurney.[230] After Kennedy had been placed in the casket, the gurney remained on the second floor, and was never placed in the corridor on the first floor. Consequently, the bullet was certainly not found on Kennedy's gurney.

Connally's gurney

If the bullet did not come from Kennedy's gurney, it must logically have been found on Connally's bed. This is the bed that hospital technician Tomlinson had put at the end of the corridor. He found the bullet on the first bed, however. If Tomlinson is correct, the bullet therefore did not come from Connally's gurney either. It *seems* to have been found on the bed of a total stranger. Maybe Tomlinson had actually placed the gurney at the front? The technician has always stubbornly insisted that this was not the case. In a television documentary in 1988, 25 years after the murder, he repeated with a sad expression that he *was* sure. On the spot, he showed how he took the bed from the elevator and placed it behind the bed that was already there and how, a little later, he found the bullet on the bed at the front with the blood-stained sheet. This was how it happened, and not otherwise.

But during his interview by the Commission, under heavy pressure from interrogator Arlen Specter, Tomlinson said just once that he was 'not really sure'. The young Specter, a brilliant lawyer, had previously spent five years as Assistant Officer for Justice in Philadelphia.[231] The war of words that he carried out with the hospital technician was too uneven. Tomlinson finally spurted out what Specter wanted to hear: '*I'm not really sure*'. Strictly speaking, the question to which this answer was given was not about the location of the bullet, but about what Tomlinson had explained to an agent in this respect. Whatever the reason, the aggressive tone of the interrogation abruptly changed to a somewhat slimy friendliness, and was then terminated in no time at all. That was also strange. Apart from the question of which bed was really concerned, Specter could also have asked other questions, such as what Tomlinson then did with the bullet, whether there was anyone else in the corridor, or about the appearance of the bullet that he found.

The Commission based their conclusion on the flimsy basis of Tomlinson's short moment of doubt:

> *Although Tomlinson was not certain [...] the Commission has concluded that the bullet came from Connally's stretcher.*[232]

This was a case of jumping to conclusions, as the question was far from clear after the interrogation of Tomlinson. Moreover, at that moment, the Commission still had plenty of time to clear this up, because they would have been able to question O.P. Wright, who had also seen the location of the bullet, and Secret Agent Johnsen. Neither was heard by the Commission, however. Tomlinson was not sure what he had said to an agent months before about where he had found the bullet, and the bullet was therefore considered to have been found on the bed of Connally. That was the logic used by the Commission, and the investigation stopped there.

The weight of a postage stamp

There is another bizarre thing about magic bullet CE399. According to the official scenario, the bullet had, among other things, shattered Connally's fifth rib and his wrist bone, one of the hardest bones in the human body. But the bullet is undamaged, apart from some flattening underneath, which led to its third nickname: the *Pristine Bullet* (Figure 13).

The ballistic experts had never seen a bullet that had caused so much damage yet still remained relatively intact. For anyone with experience in this area, CE399 looks like a bullet that had been fired into a box of cotton wool or a bucket of water. This is also the case for someone without this experience.

Figure 13 - CE399, the 'pristine bullet', is far too undamaged considering the formidable route that it took. Is this really the original bullet?

Believers rightly point out that the bullet is indeed flattened on the underside, and cannot be literally referred to as 'pristine'. But it remains indisputable that the bullet has remained straight and has hardly lost any weight. An unused 6.5 bullet weighs on average between 160 and 161 grains (1 grain corresponds to approximately 65 milligrams). After its historic journey, the magic bullet still weighed 158.6 grains.[233] CE399 thereby weighed between 1.4 and 2.4 grains less than an unused bullet.[234] That represents a difference of approximately 0.09 to 0.15 grams, the weight of a postage stamp.

We will never know how much metal the emergency rooms staff removed from Connally's wound while cleaning his wounds and how much remained in his body. Two or three fragments removed from Connally's wrist were large enough to be added to the dossier. Metal also remained behind in his thigh.[235] The missing metal is lead, as the bullet was only damaged at its base. Ninety to one hundred and fifty milligrams of lead is very little indeed.

The opinion of the doctors

On the basis of Connally's X-ray photos, Doctor Humes, the autopsy doctor, thought that it was 'extremely unlikely' that CE399 had injured the governor. He could not explain where the metal fragments on the X-ray photos had come from, taking account of the condition of the pristine bullet. ('I can't conceive where they came from this missile').[236] In addition, according to Doctor Finck, the great ballistic expert of the army, CE399 could not have broken Connally's wrist 'for the reason that there are too many fragments described in that wrist.'[237] Doctor Gregory, the doctor who treated Connally in Parkland Hospital, was in total agreement. The three experienced doctors clearly stated that too much metal had been left behind in the wrist wound in comparison with the weight loss of the bullet. Furthermore, Doctor Gregory, who treated the wrist wound, was of the opinion that the object that caused the wound must have had an irregular shape:[238]

> The wound of entrance is characteristic in my view of an irregular missile... I mean one that has been distorted. It is in some way angular, it has edges or sharp edges or something of this sort. It is not rounded or pointed in the fashion of an ordinary missile.

The 'pristine bullet' does not meet the description of a damaged object with sharp edges.

The Warren Commission

The relatively intact character of CE399 is regarded by believers as evidence of the *Single-Bullet Theory* (SBT). In this hypothesis, the passage through the body of Kennedy considerably reduced the speed of the bullet. The lateral movement along Connally's fifth rib damaged the lower side of the bullet and caused it to slow down further. By the time of the breaking of the wrist, the remaining kinetic energy was too low to cause the bullet itself to be damaged further. The speed of the bullet had then been slowed down so far that it actually came to a standstill in Connally's thigh. But it remains unlikely that the bullet was so undamaged. Ballistic expert Doctor Olivier carried out a series of tests. He was only allowed to show the Commission one of his test bullets, which was allegedly shot through the cadaver of a goat.[239] This bullet was considerably more deformed than CE399. How badly damaged were the other test bullets that we didn't get to see? You hear it said that reality cannot be imitated, and you certainly never know with bullets. But the fact remains that very unlikely events must have been taking place if the official story was to be kept afloat.

Despite all these contra-indications, the Commission argued that their statement was confirmed by *all* the evidence:

> All the evidence indicated that the bullet found on the Governor's stretcher could have caused all his wounds.[240]

Further steps in the chain of custody

'A bullet' is not specific enough, so the chain of custody immediately becomes paramount. Secret Agent Johnsen had cleaned and pocketed the bullet. He had omitted to make any kind of mark on the bullet. All standard procedures were neglected - the Secret Service simply had no experience with murder cases. In Washington, Secret Agent Johnsen handed over the bullet to his superior, James Rowley, who, in his turn, handed over the projectile to FBI agent Elmer Todd.[241] Evidence exhibit number one had thereby at last reached its final destination at the FBI. Secret Agent Rowley and FBI agent Todd also failed to place their initials on the bullet. Even so, Todd changed his statement about it later.

There is therefore not a single documented step in the chain of custody of the bullet, which had changed hands five times in the meantime. Until now, the lack of documentation and identification has only been a question of procedure, a legal problem – food for lawyers. Up to now, there is not really a practical problem with the material evidence, but we are not yet at the end of our worries.

The authenticity of the bullet

O.P. Wright, the personnel director of Parkland Hospital, stated to author Josiah Thompson (*Six Seconds in Dallas*) in 1966 that the bullet that he and Tomlinson had found had a pointed nose, whereas CE399 has a round nose. The bullet in the evidence material could therefore not be the bullet that was found in Dallas. This looks like conspiracy nonsense, because the Commission did not say a word about it in its final report. At first sight, it really seems unlikely that the magic bullet was switched during the investigation. But if that were true, then it is a problem of the first order. To the exclusion of all other weapons, CE399 came from the barrel of the Carcano. If the bullet was 'planted' evidence, it would appear that someone was trying to place the blame on Oswald.

On closer examination, we came upon Commission evidence item 2011,[242] an FBI report. This states the following about the identification of the bullet: 'he [Tomlinson]cannot positively identify the bullet as the one he found and showed to Mr. O.P. Wright.' Does this mean that CE399 is in fact a different bullet to the projectile that the hospital technician found on November 22? O.P. Wright also had the same problem:

He advised he could not positively identify C1 as being the same bullet
which was found on November 22, 1963.

Wright had therefore already stated the same thing to the FBI as he later told to the conspiracist Josiah Thompson. That is already two of the four witnesses who had seen the bullet in Dallas. Secret Agent Johnsen, who was the third person to have the bullet in his hands, said something similar on June 24, 1964: 'Johnsen advised he could not identify this bullet as the one he obtained from O.P. Wright, Parkland Hospital, Dallas, and gave to James Rowley, Chief United States Secret Service.' We hear the same from Rowley, the next link: 'Rowley advised he could not identify this bullet as the one he received from Special Agent Johnsen and gave to Special Agent Todd on November 22, 1963.' In other words, the four persons who had seen the bullet that was found on November 22, at a time that was certainly memorable, firmly stated they could not positively identify the bullet that was in the dossier as CE399 or C1 as the bullet that they had had in their hands. In any normal investigation, the following question would now arise: in what way was this bullet different from the original? But the FBI did not ask the obvious question and we therefore do not know what this 'non-identification' meant. There is only one possible reason why the FBI did not ask the crucial question: the interrogator already knew the answer and wanted to keep it out of the dossier. The bullet was specially flown in from Washington for the confrontation with the witnesses in June 1964. If you have to fly to Texas with items of evidence so shortly before the completion of the investigation, this indicates a major problem. Whatever the problem was, it did not disappear after the confrontation of the four eyewitnesses with the projectile, quite the contrary. The preferred solution was to note the statements down in very vague terms, and to then bury the items deep within the evidence. The report of the Warren Commission never mentioned a word about this again.

Another amazing fact concerns the identity of the agent who interviewed the four witnesses at the confrontation with CE399: it was FBI agent Todd, the fifth link! Todd also confronted himself with the bullet, and wrote the following about his own questioning:

On June 24, 1964, Special Agent Elmer Lee Todd, Washington D.C., identified C1, a rifle bullet, as being the same one he received from James Rowley, Chief, United States Secret Service, Washington D.C., on November 22, 1963. This identification was made from initials marked thereon by Special Agent Todd at the Federal Bureau of Investigation Laboratory upon receipt.

Todd looked at C1 and said to himself: 'This is indeed the bullet that I got from Rowley.' But Rowley told him: 'This is not the bullet that I gave to Todd.' Only one of them can be right, and Rowley does have three other witnesses who support his non-identification. Todd's counter-argument sounds good, however: his initials were scratched onto the bullet. But the initials are completely worthless as evidence. Todd did not scratch them onto the bullet in Rowley's presence, and certainly not at the time of the handover. He could just as well have picked up any test bullet in the laboratory and have put his initials on it. What we do know now, in any case, is that the bullet has not been changed since the time that Todd placed his initials on it. That's good news. If the bullet had already been changed, only Todd could have done it. But would Todd really have added his initials?

Kennedy researcher John Hunt followed up the question of Todd's so-called initials on CE399.[243] According to him, three initials can be found on CE399, originating from Kilion, Frazier and Cunningham. They were the three FBI agents who were involved in the investigation of the bullet. Hunt supported his findings with four photos in which the bullet was turned a quarter-turn each time. Todd's initials are apparently not on CE399.

Memoranda withheld for thirty years

The ARRB started its work in 1992: the ARRB was the official commission that had to make quick work of making publicly available the more than one hundred thousand secret documents on the proceedings relating to the assassination of three decades earlier. The released material contained two FBI documents of June 20 and June 24, 1964, informing the highest echelon of the FBI (including Hoover) that the first four links would not identify CE399.[244] Hoover was therefore aware that there was a big problem. If the four witnesses who were in a position to know all declared that the evidence material was not the bullet they had seen on November 22, we have to face facts: the evidence material had been tampered with. Moreover, the FBI head recommended that the commission should not be informed of this problem. The two memoranda were securely classified by the FBI under *Soviet Section*. Apart from the fact that Oswald had visited that country, the chain of evidence of the bullet obviously had nothing to do with the Soviet Union. This classification could only have been used in order to keep the document a state secret as long as possible, and preferably forever.

The chain of custody in the opposite direction

When the bullet was discussed for the first time during the work of the Commission,[245] Specter promised that the authenticity of the item of evidence would be demonstrated later. This turned out to be an empty promise. The next opportunity for identification of the bullet was the Tomlinson hearing, four days later. But Specter' intention was above all to squeeze the words 'I'm not really sure' from Tomlinson, and he did not breath a word about the bullet itself. O.P. Wright and Johnsen were, against all logic, not heard, so we also cannot find out anything here. Link four, Secret Agent Rowley,[246] was asked no questions about the bullet, and was allowed to use up the precious time of the Commission to ask for an increase in his budget. The interview filled no less than 58 pages, but there was no time for the identification of the bullet.

Against all logic, the Warren Commission preferred to work on the identification of CE399 in the opposite direction, and started at the end of the chain, with weapon expert Frazier.[247] Frazier recognized the bullet as the projectile that he had received from FBI agent Todd, and Todd had questioned himself and confirmed the authenticity of the bullet. This created the impression that the bullet in the final stage was the original bullet, but that was, of course, only a façade. In reality, the chain of evidence was as follows:

The FBI withheld the items for which the identification problem appeared in each of the first four steps, and the Commission apparently knew better than Tomlinson himself where the bullet had been found. To top it all off, the bullet did not at all look like a bullet that could have caused the official series of injuries and shattered bones. Strangely enough, the bullet had also managed to emerge from a thigh bone and slip under a mattress on its own accord.

The investigation excelled in ignorance, bias and unreliability. It was selective in the choice of witnesses to be heard and the evidence to be provided, and was cunning in the manner in which questions were asked – but even more so in the way some of the key questions were not asked, let alone answered. Yet the Commission claimed with great certainty that *all* the evidence indicated that this piece of evidence, bullet CE399, was the bullet that had been found on November 22, and could have caused the seven wounds attributed to this bullet.

Completion of the chain of evidence

The *magic bullet* was phenomenal in its performance as a bullet, but was less impressive as a piece of evidence. But where does this bullet bring us in an investigation looking for a conclusive chain of evidence from the suspect to the victim? The tentative chain is as follows:

Taking into account that four direct witnesses remember another bullet, there are serious problems with the authenticity of the bullet that was found. Hence the questions regarding the evidence. At some point in time, the bullet was fired with the Carcano that was found on the sixth floor, so we can place a tick on the link with the weapon. There is still a question mark in the direction of the victim, because of the rather poor chain of custody. No definite answer can be given as to whether the bullet actually lay on Connally's bed.

15. THE OTHER BULLETS AND FRAGMENTS

The origin of the bullets

In order to shoot, you need bullets. Oswald officially possessed exactly four 6.5 mm Carcano bullets. It would, of course, have been extremely helpful to us if we had found half a box of unused bullets in Oswald's rented room – bullets of the same type, from the same production batch, bullets that were purchased somewhere – but nothing was found. How Oswald ever obtained the bullets remains a riddle. Oswald was very stingy, but to think that he bought his bullets one-by-one – if that was even possible – is still bizarre. Bullets are sold in boxes of one hundred pieces. The FBI searched all the gun shops in Dallas and New Orleans, but no-one had sold 6.5 mm bullets to Oswald. Thousands of empty shells were also collected from shooting ranges and were then examined one-by-one, but Oswald did not appear to have practiced on any known shooting range. So there is no link between Oswald and the bullets in the material evidence. We will therefore place a cross in the evidence chain for the connection between Oswald and the bullets.

Agreement between the fragments and the bullets

Five bullet fragments were found in the presidential limousine. There were two larger pieces: evidence item CE567, a piece from the nose of a bullet, found on the front seat; and evidence item CE569, a piece from the tail of a bullet, found in the front of the limousine. Three smaller fragments lay at the front left of the passenger compartment, under the jump seat occupied by Mrs. Connally. Two fragments were also recovered from the victims, one from Connally's wrist and one from Kennedy's head. Altogether, seven bullet fragments were found.

It was demonstrated that the two larger fragments originated from a bullet fired by the Carcano.[248] Weapon expert Frazier was very sure. According to him, there is no such thing as a partial identification in this field.

> *In the field of firearms identification we try to avoid any possible chance of error creeping in.*

This is potentially a first major step forward in this investigation. If this proves to be true, this means that, in any case, Kennedy was shot at with the Carcano. But we remain cautious of the FBI in the Kennedy case, as the non-identification of CE399 is still fresh in our minds. Fifteen years after the assassination, due to lack of use and rust, this weapon could no longer be used to produce bullets as comparison material. The HSCA could only confirm that the test bullets the FBI produced in 1963 did indeed come from the same barrel as the fragments that had been found.[249] If we trust the FBI, and thereby accept that the comparison bullets were actually fired from the Carcano, then the larger fragments did indeed originate from the Carcano, to the exclusion of all other weapons.

A possible *sabot*

The agreement between the traces on the fragments and the barrel of the Carcano should prove that the Carcano is the murder weapon. But this is also not absolutely certain. It's technically possible to shoot bullets with another rifle of a larger caliber. Experts have no doubt that a 6.5 mm Carcano bullet could be shot from – for example – a Mauser 7.65. In theory, you could shoot into a bucket of water with a Carcano, recover the 6.5. bullet, fit a *sabot* – a sort of metal shell or 'shoe' – around it and then fire the same bullet with a Mauser 7.65. The bullet would then be erroneously identified in the investigation as being shot from the Carcano. A *sabot* consists of four quarters of a cylindrically shaped shell that is fitted around the originally smaller bullet. Thanks to the sabot, the 6.5 mm bullet would fit into the 7.65 mm barrel of the Mauser. When the Carcano bullet leaves the rifle barrel of the Mauser the four parts of the sabot would fly away, leaving the bullet to continue along its normal path. The traces left by the Mauser will then only be seen on the sabot, which is lost, while the bullet shows the scratches that were caused by the previous shot into the water bath with the Carcano. An example of a 12.7 mm bullet that has been fitted with a sabot in order to shoot it from a 20 mm carbine for experimental purposes is given on the website of the *Experimental Impact Laboratory* of NASA[250] (Figure 14). In the technical description of the research work, the website also reports that: 'quick sabot separation is a necessity to keep the target free of interfering debris.' Elsewhere on the site, the NASA laboratory makes it clear that:

> *We have had shots in which, for one reason or another, a piece of the sabot hit near the hole and ended up downrange, where it wasn't supposed to be.*

Figure 14 – *The first photo shows a bullet with sabot, and the following photos show how such a sabot is fitted around the bullet. In this way, the bullet can be fired from a carbine with a larger caliber.*

This technical presentation by an indisputably reliable source provides food for thought. Is this perhaps the explanation for the strange metal sliver on the outside of Kennedy's skull, ten centimeters below the place where the bullet penetrated his brain? Does this mean that a 6.5 mm bullet with the unique markings from the barrel of the Carcano could have been fired from another, much better weapon, and also by a much better marksman, with the help of a sabot? In the shot to Kennedy's head, a piece of the sabot could have traveled with the bullet, and then hit the back of Kennedy's head near the actual bullet wound. It seems a far-fetched hypothesis. There is no evidence at all of a second weapon or a second marksman, but, keeping Sherlock Holmes' motto in mind, we must always bear in mind that, when all other lines of investigation are shown to be impossible, what remains must be the explanation of what happened, even though it may seem unlikely.

The number of bullets

Oswald only had four bullets. One bullet remained unused in the weapon, one missed the limousine, and the magic bullet remained intact. This means that only one bullet comes into consideration for the fragmentation, namely the bullet that shattered Kennedy's head.

Each bullet fragment has a chemical fingerprint, which can be determined on the basis of a spectroscopic analysis. The lead in bullets always contains traces of antimony (Sb) and silver (Ag). It is therefore sufficient to determine the ppm (*parts per million*) of the two metals. In principle, the same value must be found for the fragments of the same bullet. That sounds hopeful, but this is, of course, the Kennedy dossier. The neutron activation analysis (NAA) was still a fairly experimental technique in 1964. The FBI had the test carried out on the fragments, but then chose to withhold the results. And that, of course, made the conspiracists suspicious. If the test had yielded the desired result, one can be sure that it would have been added to the file, they argue. In other words: according to the conspiracists, the fact that Hoover withheld the test results could only indicate that the investigation demonstrated that the fragments originated from several bullets. Since the official version can only work if only one bullet became fragmented, the discovery of fragments that originate from two bullets inevitably indicates that there was a conspiracy.

The analysis of the composition of the metal from the fragments was therefore very important. The commission report was not particularly illuminating regarding this important point. The Commission wrote that the bullet fragments were 'similar in metallic composition'. That is a pointless determination. An alloy of lead is always 'similar' to an alloy of lead. The question is whether the composition of the metal is *identical*. This was apparently not the case, because the report says: 'it was not possible to determine whether two or more of the fragments were from the same bullet.'[251] Did the Warren Commission circumvent a finding that was damaging for their hypothesis with vague words? In any case, the HSCA found it advisable to have the test carried out again with the NAA technique, which had been developed further in the meantime. According to Doctor Guinn, the HSCA expert, the fragment that was found in Connally's wrist did come from the magic bullet. According to him, all the other fragments were indeed from the same bullet, the bullet that hit Kennedy in the head.[252] Until then, everything was going well for the official doctrine.

But things never stay good in this dossier for any length of time. Two scientists from the Lawrence Livermore Laboratory repeated the tests. They came to the conclusion that Dr. Guinn and his team were wrong. The investigation had assumed that the metal composition of the bullets was *not* random, but their mistake was precisely here. This assumption is only true for *non jacketed* bullets, but Oswald used bullets with a metal jacket (*full jacket*). The composition of the lead is then of no importance for the quality of the bullet, and is therefore purely random data. The composition of the lead can be considerably different, not only from bullet to bullet, but also within one and the same bullet.

In 2007, the Texas A&M Center examined the case for a fourth time. Among others, the former head of forensic metallurgy at the FBI took part in the investigation. Once again, the conclusion was that the decision of Dr. Guinn was unreliable. The flaw also cannot be resolved with better techniques or new research. The Carcano bullets happen to have this specific character. They are unsuitable for the NAA test. We therefore do not know with certainty whether the fragments came from one and the same bullet.

The link between the bullet fragments and the victims

Let us reasonably assume that we could link the two largest fragments to the Carcano, in which case the next question is whether we can also link them to a victim. The victims sat in the limousine, and that is also where the fragments were found. But the car was left unattended for hours in the hands of the Secret Service. It was the agents of the Secret Service who removed the fragments before the actual investigation started. The evidence that the two large fragments were found in the limousine is therefore based entirely on the unilateral declaration of two secret agents. The agents also had no authority whatsoever to take any action in the case. Here also, the chain of custody did not start according to the rules of the art.

In 1999, the *National Archives and Records Administration* (NARA) conducted a series of tests on the five bullet fragments from the limousine.[253] They found no textile fibers that could in any way determine whether the fragments had passed through the clothing of the two possible victims. Biological material was found, but it was impossible to recover any DNA patterns. The fragments in Kennedy's head and Connally's wrist could also not be linked to the weapon. The fragments are too small to carry any useful traces from the barrel, and we only have Dr. Guinn's unreliable findings to link them to the larger fragments.

Filling in the chain of evidence

With an eye to maintaining the evidence in a criminal proceeding, the authenticity of the bullet fragments is somewhat problematic due to the flaws in the chains of evidence and custody. But we can reasonably assume that the fragments in the case come from the assassination. We also know with certainty that the bullet from which these fragments originated was, at some point in time, fired from the weapon that was found on the sixth floor. It is theoretically possible that this happened before November 22 and that the bullet was used again in the attack with the help of a sabot and a weapon with a larger caliber, for example – but not necessarily – a Mauser 7.65.

The hypothesis involving a second weapon and the use of sabots implies a conspiracy. Oswald himself would obviously not bring two weapons. As there is no evidence of a second weapon and a second shooter, this solution is only valid if all other possibilities are excluded. Suppose, for example, that Oswald had an alibi for the time of the murder. In this case, there was certainly another shooter. In that case, we may also assume that there was no real reason to use Oswald's dilapidated Carcano for the attack, and that the evidence that was found was deliberately created in order to frame Oswald. In this hypothesis, the use of a sabot is a plausible explanation, but we have not got that far yet.

The Tippit bullets

The murder of police officer J.D. Tippit provides enough material for a book in itself. It would take us far too far if we went into all the details, but I would briefly like to refer to it with regard to the bullets and shells. The problems with the bullets and the shells apparently form a recurring pattern, rather than an accidental peculiarity. In any case, Murphy's Law was also evident in the Tippit murder. The barrel of Oswald's pistol was so altered that it is impossible to link the bullets to Oswald's pistol to the exclusion of other weapons. It is therefore not proven that the bullets that were found in Tippit's body were fired from Oswald's pistol. The problem with the shells is much greater. The shells from the Tippit murder belong respectively to two Remington-Peters .38 special bullets, and two Western .38 Specials. Three Western-Winchester bullets were found in Tippit's body and only one Remington-Peters.[254] To date, nobody has been able to give a sensible explanation for this impossible combination of shells and bullets.

16. THE SHELLS

The report of the investigation at the scene of the crime

Bugliosi claims that you could throw eighty percent of the material evidence overboard and that there would still be enough left to convict Oswald. We have found problems with the evidence of the magic bullet and the five fragments. If we now jettison these, can it still be maintained that there are reasonable doubts as to whether the Carcano, and no other weapon, fired three shots at the limousine? It can, because there are still the shells. A bullet that is fired leaves a shell (case) behind. According to the official record, there were three shells in the sniper's nest and, to the exclusion of all other weapons, they belong to the Carcano. Let's take a look at this chain of evidence.

The story of the shells starts with the report of the Crime Scene Search (CSS)[255], the police report of the investigation of the crime scene. A report of this kind is a standard document in which everything found at the spot is carefully noted down. The CSS is an important step in the chain of custody. Inspector Day, the Dallas Police specialist in the field, was responsible for drafting the document in the Kennedy case. He could look back on 27 years of loyal service and was specially trained for this part of the forensic work. He had seen hundreds of homicide cases, and knew his business. His assistant Studebaker had only been working at the crime lab for several weeks and had no experience and no talent whatsoever for the job. The fact that police Superintendent Fritz, the boss of the homicide squad, also signed the CSS himself would later prove to be not without importance. Fritz was now 67 years old. He also had a lengthy and impeccable service record in homicide investigations, at least by Texas standards, where the result will prove to be more important than the procedural rules.

This report of what was found at the scene of the crime was signed by the specialist, his assistant and the aging boss of the homicide squad. The CSS was drawn up shortly after the assassination, between 13:30 and 14:15, and mentioned that 'two used shells' had been found in the sniper's nest 'by the window of the sixth floor'. Only two shells...

Documentation of the evidence

The assassination of a president is not an ordinary matter, and this can be seen in this case from the hectic movements of the material evidence. The items of evidence had already traveled from the police in Dallas to the FBI in Washington on November 22. The following night, the material returned to Dallas. When Oswald was murdered, everything went back to Washington again on November 26. The result of this was that the evidence was described at an exceptional number of points:

1. In Dallas, the police drew up a CSS;
2. The material evidence was photographed at the Dallas police station;[38]
3. A memo was drafted in Dallas;[256]
4. In Washington, the FBI drew up an inventory of what was handed to them on November 22;[257]
5. The Dallas Police Department made an inventory of the items that were returned in the night from November 23 to 24;[258]
6. The FBI compiled a 32-page list[259] of all the evidence that went definitively to Washington after the murder of Oswald;
7. The FBI again photographed the evidence that they ultimately received.[260]

All these seven documents only mention or show *two* shells: Bugliosi[261] thinks that conspiracy author Twyman, who was the first to report the 'two-shell problem', tried to deceive his readers in bad faith, and assumed that his readers were stupid and didn't know any better (underlining added):

*Unbeknownst to his readers, all Twyman had managed to prove was
something that had been a well known and established fact for years: that
<u>on the night</u> of November 22 the Dallas Police turned over to the FBI only
two of the three cartridge cases... The third shell was retained by Captain
Fritz to be used , Fritz said, 'for comparison tests'. [...] Fritz kept the shell
in his desk drawer until the early morning hours of November 27, when it
was turned over to FBI agent James P. Hosty jr..*

The third shell was therefore simply kept in the drawer of Superintendent
Fritz. The aging boss was perhaps becoming forgetful: one shell that
may have belonged to the bullet that killed the president just lay in a
desk drawer for five full days, without any documentation. This is the
official account, no conspiracy nonsense. Bugliosi reproached Twyman
for deception, but he himself also deceived his readers. He said that
Superintendent Fritz had taken one bullet into his custody only during
the night of November 22. That's not the case. The third bullet was already missing at 14:15 in the afternoon. Fritz could also do what he felt
was necessary with the evidence material. In itself, that would be no
problem if he had kept his chain of custody intact, but that's not what
happened. According to the chain of custody, there was no third shell. It
may well be a well-known and established fact that Fritz kept the third
shell, but, from a legal point of view, there were only two shells. Fritz
was obviously extensively questioned by the Warren Commission. This
interview took place very late, on July 14, 1964. The Commission was certainly aware of the strange story of the shell in the drawer, but – once
again – didn't say a word about it.[262]

An eighth document suddenly appeared (Figure 15): the list of
the evidence included in the items of evidence of the Commission.[263]
This list suddenly mentions: '6.5 spent rounds (3)'. The evidence of
the Commission thereby suddenly contained three documented shell
casings. But there is something strange going on with the '3' that refers to the shells when you compare it with the shape of the other
digits on the same page. In 1976, Gary Shaw[264] published the original
of this document, and it can be read there: (6.5 spent rounds (2)'. This
simply means that the document on Page 260 in Volume XXIV of the
Commission was a pure forgery. It has been changed from a '2' to a '3'
with a fine pen!

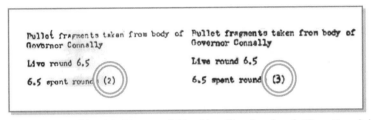

Figure 15 – Comparison of the original document (left) and the evidence item from the Warren Commission: the (2) has become a (3), according to Krush and Gary Shaw.[265]

In other words: in the evidence file, seven documents only mention two shells, while the eighth, which mentions three shells, is a proven forgery. The ninth document contains a weak explanation that the bullet had been in a drawer of Superintendent Fritz, without any chain of custody.

There is another piece of evidence that would prove the presence of three shells: the photos of the sniper's nest. According to the rules of the profession, the evidence must be photographed immediately and without any re-arrangement of the spot. We do in fact see that there are three shells lying on the floor in the crime scene photos. But were the photos taken in the way they should have been? We will return to this in Part 4, when we investigate the scene of the crime.

The chain of custody for the shells

The shells were in an envelope when they arrived at the police station in Dallas. The envelope itself was an intermediate step in the chain of evidence and perhaps helps us to move forward. To start with: who placed the shells in the envelope? According to Inspector Day, it was Detective Sims,[266] but the latter thought that Day himself had picked up the shells. What then happened with the envelope? Sims was no longer too sure, but his memory was refreshed after a discussion with Superintendent Fritz. He had indeed placed the envelope with the shells into the pocket of his overcoat. He couldn't remember in which pocket. According to Sims, the envelope was brown, but Day said that it was a manila colored envelope. When Sims was asked how large the envelope was, his memory let him down again. He could also no longer remember whether he had placed his initials on the shells or on the envelope. What is certain is that the envelope, contrary to all the rules, was not sealed, so that there is yet another flaw in the chain of custody of the shells.

Markings on the shells

We throw all the previous evidence (CSS, photos, inventories of the items of evidence, envelope, statements…) overboard once again and see what still can be found in the dossier regarding the authenticity of the shells. Let's consider the markings on the shells in more detail. It's standard procedure that non-unique items of evidence should always be individualized. In the case of bullets and shells, this is done by applying your initials with a diamond pin. No doubt can then arise that the evidence was found at the scene of the crime and that it is still the same item.

Inspector Day told the Commission that he had indeed marked the one 'unused bullet' that came from the gun according to the rules.[267] He knew how it had to be done. But what had he done with the empty shells that he had found just before? In an interview two weeks before his hearing by the Commission, inspector Day was still insistent: he '*marked all empty shells at the scene*. Fourteen days later, he could no longer confirm that significant statement (underlining added):

> It was further confirmed today when I noticed that the third hull, which I did not give you, or come to me through you, does not have my mark on it.

No initials from Day on the third shell means that there is also no chain of custody for the shell. As an item of evidence, the third shell is well on its way to the trashcan. In the meantime, Day is now in his second version of the facts. On April 22, the Commission[268] asked Day whether he was sure that the third shell was found in the TSBD. Day could only stammer '*I think it is*'. That is only a weak confirmation from the crime specialist who stepped into the site of the assassination of the President. Were there two or three shells lying on the ground? Day 'thought' that there could have been three. He thought that because Superintendent Doughty had placed his initials on it. But it soon became apparent that Doughty was not at the scene of the crime.

We now have the two shells with Day's initials and one with Doughty's initials. At the first glance, we also have an intact chain of custody for the two Day shells. According to all the statements and documents, the shells went to Washington on Friday evening. Because they were included in the FBI file from an early stage, they were also given low numbers as items of evidence: 'Q6' and 'Q7'.[269] The famous third shell, which first took a break in a desk drawer, went to the FBI five days later, and was only 'Q48'. If the story of Day and all the related documents in the file are correct, the shells Q6 and

Q7 bear his initials, but not Q48. But, strangely enough, there are no initials of Inspector Day on Q6, but of Superintendent Doughty ('GD'). This means that Q6 must have been the bullet that was lying in the drawer of Fritz. But Q6 was brought to Washington on November 22, and could therefore not be in Fritz' drawer at the same time. Moreover, Q6 was allegedly picked up and marked in the sniper's nest, and Doughty had never been there. Day therefore tried to limit the damage on the day after his appearance before the Commission. He wrote the following to the Commission on April 23:[270]

> In regard to the third hull which I stated has GD for George Doughty scratched on it, Captain Doughty does not remember handling this.

Doughty's initials can therefore be found on a shell that he never had in his hands. In his letter, Day wanted to clarify why, contrary to all statements and documents, there were no Doughty initials on Q48, the bullet that was sent to Washington later. But this attempt to damage limitation only made matters worse, because the initials of Doughty were still on Q6, where they really couldn't be. Day was therefore not able to uphold his third version either.

This certainly caused some emergency consultation at the police office in Dallas. Those involved eventually saw only one way out: there had to be a story in which unscratched shells Q6, Q7 and Q48 were located at one and the same place, and this place could no longer be the TSBD. Moreover, Day and Doughty had to have both been present at this location without any third parties. We are supposed to believe that one agent then arbitrarily placed his initials on two shells while the other one scratched the third shell. Two of the three shells were then randomly chosen to be handed over to the FBI, and the third shell had five days' rest in a desk drawer. That was the only way to explain Doughty's initials on Q6 and those of Day on Q7 and Q48. Day launched this unlikely story, version four, on May 7 via an *affidavit*,[271] a hand-written statement under oath, confirmed by a public official. Day's statement that the shells had been lying around without any identification up to 22:00 probably resulted in him receiving a reprimand that caused the whole FBI office to shake to its foundations, because, as early as June 23, with a very red face, he had to dictate a new affidavit. Day's fifth version about the marks on the shells was now worded as follows:

> Both Detective R.L. Studebaker and Detective R.M. Sims, who were present at the window when the hulls were picked up, state I marked them as they were found under the window.

The inspector had become very cautious, as he had brought himself well into perjury territory in the four previous versions, and gradually found himself on the brink of an ignominious end to his career. He himself said nothing this time; he simply *reported* that two other officers had stated what had happened. According to Day, his colleagues would claim that he had marked the shells on the spot in the TSBD. Day cunningly avoided mentioning the number of shells that he was supposed to have marked. This time, he clearly thought about what he was going to put to paper.

If, like the Commission members, you only read the last statement and were not too suspicious by nature, you would therefore think that Day had marked the three shells at the scene of the crime, perfectly in accordance with the rules. The Warren Commission, which nevertheless called in more than five hundred witnesses, found that Superintendent Doughty was not important enough. All's well that ends well, they must have thought. But we, of course, are suspicious, and we have read the five consecutive versions, which point towards perjury, lies and shocking procedural errors. In short, the chain of custody of the three shells doesn't make any sense.

Completion of the chain of evidence

Where do we stand in the meantime with the links between the suspects and the victims?

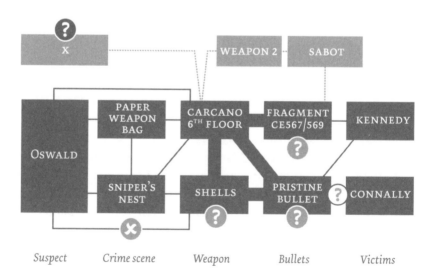

The chain of evidence for the shells is too problematic. There was not only the mystery about the number of shells that was 'cleared up' by means of a falsified document, but, on top of that, the principal investigator repeatedly committed perjury. There are initials on the wrong shells and one of the persons involved also does not remember having applied any initials. The envelope in which the shells were transported was not sealed. One shell lay lost in a drawer without any documentation for several days. The shells are also flawlessly free of fingerprints. It also appears that Oswald never bought any bullets. The list of problems in connection with the shells is even longer, but the difficulties here are already sufficient to show that the shell cases are no good as evidence. If the shells are also unreliable as evidence, the only link between Oswald and the victims in the above diagram is via the weapon. The Carcano that was found on the sixth floor could maybe help the investigation further.

17. THE WEAPON

The weapon that was found on the sixth floor was a 6.5 mm Mannlicher-Carcano[272] with serial number C2766. The Commission assigned evidence number 'CE139' to it (Figure 18). The Carcano is a military weapon of Italian origin that experienced its heyday during World War One. The type that Oswald owned was a Modello 91/38, caliber 6.5, and was only produced in 1940. The weapon is 102 centimeter (40.2 inches) long. Disassembled, the longest part of the weapon is 88 centimeters (34.8 inches) long.[273] A very cheap Japanese telescopic sight (scope) was mounted on the weapon[274] that provided a 4x enlargement. The weapon found in the TSBD was 'well-oiled', which would suggest that it was in a reasonable state of maintenance.

Oswald and the Carcano in the TSBD

Oswald had purchased an old military weapon by mail order on March 12, 1963. Using the alias 'Hidell', he answered an advertisement from the *Klein's Sporting Goods* company in the *American Rifleman* magazine. The price was 19.95 dollars and 1.5 dollars shipping costs. We shouldn't try to read too much into Oswald's childish predilection for using a pseudonym. From an early age, Oswald had been fascinated by espionage stories and, in his youth, had breathlessly followed the television series *I led three lives*. He was perhaps above all a master spy in his own imagination. There is no doubt that this peculiarity made him very vulnerable to manipulation, for example, by the CIA. But if he was planning a murder, he could easily have bought a weapon without leaving any trace in 1963. The Hidell alias was not a sign of cunning cleverness, but rather of adolescent naivety. The weapon was delivered via Oswald's post office box number 2915 in New Orleans.

There are a few problems with the post file, but there was indeed a weapon stored in the garage of Mrs. Paine. We can therefore be sure that Oswald had a Carcano in his possession.

Deputy Sheriff Weitzman found the weapon on the sixth floor of the TSBD at 13:22 on November 22. As the former owner of a gun store, Weitzman was a real weapon connoisseur. Nevertheless, he was still describing the rifle as a Mauser the next day, and not as a Carcano. That caused some confusion, and there was even talk of a British weapon, an Ensfield 303.[275] But, in any case, a Carcano was found on the sixth floor: reporter Tom Alyea filmed the moment when the police found it. The Dallas police again showed itself from its best side through the official indictment stating a '6.25 Carcano' instead of a '6.5'. This indicates the profound nonchalance with which they handled the matter. In Texas, the indictment must be proven in all its components[276] and any silly mistakes in the indictment would be very detrimental with regard to the subsequent prosecution of the suspect. But, for the time being, silly mistakes are still the least of our concerns in this dossier.

Prints on the weapon

The weapon was in the care of Inspector Day until 23:45 on Friday night. No fingerprints were initially found on it. A few partial and blurred prints on the trigger were too unreliable for identification. Oswald's fingerprints were not on his own rifle. Day then dismantled the carbine in the police station and did find a usable palm print under the wooden butt, although it was an old and latent print, an invisible or less visible print that requires enhancement in order to be seen. He thought that he could perceive some of the characteristics of Oswald's palm print. Unfortunately, the inspector forgot to inform his superiors of his happy discovery. He also didn't take a photo of the palm print. In the evening, at around 20:00, he photographed various aspects of the weapon, but he didn't find a minute to take a picture of the palm print in the more than three hours up to 23:45, when he handed over the weapon to the FBI,[278] This is even stranger when you realize that Inspector Day was a specialist in latent fingerprints and had developed a highly individual method for photographing latent prints. With a world's first in his hands, he did not even attempt to put his fantastic technique into practice. He did take the palm print from the butt using adhesive tape.

He applied the adhesive tape to an index card and thereby preserved the palm print for all eternity.[279]

But the Dallas police were then abruptly taken off the case. Shortly before midnight, the FBI took all the material evidence with them to Washington. Day claimed afterwards that he had informed the FBI agent about the palm print, but the agent in question could no longer remember anything about this. We may assume that an FBI agent would certainly have remembered the ultimate evidence that Oswald was the perpetrator. Day was therefore lying again when he claimed to have pointed out the palm print. But even without Day explicitly drawing attention to it, the palm print could not have gone unnoticed by the FBI. Even after the use of the adhesive tape, Day claims that the print could still be seen with the naked eye.[280] In Washington, they not only knew nothing about a palm print, they also didn't notice one. Fingerprint expert Latona from the FBI did not find any usable fingerprints in Washington on November 23, and saw not a single trace of a palm print in the place where it had been found in Dallas.[281] In the FBI laboratory, they found absolutely nothing under the butt, and did not even detect that the weapon had been treated with carbon. It wasn't Inspector Day's day, because he also forgot to hand over to Washington the index card with the adhesive strip from the print. He also forgot to report the existence of this piece of evidence. As a result, the card with the super-important palm print was not mentioned anywhere in any inventory of the material evidence. The FBI only received the card with the palm print for the first time nine days after the assassination. While every possible piece of evidence against Oswald was trumpeted all around, nobody said a single word about the print that would make Oswald's guilt undeniable. Superintendent Fritz even replied in the negative to the question from the press as to whether any fingerprints had been found on the weapon.[282]

Apart from the once more incomplete and implausible chain of custody, one latent palm print, and that under the butt, seems a little thin. Oswald's only official motive was to acquire eternal fame. Why then would it make any difference to him whether his fingerprints could be found on his own weapon? The weapon had been purchased through his post office box and would certainly be found on the sixth floor. Why would Oswald carefully clean his weapon, the shells, the unused bullet and the magazine? Cleaning would cost him time, time in which he could be noticed with the weapon in his hand, time that he could make better use of in an attempt to escape. It would soon come to light that he was the perpetrator. Did Oswald really think that, after assassinating the President on Friday, he could just return to his 1.25 dollar an hour job again as usual on Monday? Moreover, he had managed to leave the only print that he could have removed during his preparation, an old print under the butt. And there was also no rag found anywhere on the sixth floor.

Post-mortem prints

There were incredibly few fingerprints, and then a latent print suddenly emerged, a palm print that was first mentioned the morning after Oswald's death.

The timing raises questions among the conspiracists. Some claim that the print could have been applied after Oswald's death. However crazy that sounds, there are undisputed facts that provide some support for that story. For example, mortician Paul Groody, who laid the murdered Oswald in his casket on the night of November 24, reported the following:

> Some place in the early morning agents came, [...] they carried a satchel and equipment and asked us if they might have the preparation room to themselves, and after it was all over we found ink on Lee Harvey's hands showing that they had fingerprinted him and palmprinted him, we had to take that ink back off in order to prepare him for burial.[283]

Rusty Livingstone, a colleague of Inspector Day in the crime lab, confirmed the nocturnal visit to the morgue. Taking finger and palm prints from a deceased person was standard procedure, he claimed.[284] But if you already have prints from the living person, a post-mortem examination is, of course, pointless. Oswald spent two days in the police station while still alive, and, according to Inspector Day, his fingerprints were taken three times. What had to be carried out so urgently that night? Furthermore, it goes without saying that the file contains not a single trace of the nocturnal activity and even less of even a hint of an explanation of who and why. Was the palm print on Day's card actually created after Oswald's death[285], and then preserved with sticky tape and glued onto the index card? It sounds crazy, but we are getting used to this. The conspiracists are also uneasy, because they believe that the place where the print was found on the weapon was curved, whereas the palm print on the card appears to have come from a flat object.

Here also, Hoover himself provided assistance. On September 9, 1964, he wrote the Commission a letter in which he confirmed that the palm print on the card had indeed come from the Carcano. The print showed the same irregularities as the Carcano. The annex to Hoover's letter also stated that 'Inspector Day continues to refuse to explain anything about the palm print in writing'. The Inspector was clearly becoming more cautious in his statements.[286] The Commission did not ask FBI expert Latona anything about the confirmation that the print on the card had come from the Carcano.

Use of the Carcano in the attack

FBI firearms expert Robert A. Frazier was questioned by the Warren Commission about the condition of the weapon on March 31, 1964. He reported that the barrel showed signs of rust *'Metal fouling'*.[287] This would indicate that the weapon had not been used for some time. After firing three bullets on November 22, the barrel would normally have become clean again. For once, the Commission asked a pertinent question: was this aspect investigated? The expert replied in the negative. Nobody had thought of checking whether the Carcano had recently been fired. This seems so unlikely that conspiracists believe that it was indeed investigated, but that the results were removed from the file when it appeared that the Carcano hadn't been fired recently.

There is yet another technical problem with regard to Oswald as the perpetrator. The Dallas Police had carried out a paraffin test on his hands and cheek. This test indicates the presence of nitrates, which means that the person concerned has used a firearm in the 24 hours before the test. Oswald tested positive for his hands, but negative for his cheek. This would suggest that his cheek had not been near a shot, and that he had therefore not fired a carbine. The FBI repeated the test by having Agent Killion shoot with the Carcano and then carrying out the paraffin test on him. The test was also negative for the FBI agent.[288] After being loaded with the *bolt-action* loading system, the bullet is completely shielded in the Carcano, with the result that no traces of gunpowder can escape, and the weapon will give an incorrect negative result in the paraffin test.[289] Conspiracists again suspect bad faith here. According to them, the Commission would have certainly considered a positive test to be reliable, but a result that was favorable for Oswald could only mean that the test was unreliable. The white marble did not count. Besides, if the paraffin test was so unreliable, why did it belong to the standard arsenal of police investigations? In any event, it is a fact that Oswald tested negative. If he had been the shooter, it was unlucky for the investigation that it was precisely the Carcano that was unsuitable for this test. The paraffin test on the hands does seem to indicate that Oswald fired a pistol on November 22. But this test also sometimes returns incorrect positive results, for example, as the result of urine traces on the hands. But, at this point, the test is still a strong indication that Oswald could have shot Tippit.

The Carcano provides yet another technical riddle, because the weapon had been adjusted for a left-hander, although Oswald was right-handed. The FBI noted this in a memorandum that was included in the items of evidence of the Commission:

> The gunsmith observed that the scope as we received it was installed as if for a left handed man.[290]

This problem was not discussed any further.

The weapon soon became the subject of controversy. Harold Weisberg was the first to launch an attack in his self-published series of *Whitewash* books. He pointed to the technical impossibility of firing three shots from such an antiquated weapon in the limited time available.[291] The doubt has never really disappeared since then. The Mannlicher worked with a *bolt-action* loading system, which is both time-consuming and impractical. The loading system also jammed regularly. According to a test by the Discovery Channel in the *Unsolved History* program, the weapon jammed in more than twenty percent of the cases. The weapon had a bad and simultaneously good reputation as 'the humanitarian rifle', precisely because it was so unreliable and because, in many cases, no usable shot occurred when the trigger was pulled.

Oswald's Carcano was clearly old. A Carcano is by nature a cheap weapon, and the one owned by Oswald was not in the best state of maintenance and had not been adjusted after its assembly. That does not, of course, mean that it could not have been fired. Bugliosi said that conspiracy author Walt Brown[292] incorrectly claimed that Oswald's weapon was 'a piece of junk' [...] 'that lacked accuracy'. Brown was said to have been dishonest in this respect by withholding information from his readers.[293] Bugliosi admitted[294] that the Mannlicher Carcano was not exactly the best rifle, but he referred to Ronald Simmons, the military weapon expert who testified before the Warren Commission. According to Bugliosi, Simmons declared that the weapon was 'quite accurate', even 'as accurate as the M-14 rifle, the rifle used by the American military at the time.' The American military were not armed with cheap Carcanos in Vietnam, so we should take the assertion of its equivalence with an M-14 with a pinch of salt.

Let us take a look at Volume III of the Warren Report and examine what Simmons actually said. Simmons first had the weapon adjusted.[295] Two *shims* were applied in doing this (small plates that are clamped under the sight in order to adjust its height). The test was carried out using stationary targets and with an unlimited aiming time for the first shot.[296] The shooters were *masters*, 'highly qualified rifle men', who had taken part in the national competitions of the *National Rifle Association*[297] and who had practiced with the weapon beforehand. What's more, they also worked under less stressful conditions than Oswald on Dealey Plaza. Last but not least, there was also some cheating in the test, as too many attempts missed the second target, but, under the circumstances, the shooters were reasonably accurate with the Carcano. In one attempt, 'Specialist' Miller succeeded in firing three shots in the test within 4.6 seconds. Weapon expert Frazier also had the weapon tested on November 27, five days after the murder. The bullets were well grouped on the target, but invariably too high and too far to the right. The upwards deviation over the distance of the fatal shot was more than half a meter, and the deviation to the right was 15 centimeters. Frazier also considered 4.6 seconds to be the minimum time needed to fire three shots with the Carcano 'as fast as the bolt can be operated, I think.'

Therefore, after adjustment and practice, you can fire three shots at a stationary target with a quite inaccurate weapon at intervals of 2.3 seconds. But will that still work in one movement and with a moving target?

Reconstruction of the shots at a moving target

On YouTube, you can admire numerous attempts of amateur marksmen who try to match Oswald's performance. Everyone on the Internet seems to agree that it is very difficult and that it is even more dangerous for the shooter than for the target. The test is also organized and carried out by a team from Discovery Channel in the *Unsolved History* series. The sharpshooter employed, Michael Yardley, was described as a 'supreme marksman'; and effortlessly shot three skeets to shreds from the hip. The man could certainly hit a moving target. A telescopic sight is, of course, not too important for someone who can hit a clay pigeon from the hip. The use of a sight inevitably causes a delay. After loading, the sight makes it more difficult to quickly re-aim, because, of course, you first have to find the target again, like when using binoculars. Yardley hit the moving target three times in 7.87 seconds. It is striking that five of the 21 shots were 'misfires'. In other words, the carbine refused to fire in 23 percent of the shots. Yardley had no doubt: the Carcano was 'a very inferior weapon'. From a technical point of view, however, the shots were perfectly possible for an 'excellent marksman' like Yardley.

Oswald was not known as a very good shot in the Marine Corps. He often scored a red flag, which his colleagues mockingly referred to as 'Maggie's drawers '. A red flag means that the shooter did not even hit the target. In December 1956, Oswald achieved a score of 212 'under ideal circumstances', whereby he could refer to himself as a 'sharpshooter'. Sharpshooter sounds impressive, but the score was a mere point above the lowest qualification, 'marksman'. In addition, an intensive training period also preceded the test and, of course, Oswald did not take the test with an incorrectly adjusted Carcano. About two years later, in May 1959, he only achieved 191 points, one meager point above the minimum level for 'sharpshooter'[298]. It is not inconceivable that his superiors turned a blind eye and granted him the absolute minimum plus one point in order to prevent him having to stop his training. There is no evidence that Oswald trained again with firearms in the subsequent four and a half years. His quality as a shooter in 1963 must certainly have been a lot lower than the score in May 1959. But, in his statement to the Commission, Major Anderson confirmed that Oswald was a 'good to excellent' shot in comparison to a citizen that had not had any intensive training.[299] An ex-Marine will indeed shoot much better than the average grocer, and shooting at a moving target will certainly have been part of his training. If you look out of the window on the sixth floor of the TSBD, it also does not appear insurmountable to shoot at a limousine in Elm Street with a telescopic sight that brings the target four times closer. Incidentally, it does not matter whether or not Oswald was a poor shot. Indeed, it can never be proven how good Oswald was this one time.

The firing tests of both Frazier and Simmons were carried out on a stationary target, but, in its questions, the Commission ventured into the field of moving targets. In order to shoot at a moving target, the shooter takes account of a '*lead*', a deviation between his aiming point and his actual target. How close he aims to the target will depend on the distance of the shot and the speed and direction of the movement. How much *lead* should the shooter take into account in order to hit the president? According to Frazier, you would aim above and to the right of the target in this case. While the bullet is traveling, the limousine is also moving, so you need to aim next to and above the target in order to make a hit. By coincidence or not, the incorrect adjustment of the Carcano made the weapon always shoot above and to the right of the target. The deviation of the weapon was thereby perhaps an advantage. The limousine drove in a direction that almost perfectly anticipated the deviation of the weapon (Figure 16). This gave the shooter the *lead* that was necessary to hit an object moving at 15 km an hour on Elm Street, free-of-charge as it were, with the incorrectly adjusted sight. Provided, of course, that he aimed at, and not next to the moving target (as an experienced shooter would do). As an ex-Marine, Oswald undoubtedly knew that you should never aim directly at a moving target if you wanted to hit it. But this didn't apply to this particular Carcano. The sniper didn't hit the target once, but twice. Was he incredibly lucky, or did he know that the deviation of the weapon and the target corresponded, and deliberately used the incorrect adjustment in order to make it easier to hit the moving target under these circumstances?

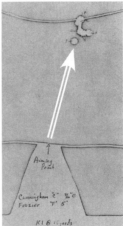

Figure 16 – Left, the target seen from the sniper's nest, right the deviation of the Carcano. Was it luck or coincidence?

The serial number

Every weapon has a serial number. The Carcano that Oswald bought certainly had the serial number C2766[300]. The Warren Report contains a copy of the order form. The weapon that was found in the TSBD also bears the serial number C2766, with the last '6' engraved somewhat too high. According to the Commission, a serial number is unique[301], but this was apparently naive reasoning. In his book *Kennedy & Lincoln*, believer John K. Lattimer described how he carried out an experiment with a 'Mannlicher Carcano 91/38 rifle with a serial number of C2766' in the seventies.[302] If the Commission members had thought logically for a moment, they would have realized that the Carcano could not have had a unique serial number. The number only consists of four digits and one letter, but millions of Carcanos were produced. The weapon that Oswald bought came into the USA in 1958 as part of a purchase of up to 500,000 units by Crescent Firearms. There are several models of the Carcano and the production of the weapon took place in five different factories.[303] If we place that information in the letter C, that only leaves four digits. This is only enough to provide 9,999 weapons with a unique number. There were therefore certainly other C2766 numbers in the stock held by Crescent Firearms, or a C276 to which the number 6, engraved slightly too high, could be added.

In November 1983, Michael O'Neill photographed the Carcano in the National Archives for a commemorative issue of *Life Magazine*. The serial number can be seen clearly in one of the photos. The conspiracists immediately took out their best magnifying glasses. According to them, the 'C' in the photo from O'Neill in *Life Magazine*[304] was a round 'C', while the 'C' on evidence item CE541 of the Warren Commission[305] clearly had a straight edge that made the letter look more like a 'G'.

The temptation to sound an alarm is great here, but the lighting and the angle from which the photos were taken were different. Moreover, important similarities can also be established between the weapons in the two photos. Hence there is no doubt that there is only one Carcano in the material evidence. We are looking at this easily refutable photographic evidence here as a warning regarding the following point: comparing photos and then coming up with far-reaching conclusions on the basis of this is very dangerous.

Photos of Oswald and his weapon

In any case, we know that Oswald owned a Carcano because there are photos, the so-called 'backyard photos' (Figure 17), in which he can be clearly seen with his weapon. The photos were only found on Saturday, during the second search in the garage of Mrs. Paine. Marina Oswald was asked to take a number of cool photos of Oswald – in a black polo shirt and black pants – with a Carcano prominently in one hand, a pistol in his belt and two communist newspapers in his other hand. When Oswald was confronted with these images, he condescendingly said that they were forgeries. The conspiracists can spend hours playing around with this: They see a chin that is too square or the line from the collage of another body, onto which Oswald's head has been placed. Some find that the shadow that gives Oswald a Hitler moustache does not correspond to the position of the sun and of the other shadows in the photos. The garden plant has too many leaves for the alleged time of year or the foliage in the background is completely identical in the various photos, which would, of course, suggest a photo-montage. But the photos are genuine. The HSCA devoted 81 pages of Volume VI to substantiate this. The conclusion was: 'The panel detects no evidence of fakery in any of the backyard picture materials.'[306]

Figure 17 – The backyard photos are genuine, but is the weapon in the photo also the murder weapon?

There is another simple, yet convincing, argument that the photos are real: nobody would make three forgeries of the same item. If the photos are real, they can provide an answer to another question: is the Carcano in the material evidence the same Carcano as in the photos in the backyard? This is not an academic question, because if Oswald's Carcano is not the murder weapon, this would indicate a conspiracy. Oswald could have bought a second Carcano, but this would not have had the same, identical serial number. Why would Oswald have replaced an outdated, unreliable weapon with another that was also outdated and unreliable? And if another Carcano with the same serial number surfaced in the TSBD, this could only mean that someone wanted to place the blame on Oswald.

The fixing ring for the strap

Figure 18 – The Carcano found on the sixth floor. Below: Oswald's Carcano. Is this the same weapon?

The assumption that someone brought a second Carcano into circulation sounds a little unlikely, but we cannot exclude this a priori. CE139, the Carcano in the dossier had a dark-colored carrying strap that was attached to the side. The conspiracists are convinced that the 'sling' in the backyard photos is attached to the bottom of the butt and the barrel, and not to the side (Figure 19).

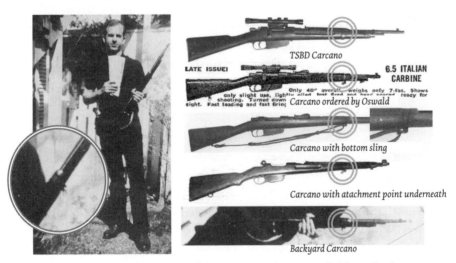

Figure 19 Backyard photo 313. A with magnified inset. Figure 20. Five Carcanos: find the one that does not belong in the list. TSBD Carcano - Carcano ordered by Oswald - Carcano with bottom sling - Carcano with attachment point underneath - Backyard Carcano

There are various models of the Carcano. In the model that was found in the TSBD (Figure 18) the attachment for the strap (sling mount) is on the side, while the attachment is at the bottom in the model shown below.[307] (Figure 21)

In the backyard photo CE133-B, the white cord seems to be attached with a knot to the attachment point on the underside of the weapon. This is a big problem, because the weapon in the material evidence has no such attachment point. In the Warren volumes[308], the backyard photo CE133-B is gray, and has been printed so small that it is completely impossible to determine this important element. The way in which the strap of Oswald's Carcano was attached can be seen clearest on one photo, which has been called CE133-C. This CE133-C was not part of the evidence of the Warren Commission. The photo was only found thirteen years later by Roscoe White, an agent of the Dallas Police, who confused the investigation with a hunt for souvenirs.

The groove and the tab

If a weapon with serial number C2766 was delivered to Oswald, and the weapon found at the scene of the crime had the same serial number, there is a strong supposition that it was the same weapon, despite the apparent differences in the photos. The believers also have the experts on their side in this area. The *Photographic Evidence Panel* of the HSCA closely examined the backyard photos and confirmed that the weapon in the pictures was identical to the weapon that was found on the sixth floor:

> *The rifle in these photographs can be positively identified as the same rifle that is presently in the custody of the National Archives.*[309]

The panel even found a marked 'groove S' on the original backyard photo, which is also claimed to be visible on the weapon in the evidence materi-al.[310] Claimed to be visible, because, even in the backyard photos with the highest resolution, this groove cannot be detected anywhere. The photo material provided by the photographic panel itself is also not very en-lightening.[311] The sharper version of backyard photo 133A, in which the groove should be visible, was also not available to the Commission in 1964. The wife of Baron de Mörenschildt found this best-quality backyard photo four years after the assassination among her husband's papers.

Why the copy from de Mörenschildt has more detail than the original is just as puzzling as the question of why the baron never informed the Warren Commission about the existence of the photo. In the meantime, the Dallas police had also managed to lose one of the two negatives that had been found.[312]

The presence of the groove on the weapon *after* the assassination can be confirmed. There is a sharp photo in the police file in which the groove can indeed be seen, and, with a little goodwill, it can also be recognized in a still image from the Alyea film at the moment that Inspector Day held the weapon in his hand. But was the groove also present on the backyard weapon? In no version of the backyard photos known to me can I see the groove at the place indicated by the panel.

What can be clearly seen in the backyard photos is the metal tab on the underside of the Carcano. The report from the HSCA experts didn't say a single word about this. The square hole in the tab cannot be overlooked, however (Figure 21). The hole in the backyard Carcano seems to be located somewhat closer to the end of the tab, but this is only due to the fact that the weapon in Oswald's hand is tilted towards the camera. Belief or suspicion is often a matter of one detail that sticks in the observer's mind. Here, for me, it is the square hole. The agreement of this specific point with the photos of Carcano models with the attachment point underneath seems undeniable. In any case, the Carcano found in the TSBD is not the model with the attachment point underneath. It does seem unlikely that one Carcano would be replaced by another. But, ultimately, it comes down to this one question: Who do you believe: the research panel of the HSCA, or your own eyes?

Figure 21 – Did Oswald's Carcano have a tab for the attachment of the strap? The photos on the left and middle show a Carcano model with this kind of tab, while the right photo shows the backyard Carcano. The Klein's Sporting Goods ad (above) also shows a Carcano with tabs at the bottom. The TSBD Carcano has no tab.

Filling in the chain of evidence

In all objectivity, and in view of the doubts regarding the integrity of the investigation, it seems that the link between Oswald and the weapon that was found in the TSBD has not been established sufficiently. It is uncertain whether the Carcano that was found on the sixth floor was the same weapon that Oswald is showing on the backyard photos. For the time being, I tend to trust my own eyes more than the experts from the HSCA. Moreover, the single, old palm print that subsequently also disappeared, and about which Inspector Day held back the documentation for days, is slender evidence for putting someone in the electric chair.

At this point of our investigation, we now have the following picture:

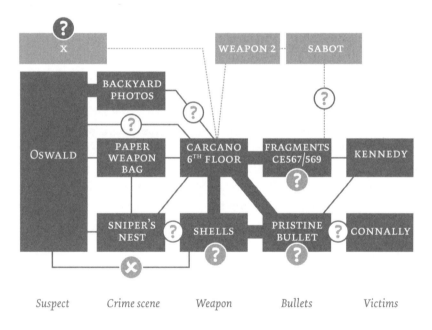

| Suspect | Crime scene | Weapon | Bullets | Victims |

The Carcano that was found cannot be linked to Oswald with certainty, either directly through the fingerprints or indirectly via the backyard photos. Was the Carcano that was found Oswald's carbine? This is crucial data for the investigation. We will leave the question open for the moment. We can perhaps prove that Oswald brought the weapon into the TSBD; that would make it much more likely that it was indeed his Carcano that was found there. If Oswald brought the weapon into the TSBD, it was in the paper bag that he was carrying on Friday morning.

18. A LONG PAPER BAG

If Oswald was the sole perpetrator, he must have brought the weapon into the building on Friday morning. On that day, Oswald was driven to work by his colleague Buell Wesley Frazier. When he got into the car, he laid a brown paper bag on the back seat. He told Frazier that it contained curtain rods for his rented room. In Dallas, Oswald quickly stepped out of the car and left with the parcel. No curtain rods were found anywhere in the TSBD after the assassination.[313] But Oswald's rifle had certainly gone from Mrs. Paine's garage in the meantime. The logical conclusion is that the weapon was in Oswald's parcel. If Oswald lied about the curtain rods during the interrogation, he must certainly have had a good reason for this.

The longest component of a dismantled Carcano is 34.6 inches long. This length would fit into the brown paper bag that is included in the evidence, which is 37.8 inches long. A palm print of Oswald was also found at the bottom of the bag. According to the believers, the print corresponds with the way that Oswald carried the bag close to his body, clamped under his arm. But there are still a few problems.

Problems with the paper bag

The FBI played about with chemicals on the original bag, with the result that it took on a completely different appearance and became dark brown.[314] A replica of the bag was then made to replace the original.[315] But that is the least of the problems. Much worse is the fact that the place where the bag was found is questionable. No photograph was taken of the original situation in the sniper's nest. This error is not insurmountable. The Commission found an original solution: as evidence, they produced a photo with a dotted line showing where the bag 'would have been'. There is also a problem with the important early witnesses of the sniper's nest. The deputies who found the nest did not remember any paper bag at the site. There is also the question of whether the weapon was ever in the bag. FBI expert Cadigan found no trace of this. If the Carcano had ever been in the bag, it couldn't have moved very much.[316] That's strange, because the Carcano was 'well oiled' and the bag moved a lot that day. Well oiled could have meant just one drop in the right place of the mechanism, but it's strange that not a single trace of the weapon was found in the bag, and only limited movement also does not sound very likely.

The size of the bag is the next problem. According to two witnesses, namely his colleague Frazier and the latter's sister Linnie Mae Randle, the bag that Oswald had with him in the morning was about 24 inches long. That is about 11 inches shorter than the dismantled weapon. Frazier had looked at the parcel on the back seat over his shoulder: 'I would say roughly around 2 feet of the seat.'[317] People are sometimes poor at estimating sizes, but no-one makes a mistake in the difference between two and three feet, or between 24 and 35 inches. There are even indications that the package was shorter. In his first affidavit on the day of the assassination, Frazier said that Oswald had carried the package under his armpit with outstretched arm.[318] This would correspond to about 24 inches. Thirty-five inches would have protruded above the shoulder. Frazier, who was initially regarded as a possible accomplice, is certain to have considered things carefully before he stated anything. He was subjected to a test with a lie detector on November 29. This confirmed the sincerity of his estimate of two feet. Linnie Mae Randle is said to have declared on November 22: '[I] saw him put a long brown package, approximately 3 feet by 6 inches.' The package is suddenly just long enough for the dismantled Carcano. This statement is not her signed statement, however. It is a report from the FBI regarding what Randle *is said to have stated*.[319] The FBI has not yet built up much credibility in this affair. Distrust is also justified here. During her interview by the Commission, Randle could provide her own statement, and she stated '24 inches'. She also described what she saw that morning though her kitchen window: Oswald held the package firmly from the top, against his body, and it did not touch the ground. It is not possible to carry a 35 inch package with your arm outstretched without it touching the ground.

The link to Oswald

The palm and finger print found on the bag are also grist to the mill of the conspiracists. Inspector Day, the great specialist in latent prints, found *no* fingerprints on the bag on November 22, but there suddenly *were* finger-prints on November 24. The FBI discovered the latent print of the ball of the thumb of a left hand and the latent print of the index finger of a right hand. In order to find the prints, powerful chemicals were used, such as silver nitrate. This made the bag – which was, after all, crucial evidence – un-recognizable through its change of color. The print was also 'latent' again, which means that it was very weak and susceptible to errors in identifying the print.[320] A latent palm print and a latent print from a finger seem to be a poor return from the many radical manipulations that Oswald carried out with his bare hands. Oswald had made the bag from wrapping paper and adhesive tape that he had fetched himself from the roll in the TSBD. He had taken the bag with him to Irving and had put a rifle into it. He had then carried the bag to the car, laid it on the rear seat and had later fetched it from the car. Subsequently, he had taken the bag into the TSBD, hidden it on the sixth floor and fetched it from its hiding place at noon, removed the weapon, and finally folded the bag and put it away. The evidence material of the Commission shows that the only palm print on the bag had nine points of resemblance to Oswald's palm print. Courts often require a minimum of twelve points of resemblance for a positive identification.[321] FBI expert Latona said that this was not a sacred number, however. A great deal depended on the experience of the analyst. Other sources confirm this view[322] and we may assume that the palm print on the bag with nine points of agreement can be attributed to Oswald. But it's not inconceivable that a criminal court would deem the identification to be inadequate.

A few fibers were also found in the bag and some of these had 'possibly' come from the blanket in which Oswald had wrapped the weapon in Mrs. Paine's garage. Those who consider that this is the proof that the weapon was in the bag should take a look at the following photo (Figure 22). In this photo, we can see the evidence material in Dallas, and the blanket is ly-ing nicely just above the opening of the paper bag. It looks as if the police didn't want to miss any chance to contaminate the evidence. Incidentally, please note the two shells in the lower left-hand corner of the photo with the evidence material.

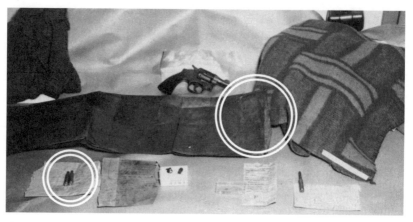

Figure 22 – The blanket in which the weapon was wrapped in Mrs. Paine's garage lies above the opening of the paper bag. Afterwards, the fibers would be used to prove the link between the bag and the weapon.

The curtain rods

In any case, Oswald did carry a brown paper bag into the TSDB. His statement that it contained curtain rods is implausible. No package of curtain rods was ever found. Truly confirmed to the Commission that no such package was found in the months after the assassination.

Yet there is also something strange going on with these curtain rods. Gene Daniels from the *Black Star Agency* wanted to take some photos of Oswald's rented room, but the landlady asked him to wait until the curtains had been hung. Daniels was in Oswald's rented room less than 24 hours after the assassination, and curtains were quickly being hung at precisely that moment,[323] which, for the conspiracists, gives a little more credibility to the account of the curtain rods. Patricia Hall, the grand-daughter of the then owner confirmed to me that there were certainly curtains in Oswald's room. That seems very credible. Oswald was always a bit of a troublemaker, and he would never hang up curtains at his own cost in a rented room where he would perhaps no longer be staying a week later. Mrs. Hall also emphasized that the possession of weapons was not permitted in the house. As the small and sparsely furnished room was cleaned twice a week, it was quite possible that Oswald's pistol would have been discovered, and then he would certainly have been thrown out of the room. This idea alone would have been sufficient to stop the miserly Oswald becoming involved in any additional costs. That morning, after a failed attempt to get together with his wife again, Oswald had left his wedding ring in a tea-cup on the Paine's breakfast table. This was a very emotional and far-reaching decision. You don't simply leave your wedding ring behind without a deep sigh. Is it credible that your next thought would be about curtain rods?

We may assume without any reasonable doubt that Oswald's story about the curtain rods was a lie. But that does not remove the other major problems with regard to the paper bag, and there are even more to come.

The wrapping paper

The FBI tried to prove that the bag had been made from wrapping paper and adhesive tape that originally came from the TSBD. Nobody had seen Oswald at the packaging desk, however,[324] but he did have access to this part of the building. Nobody had also seen Oswald busying himself with wrapping paper in the Paine household. But if the paper of the bag corresponds to that from the TSBD, we will have come one step forward.

The Dallas police had been smart enough to take a few samples of the wrapping paper from the TSBD on Friday afternoon. We can read the following on page 129 of the FBI report dated November 30 (underlining added by the author):

> *This paper was examined by the FBI-laboratory and found to have the <u>same observable characteristics</u> as the brown paper from the roll that was used in packing books by the Texas School Book Depository.*[325]

Once again, this doesn't sound very convincing. The brown paper had the same 'observable characteristics' as other brown paper. You wouldn't need the most specialized crime laboratory in the world to determine this.

We know in the meantime that we need to watch out for the vague expressions and euphemisms of the FBI. Indeed, further research again leads to a more significant underlying problem. It appears that the cited page 129 was changed by the powers that be after the definitive signing of the report. On December 18, the FBI in Dallas sent a telex to Hoover[326] with a new version of page 129. We can find the explanation for why the change was necessary elsewhere in the file of the FBI headquarters.[327] Note 11 reads as follows (underlining added):

Line 10 indicates the paper from the TSBD when compared with the brown
paper by our laboratory <u>was found to be identical</u>. As you are aware our
laboratory did find it <u>SIMILAR</u> as shown on page 165. Handle corrections.
(underlining added)

The FBI made an effort to not find the bag 'identical', but only 'similar'. The agency thereby apparently weakened the evidence, and that is strange, because the FBI expert who examined the bag carried out his work very thoroughly. He had compared the paper and the adhesive tape from the dispatch room with the bag. Four different kinds of lighting were used, together with a microscope and a spectrograph. He examined the structure and the production properties, and measured the thickness of the paper down to one thousandth of an inch. The result of this thorough laboratory investigation was as follows (underlining added):

The presumed and known items were <u>identical</u> for all properties that were
measured in these tests.[328]

Expert Cadigan confirmed this again, contrary to the final version of his own report, when he was interviewed by the Commission.[329] In reply to the question 'Did you find any points of nonidentity?' his answer was: 'I found none'. The question was repeated. 'They were identical on every point on which you measured them?' The answer is clear: 'Yes'. The paper from the bag and the paper from the roll in the packing desk on November 22 were thereby *identical*. The change imposed from above by the FBI was a blatant lie. But why did the FBI want to absolutely eliminate this fact from the dossier and to weaken the finding of the investigation from 'identical' to 'similar', contrary to the findings of their own expert?

Something else was determined by the laboratory investigation: paper from different rolls was *not* identical. A replica bag had been made on December 1, and the TSBD paper from December 1 was definitely different from the paper from the roll that was in use on November 22. 'Identical' paper therefore came from one and the same roll, while 'similar' paper came from different rolls. In fact, the laboratory had determined that the roll of paper had not been replaced between the time of the manufacture of the long bag and Friday afternoon. The FBI's problem apparently related to the time at which Oswald made the paper bag. But it is not immediately clear what the problem could have been. The TSBD had purchased 58 rolls of paper on March 19, which should have been sufficient to cover their needs up to around January 1964.[330] One roll of paper was therefore sufficient for around three to four days at the TSBD. Oswald could therefore have taken paper on November 21 to make the bag that he brought into the building on November 22. Without any problem, this paper could have been from the same roll from which Inspector Day took a sample for comparison on November 22. But, on the photo of the packing desk that was taken by the police after the assassination, we can see the roll of paper that was in use. The roll appears to have been hardly used (Figure 23). Could it be that the roll was replaced on Friday morning? It occurred to nobody to ask the question. If the answer had been affirmative, how then could the paper that Oswald allegedly took with him on Thursday be identical to the paper on this roll? Was this a problem that was serious enough to compel the FBI to change the facts that had been determined in a solid and conclusively finalized report?

Figure 23 – There still seems to be plenty of paper on the paper roll in the packing desk. Was the roll changed on Friday morning?

The adhesive tape

There is a similar problem with the tape. This was also identical according to the laboratory investigation. Apparently, the last time that the TSBD had purchased adhesive tape was on March 29:[331] fifty cartons, each containing ten rolls of 3-inch wide gummed tape. There was only one tape dispenser in the shipping room of the TSBD.[332] There was also only one supplier of adhesive tape.[333] Researcher Gil Jesus[334] made the logical assumption that the orders for paper and adhesive tape would be placed for the same period. If that's correct, there would be five hundred rolls of adhesive tape for 58 rolls of paper. This means that a roll of adhesive tape would be used up in around three and a quarter working hours. That's not entirely true, because nobody has figured out how often the tape was purchased. It is inconceivable, however, that the gummed tape would be purchased for several years. If the tape is only purchased once a year, this means that a roll of adhesive tape would last for about 3 hours and 45 minutes on average. Logically, this means that at least one fresh roll of adhesive tape was put into use, and possibly also a new roll of paper, during the course of Friday morning.

If the material for the paper bag was *identical* to the material that was found on the packing desk after the attack, it seems that the only possible conclusion is that the paper bag was made on Friday. Oswald could then not have brought in the bag that is part of the evidence in the early morning of Friday, because the bag did not exist at that time. Whatever the problem was, it was in any case serious enough to compel the FBI to falsify the evidence, which, in this case, was made up of the findings of a scientific investigation by its own expert.

A bag in the mail

And then, to top everything off: on December 4, 1963, twelve days after the assassination, a package addressed to Oswald was found in the dead letter department of the post office in Irving. The address (W Nassau Street 60, Dallas) did not exist, and so the package was undeliverable. Oswald had been world famous since November 22, which was why the package stood out. When it was opened, it was found to contain a long, brown paper bag. This bizarre fact only came to light in 1967, when an unfinished FBI report about it appeared in the National Archives. Logically, this package must have been sent before November 22, because any package addressed to Oswald would not have been casually classed as undeliverable mail after that date. Yet another unsolved mystery.

Filling in the chain of evidence

What remains at the end of the whole paper bag story? The only incriminating fact is that Oswald had a package with him and that he allegedly lied about it during an interrogation, for which there is incidentally no official police report. All the other information is questionable. We have to place a question mark against the bag itself, as well as on the lines connecting it to the weapon, the sniper's nest and the suspect. The investigation into the paper bag has not helped us move forward at all. Quite the contrary. Our confidence in the investigation and the FBI has once again been seriously shaken. The chain of evidence now looks as follows:

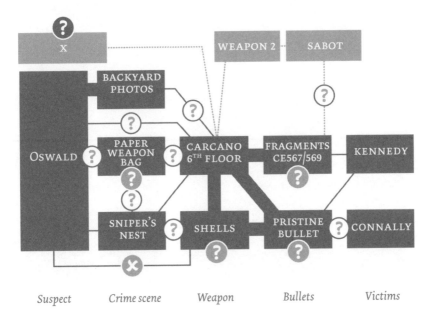

There is still one route open. We may be able to prove Oswald's presence in the sniper's nest at the moment of the attack. If he was there, it would also be his weapon that was found there. It's time to move to the scene of the crime.

PART 4

THE SCENE OF THE CRIME

19. SNIPER'S NEST

The TSBD was a cluttered, old-fashioned warehouse six stories high. A barricade made of book boxes was discovered in the south-east corner of the sixth floor, and the assassination was allegedly carried out from this sniper's nest. Film and photo reporter Tom Alyea of WFAA-TV was one of the first to reach the sixth floor. Later, in an interview with Connie Kritzberg,[335] he stated that the sniper's nest as we know it today from the official evidence is a fake:

> *The actual positioning of the barricade was never photographed by the police. [...] The police photo showing the shell casings lying next to the brick wall was staged later by crime lab people, who did not see the original positioning. [...] The photo I have seen of the barricade wasn't even close.*

Tom Alyea

The first question is whether a reporter actually followed the police officers who discovered the sniper's nest. It sounds unbelievable, but was in fact true. Deputies (deputy sheriffs) Mooney, Vickery and Webster entered the TSBD from the rear many minutes after the assassination, yet all the doors were still wide open. The *big gates*, as Mooney explained it to the Warren Commission later on. The trio checked the sixth floor and then the seventh floor. They didn't spot anything suspicious, and returned to the sixth floor.[336] Mooney made the following statement to the Commission: 'At that time, some news reporter, or press, I don't know who he was--he was coming up with a camera.'[337] This is a serious infringement of all procedural rules, but obviously also good news. The reporter and his picture material are a unique source of information on the original condition of the sniper's nest. The Commission showed no interest at all, either in the procedural error or in the unique picture material. Neither did it interview Deputy Sheriffs Vickery and Webster. Of the four people who witnessed the original condition of the sixth floor, only Deputy Sheriff Mooney was cross-examined. Mooney's reference to 'some news reporter or other' is, in fact, the only reference to Alyea's presence. All the other witnesses kept silent about the presence of a reporter.

Alyea managed to smuggle out his unique, historic pictures by dropping the film to a colleague on the Dealey Plaza through the sixth floor window. This original and complete film record subsequently disappeared without a trace, however. Only incomplete fragments remain. However incomplete, these fragments are still significant evidence. Moreover, they at least register the time the camera man recorded the images.

Discovery of the sniper's nest

Another striking fact is the time it took to locate the sniper's nest. Spectator Brennan was sitting on a wall opposite the TSBD when the president drove by. He provided the police with a very vague description of a man who, by any reasonable standards, he could hardly have seen, but immediately identified the sniper's nest with great accuracy: the corner window on the sixth floor. Nevertheless, the Dallas police department appeared not to know where to look. In the time it took the police to finally locate the sniper's nest, Oswald would:

- talk to officer Baker;
- leave the TSBD;
- walk seven blocks up Elm Street;
- take the bus back in the direction of Dealey Plaza;
- step down from the bus and take a taxi;
- drive to Beckley Street to five hundred meters past number 1026;
- walk five hundred meters to his lodgings at number 1026;
- change;
- wait for the bus in the direction of Dealey Plaza;
- walk to 10th Street in the opposite direction;
- talk to officer Tippit ;
- murder officer Tippit at 1.15 p.m.

Only then do we reach the point, at exactly 1.15 p.m., when Sergeant Hill, who had also searched the sixth floor in the meantime, heard Deputy Sheriff Mooney shout: 'This is it!'[338] The sniper's nest had been found. Mooney leaned out of the window and called Captain Fritz, who was downstairs, standing on the steps of the TSBD. Sergeant Hill ordered the deputy sheriffs not to touch anything, went downstairs and, on the way, encountered his former boss, Captain Fritz, who was on the way up with his assistants Boys and Sims. Fritz arrived on the sixth floor around 1.18 p.m. Having arrived downstairs, Hill also sent the crime lab men, Lieutenant Day and his bright assistant Studebaker, to the sixth floor. Fritz, Boyd and Sims were alone in the sniper's nest for just a few minutes with the three deputy sheriffs Mooney, Webster and Vickery, and, obviously, the reporter Tom Alyea.

Years later, Tom Alyea told his remarkable story for the first time, to the journalist Connie Kritzberg.[339] In the few minutes following Captain Fritz' arrival upstairs, and before the arrival of Lieutenant Day, Alyea wanted to film the shells lying in the sniper's nest. But the barricade made of book boxes was too high. Captain Fritz then walked into the sniper's nest, and, to Alyea's amazement, picked up the shells and held them up in his hand to enable the reporter to take even better pictures. Alyea filmed the shells in the captain's hand for several seconds. Alyea subsequently confirmed this for the most part to another investigator.[340] Fritz picked up the shells and allegedly even put them in his pocket. This is so unimaginable that we have to provisionally give Captain Fritz, an experienced hand, the benefit of the doubt over a journalist who related a spectacular account years later.

In any event, Captain Fritz did his job. He ordered Officers Montgomery and Johnson to closely guard the sniper's nest. The crime lab team had meanwhile reached the sixth floor. One minute later, at 1.22 p.m., the weapon was discovered, and the focus on the sniper's nest largely disappeared.

The barricade

Alyea kept back yet another startling revelation. He said that the barricade of book boxes had never been photographed in its original situation. There is a photograph in the evidence, recorded as reference CE508[341] (Figure 24, left). Mooney stated that the photograph 'more or less' reflected the original configuration of the boxes. He emphasized that there was definitely no direct opening in the east wall, the side wall of the TSBD. The photograph on the right is CE734[342]. This photograph gives the false impression that the marksman could leave the Sniper's Nest without passing any obstacles.

Figure 24 – Left: the barricade as it would probably have looked. Right: a photograph of the alleged location of the marksman. Is the configuration of the boxes compatible in both photographs?

There are various, highly contradictory photographs of the sniper's nest in circulation. For example, there is a major difference in the position of the third box, which is said to have been used as support for the weapon. It is sometimes specifically stated that a photograph is in fact merely a 'reconstruction',[343] but more often than not there is no such qualification. Other than a few family pictures, Studebaker, Day's inexperienced assistant, had never taken photographs before, and appeared to be not too concerned about the fact that he had moved the boxes before photographing them.[344] When the Warren Commission asked Detective Sims whether the barricade had been photographed in its original state, his reply was rather vague. The Commission then decided not to question any of the others who had been present any further regarding this thorny issue.

Alyea was consequently correct in saying that no systematic photographs had been taken of the original situation of the book-box barricade. CE508 comes the closest, and shows a completely different sniper's nest from the other photographs, which were apparently taken *after* some boxes had been moved and an access path had been opened up. The police dossier also contains a rough sketch of the complete sixth floor,[345] but it is too vague to be of any use.

The brown paper bag

The fact that there is no photograph of the sniper's nest before anything was touched definitely has one frustrating consequence: there is no photographic evidence of the presence of a brown paper bag, which should have been there immediately after the assassination. The witness statements are again of little or no use.

Mooney, the first deputy sheriff to arrive on the scene and the only one questioned by the Commission, was asked whether he had noticed any object lying in the corner of the sniper's nest. His reply was quite clear: 'No, I didn't see anything lying in the corner.'[346] The other two deputy sheriffs to arrive first at the site were not questioned. Deputy Sheriff Roger Craig arrived shortly after the discovery of the sniper's nest.[347] We know this because he appears in Alyea's film. Craig was cross-examined by the Commission, but not about the sniper's nest or the shells.[348] However, Craig told the author Barry Ernest : 'I never saw the rifle bag, and I was one of the first to arrive when that area was discovered. It just wasn't there. I could not have overlooked it if it was in there. [...]'[349] Motorcycle officer Haygood maintained that he had seen the paper bag at an early stage of the proceedings,[350] but, in his opinion, the bag was of a similar length to a rifle. This would make the bag 3.5 feet long, even though there was only just that much space in the corner (Figure 25). Whereas a folded bag may well have remained unnoticed, a fully opened bag would undoubtedly have been noticed. Haygood also confused the sixth and seventh floor, didn't know where the shells had been found, who had found them and what had happened subsequently. He was a dedicated member of the police corps, but a poor witness.[351] The guards posted at the sniper's nest by Fritz, Officers Johnson[352] and Montgomery,[353] also maintained that they had seen the bag. Apart from these three officers, all other officials responsible for the investigation were extremely vague about the presence of the bag.

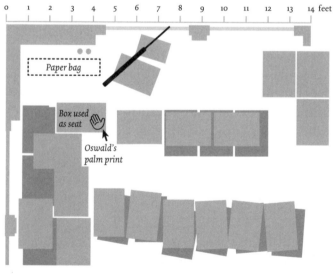

Figure 25 – Situation sketch of the sniper's nest, with the dotted line indicating the length of the paper bag if it had been lying in the corner completely unfolded.

Did Detective Boyd see the paper bag? 'I don't recall any if I did.'[354] His colleague, Sims maintained that he had seen the paper bag, but he couldn't remember it clearly (underlining added):

As well as I remember - of course, I didn't pay too much attention at that time, but it was, I believe, by the east side of where the boxes were piled up -that would be a guess- I believe that's where it was.[355]

If, on the basis of various television series, you have a high opinion of the powers of observation and memory for details of detectives, you now urgently need to revise your opinion. Sims' statement cannot be understood in any other way than as an attempt to confirm a fix, while at the same time steering clear of the serious crime of perjury. 'I didn't pay too much attention at the time' is a peculiar statement from a homicide squad detective. And 'I believe', 'That would be a guess' is not much use either.

What did Fritz, Boyd and Sims' boss really see? We can see Captain Fritz with the white hat in Alyea's film. He is standing quite conspicuously in the sniper's nest, his feet positioned where the bag must have been lying. Somebody must have told him about this significant find? The Commission didn't question Fritz about the bag, and he didn't say anything about it. There is no trace of the paper bag in the other photographs of the crime scene either, which brings us to another important point of controversy.

Origin and timing of the photographs

Photographs of the crime scene are elementary evidence in any murder investigation. In this case they were also added to the dossier. But do these photographs reflect what they are supposed to show, i.e. the original situation in the sniper's nest?

The deputy sheriffs don't shed any light on this. Mooney wasn't asked about the photographs, and Vickery and Webster weren't questioned at all. Which brings us back to the homicide squad, the men wearing Stetsons. The first is Captain Fritz. When enquiring whether Lieutenant Day took photographs of the sniper's nest, the Commission received a very evasive reply: 'I feel like he did but I don't know because I didn't stay to see whether he could.'

'I feel... I don't know...' This again appears to be a transparent attempt at avoiding perjury, because Fritz obviously *knew* whether photographs had been taken of the location of the crime. How incompetent would that have made him look as captain of the homicide squad if he had not been aware of it? Fritz made this statement in fact on April 22, 1964, by which time he would have had five months in which to ask Lieutenant Day whether he had observed the standard procedure or not. Moreover, photos had been part of the dossier for some months, and were included in their own police file. The explanation for his bizarre reply is clear. He could neither deny, because the photographs did exist, nor confirm, because he would then obviously create an even trickier problem. The former captain could therefore only answer with a humiliating 'I don't know'.

It becomes quite clear that something was amiss when his assistant Boyd's memory also let him down. Were photographs taken? 'Well, let me see... I think...' Detective Sims, the third member of the homicide squad, also said 'I think', and then confirmed that he had seen someone taking photographs, but couldn't remember who. He assured the Commission, however, that the shells had remained in their original position until the photographs had been taken. The dutiful officers Montgomery[356] and Johnson, who were guarding the sniper's nest, did know, however. Their memory was also much better in this respect. Yes, photographs were taken. That was no doubt the case, the reverse would be unthinkable. The officers were confronted with the photographs following their candid answer, however, which is exactly what the detectives had wanted to avoid with their vague denials. Was Alyea right after all when he maintained that the pictures of the shells 'were staged', or in other words, recreated at a later stage? Did *something* happen in the sniper's nest in the few minutes before the arrival of the crime lab that went against the rules, and subsequently needed to be removed from the records at all costs?

Position of the shells

Officer Johnson looked at the photograph and replied quite formally: the shells in the photograph were *not* in their original position. He remembered the shells being much closer together than they were on the photograph.[357] Mooney, who was the first to see the shells, confirmed this. When the commission asked whether he meant that shell 'B' should be closer to shell 'C', he replied: 'Closer to C, yes, Sir.'[358] When asked whether he might have moved the bullets, he replied that he hadn't touched anything until Captain Fritz arrived. Deputy Sheriff Craig agreed with this. He told the author Barry Ernest the following about the shells: 'They were lined up uniformly, no more than two-and-one-half to three inches from each other... all facing the same direction.'[359] It seemed as if the shells had been positioned there, rather than ejected by a weapon as Craig maintained. Finally, the reporter Tom Alyea also stated that on November 22 the shells had been lying much closer together than on the photograph.

The question as to whether the photographs reflected the original situation was subsequently conspicuously avoided when members of the homicide squad and the crime lab were questioned. The detectives also did not feel compelled to report that there was a problem with the photographs of their own accord. The main problem appears to relate to the location of one particular shell. The two shells near to the wall appear to be more or less where they should be, but the third one isn't. Presumably that is the crux of the matter.

Where the weapon was found

The search on the sixth floor continued meanwhile unabated. The weapon was found a few minutes after Fritz' arrival. The Alyea film shows an officer indicating the location where the weapon had been found, while drawing heavily on a cigarette. With all the rubbish and paper lying about, we should consider ourselves lucky that the Dallas Police didn't burn down the book warehouse that day. Captain Fritz made the following statement concerning the discovery of the weapon:

> A few minutes later some officer called me and said they had found the rifle over near the back stairway and I told them the same thing, not to move it, not to touch it, not to move any of the boxes until we could get pictures, and as soon as Lieutenant Day could get over there he made pictures of that.[360]

Once again, this appears to be a half truth, because the boxes had already been touched earlier. The Alyea film shows how the photograph of the location of the Carcano rifle was taken. The Commission confronted Mooney with this photograph (CE514) and asked: 'Does it look anything like that?' Mooney replied: 'Yes Sir, with the exception there was (sic) more cartons around it than that.' We cannot blame Fritz for the fact that boxes were moved during the search, otherwise the rifle would not have been found if it have been lying underneath the boxes. But Fritz was so keen to emphasize once again that he had arranged for the crime scene to be photographed in its original state that he lied yet again.

Once again, this has a significant consequence for the dossier. If photograph CE514 does not reflect the correct position of the boxes, Oswald could not have hidden the rifle there in the way in which it was assumed in the reconstruction. The film of the reconstruction shows the man pretending to be Oswald just putting the weapon down between the boxes. The real Oswald would have needed more time to place boxes on top of the rifle. Weitzman, who found the weapon together with Boone, clearly stated the following to the Warren Commission:

> It was covered with boxes.[361]

Deputy Sheriff Boone also told the Commission that there was a box on top of the two rows between which the weapon was hidden:[362]

> I caught a glimpse of the rifle, stuffed down between two rows of boxes with another box or so pulled over the top of it.

Lieutenant Day picked the weapon up from between the cardboard boxes. He stated:

> Captain Fritz was present. After we got the photographs I asked him if he was ready for me to pick it up, and he said, yes. I picked the gun up by the wooden stock. I noted that the stock was apparently too rough to take fingerprints, so I picked it up, and Captain Fritz opened the bolt as I held the gun. A live round fell to the floor.[363]

On November 23, the day after the events, Weitzmann stated in his affidavit, i.e. under oath:

> The time the rifle was found was 1:22 p.m. Captain Fritz took charge of the rifle and ejected one live round from the chamber.[364]

Would Fritz have touched the weapon and opened the lock before the Carcano had been checked for finger prints? Fritz obviously denied this in the strongest possible terms: 'I let him dust first before I ejected a shell.'[365]

He was lying. Alyea's film shows how Lieutenant Day picks up the weapon by its strap and then immediately hands it over to Fritz. The film then jumps, and the next fragment suddenly shows Lieutenant Day again holding the weapon in his hand. Is it possible that Alyea did not film the ejection of the live round? If we refuse to believe that, the only alternative explanation is that the film was censored. There must have been a serious motive for this, and the obvious conjecture is that Fritz manipulated the weapon before it had been tested for finger prints.

An extra shell on the photograph

The photographic material in the annexes to the Warren Commission also shows a 'printing error' or scratch, in a crucial location (Figure 26). In the low-resolution print of the Warren Report the scratch looks amazingly like a bullet shell. In CE512[366], the photograph on the left, the circled 'shell' on the extreme left isn't a shell at all. The photograph on the right, which is also part of the Commission's evidence under reference CE716,[367] should show the same as the photograph on the left. There is clearly something amiss with a shell that appears to be leaning against the wall in CE512. It is difficult to interpret this 'printing error' as anything other than a shell. It was only when I obtained the picture from NARA in high-resolution that it became obvious that it was indeed a scratch on the photo (Figure 26 circled and overlay).

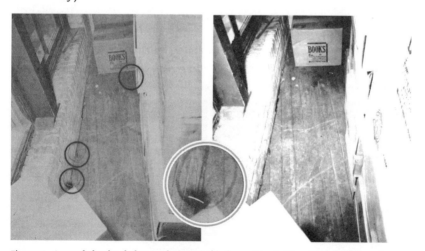

Figure 26 – A scratch that (on the low-resolution print) looks suspiciously like a shell in the Warren Report.

The time at which the picture with shells is taken is also uncertain. An identical photograph (Figure 26 right) is as photograph number 390 part of a series available at the Dallas Municipal Archives.[368] Looking at these and many other photographs in the same police folder, it is quite clear that they were all taken at the same time, i.e. the hard contrast of the pictures, lighting, absence of police officers... If photo number 390 had been taken at the time it was said to have been, the sixth floor would have been swarming with policemen in photo 385 (Figure 27 left). The photograph with the three shells in Figure 26 is therefore part of a series of photographs that were *not* taken immediately after the discovery of the sniper's nest. The police catalogued the photographs with the indication 'date unknown' and 'unknown author'.

Figure 27 – Some of the photographs in the police dossier, including the photograph with the shells. Date unknown, unknown author.

The series of photographs in the police archive includes other photographs showing the third shell, such as photograph number 80 (Figure 28 right and inset). This photograph is unique, because it enables us to see Houston Street through the window at the time it was taken. We notice a remarkable white van, which is still there in photograph 421. There seems to be very little movement in the square, but stills from the Alyea movie on History.com confirm that there were relatively few bystanders in Houston Street at the time at which the sniper's nest was found. Photo 80 (Figure 28 right) does indeed appear to be an early photo with three shells on the floor of the sniper's nest.

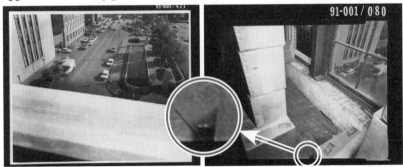

Figure 28 – Photograph of Dealey Plaza. The white van demonstrates when the photograph with the third shell (circled and overlay) was taken in the sniper's nest.

It therefore appears that photographs were indeed taken of the sniper's nest shortly after the arrival of Day and Studebaker. The contrary would, in fact, be unthinkable. Whether those photographs were taken immediately and before anything was touched is a very different question. This is what is claimed by Inspector Day.[369] Criminal courts apply a zero tolerance position in this area. If the photos are not what they claim to be, i.e. the situation before anything was touched, they constitute no valid evidence whatsoever. It is quite likely that Fritz did pick up the shells, and then replaced them in a different position than where they were originally. And why is there no photograph in which the paper bag can be seen among the early photos?

The Captain's draft report

The Dallas Municipal Archives also contain a draft report on Oswald's interrogation.[370] It was written by Captain Fritz. It appears that he had started writing a report at some time, but he no longer considered it sufficiently important to complete it after Oswald's murder. Fritz also didn't appear to care too much about the number of untruths in the draft report. For instance, he stated that three shells were found and 'these pieces of evidence were protected until the crime lab could get pictures and make a search for fingerprints.' The following sentence in the draft report is also suspect:

> After Ltd. Day, of the crime lab, had finished his work with the rifle, I picked it up and found that it had a shell in the chamber, which I ejected.

There is too much emphasis on the fact that Fritz wanted to confirm that standard procedures had been strictly observed at the crime scene. In the meantime, it has become quite clear how much of this can be believed.

A hypothesis

If we try to put all this in a logical sequence, we arrive at the following possible explanation for the confusion surrounding the paper bag, the shells and the pictures of the sniper's nest:

1. There were initially three shells, as confirmed by Deputy Sheriff Mooney, the two officers and Alyea. They should know, as they saw the sniper's nest before the arrival of Captain Fritz.

2. Fritz did something moved the shells, and even put one in his pocket. Lieutenant Day and homicide detectives Boyd and Sims then arrive, and e few minutes later the rifle is found and becomes the focus of everyone's attention.

3. Among other photos of the sixth floor, Day and his assistant Studebaker also took pictures of the Sniper's Nest on November 22. If Day and his assistant took photographs of three shells, it is inconceivable that they would have drafted a CSS for two shells immediately afterwards. The original photographs probably only showed two shells.

4. The photos were restaged afterwards with three shells in place. The photographs in the dossier are not the ones taken *in situ* on November 22, before anything was touched. This is clear from several mutually reinforcing elements:
   a. There are no photographs of the barricade in its original state;
   b. There are no photographs of the paper bag.
   c. The location of the two shells was known, The third shell was placed in the wrong position on the falsified photographs. The witnesses who had seen the original three shells highlighted the striking difference;
   d. The pictures in the police file were classified as 'date and time unknown' and 'author unknown' which is clear enough in itself. It means that the date and time were *not* 22 November 1:22 p.m., and that although it concerns historic pictures of the utmost importance, nobody wanted to see his name associated with them.

5. The subsequent story of the forgotten shell in Fritz' drawer is just as implausible as the other attempts to solve the problem with the shells.

6. Fritz also made a blatant mistake when he found the weapon and opened the magazine before the weapon had been checked for fingerprints. These images also disappeared from Alyea's film. Fritz had given the reporter the scoop of his life, and Alyea was prepared to remove the scenes that would compromise the captain. The reporter's conscience got the better of him after Fritz' death, however, and he told the unbelievable tale to Kritzberg.

The homicide squad generally conducted its activities without onlookers, and the police officers in Dallas probably assumed that they were tackling the case correctly. The FBI snatched the dossier from them even before the sun went down, however, and they were faced with several significant problems from then on, i.e. a shell for the purpose of comparison in Fritz' jacket pocket; photographs showing only two shells; a film in which the captain contaminates the main pieces of evidence... Efforts were clearly made at a local level to brush things under the carpet. The only valid photographic evidence, i.e. the photographs taken by Studebaker on Friday afternoon, was destroyed and was substituted by photographic evidence that was totally unacceptable. The Dallas Police Department preferred to manipulate the evidence rather than allow its captain to lose face with the FBI.

Finger and palm prints found at the crime scene

The police found one of Oswald' palm prints in the sniper's nest, on the box on which the sniper was supposed to have been sitting when carrying out the assassination. Detectives found further fingerprints belonging to Oswald on the barricade boxes. They did not constitute criminal evidence as such, because Oswald worked in the building and could have moved the boxes whilst carrying out his tasks. Most of the fingerprints uncovered at the site were subsequently found to belong to the police officers themselves, with Studebaker being the main culprit with 18 out of 25 found fingerprints being his. It seems as if he went out of his way to touch everything at the scene. Only one non-identified fingerprint was eventually found and, according to investigator Walt Brown, it belonged to Malcolm E. 'Mc' Wallace, a convicted murderer with links to Lyndon Johnson. Nathan Darby, a military fingerprint expert with 35 years of experience, supposedly noted fourteen similarities between the fingerprint on one of the boxes in the barricade at the sniper's nest and Wallace's fingerprint. In any event, the evidence appears to indicate that, if nothing else, Oswald was definitely involved in the creation of the sniper's nest.

Filling in the chain of evidence

If we logically analyze the situation at the crime scene, it appears that (unnecessary) confusion was mainly created by procedural faults by the

Dallas Police Department. The weapon – whether or not the same as in the photographs – was found on the sixth floor. In all likelihood, we can also assume that there were actually three shells in the sniper's nest. We cannot merely disregard the procedural faults and manipulation of the dossier, however. Whether or not there was a folded paper bag in the corner is not that important. The link between the paper bag and the sniper's nest does not really help us at all without a definite link with the weapon and with Oswald. We can assume that there was a paper bag in the sniper's nest. The fact that it is not shown in the photographs is merely due to the time the photographs were taken.

Our chain of evidence now looks as follows:

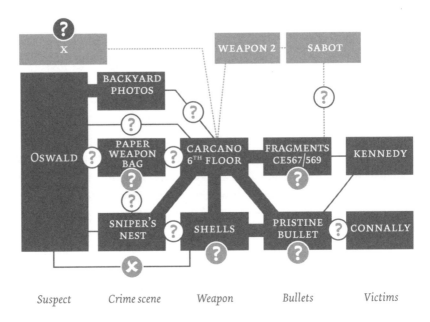

| Suspect | Crime scene | Weapon | Bullets | Victims |

As a potential perpetrator, we still need to be able to link Oswald to the sniper's nest. Until we can clarify this, we must reserve judgment on the similarity between the weapon and the backyard photographs. With regard to the victims, we need to link the discovered bullet and fragments to Kennedy and Connally. The key question is whether there was indeed a magic bullet. If so, all the other problems would be put into a completely different perspective.

In order to assess the possibility of a magic bullet we need to leave the sniper's nest and concentrate on the limousine and Dealey Plaza.

20. CRIME SCENE ON WHEELS

Citizen X was a film made in 1995 about the hunt for Chikatilo, a pedophile and serial killer in Russia just before the fall of the Wall. The talented, tenacious forensic police officer Burakov is hot on the heels of Chikatilo. Several battered little bodies are discovered alongside the electrified railway line. Each time, Burakov emphasizes the importance of safeguarding the integrity of the crime scene at all costs. A blade of grass, a casually discarded cigarette or a vague track with mud unfamiliar to the local environment can provide a breakthrough after years of unsuccessful investigation. The film also highlights the catastrophic consequences of any kind of bureaucratic interference in the investigation. Burakov had already come to that conclusion himself, from lessons learned from his guiding light and grand master in investigation techniques, the FBI.

In 1963, the FBI also had to defend a reputation that had been carefully built up over twenty years. The Kennedy murder represented a unique opportunity to raise this reputation even higher. As well as Marcello, Hoover must have pinched himself that day to make sure he wasn't dreaming. Kennedy, the degenerate, was dead. Hoover's friend and neighbor Lyndon Johnson, who until the day before had been facing the edge of the political abyss, suddenly found himself in the Oval Office. Arch-rival Robert Kennedy had suffered a devastating blow. Moreover, the cherry on the cake was that, once and for all, the FBI could establish its position in the collective global memory as the ultimate standard for police efficiency, scientific approach, objectivity and integrity. Only a perfect investigation would be acceptable in the circumstances.

Hoover's officers Sibert and O'Neill were already keeping a critical eye on, and looking over the shoulders of the hopelessly inexperienced pathologists in Bethesda. Their report would subsequently glaringly highlight the bungling by the doctors and all the resulting contradictions. Oswald was in the hands of an inept Dallas Police force, but all the ballistic evidence, the weapon and other confiscated paraphernalia concerning Oswald had been handed over to the FBI in the meantime. Only the limousine, the location of the actual murder, was still in the hands of the Secret Service. The vehicle landed in Washington at *Andrews Air Force Base* on Friday night at 8.00 p.m. on board a C130. The limousine was then driven to the White House under police escort, where it arrived shortly after 9.00 p.m.

SS-X-100

The SS-X-100, or X-100, as the limousine was referred to by the Secret Service, was a *custom*-built Ford Continental. The vehicle had cost approximately 200,000 dollars, a colossal amount in those days. The Ford Motor Company leased the vehicle to the president at a cost of five hundred dollars per annum.[371] It was in no way armor-plated or equipped with other special safety features. (J. Edgar Hoover had the use of no less than four armor-plated limousines.) The limousine was 194 cm wide[372], no wider than a standard car at that time. When a vehicle is converted into a limousine it is lengthened, but not widened. The convertible came with a transparent plastic hardtop, a bubble top for rainy days and a leather top. Unfortunately, it did not rain on November 22. There is no doubt the Plexiglas top would have registered the impact of the first bullet and would have resulted in swift reaction. It might even have changed the trajectory of the bullet or marginally hampered the sniper's vision. The political animal in JFK opted for maximum visibility, however. He was not bothered about safety aspects. If someone wanted to shoot him, they could just as well do it inside a church, was Kennedy's motto. As far as he was concerned, the risk of assassination was part of his job. His war experiences and his medical pre-history had also made him aware of the finality of the human existence. 'We are all mortal,'[373] he had emphasized during a speech in June. He also had a natural flamboyance, and thrived on risk. Self-confidence was an inherent part of his charisma. In this respect, he was also to some extent responsible for the safety risks that were taken in Dallas. He wanted to show the right wing rabble in Dallas that he was not afraid, and the X-100 convertible was the ideal vehicle for this purpose. Kennedy was the last president to travel through a major American city in an open-top car.

The limousine had a very long trunk, which was also used to store the removable Plexiglas hardtop. The vehicle was also equipped with a step behind the trunk to accommodate secret service agents. Because the limousine had three rows of seats and the hood was very long, even on a standard version, it was 256.10 inches or 6.5 m long. A commercial photograph of the Ford clearly shows the interior and the passenger space (Figure 29). The jump seats were spaced quite far apart on either side of the central drive shaft. The sides of the limousine alongside the rear seat were quite straight, which made it possible to sit right up against them, with an arm on the side of the vehicle. The sides of the car were also slightly narrower near the rear seat, because of the long, wide doors that opened to the right.

Figure 29 – Photograph of the limousine's interior

The limousine held the key to many secrets associated with the murder investigation. If the official version is correct, every bullet fragment, however small, originated from one and the same bullet. The fragments in the limousine, however small, could have contained traces of blood, tissue or clothing. According to the official version, they could only have originated from Kennedy. The front windshield was cracked, the chrome edge was damaged and a study of the photographs also shows that the back of the rear-view mirror was damaged. Perhaps more could have been found - who knows? Did the car paint contain traces of fragments that spattered in the vicinity of the vehicle? Did blood stains provide an indication of the direction of the spatters? The proportions inside the limousine, and in particular the difference in height between Kennedy and Connally, also define the direction from which the shot must have been fired. In order to produce a successful reconstruction of the assassination, it was absolutely necessary to have access to a vehicle with exactly the same unique dimensions. The X-100 held the answers to many questions. If the FBI wanted to take the investigation seriously, they had to take the limousine seriously. A lawsuit against Oswald would only have considered the evidence from the limousine if it was sufficiently clear where and how this evidence had been gathered. And that's without mentioning the historic significance of the car. The theater chair in which Lincoln was murdered has been very carefully preserved with blood stains and all. The limousine was unfortunately not granted this honor...

The limousine's return journey to Washington

From the outset, scant attention was paid to the fact that the limousine was a crime scene. Captain Cecil Stoughton, the presidential photographer, took a picture at the entrance to Parkland Hospital (Figure 30). It shows Secret Agents Kinney and Hickey busy with a bucket and sponge in and around the car.[374] This complete obliteration of evidence was totally repressed in subsequent reports, cross-examinations and letters in the Warren Commission report. In their reports, the Secret Service agents in question merely mentioned mounting the hardtop,[375] but did not say a word about a bucket and sponge. They presumably realized later that had made an irreversible mistake. But they didn't have to worry, as neither agent was questioned by the Warren Commission.

Figure 30 – Secret Service agents cleaning the limousine with a bucket and sponge.

Nevertheless, the commission must have been aware of the inconceivable intervention, as it had been widely discussed in the press.[376] The picture material was kept under wraps for some time. The photograph taken by Stoughton was not published until 1983, when it appeared in *Life Magazine* with the following caption: 'Outside Parkland, agents clean the bloody limousine.' Only in 2003 did Gerald O'Rourke, a member of the president's Secret Service team at the time, tell *Rocky Mountain News* for the first time 'that on the day of the assassination, one agent was ordered to clean out the cars used in the motorcade, getting rid of blood and other evidence.'

Once cleaned, the car was driven to Love Field airport and loaded onto a C130. During the flight, the vehicle was constantly guarded by Secret Service Agents Kinney and Hickey.[377] When the C130 landed in Washington, Kinney drove the car to the White House garage; Secret Service agent Taylor sat alongside him on this journey.[378] It was presumably considered a good idea for an additional agent to sit on the evidence.

Cleaning the car, driving it to and from an airport, flying it back and then having it moved again by FBI agent Orrin Bartlett[379] at the start of the investigation is already a serious manipulation of the unique setting in which the president of the United States had been murdered, nota bene before any investigation had taken place. Who can tell what evidence was lost because it stuck to the agents' clothing and shoes? What traces were eradicated and/or superimposed? In any case, the crack in the windshield worsened considerably during transport. There was no reason at all not to leave the vehicle in Dallas and to examine it there in its original condition. But it was, of course, too late for that now.

The garage

On arrival at the garage of the president's official residence, Kinney handed over the limousine to the White House Secret Service department. There were still skull and tissue fragments on the floor of the vehicle. In view of the fact that these were part of the president's mortal remains, the Secret Service agents called in Admiral Burkley, the president's personal physician. A number of color photographs were apparently taken subsequently. The vehicle was then covered with a plastic tarpaulin and placed under the protection of two secret agents.[380] At 10.00 p.m., the plastic cover was briefly removed and employees of Admiral Burkley removed a triangular piece of human skull, approximately 7.5 cm in size, and some 'brain tissue'. In a sudden burst of helpfulness, Paul Paterni, Deputy Director of the Secret Service, swept his hand across the front seat and found a metal fragment 'in the area between the left and right front seat'. This bullet fragment later became Exhibit CE567. Paterni's colleague Mills also wanted to do his bit, and found Fragment CE569 on the floor on the right side in front of the front seat. Swiping your hand across the area where the victim was murdered before the start of the official investigation does not bear witness to a particularly careful and forensic approach. There are obviously no photographs of the location of the fragments. The Secret Service did forward the two fragments they found to the FBI lab[381] and, as such, acted at least in this matter correctly.

At 1 o'clock in the morning, during the night from Friday to Saturday, a five-man FBI team led by ballistics expert Frazier, finally examined the limousine.[382] Two secret agents also took part in the investigation.[383] Bearing in mind that seven people examined the vehicle until 4.30 a.m., there is no official FBI report of the nocturnal examination of the president's car. 'No report of their examination was furnished to the Secret Service', dryly remarked Secret Service Director Rowley twice in his letter to the Warren Commission.[384] There is no direct report of the nocturnal FBI investigation in either the Commission's evidence, the FBI documentation and all documents submitted subsequently. Fortunately, the two secret agents did write an extensive report, which Rowley attached to his letter as an appendix. Rowley indicated that 'three metal fragments [were] recovered from the rear floorboard carpet.' Furthermore, fragments had been scraped from the inside of the crack in the windshield. The Warren Commission did not summon the FBI, and did not request the urgent submission of the limousine's investigation report. In the end, five bullet fragments were found, two somewhere on the front seat picked up via the 'loosely-swiped method' and three on the carpet in the rear of the vehicle, the exact location of which is unknown. There was a crack in the windshield and the chrome edge above the centre of the front windshield was also damaged. There was no mention of damage to the rear-view mirror,[385] nor of any other damage to the car.

More than thirty years later, Anthony Marsh found photocopies of the original notes made by the agents involved in the limousine examination (figure 31), and photographs of the limousine in a folder in the *National Archives*.

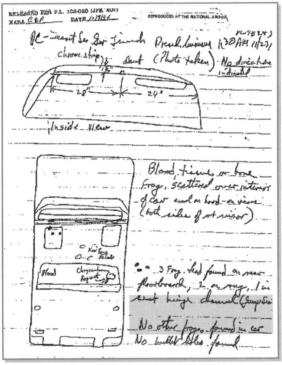

Figure 31 – A sketch of the investigation of the limousine by the FBI turned up thirty years later. There is no official report of the investigation.

Marsh wrote:

I'm not sure who wrote the sheets and exactly when they were written[386]*, but the sheets record the observations of the examination team that night. They mark the exact locations of the fragments recovered.*

The three bullet fragments in the rear of the car were apparently found underneath the jump seat that was being used by Mrs. Connally. Thirty years after the investigation, we find that no other signs of bullet impact were found in the car. The FBI also took six black and white photographs.[387] What the investigators were doing the rest of the time is unknown. The Secret Service also released the following statement concerning the FBI's 'secure examination' of the limousine: 'A meticulous examination was made of the back seat of the car and the floor rug, and no evidence was found.' It does seem rather strange that they did not find any evidence on the rear seat and floor carpet. Three fragments were found on the carpet and the rear seat was still covered in 'miscellaneous debris', as demonstrated by the photograph (Figure 32), and subsequent developments. Since when are blood stains and the pattern of blood spots no longer considered to be evidence?

Figure 32 – No further evidence on the rear seat?

As a result of the nonchalant, negligent and clumsy approach to the investigation, we consequently know nothing about the location and type of blood spots. If the bullet that shattered Kennedy's skull came from the rear right, it would undoubtedly have had an impact on the location of the blood spots and brain tissue in the vehicle. It appears that the FBI did not want to know this. The exact dimensions of the limousine were also not recorded anywhere. The height measurements of the limousine, the rear seat or the jump seat have still not been found to this day, and are certainly not included in the Warren report, its appendices and the extensive *Commission Documents*. It also seems that they are not included in the HSCA investigation. The reason is simple: the FBI failed to measure and record the exact dimensions that night. Believers keep stressing the fact that the conspiracists never mention that the folding seat was lower than the back seat when criticizing the one-bullet theory. But this is again the result of the FBI and the commission not having investigated, or included this kind of data in their documentation.

The examination of the limousine is mentioned indirectly once again in the FIB files in a memorandum dated November 23, which was a kind of general summary regarding the status of the dossier the day after the murder. Reporter Devons tells us that it was a 'detailed examination', as if a superficial examination would also have been an option...[388] But apart from that one paragraph in the memorandum, no trace can be found of a signed report in which the investigators recorded their findings about the limousine and authenticated the starting point of the evidence chain for the recovered fragments. The map of the limousine[389] made available by the Commission is not exactly an example of clarity, legibility and reliability either, and there is no vertical view at all. It defies all logic that no-one involved in the investigation into the president's assassination had a problem with this modus operandi. And that's not the end of it...

Operation *Quick Fix*

In the early hours of Saturday November 23, the Secret Service called Mr. Ferguson of the Ford Motor Company. At 10.00 a.m. he was already present in the garage at the White House to arrange a replacement of the front windshield. The Secret Service wanted to have the car cleaned at 4.30 p.m. The FBI did not object to this, as they considered the examination of the limousine to be complete. And the surveillance of the garage was called off

at the same time. 'The flowers, torn pieces of paper, and other miscellaneous debris' still left behind in the car were collected and handed over to the
FBI's *Washington Field Office*.[390] On Saturday night, Hutch, the duty police
officer, was given permission to use a bucket and sponge to remove odor
and blood stains from the limousine. Whilst cleaning, Hutch found more
miscellaneous debris, 'bone and hair fragments' originating from the fallen
Commander-in-Chief's head. The instruction to replace the front windshield had meanwhile been followed with great urgency. According to the
logbook in the White House garage, the glass was replaced on November
26, at 11.15 a.m. It had to be done quickly. Ferguson referred to the rather
unorthodox approach when removing the glass: 'The Arlington Glass personnel did remove it by putting their feet against the inside of the windshield and pushing it out. In doing so, additional cracks formed.' The crack
in the front windshield was crucial ballistic evidence, but it appeared not
to be a problem to push out the glass with a couple of firm kicks![391] With
almost surrealistic earnestness, Director Rowley then arranged for the
windshield, which had been removed with brute force, to be securely protected and watched around the clock.[392] The new carpet was delivered halfway through the week, and was fitted on November 29. The original carpet
containing the blood stains, and no doubt various other traces significant
to the investigation, disappeared in the waste container at the Ford garage.

A commission was then set up as a matter of great urgency to completely refurbish the X-100. The commission consisted of thirty members working for the Secret Service, the army, limousine builder Hess &
Eisenhardt and the Pittsburgh Glass Company. The commission worked
well. President Johnson was able to approve the plan for the total conver-
sion of the X-100 on December 12, 1963. This was barely three weeks after
the assassination, and eight days before the Warren Commission released
the vehicle. In addition to the name *Project D-2*, the project was also giv-
en the code name *Quick Fix* by the very active commission.[393] It was all finished very quickly indeed. Why did the windshield and carpets have to be
replaced as a matter of urgency at the end of November when the vehicle
was due to be completely refurbished and stripped down to bare metal a
few weeks later?

According to Rowley, the limousine was sent to Ford in Dearborn,
Michigan for refurbishment on December 20, and to Hess & Eisenhardt
in Cincinnati, Ohio on December 24. Willard Hess, co-founder of Hess
& Eisenhardt, strenuously denied that the car came to his company during the night of Christmas Eve: 'This could not have happened, and did

not happen.'[394] Hess was convinced that the limousine was already in Cincinnati on December 13, and had been flown in by plane. A United Press International report dated December 18 records the following:

> *Detroit, Dec. 18. The car in which President Kennedy was assassinated is being refitted with bulletproof glass and armor plate for use by President Johnson. The work on the famous 'bubbletop' presidential Continental is being done at Ford Motor Co. Experimental Garage in suburban Dearborn, but Ford officials and the Secret Service declined to comment.*[395]

Contrary to the official account, the limousine had already arrived in Detroit on December 18 at the latest. The official date was probably falsified to ensure that it at least occurred after the release of the limousine by the Commission on December 20. However, December 13 or 18 or 20 or 24 makes little difference. The real question is how the Warren Commission could have assumed that it would no longer need the vehicle and it remains a fact that the limousine with its unique dimensions, which were of crucial importance for the reconstruction of the crime, was no longer available as evidence.

The refurbished vehicle was ready to be used again by the new president in May 1964,[396] but he decided to leave it in the garage as long as the color was still 'Kennedy blue'. Johnson would only use the limousine again after it had been sprayed black. This was in October 1964. So it appears that the refurbishment wasn't that urgent after all.

The limousine in the reconstructions

The speed and efficiency displayed in eliminating the limousine as potential evidence made it necessary to use other vehicles during the reconstructions. In both cases, the vehicle in question was totally unsuitable for the intended purpose. While a standard vehicle was used for the initial reconstruction (Figure 33 left), the support vehicle used by the Secret Service, a huge converted 1956 Cadillac, was used for the second reconstruction (Figure 33 right). It was immediately behind the X-100 in the motorcade on November 2, and was referred to as the *Queen Mary* because of its enormous dimensions. The second reconstruction was staged to test the single-bullet theory on the terrain. But the Cadillac was 31.7 cm shorter than the X-100 and the passenger area was located further back. The important distance between the rear and intermediate seats was also different in both cars and the difference in seat height was no less than 24 cm... These cars could consequently not really be considered comparable in order to test the single-bullet theory.

With a little creativity, the investigators could still have rectified quite a lot, even after the X-100 had been converted with undue haste. Nothing prevented the technical department of the FBI, which produced a scale model of Dealey Plaza within a couple of weeks, from also designing a vehicle – a driving platform – on which the investigators could mount the seats occupied by Kennedy and Connally in the right proportions. If necessary, the actual rear seat and folding seat could have been collected from Hess & Eisenhardt in Cincinnati. But no one appeared to come up with that idea. The Warren Commission had no problem with reconstructions that would only lead to unreliable conclusions, and thereby once again created a source for further conspiracy theories.

Figure 33 – Reconstructions with totally unsuitable vehicles. In the first, using a standard vehicle, Kennedy's and Connally's seats are not at all representative. The Queen Mary, which was much too large, was used for the second reconstruction.

The limousine in the Warren Report

In the end, the Commission devotes a mere eighteen lines to *The Presidential Automobile*.[397] That was it. We are told how many bullet fragments were found, how heavy they were and roughly where they were found (e.g. 'on the seat alongside the driver'), but that's all. Eighteen lines about the scene of the crime... These lines are followed by another three paragraphs in the Warren report. The first one states that the bullet fragments were *similar* in terms of their metal composition; the second one describes, on the authority of Robert Frazier, that the front windshield had been damaged from the inside and the third paragraph deals with the damaged chrome edging. The Commission also needlessly raised further doubts as to whether the damage had been inflicted on November 22: 'there is some uncertainty whether the dent in the chrome on the windshield was present prior to the assassination.' Did no one take the time to check the photographs that reporter Dillard had taken prior to the departure of the motorcade? Did no one check whether the damage was actually caused by the impact of a bullet or a bullet fragment?

Conclusions regarding the limousine

The intervention of the Secret Service with a bucket and sponge and the removal of the limousine, which greatly compromised the authenticity of the findings, appear to have been pure improvisation. It appears that no one had the presence of mind to impose adequate measures to preserve the crime scene. And it became even worse, because the FBI's findings were not recorded in any report, and instructions were given to completely destroy the interior of the vehicle less than a month after the murder. The latter action was a deliberate attempt to obliterate evidence in a murder case - no other explanation can be found. The Secret Service, and therefore its commander, President Johnson, were responsible for these actions.

21. GROUND ZERO

Dealey Plaza is an open space in which three wide, parallel streets - Elm Street, Main Street and Commerce Street – come together in the shape of a funnel and then continue underneath a railway viaduct, the so-called *Triple Underpass* (Figure 1). When Dallas was founded in 1841, the square was referred to as the central *Courthouse Square*, the only open space in the checkerboard pattern of the layout of the city. On the arrival of the railroad, the Triple Underpass was referred to as the 'front door' to Dallas. Main Street and Commerce Street were the main thoroughfares in this young city. The 'art deco structures' and the park were added just before the Second World War. The name of the square refers to George Dealey, the owner of a local newspaper, *The Dallas Morning News*.

Houston Street is on the east side of the square, and is bordered by a number of government buildings, an old courthouse building, the local criminal court buildings and an archive building used by the local administration. The Dal-Tex building, which is in the northwestern corner, used to house a number of textile businesses, such as *Jennifer Juniors*, and Zapruder's business in the sixties. The Dal-Tex building is, in fact, located on the corner, rather than actually on the square, but it does have a view of Dealey Plaza from two sides. In actual fact, the Dal-Tex building was an ideal location from which to assassinate Kennedy, as he would continue to move along directly in front of the sniper without any trees impeding the view.

The crucial seconds of the assassination took place on Elm Street, a three-lane, one-way avenue that drops fairly steeply in the direction of the tunnel. The presidential motorcade proceeded along Main Street. It then had to pass through the tunnel, via Dealey Plaza, in order to drive onto the highway heading north. The president was to hold his lunchtime address a few miles down the road at the Trade Mart, which was full to the rafters. Regular traffic making its way to the highway from Main Street had to turn right into Houston Street on Dealey Plaza, and then make a sharp left turn to proceed underneath the railway via Elm Street. For the visit of the president, it would have been better for safety reasons if the presidential motorcade had continued straight ahead on Main Street in order to cross Elm Street after the railroad – following a few changes to both lanes – and thus reach the highway. Not only the buildings with open windows, but, more specifically, the 120-degree turn from Houston Street into Elm Street could have been simply avoided this way. But they opted for the easy solution, the regular route that applied to everyone, including the hairpin bend[398] to the left and past the steps of the Texas School Book Depository. According to the official version, Oswald fired at the presidential motorcade through the most easterly window on the sixth floor of this corner building in Elm Street. The distance from the steps directly below the sniper's nest to the railroad viaduct is approximately 150 meters.

A pergola or colonnade had been built in the shape of a quarter circle about halfway along Elm Street. Similar architectural features were added to the square at four locations in an attempt to make it more attractive and give it an individual character. Elm Street slopes downhill in order to pass underneath the railroad. The height difference between the steps below the sniper's nest and the railway amounts to 6.4 meters (almost 21 feet) along the entire trajectory, a gradient of 4.2% or 3.4 degrees.[399] A grass verge – referred to since November 22 as the *Grassy Knoll* – connects the different levels. A wooden fence, referred to as the *Picket Fence*, stands behind the colonnade and grass verge, bordered at the rear by a parking lot. You would have a perfect shot at the front of the limousine for several seconds from the *picket fence*. Tailor Abraham Zapruder had taken up position with his new camera on a concrete platform near the colonnade on Elm Street. Several storm sewers were located at the edge of Elm Street to drain away any excess water. The nearby Trinity river is only a small stream in November, but when it rains in Dallas it really rains, and the Trinity can quickly become a torrent. The storm sewer pipes, which were designed to meet this situation, are large enough for a man to stand upright in them. It would theoretically also have been possible to fire at the limousine from there, from below the sidewalk. This extremely far-fetched hypothesis has several ardent followers amongst conspiracists.

Source material

A decent map of the crime scene would be the least you might expect from an in-depth investigation into the murder of a president. Surveying isn't exactly rocket science, but nothing can be taken for granted in the Kennedy dossier. The Warren Commission's report – the first book of which contains 888 pages – does not include a single plan of Dealey Plaza. The report does contain a full-page plan of the cellar of the Dallas Police Department,[400] but of the Dealey Plaza... nothing. The 26 volumes of evidence subsequently published by the Commission contain four maps,[401] or rather 'concise maps', that cover two pages in total. The description of the graph of Ruby's lie detector test covers no less than 63 useless pages.[402] A photograph of Oswald's pubic hair[403] is given the same space as the largest map of Dealey Plaza. To add insult to injury, three of the four maps in the appendices are almost identical. However, the differences between the maps again tell us quite a lot about the authors' motives. Cutler referred to the Commission's attitude with respect to the manipulation of the maps as unethical, clumsy and puerile.[404] We can only confirm this. Ignoring the identical copies, we are left with only two maps that were composed before[405] and after[406] the formulation of the single-bullet theory. The first map, CE585, is a premature remainder of the initial theories on the timing of the shots. Eventually, both inadvertently and unnecessarily, it did become part of the official evidence.

The unreadable maps with many unnecessary errors are also symptomatic. After all, the FBI was well aware of the exact dimensions of Dealey Plaza down to the last detail (Figure 34). The Commission was given a room-sized scale model[407] of Dealey Plaza for its own use by the FBI. In five weeks, the team of Inspector Leo J. Gauthier from the FBI's *Official Evidence* department had created a scale model measuring 3 x 3 m – a remarkable piece of craftsmanship and precision. Hoover was so pleased with the result that he even felt at liberty to make a joke about Chief Justice Warren's demand for more original and hard evidence. Hoover happily remarked:

> *Better have some extra wood and nails as Warren may want to see the raw materials.*[408]

The scale model was also made as proof for the FBI theory of 'three shots, all hitting their target', with fluorescent tape from the sniper's nest to the (totally incorrect) positions according to the FBI's timing of the shots.

POSITIONS OF PRESIDENTIAL CAR WHEN SHOTS ONE, TWO AND THREE WERE FIRED, AS VIEWED FROM THE SOUTH SIDE OF THE PARKWAY LOOKING TOWARD PERGOLA (LINE OF FIRE INDICATED BY STRING LEADING TO EACH CAR).

Figure 34 – The FBI was able to build an impressive scale model of the plaza, even though the dossier does not contain any detailed three-dimensional measurements of the square.

However, the existence of the scale model definitely proves that the FBI did have highly detailed information on the three-dimensional measurements.[409] Time and time again, it becomes clear that the FBI must have had access to much more information than can be found in the archives today.

New site map

The Commission gradually became aware that the timing of the shots proposed by the FBI was impossible. The fact that the official version departed from the truth appeared not to be an insurmountable problem. The Zapruder film, however, represented the real problem, and was dangerous according to commission advisor Arlen Specter. After all, one could never exclude the possibility that the public might gain access to the film at some point, despite the authorities' stringent efforts to prevent this at any cost. If the Zapruder film became public, it would become clear to all and sundry that the scenario with the three shots hitting their target was pure fiction. Specter was one of the first to understand that the problem with the timing was insurmountable. Kennedy had not yet been hit at the time he disappeared behind the Stemmons freeway sign in Z205. Connally was definitely already injured in Z237. If Kennedy and Connally were hit by two bullets, a maximum of 29 Zapruder frames would have elapsed between the two bullets, which represents only 1.6 seconds. No matter how willing you are to elevate Oswald's shooting skills to the absolute world top, shooting twice within 1.6 seconds was physically and technically impossible.

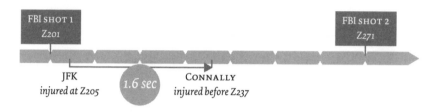

It took many months for the Commission to pluck up the courage to acknowledge that the FBI had got it completely wrong, but, in the end, the only remaining option was to carry out the investigation again. This resulted in lost time and increased confusion on the one hand, and in the need for a new map and a reconstruction on the other. This initiative was not without risk either. Hoover was not exactly the kind of person who would take kindly to public loss of face. The 833-page FBI report (including appendices) only devoted one paragraph to the actual assassination: 'Three shots rang out. Two bullets struck President Kennedy, and one wounded Governor Connally.' As soon as the ink was dry, Hoover made sure that the conclusion of the report was leaked to the press. During their initial executive session,[410] the members of the Commission noted to their surprise that there was nothing in the FBI report that they hadn't already read in the papers. By means of a pre-emptive strike, the FBI had already etched the personal view of its vain director as the definitive truth in the mind of the general public.

A Commission standpoint that differed from the FBI report also met with internal opposition. Chief Justice Warren was and remained convinced that the Commission didn't need to instigate its own investigation.[411] President Johnson had assured Warren that the commission only needed to quickly check the FBI investigation and then approve it in its entirety. Chief Justice Warren literally said: 'Our job here is essentially one for the evaluation of evidence as distinguished from being one of gathering evidence'. The FBI still had an unassailable reputation in those days. Commission member Allan Dulles referred to his extensive experience with the Bureau: the FBI only reported facts, facts and more facts – based on fact.[412] Therefore, when the FBI unequivocally stated in a report that 'two bullets struck President Kennedy, and one wounded Governor Connally', it was an assertion that a Junior Counsel such as Arlen Specter could not ignore lightly.

But there was no escape: the Zapruder film was too clear, and 1.6 seconds was not enough. With three-quarters of its allocated time elapsed, the Commission consequently had no other choice than to drastically change course and to recalibrate all the evidence on the basis of the single-bullet theory. The Commission then instructed Robert West, a surveyor, to produce a new site map. It was completed on May 24, 1964, and was incorporated into the evidence as CE882.[413] The new map included some additional data, and rectified a number of striking errors. But, once again, the Commission printed the map in a ridiculously small format. The new map was set to a scale of 1/240 and was therefore four times larger than CE585. If the new map is printed equally small in the appendices, then, paradoxically, the largest map suffers the greatest disadvantage. If a draftsman increases the scale, he increases the size of the drawing but not the letters. If the map is then printed in a smaller format, the largest map will be the least legible. It is impossible to understand why the map was reduced to a completely illegible format. Did the Commission suddenly want to save one page amongst the many thousands of pages?[414] Why was it such a problem to add one map in a legible format to the 27 volumes? The original version of the site map was approximately 1 m x 1.60 m in size, i.e. 16,000 cm2, which was then reduced to 100 cm2. The map was consequently 160 times smaller than the original and when a letter or figure is reduced 160 times, it obviously becomes illegible. Critics suspect malicious intent by the Commission, which is said to have purposely sabotaged the evidence in order to prevent later verification or to make it as difficult as possible. The commission probably did not pay enough attention to this matter, however, as it considered it to be highly unlikely that anyone would take the trouble to read the report.[415] How much less did the Commission expect that, fifty years later, hundreds of investigators would still be uncomprehendingly poring over the site map with magnifying glasses until it gave them a headache?

Item CE882 includes a table of figures in the top left corner. The table, consisting of seventeen rows and seven columns, is exactly 1.6 cm2 (1.1 x 1.45 cm) in the published evidence. Even for the Warren Commission, the half-page print-out of CE882 was not quite legible enough, and the table was therefore inserted separately under Reference CE884.[416] This is a highly significant table, as it links the position of the limousine to the Zapruder frames and calculates the downward angle from the sniper's nest for each frame.

HSCA map

For the purpose of this investigation, we eventually based our research on the clearest and most complete site plan,[417] a map created by the HSCA (Figure 35).

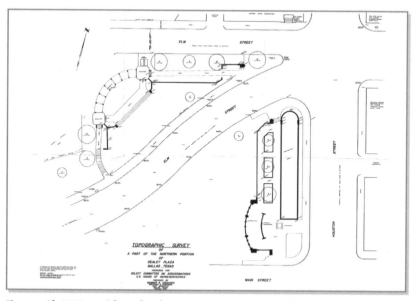

Figure 35 – The HSCA map is better than the Warren Commission version, although many elements were no longer available for surveying purposes after fifteen years. For example, the Stemmons freeway sign and the road markings are no longer included in this map.

The disadvantage of the creation of the map in 1978 is that, fifteen years after the murder, researchers could no longer survey essential reference points, such as the Stemmons freeway sign and the correct road markings, so that these are missing on the HSCA map. For the purpose of our investigation, we have added the freeway sign, the road markings, the curb stone at the feet of Jim Tague, and the decorative colonnade across from Main Street to the map again. Having collated the various components, we also added a coordinate system with the north-east corner of the TSBD as the reference point (zero). This enabled us to add coordinates to an accuracy of 1 ft (30 cm) in order to give each point on the map a unique location. This comes close to providing us with a functional map of the scene of the crime.

A reliable map with coordinates would have avoided many point-less misunderstandings in the Commission's report and investigations. How easy it would have been to clearly position a witness at the start of a cross-examination using two simple coordinates. But no one came up with such a straightforward idea. We will mainly use the map to test the single-bullet theory. Once you know the correct coordinates, many ballistic questions can be answered using simple trigonometry.

The map in the Commission evidence also does not indicate where exactly the weapon would have been. The window from which Oswald was said to have fired is obviously not right at the corner of the building. The police archive[418] does include a rudimentary sketch of the sixth floor drawn on graph paper. According to R.B. Cutler, the muzzle of the weapon would have been located 90 inches or 229 cm from the corner.[419] This measurement can be confirmed.

Another missing element on the HSCA map is the road markings between lanes. They could obviously no longer be measured exactly after 15 years. We have divided the width of Elm Street into three equal lanes. The Z-frames before the freeway sign show that the limousine was driving with its left front wheel close to the left-hand side of the middle lane. There is still a lot of space in the middle lane to the right of the limousine. The photograph taken by the photographer J.W. Ike Altgens immediately after JFK had been hit (Figure 36), shows that the limousine is still very close to the left-hand side of the center lane. Along the entire trajectory, Kennedy's head is positioned approximately on the imaginary center line of Elm Street.

Figure 36 – The Altgens photograph. The limousine is driving right alongside the road markings. Kennedy has raised his arms to his throat. The secret agents are turning around to look behind them. The door to the white vehicle containing Johnson's security guards is already open. They are reacting quickly to protect the Vice-President. The fire escapes of the Dal-Tex building are visible in the background.

The limousine's position with respect to the road markings may appear obvious, but as far as the Warren Commission was concerned it was anything but. Item CE875 (Figure 37) is one of the photographs of the initial reconstruction on December 5, 1963. It appears that the investigators were not too worried about the position of the vehicle with regard to the edge of the lane. Another good question is why Oswald's stand-in aimed at Jacqueline Kennedy, and not at the president.

Figure 37 – The vehicle's position according to the initial reconstruction.

Finally, we briefly focus on Jim Tague once again, the third victim on Dealey Plaza. He was standing on the south side of the central tunnel, quite a long way away from the TSBD. Tague pointed out to a police officer the damage to a curb stone, allegedly caused by the impact of a bullet. CE882 indicates where the curb stone was removed and this information is corroborated by other maps. We can, therefore, also include this point in the HSCA map (Figure 38).

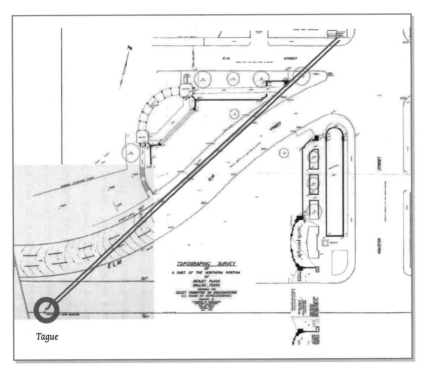

Tague

Figure 38 – Position of the curb stone that was hit, resulting in a fragment flying off and hitting the face of an onlooker, Jim Tague.

PART 5

THE VICTIMS

22. A LIGHTWEIGHT, GRAY SHIPPING CASKET

Arrival at Bethesda

The arrival of Kennedy's body at the Bethesda Naval Hospital again leads to an incomprehensible observation. The conspiracists who argue that Kennedy's body was abducted and touched up before the autopsy are a class apart. Yet no sooner do you think that you should be at least spared this type of nonsense, an astonishing document surfaces. The document in question was written by the undertaker. The Gawler company in Washington was entrusted with the organization of the funeral. The first document the funeral home dedicated to the task was an 'order form' (Figure 39).[420]

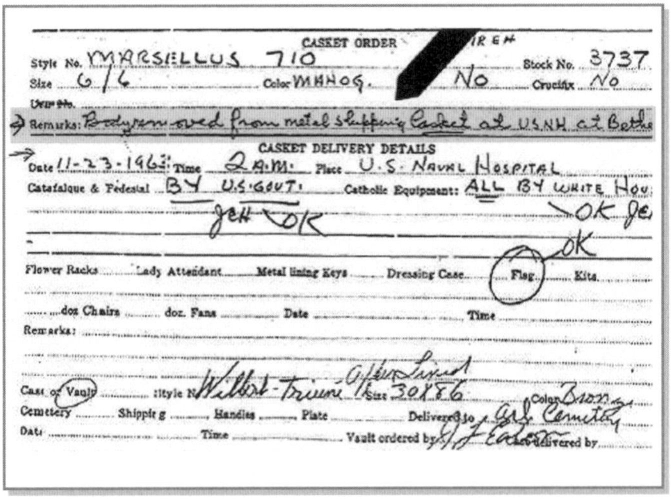

Figure 39 – The undertaker noted: 'Body removed from metal shipping casket'.

Under the heading 'Remarks', the White House undertaker noted that Kennedy's body was removed from a lightweight metal shipping casket at Bethesda Hospital. But everyone in the world had seen on television how President Kennedy's body had been transported in a heavy bronze casket in Dallas. The Commission did not waste any words on this, and the FBI did not conduct any further investigation. Is this perhaps an incomprehensible mistake by one of Gawler's staff members, or is there – again – more to it? There are at least three other witnesses who state independently from one another that Kennedy's body did not arrive in Bethesda in the ornate bronze casket. As a staff member of the Assassination Records Review Board (ARRB), Douglas Horne took down a telephone statement[421] from Dennis David, the Chief of the Day at the Medical School in Bethesda. In 1997, David testified that he was present while the casket in which President Kennedy was transported was unloaded from the black hearse. He referred to a lightweight metal casket; a kind of aluminum box, commonly used for fallen soldiers. In his statement, he referred to a black hearse, and this is also strange, because everyone had seen how the body of Kennedy was taken away in a gray hearse after the plane had landed. In an interview with conspiracist David Lifton, David also confirmed that the autopsy physicians Humes and Boswell were present when the aluminum casket arrived.[422] David also stated that the casket was not empty. Because of the weight, seven or eight people were required to carry it. Approximately half an hour after the pale gray casket had been carried in, David proceeded to the front of the hospital. The main lobby consisted of a rotunda with a balcony on the second floor, and David saw the gray hearse arrive from this balcony.[423] Jacqueline and Bobby Kennedy entered the building and took the elevator to the seventeenth floor, where a suite was available. In the report of the telephone interview with Dennis David in 1997, the ARRB stated: 'He was firm in his recollection that the motorcade out front with the gray ambulance arrived well after the gray shipping casket at the rear loading dock.'[424]

The second witness was Paul O'Connor, a medical assistant who was present at the autopsy. The HCSA interviewed him on August 25, 1977 and noted down the following: 'O'Connor said that the casket was a pink shipping casket and it arrived approximately eight o'clock.'[425] He also stated that the body was placed in a body bag and that he was shocked by the enormous damage to the head ('nothing left in the cranium but splattered brain matter'.) This statement not only confirmed that there was a lightweight metal casket, but also that Kennedy's body had been placed inside this casket in a body bag, while it had left Parkland Hospital wrapped in sheets.

David Lifton, who stubbornly specialized in unraveling all autopsy problems, also interviewed Paul O'Connor, and rendered the latter's description of the casket as follows:[426] 'Well, I used to work in a funeral home as a kid, and a shipping casket is nothing but a cheap casket. It was a kind of pink gray, [...] It's nothing fancy. It's just a tin box.'

Jenkins, a colleague of O'Connor, was the third witness, and he stated to David Lifton: 'It was not a really ornamental type thing... it was kind of plain casket?' 'Awful clean and simple. As a matter of fact it was nothing you'd expect a President to be in.'[427] Witness four was Sergeant R.E. Boyajian, the officer in command for the Navy. He prepared a report on the arrival of the presidential casket at Bethesda immediately after the events, and wrote down the following: 'At approximately 18:35 the casket was received at the morgue entrance and taken inside.'[428] This was logistically possible, because the plane had landed in Washington at 18:00. But the gray hearse in which the bronze casket had left the airport only arrived at the main entrance of Bethesda at 18:55, and remained there for another twelve minutes. At 19:07 the hearse followed an FBI vehicle that lead it around the building to the loading dock at the back. Press people who were present at both places have confirmed these times. Kennedy could not have arrived at the morgue at 18:35 in the bronze casket that only appeared at the loading bay of this morgue at 19:07.

None of the persons involved were questioned by either the FBI or the Warren Commission in 1964. Nowhere does the official account make any mention of a light gray, metal casket, a black ambulance, or the arrival of Kennedy's body at Bethesda at 18:35.

A wild chase?

Conspiracist Lifton also treated his readers to an exciting story. The guard of honor escorted the hearse with the bronze casket from the front to the back of the Bethesda Hospital. In this short trip, the guard of honor is said to have lost sight of the hearse, after which they followed the wrong ambulance, before the correct vehicle came into view again.[429] But a sober witness of this peculiar incident, Bethesda pharmacologist Sorrell L. Schwartz, contradicted Lifton's account. He wrote a reader's letter to *Time Magazine*[430] in 1981. According to him, the car that drove ahead had simply driven off too quickly, assuming that the hearse would follow. When this was not the case, the car returned to the main entrance, and the gray hearse did follow it this time. He concluded his letter with the following words:

At no time was the ambulance out of sight of at least several hundred peo-
ple, from its arrival at the center until the bronze coffin was unloaded at
the morgue.

Our preference is for this version, without the wild chase and crazy ride
behind the building.

Deliberate choice of a second hearse

Donald Rebentisch was a student at Bethesda Hospital. He was mentioned by witness Dennis David as one of the persons who was present
when the aluminum casket was unloaded. Rebentisch would later declare that the use of a second ambulance had been a deliberate decision
to mislead the curious spectators who had gathered at the front of the
hospital:

> *The chief said we got all the [...] ghouls and reporters and the TV and*
> *everybody at the front of the hospital. He said there would be an empty*
> *casket in the ambulance. He said the President's body would really come in*
> *the back. [...] This made sense to me. I felt there was nothing wrong with*
> *this. I just bought it, as did the rest of us.*

Furthermore, according to Rebentisch, the president's casket was unloaded from a black hearse 35 to 40 minutes before the car with the empty casket arrived at the front.[431]

Robert Muna, a dental technician who was also present at Bethesda that
evening, confirmed Rebbentisch's account:

> *There were two ambulances that came in. One was lighted. It came up to*
> *the front door. The second one they kept dark and it went around to the*
> *back. That was the one that had Kennedy in it. It was common knowledge*
> *that there were two caskets.*

This only tells us that there was something going on that involved more
than one hearse. What difference it would have made to the tabloids
whether an empty casket or a casket containing the body was carried in
is not quite clear. The story about the deliberate decision to opt for two
caskets is therefore nonsense. What does remain, however, is that there are

two more confirmations that there were indeed two caskets at Bethesda. With Rebentisch and Muna, this brings us to at least seven witnesses.

The believers consider the story of the shipping casket to be completely crazy. They point out that the Kennedy clan remained very close to the heavy bronze casket at all times. The scenarios proposed by the conspiracists do not excel in credibility, to be honest. But the believers also fail miserably. Their strategy of denial does not address the problem of the lightweight gray casket and the black ambulance. We can fully agree with the fact that it *sounds* unbelievable that the president was removed from the original casket and arrived at Bethesda in a shipping casket. But the written note of the undertaker is and remains a fact, incredible as it may sound. It is one of the pieces of a puzzle for which we need to find a place in the context of this account.

23. THE DEVELOPMENT OF
THE AUTOPSY REPORT

In a homicide case, the body of the victim constitutes the *best evidence*, the evidence that is strongly preferred when it comes to resolving the case. In this dossier however, the autopsy also went seriously wrong. Many Kennedy books are exclusively devoted to the medical-forensic issues. It is not our intention to fully explore these issues in this book, but we cannot ignore the remarkable autopsy examination.

With a full gallery

According to FBI agents Sibert and O'Neill, 28 attendees, including themselves, witnessed the president lying naked on the autopsy table before, during and after the actual autopsy. Historian Walt Brown even counted 34 attendees.[432] Below is an overview:

AUTOPSY DOCTORS	AUTOPSY PERSONNEL	MILITARY PERSONNEL	FBI AGENTS
1. Humes	9. Jenkins	19. Osborne	28. Sibert
2. Boswell	10. Custers	20. Canada	29. O'Neill
3. Finck	11. O'Conner	21. Stover	PERS. PH. PRESIDENT
4. Karnal	12. Reed	22. Cross	30. Burkley
SECRET SERVICE	13. Riebe	23. Galloway	UNDERTAKERS
5. Kellermen	14. Pitzer	24. Boyers	31. Hagen
6. Hill	15. Stringer	25. Bakerman	32. Van Hoesen
7. Greer	16. Ebersole	26. McHugh	33. Stroble
8. O'Leary	17. Rudnicki	27. Wehle ·	34. Robinson
	18. Metzler		

There could have been even more people. General Curtis LeMay, USAF Chief of Staff is not listed, for example. During the missile crisis, LeMay was in favor of bombing the missile installations in Cuba, an initiative that would probably have lead to an escalation of the Cold War. LeMay considered Kennedy's efforts to come to a diplomatic solution to be a rather weak alternative (the general was not exactly a Kennedy sympathizer). Medical assistant Paul O'Connor claimed that LeMay was present at the autopsy with his inseparable cigar in his mouth.[433] We cannot be sure whether this is true or not, because there was not even a list of who wandered in and out of the morgue while the autopsy was in progress.

The presence of unauthorized persons was in any case a serious error according to the *HSCA Forensic Pathology Panel*, which, in 1979, made a list of everything that went wrong during the Bethesda autopsy.[434] The doctors who had conducted the autopsy were later not allowed to see photographs of the president's back – out of great respect for the president. But while the president was lying naked on the autopsy table and was being cut to pieces ('The body was literally butchered.'[435]), dozens of curious people were looking over the shoulders of the doctors. We have no idea what all those people were supposed to be doing there, because only three of the 34 people present were interviewed by the Commission: doctors Humes, Boswell and Finck. Secret agents Greer, Kellerman and Hill were also interviewed, but mainly about the motorcade in Dallas, not about the autopsy.

Not only were there too many people present, attempts were also made to influence what was happening. Radiology technician Jeroll Custer stated in front of the ARRB in 1997 that spectators were constantly interfering with the autopsy process.'[436] Autopsy technician Paul O'Connor spoke about 'apparent control over the autopsy by persons whispering in the morgue' and James Jenkins stated: And of course, the gallery had to stick their two cents in, and – it had to be most of the night.'[437]

Officially, Jacqueline Kennedy had opted for the Bethesda Hospital because Kennedy had been a naval officer. Whether this sentimental preference was the true reason is uncertain. Many decisions in the dossier are attributed to the Kennedy entourage. As a rule, however, these decisions were, on reflection, always an unfortunate choice with regard to the investigation, but rather a convenient option for a cover-up operation. But in the context of the autopsy, interference by the Kennedys is a plausible option, because they undoubtedly had an interest in the discrete treatment of the medical condition of the deceased president.

The alleged throat wound

The alert FBI agents Sibert and O'Neill wrote the first report on the progress of the autopsy.[438] They allegedly had been present throughout the entire autopsy. In their report, Sibert and O'Neill stated that the doctors were sure that a bullet had remained in Kennedy's back, and that they assumed that this bullet had later become dislodged from the body as a result of the heart massage.[439] The FBI report writers mentioned another interesting detail:

> It was also apparent that a tracheotomy had been performed, as well as surgery of the head area, namely, in the top of the skull.[440]

Only emergency care had been administered in the Parkland Hospital in Dallas, however, and no surgery had been performed on the head of the president at all.

This emergency care included making a cut underneath the Adam's apple. When Kennedy was brought into Parkland Hospital, he had a small, circular bullet hole just below his Adam's apple. In order to resuscitate him, a horizontal, classical tracheotomy was applied to the windpipe. The cut ran through the throat wound. The autopsy doctors in Washington had apparently not been informed of this significant fact. Secret agent Clinton Hill[441] was called in at the end of the autopsy, before the staff of undertaker Gawler started their work. He was the security guard of Jacqueline Kennedy, and was permitted to briefly see the president in case Jacky had any questions later regarding the injuries.[442] Hill testified before the Commission regarding the throat wound: 'It was my understanding at that time that this was done by a tracheotomy.'[443] Commissioner Specter quickly interrupted the witness, but Hill had already said it: at the end of the autopsy, just before the undertaker started his work, there was no mention at all at Bethesda Hospital about a throat wound. Secret agent William Greer, Kennedy's driver, also confirmed that there was no mention of a throat wound during the autopsy, let alone a passage from the back wound to the throat. On the contrary, according to Greer, it was established that *no passage* had been found when checking the direction and the depth of the back wound.[444]

Admiral Burkley, the president's personal physician, attended the autopsy and prepared the official death certificate. There is no mention in the death certificate of a bullet wound in the anterior neck. Burkley was also present in Parkland, but only arrived there after the tracheotomy had already been carried out. He was therefore not aware of the original wound below the Adam's apple that was subsequently enlarged by the tracheotomy.[445] The death certificate re-confirmed that the existence of the bullet hole in the anterior neck remained unknown during the autopsy. Burkley, the president's personal physician, and moreover the only doctor who was present at both Parkland and at the Bethesda Hospital, was never interviewed by the Commission.

It is a hallucinatory fact: the doctors who carried out the autopsy at Bethesda Hospital did not know anything about a wound to the throat, an essential piece of information that was meanwhile known by millions of Americans. Dr. Perry of the Parkland Hospital had, in fact, mentioned the injury to the anterior neck of President Kennedy during a press conference that was broadcast live and on national TV on Friday afternoon. He described the original throat wound as an entrance wound during this press conference. It was his distinct professional opinion that an exit wound would have been larger and less neat.[446] Dr. Perry was soon to bitterly regret his honest statement. On Saturday morning, nurse Audrey Bell, operating room coordinator at the Parkland Hospital, met him in the hospital. 'He *looked as hell.*' In front of the ARRB, Mrs. Bell testified that the doctor had claimed to have hardly slept that night because 'people from Bethesda Naval Hospital had been harassing him all night on the telephone, trying to get him to change his mind about [...] that President Kennedy had an entrance wound in the front of his neck.'[447] The doctor was concerned. The withdrawal of his position that was demanded was at odds with his professional pride. 'His professional credibility was at stake', testified nurse Bell. At that point in time, Dr. Perry was not quite sure yet how to handle this situation. The testimony of Audrey Bell was an official statement before the newly established, independent, federal agency ARRB, which had been established in 1992, and not gossip by some conspiracy author. ARRB member Horne said of Audrey Bell that she was an 'unimpeachable witness of sterling character with tremendous credibility'.

Dr. Perry was not alone in his assumption that the original throat injury was an entrance wound. His colleague Jones expressed it as follows:

> The hole was very small and relatively clean cut, as you would see in a bullet that is entering rather than exiting from a patient [...] you would expect more of an explosive type of exit wound, with more tissue destruction.[448]

The main problem was that Perry not only had an opinion, but had also given a press conference. Someone also tried to find a way around this as well. On March 25, 1964, the Warren Commission was looking for images from this press conference. The correct body to retrieve visual or sound material from this press conference was the Secret Service, but Director Rowley had to disappoint the Commission: the images and the transcript of the interview of Dr. Perry were nowhere to be found. Not a single television station, either locally or nationally, had preserved anything of this press conference, which was world news at the time. Apparently, channels such as NBC, ABC and CBS had collectively decided to destroy unique, historical footage. Conspiracy author Lifton claims that Joe Long, Executive Director of the Dallas-based KLIF radio station, told him that the original footage had been confiscated by the Secret Service. We cannot be certain that the KLIF Director spoke the truth, but it is certain that Rowley lied once again. Douglas Horne later came across a transcript of the press conference by accident among some random papers of the *Johnson Library*.[449] The document reference was 'White House Transcript 1327-C', and bore the stamp 'Received U.S. Secret Service 1963 Nov. 26 AM 11:40 Office of the Chief'. Rowley's own department had clearly received the transcribed text of the press conference, and was in possession of this text when Rowley informed the Commission that the interview was nowhere to be found.

It is clear what the problem was: an entrance wound in the throat would obviously provide the evidence of a conspiracy, and that was the last thing the authorities needed. Perry's press conference had already been a major setback. Perry, an experienced emergency doctor in Dallas, where shootouts were a regular occurrence, had given a correct description of the wound and had provided his conclusions based on his professional experience with it. Whether he was right about the throat wound being an entrance wound is neither here nor there. In any case, the exertion of pressure on a witness and the withholding of evidence by a public authority is certainly not the correct method to address a problem in an investigation. Intriguingly, the pressure was exerted on Perry by the Bethesda Hospital, in other words by the people who had been present at the autopsy. Someone on the long list of those who had been present in the autopsy room evidently had known about the throat wound in question, but doctors Humes, Boswell and Finck, in the very same autopsy room, remained unaware of what the rest of TV-watching America knew. Those who neglected to inform the autopsy doctors were manifestly guilty of obstruction of justice.

No further investigation desired

But lack of verbal communication with the doctors was not the main reason why information was not flowing. Medical assistant Jenkins had been present in the autopsy room until 9 o'clock in the morning. He reported heated discussions with men in civilian suits,[450] and had the impression that Dr. Humes was clearly under severe strain. According to Jenkins, Humes was the kind of career person who would yield to such pressure. The doctors had probed the back wound, and Humes could feel the end of the back wound with his finger. According to Jenkins, the physicians determined that there was no passage.[451] An attempt was made to insert a metal probe through the back wound to see where it would emerge. At that point, the men in suits intervened and insisted that further investigation into the path of the bullet in the back was unnecessary. The fact that, at the same time, they also neglected to point out to Humes that there was a wound to the anterior neck beneath the tracheotomy can only mean that the 'men in suits' did not take the possibility of a path from the back wound to the throat wound into consideration for the explanation for the bullet wound below the Adam's apple. They therefore assumed that the throat wound was indeed a frontal entrance wound.

Who were these autopsy saboteurs? The military was certainly helpful in the cover-up operation. All who had seen the wound at the Bethesda Hospital had to keep their mouth shut – on pain of court martial. Radiology technician Jerrol Custer even called it a traumatic experience:

> *I was told if anything – no matter what – got out, it would be the sorriest day of my life. I'd spend most of my life behind prison walls.*[452]

But, according to all witnesses, the active obstruction of justice was carried out by men in civilian dress. There were six 'civilians' among the spectators: FBI agents Sibert and O'Neil, Admiral Burkley – who was not in uniform – and several secret agents. We can disregard Sibert and O'Neill as potential candidates for exerting pressure on the doctors. Admiral Burkley knew nothing of the throat wound, as he had arrived at Parkland late, and the wound was not mentioned in the death certificate. This means that the pressure had to be exerted by secret agents Kellerman, Greer and O'Leary, loyal members of the Kennedy staff. The strongest argument of the *believers* in excluding any surgery prior to the autopsy was the presence and the loyalty of these men. According to the *believers*, they would never have allowed the autopsy to be sabotaged in any way at all. We don't know whether they permitted the President's body to be removed from the bronze casket, but, in any case, it was the people who had guarded the casket who later applied pressure on the doctors during the autopsy. It was these men who omitted to inform the doctors about the throat wound underneath the tracheotomy. From the Bethesda Hospital, one of them pressed Perry hard to change the throat wound into the exit wound of the bullet through the back.

An enlightening phone call

The two main doctors, Dr. Humes in Washington on the one hand, and Dr. Perry in Dallas on the other, at last spoke to each other on the phone on Saturday, November 23. At that time, Dr. Perry had not yet decided whether or not he should give in to the pressure and declare that the throat wound was an exit wound after all. Dr. Humes, on his part, had apparently still not found the time to read a newspaper, because he still knew nothing about the throat wound. Perry finally updated him accordingly during this telephone conversation. It seemed that the pieces of the puzzle only finally fell into place for Humes then. A through-and-through wound would naturally be the solution to the riddle! In reality, both Humes and Perry were convinced that there was no passage wound, although for different reasons. Perry was convinced that the throat wound was an entrance wound. 'My professional credibility is at stake here,' he had said. This could only mean that he was struggling to accept the step to the exit wound scenario because this was not in line with his professional conviction. Humes did not believe the passage wound solution either. He had seen and felt the back wound, and had probed it with a metal probe. He had not found any outlet, and specifically no outlet that ended in the throat. But both doctors were under the same heavy pressure to conclude that it was a through-and-through wound after all. Under no circumstances could the bullet wound to the throat be seen as an entrance wound. A frontal shot would imply a conspiracy, and was therefore beyond discussion.

The magic bullet with its seven injuries was not yet conceived on November 23. The planned course of the investigation at that point in time was still 'three bullets, three hits'. The official working hypotheses were therefore sequentially as follows:

1. Three bullets were fired: one bullet hit Kennedy's back and was dislodged from the body as a result of the CPR, one bullet hit Connally, and the last bullet went through Kennedy's head;

2. Following the commotion regarding the throat wound, there were still three bullets: a bullet that penetrated Kennedy, one bullet for Connally, and one bullet through Kennedy's head;

3. The magic bullet only made its appearance in the last scenario. The official version then became the following: one complete miss, the magic bullet, and one bullet through Kennedy's head. The Warren Report was not even conclusive about the sequence of these bullets.

In the messy situation surrounding the autopsy, the discussion on the working hypothesis mainly involved the transition phase between scenario one and two.

The autopsy report

According to the official fairy tale, the case suddenly became crystal clear to Dr. Humes following his conversation with Dr. Perry on Saturday morning. A sudden unlawful impulse caused him to burn his original notes, which were evidence in a homicide case, and he prepared the autopsy report we now know as CE387[453] (Figure 40). The report deviated thoroughly from the observations that were made during the autopsy examination. That did not prevent the other two doctors at Bethesda Hospital being completely in agreement with the findings. All three physicians signed the report, but nobody remembered to also date the document.

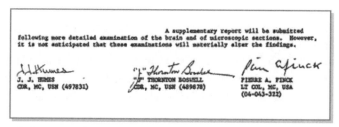

Figure 40 – The three autopsy doctors signed the undated autopsy report.

The autopsy report does not show any date whatsoever, on neither the front nor the back. Anyone who has ever signed an official document knows that this is nonsense. This could only mean that the signatories did not want to reveal when the document had been signed. It therefore remains an open question as to whether the autopsy report in its final form had been prepared on November 24, or at a later date.

The FBI and the Secret Service

The chronological account of the autopsy report is totally incomprehensible, but it takes a while before it becomes clear why this is so. The two stories do, in fact, cross each other in the chronological overview. It is as if two radio stations were transmitting simultaneously on the same channel. Only when you recognize and distinguish the two sources of information does the information becomes somewhat more understandable.

The first story is about the intransigence of the FBI. We already know that FBI agents Sibert and O'Neill were present at the autopsy, and prepared a detailed report immediately afterwards.[454] On December 26, they reported that only the back wound had been established during the autopsy. The distance the bullet had travelled in Kennedy's back was very short, and the bullet had become dislodged from the body as a result of the CPR that had been administered. This version perfectly fits the scenario the FBI had initially opted for, i.e. three shots that hit the target. On the occasion of the third anniversary of the assassination, Hoover stated on the front page of the *New York Times* that the FBI reports on the medical aspects had only been preliminary, and moreover were also based on incomplete information. The report by Sibert and O'Neill had only been drafted in anticipation of the final autopsy report.[455] What ultimately mattered was the final opinion of the doctors. That sounds logical. One would therefore expect that the FBI, who was ultimately responsible for the full investigation, would then have requested the autopsy report on the first working day following the assassination. If the autopsy report of November 24 proved to be different from the report provided by agents Sibert and O'Neill, the FBI would immediately adjust its view to the vision of the better-qualified doctors, or at least that's what Hoover seemed to imply. But on December 9, the FBI still stated in a 'Supplemental Report' that the bullet was stuck in the back.[456] So what about this tiresome wound to the throat? On December 18, the *New York Times* reported the following, quoting a source that was familiar with the autopsy report (underlining added):

> *The first bullet made what was described as a small neat wound in the back and penetrated two or three inches [...]. The pathologists at Bethesda, the source said, concluded that the throat wound was caused by the emergence of a metal fragment or piece of bone resulting from the fatal shot in the head.*[457]

The first part of the report in the *New York Times* is peculiar. We certainly cannot call the *New York Times* a tabloid paper. But why then did this influential newspaper still report a back wound with a depth of only up to 3 inches almost one month after the assassination – on the basis of a source 'that was familiar with the autopsy report'? What about the autopsy report dated November 24 that described a transit wound to the throat? But it's the second part of the quotation that is not only peculiar, but downright nonsensical. Kennedy was already reaching for his throat at Z223 (Figure 62), while the shot to the head was only fired at Z313. Whatever the injury to the throat was, it was certainly not a fragment of a bullet that was fired at time frame Z313. It would appear that the FBI, the presumable source of the *New York Times*, had to leak *something* to explain the wound to the throat within the theory of the three hits, while still maintaining that there was no passage.

The FBI report of December 9 is still somewhat understandable, because, according to the official chronology, the FBI had not yet received an autopsy report at that time. This fact in itself is, however, already astonishing. In any homicide case, the autopsy report is usually among the top ten documents that are required to conduct the investigation. In this case, the FBI waited patiently until the Secret Service handed over the autopsy report on its own initiative, and this only took place on December 23. It took one month for the Secret Service to provide the FBI with the autopsy report after the assassination. Better late than never, and, if we can believe Hoover, the FBI would now at least realize its mistake, and align its position with that of the autopsy doctors. But the FBI did not admit defeat in the least. On January 13, 1964, three weeks after the receipt of the autopsy report, the FBI added a *Supplemental Report*[458] to the dossier. This report was prepared and signed by J. Edgar Hoover in person – just like the initial *Summary Report*. It states the following: 'Medical examination of the President's body had revealed that the bullet which entered his back, had penetrated to a distance of less than a finger length.' In the FBI version, there is not yet any mention of a throat wound or a through-and-through wound. The FBI still based its statements solely on the report prepared by Sibert and O'Neill. The agency again ensured itself the necessary backing by making use of the obedient press. On January 26, the *New York Times* reported that: 'investigators were satisfied that the first bullet hit the President in the back and that 'that bullet lodged in his shoulder.'[459] The FBI aimed to impose its version of the facts on public opinion and the Commission through press leaks. An executive session of the Warren Commission was scheduled for January 27, the day after the article appeared in the NYT.[460] General Councilor Rankin expressed his frustration with the diligence of the FBI:

Part of the difficulty in regard to it is that they [the FBI] have no problem. They have decided that it is Oswald who committed the assassination, they have decided that no one else was involved, they have decided.

That makes 'decided' three times. Commissioner Russell could only agree with this: 'They have tried the case and reached a verdict in every aspect.' Commissioner Boggs also agreed: 'You have completely understood.' But the childish attitude of the FBI was, in retrospect, only a jamming station on the channel. We can only ascribe this to Hoover's obstinacy, and simply disregard any newspaper articles further, because we do not learn anything about the origins of the autopsy report from them. Whether this report had been finished on November 24, on December 19, or mid-January, made no difference whatsoever to Hoover. In each of the three cases, he completely ignored the content anyway.

The second transmitter on the same channel was the Secret Service. On December 11, several secret agents turned up at the Parkland Hospital[461], including Elmer Moore, with an autopsy report under his arm. Moore was not a schoolboy inside the Secret Service. He was the '*Liaison Officer*' between the Secret Service and the staff of the Warren Commission. He turned out to be the man who had pressurized the Parkland Hospital doctors. For the Secret Service, the throat wound could not be an entrance wound, and transit wound was the word of the moment. Fifteen years later, the HSCA tried to sort out what had happened. But Moore rather bluntly refused any statements. He could not remember anything. The HSCA then contacted James Gochenaur,[462] who had had a five-hour interview with Moore regarding the Kennedy dossier several years before, in 1970. Unlike Moore, Gochenaur's memory was still excellent. Moore had allegedly said that 'he had badgered Dr. Perry into changing his testimony.' Moore had not felt at all comfortable with this, but he had no choice: 'We had to do what we were told in connection with, you know, the way they were investigating the assassination, or our heads would roll.'[463] Gochenaur could, of course, have made the story up, but it's all we have, and if Moore himself bluntly refused to provide an official statement, he probably had a good reason for this.

There is also *circumstantial evidence* about Moore's role. Once again, this relates to a newspaper article. By coincidence, precisely one day after

Moore had been at the Parkland Hospital applying heavy pressure to the doctors, either willingly or not, an article appeared in the *Dallas Times Herald* that mentioned the through-and-through wound scenario for the first time. One thing is certain: the Secret Service also tried to push its through-and-through wound solution via the press. Soon afterwards, on December 20, Head of the Secret Service Rowley finally shared the autopsy report with the Commission[464] (Figure 41), and, another three days later, with the FBI.

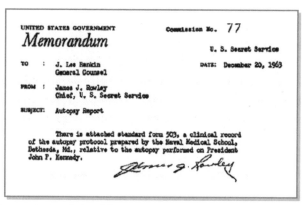

Figure 41 – *The Secret Service only shared the autopsy report with the Commission on December 20, and waited a few more days to inform the FBI. Yet the autopsy report had allegedly already been finalized and signed on November 24.*

Why did the Secret Service leave the autopsy report that had allegedly been finalized on November 24 lying around for almost one month, and why did secret agents still apply heavy pressure to the doctors of Parkland Hospital if the autopsy report had already been conclusively completed weeks ago at that time? The only explanation is that the final version of the autopsy report, including the through-and-through wound scenario, did not arise until the second half of December. That would explain why the date is missing from the document, and why the Secret Service had to exert pressure on the Parkland Hospital doctors. As long as the doctors were not willing to modify their entrance wound theory, there could be no definitive autopsy report.

If the events in the accounts of the FBI and of the Secret Service are combined and then read in chronological order, it's impossible to make head or tail of it. The Warren Commission had the same problem. Commissioner Rankin had no idea what to do with the contradictory information during the executive session of January 27. Rankin referred to 'this point of exit or entrance of the bullet in the front of the neck' and quoted annoyed the contradicting sources. The reason for the incomprehensible mess was the cops' war between the FBI (shallow bullet in the shoulder, no throat wound) and the Secret Service (passage wound to the throat), in which neither party wanted to give in. Strangely enough, neither of them actually believed that the solution they wanted to push through was consistent with the truth. Hoover had no explanation for the throat wound, and the Secret Service deemed the hard approach necessary in the conviction that, in reality, there was no passage to the throat.

The original autopsy report

The assertion of the subservience of government to the individual is an important achievement in the United States. The American public is entitled to request the disclosure of government documents via the *Freedom Of Information Act*, or FOIA. In the case of the Kennedy dossier, the government decided that it would be better to avoid this. The Secret Service therefore came up with a smart legal trick. The medical documents were initially transferred to the Kennedy family, which ensured that, as private documents, they were safe from unwanted curiosity. In October 1966, the family transferred everything to the National Archives through an act of donation, under the strict condition that the documents would not be accessible by the general public. This seemed like a waterproof scenario to keep the documents secret in perpetuity, but an inventory list of the transfer itself was, of course, prepared, and the administration also wrote several memoranda on the subject. Conspiracist David Lifton succeeded in obtaining this secondary information through an FOIA procedure. As a result, at least the inventory of what had been transferred to the Kennedys in 1965 is available. This inventory was prepared by Admiral Burkley. The list is very accurate, and includes an original, signed autopsy report: *Complete autopsy protocol of President Kennedy (orig & 7 cc's) Original signed by Dr. Humes Pathologist.*' This last item is peculiar in view of the otherwise very precisely formulated list. The original autopsy report, which we know as CE387, bears three signatures. Could it be that the Kennedys had, in fact, obtained another report, a more recent version of the autopsy report? Moreover, the NARA had to admit that the autopsy report that was allegedly transferred by the Kennedys had vanished. But then, on October 2, 1967, the report suddenly surfaced after all. Director Rowley of the Secret Service was the person who transferred it to the National Archives.[465] The report that Rowley forwarded had three signatures and was undated. The original 'original report' apparently had only one signature and was undoubtedly dated, but has gone up in smoke. The three signatory doctors, of course, swore solemn oaths that they had only signed one original report.

Although it is completely beyond discovery now, the facts strongly point in one direction. There was a signed version of the original report of November 24 that presumably supported the scenario without the passage wound. This document had to disappear. Only when this fact was brought to light by accident did the Secret Service replaced the vanished document of November 24 by the second autopsy report, a report that was established mid-December and that – after appropriate manipulation of the Parkland Hospital witnesses – fully endorsed the passage wound theory.

Parkland Hospital buckles under pressure

That the Secret Service had indeed exerted heavy pressure on the Parkland doctors became clear when Dr. Perry appeared before the Commission to testify. The maneuver had had its effect: on November 23, the doctor had yet to make a decision on the dilemma that had caused him great worries about his professional reputation. But before the Commission, Perry remorsefully stated that the view reflected in his press conference contained 'gross inaccuracies'. He had said nothing about an 'entrance wound', but would only have referred to a 'small wound'. The AMA, the surveillance body of the medical professions, had reassured Perry: if the press had quoted him wrong, he would not be punished and would not have to fear any disciplinary sanctions. From now on, the press was officially to be blamed. Meanwhile, the transcription of the press conference, with Rowley's stamp, which was later recovered by accident, makes it clear that the press had, of course, printed Perry's statement correctly. But as far as the official historiography goes, Perry had become the victim of a flagrant misrepresentation of his words in the papers: 'it is harmful to me as a member of the faculty of the medical school to have such an article in print.' When Commissioner Specter asked him about the autopsy report, Perry asserted that he had no problem whatsoever with it. Commissioner Gerald Ford also put in his two cents worth: 'There is no basic conflict between what you have testified to or what you have said previously, and the autopsy report?' Dr. Perry confirmed: 'None at all.'

During his testimony, he vaguely recalled having been visited by secret agents, but any details, dates or names completely eluded him, and he didn't breathe a word about any pressure with regard to changing his point of view.

What was the threat that made this competent and honest physician eat humble pie like this? It is understandable that agent Moore did not feel at all comfortable in the role he had to take in this unsavory matter, apparently also under severe threat. The same question applies to the Bethesda doctors. They kept obstinately silent about what really happened for the rest of their lives. What sword of Damocles was hanging over their heads?

Commissioner Specter still grilled Perry on the question as to whether the throat wound was really an exit wound. Below is a gem from his interrogation technique (underlining added):

> Permit me to supply some additional facts, Dr. Perry, which I shall ask you to _assume_ as being true for purposes of having you express an opinion.
>
> _Assume_ first of all that the President was struck by a 6.5 mm. copper-jacketed bullet [...] striking the President on the upper right posterior thorax [...], and then exiting from the hole that you have described in the midline of the neck.
>
> Now, _assuming_ those facts to be true, would the hole which you observed in the neck of the President be consistent with an exit wound under those circumstances?
>
> Now, _assuming_ one additional fact that there was no bullet found in the body of the President, and _assuming_ the facts which I have just set forth to be true, do you have an opinion as to whether the wound which you observed in the President's neck was an entrance or an exit wound?

Poor Dr. Perry could only admit: 'with these assumptions, I believe that it was an exit wound.'[466] The question was obviously absurd. Perry quite rightly started his reply with 'With these assumptions...' He had one more chance to resist any manipulation when Commissioner Boggs, who had apparently missed the epic technical and strategic beauty of Specters question covering multiple hypothesis, asked him: 'This neck wound, was there any indication that that wound had come from the front?' Perry replied: 'There is no way to tell, sir, for sure.' By saying that nobody knew the answer, Dr. Perry at least managed to hold on to a fraction of his reputation and professional honor.

The Warren Report

The Commission now had everything it needed to write with great certainty in its final report on the autopsy that the claim suggesting that the bullet had only caused a shallow wound in Kennedy's back had been pure speculation. Their conclusion on page 88 read as follows (underlining added):

> _Further exploration during the autopsy disproved that theory._ The surgeons determined that the bullet had passed between two large strap muscles and bruised them without leaving any channel, since the bullet merely passed between them.

That is a blatant lie. In no way had the autopsy doctors carried out an examination during the autopsy to confirm a hypothesis that would only be thought up the following morning at the earliest. The fact that the Commission had no scruples to lie about this is very serious. The autopsy report should have been the best evidence.

In 1967, Arlen Specter provided some afterthoughts. He was now District Attorney of Philadelphia, Pennsylvania, and felt compelled to explain to Dr. Humes[467] in writing, on December 11, 1967, exactly what had gone wrong with the 'autopsy bungling' that had taken place in Bethesda. From this detailed letter, it's clear that Specter had already been perfectly aware of what went fundamentally wrong with the Kennedy autopsy, even in 1964. The sharpest critic of the Warren Commission couldn't have listed the mistakes any better. Strange as it may sound, Specter also criticized the use of hypothetical questions that could cause confusion, or having the witness reply to questions as to what could possibly have happened. Hopefully, this was a form of healthy self-criticism. One shortcoming from the list is striking. Specter emphasized the necessity of a 'prompt, complete written report'. Was the autopsy report then not 'promptly' finalized? Was it not already officially available on November 24?

Conclusions regarding the autopsy report

The autopsy should, of course, have taken place in Dallas. This would have complied with the law, and it would have been much better for the dossier. The autopsy reports of Tippit and Oswald, which were prepared in Dallas in the days following the event, are technically of impeccable quality. There are no ambiguities, no discussions and certainly no lies, no destroyed documents, no missing data, no vanishing reports, and the time that elapsed between the autopsy and the provision of the report was nowhere near a month.

The Bethesda autopsy was poorly conducted by physicians without any pathological experience, was poorly documented and some of the autopsy findings that were contrary to the desired scenario were adjusted accordingly, even after Kennedy had already been buried. The report showed obvious gaps. There was no mention of the symptoms of Addison's disease, for example, which must have been clearly visible. The report did not say a word about the signs of prior surgery to the head mentioned by the FBI agents, or about the slight injury caused by a metal flake to the back of the head. The information that was provided was often demonstrably wrong. In 1979, the HSCA Forensic Pathology Panel confirmed the following about the way in which the autopsy had been conducted and about the destruction of the original notes: '[...] in the event of legal dispute could adversely affect the outcome of subsequent criminal litigation.'[468] The FBI did not play a significant role in the autopsy account. Hoover stuck to his own scenario and was not interested in the actual autopsy findings. The initial autopsy report was probably also already prepared according to this hypothesis, a scenario that had also already been included in the report of the FBI agents: Kennedy only had a shallow back wound. Later on, the realization dawned that the throat wound also had to fit into the story. In view of the fact that a frontal shot was taboo, and that the explanation the FBI dreamt up for the throat wound was too strange for words, only the scenario with the passage wound was left. The first version of the report and the original autopsy notes had to be destroyed at this point. This took place under the transparent pretext that these papers could give rise to 'unhealthy interest'.[469] This was a pure lie, because Dr. Humes also declared the following to the Commission: 'In the privacy of my own home, early in the morning of Sunday, November 24th, I made a draft of this report [...]. That draft I personally burned in the fireplace of my recreation room.'[470] The fact that the draft report that Humes had written at home also had to be destroyed clearly indicates a problem with the content. It was not a matter of respect or good taste, as there could have been no serious problem with this draft version. Other notes relating to the autopsy apparently also disappeared. Biochemist Leonard Saslaw heard Dr. Finck talking irritably during the week of November 22. The doctor stated that his autopsy notes had disappeared without a trace while he was washing after the autopsy. Several colleagues had helped him to search for them, but the notes had gone.[471]

The Secret Service exerted heavy pressure on the Parkland Hospital doctors during the autopsy and in the weeks that followed to ensure the modification of the statements. As soon as the Parkland Hospital had given in, the new autopsy report could at last be finalized in mid-December. From then onwards, the theory of the passage wound was the official truth.

None of the stakeholders were certain of their case at the time the passage wound was declared as ultimate truth. During the executive session of January 27, Rankin expressed what everyone was thinking: how on earth could a bullet descend from the shoulder blade into the Adam's apple? The doctors had not established the necessary findings during the autopsy. The examinations that *had been* carried out seemed to exclude a passage wound. The nagging feeling of the secret agent on duty with the crackdown on the Parkland Hospital doctors also speaks volumes. He certainly did not seem to feel that his intervention had served the truth. The FBI was ultimately not at all sure that the passage wound solution was consistent with the truth. Still, this version had to be passed as the definitive conclusion of the autopsy report, at whatever cost. The passage wound solution immediately propelled the official investigators into a new minefield, however. Because, in that case, what had happened to the bullet after it had emerged from Kennedy's throat? And new life was breathed into the passage wound solution here. According to Commissioner Arlen Specter, the bullet continued its natural trajectory – in the direction of Governor Connally!

It may be possible that the autopsy report, despite all its flaws, accidentally hit upon the correct conclusions in the end, but this does mean the fact that the way in which it was prepared made a mockery of all the rules. To start with, the autopsy should never have been carried out in Washington. The law provided for an autopsy in Dallas. Humes destroyed evidence in a homicide case, and Finck's evidence had been stolen. Perjury, blackmail, theft, forgery of documents and obstruction of justice was committed. The autopsy report, one of the major pieces of evidence, was therefore also severely compromised, and we can add it to the long list of evidence material that would – without mercy – be declared inadmissible in any normal criminal proceedings. Another consequence of these findings is that we cannot rely on the autopsy report in order to be certain about the positions of Kennedy's various injuries, and these injuries are of crucial importance to the investigation. We can only establish whether or not there was indeed a magic bullet on November 22 on the basis of the correct location of Kennedy's back and throat wounds. We must therefore search for alternative sources in order to find out with sufficient certainty where exactly Kennedy's wounds were situated.

24. KENNEDY'S BACK WOUND

The exact location of the wound on Kennedy's back is essential for the investigation into the magic bullet.

The location of the back wound

Kennedy remained on his back while in Parkland Hospital, and therefore nobody saw the wound in his back. The first person to note down information regarding the back wound was Dr. Humes, during the autopsy in Washington. On the *Autopsy Descriptive Sheet*[472] (Figure 42), the wound is situated '14 centimeter below tip' (of the shoulder). According to the sketch, the wound is clearly situated on the back.

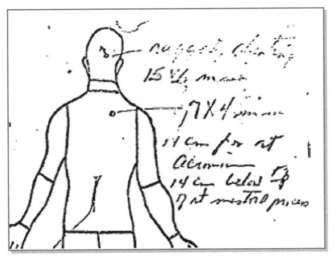

Figure 42 – Autopsy sketch by Doctor Humes: Kennedy's back wound.

In their report, FBI agents Sibert and O'Neill wrote the following regarding the progress of the autopsy: 'The pattern was clear that one bullet had entered the President's back and had worked its way out during external cardiac massage.' The FBI also situated the wound in the back.

Kennedy's shirt and jacket also left little opportunity for dispute. The hole in the jacket (Figure 43) was fifteen centimeters (six inches) below the collar.[473] The collar of a shirt or jacket is usually situated three to five centimeters above the shoulder line. The bullet hole in the shirt corresponds with the position of the hole in the jacket. On the basis of the clothing, the wound was therefore situated approximately 10 to 12 centimeters (4 to 5 inches) below the shoulder line.

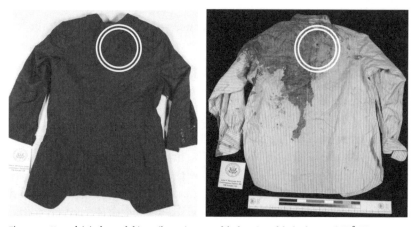

Figure 43 – Kennedy's jacket and shirt – silent witnesses of the location of the back wound. [474 & 475]

There is another medical document that cannot be overlooked: the death certificate that was prepared by Admiral Burkley, the personal physician of the President.[476] This includes the following statement: 'a second wound occurred in the posterior back at about the level of the third thoracic vertebra.' The third thoracic vertebra is clearly a position in the back (Figure 44).

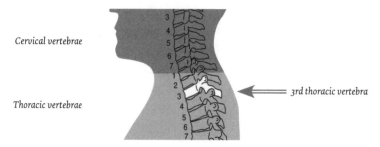

Figure 44 – Position of the third thoracic vertebra

It again becomes clear how hard the game was being played here. Even the official death certificate of the president, prepared by an admiral, disappeared from the dossier as soon as the information it contained no longer suited the investigators. This unique historical document would only re-emerge many years later. Dogged researcher Barry Ernest was searching for any snippet of information he could find on Vickie Adams, the girl who came down the staircase at the TSBD without meeting Oswald. In the National Archives, he had just started on another box containing boring documents when, to his amazement, he came across the death certificate.[477] If the original death certificate of a President of the United States is dumped into administrative oblivion, there is no way that this can be put down to a mistake; this is malevolence.

A new starting point

The investigators assumed that the downward trajectory from the back to the throat was only possible with a significantly higher starting point than the location where Kennedy had been wounded near his shoulder blade. The back wound consequently made an inexplicable jump upwards in the official account.[478] Suddenly, the 14 centimeters that were mentioned on the autopsy sketch of the autopsy report were measured starting from the bony point of the skull behind the ear (the mastoid process). As a result, the wound was repositioned rather higher than the initial fourteen centimeters below the shoulder line on the sketch of the doctors. Everyone agrees that the reference point behind the ear is unsuitable to locate a wound in the back. The mastoid process is not a fixed point. It varies with regard to the back when the head moves. The autopsy doctors certainly had not measured the location of the back wound on the basis of this flexible point, but a higher starting point was the only way of maintaining the measurement of fourteen centimeters while achieving the higher position of the wound that was deemed necessary.

The Rydberg drawings

The doctors were undoubtedly aware that they were venturing onto dangerous grounds with this manipulation, but there was no way back. Moreover, the autopsy photograph of Kennedy's back would immediately expose the lie. An alternative for the photograph was therefore required. In view of their appearance before the Commission, the doctors therefore resorted to having a drawing made by a serviceman with limited talent and no experience as a medical illustrator. The young Rydberg was given two days to produce the sole piece of evidence that would inform the world about the location of Kennedy's injuries. This is how piece of evidence CE386 (Figure 45) was forced upon the Commission, and upon later readers of the Warren Report – with the wound in the back being too high and too much to the right. Had Dr. Humes lost his mind as a result of the traumatic events? Humes had said that the bullet in the back had been dislodged from the body due to the reanimation efforts. Did he believe that the doctors in Dallas administer heart massage to the right shoulder?

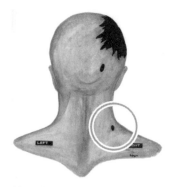

Figure 45 – Evidence CE386, one of the Rydberg drawings in the Commission report.

Humes made the following statement before the Commission: 'Attempts to probe in the vicinity of this wound were unsuccessful without fear of making a false passage.'[479] His colleague, Dr. Finck, had made an attempt to find the trajectory of the bullet.[480] Secret agent Kellerman had asked him: 'Colonel, where did it go?' Finck had replied: 'There are no lanes for an outlet of the entry in this man's shoulder.' But how could a wound at the height drawn here become a problem when tracing the passage? During the autopsy, had Finck been searching for an outlet of the bullet with his probe a few centimeters away from the lower neck? And then the passage wound. Where was Kennedy's Adam's apple situated according to Humes, Boswell and Finck if there was supposedly a passage wound to the center of the throat from this back wound? Commissioner Specter explicitly asked Humes whether he had checked the drawings of the medical illustrator for accuracy.[481] The question had undoubtedly been agreed with the doctor in advance, and he therefore replied with a clear 'Yes.' Specter was well aware that the drawings were far from accurate, however. He expressed his concern about this in a letter of April 30 addressed to Rankin, the big boss of the Commission staff (underlining added):[482]

> Commission Exhibits Nos. 385, 386 and 388 were made from the recollections of the autopsy surgeons as told to the artist. _Some day someone may compare the films with the artist's drawings and find a significant error_ which might substantially affect the essential testimony and the Commission's conclusions.

Specter clearly stated that the drawings were inaccurate, and that the credibility of the Commission's conclusions would be seriously at stake if this would ever be exposed. Yet he did not address the problem any further after the confirmative answer from Humes. Humes did not feel comfortable either, because he kept some options open and, at the same time, toned his confirmation down somewhat:

> I must state these drawings are in part schematic. The artist had but a brief period of some 2 days to prepare these. He had no photographs from which to work, and had to work under our description, verbal description of what we had observed.

They were only sketches, there was little time, the artist had no photographs available and had made his drawings on the basis of verbal instructions. That's a lot of superfluous excuses for the drawings that Humes had checked for their accuracy. In any case, Humes at least knew what code language was expected of him, and only referred to 'the wound in the low neck' during his interview. Nobody had used the description 'low neck' at the time of the autopsy. Reference had only been made to Kennedy's 'back' at that time. The Commission also asked Humes how he could explain the difference between the Rydberg drawings and the bullet holes in the clothing of the President (Figure 46). Humes could only admit that the shirt and the jacket created the impression that the wound might perhaps have been a little lower than what was shown on the drawings (underling added):[483]

> Humes: They _give the appearance_ when viewed separately and not as a part of clothing of a clothed person as being _perhaps, somewhat_ lower on the Exhibits 393 and 394 than we have depicted them in Exhibit N° 385.

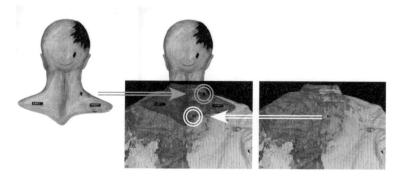

Figure 46 – Comparison between the back wound in the Rydberg drawing and the bullet hole in the shirt of the President.

The Commission was then presented with the tale of Kennedy's jacket riding up. The President's tailored suit had allegedly been pushed upwards during the drive in the car, and this explained why the bullet hole in the clothing no longer corresponded to the wound in the back. A jacket that had been pushed upwards would explain a difference of perhaps two centimeters, but a shift of almost 10 centimeters is rather a lot for a tailored presidential suit. Moreover, not only would the jacket have been pushed upwards, but also the shirt underneath the jacket. A shirt that shifts to the right at the level of the collar is a strange tale for anyone to accept, except for the Commissioners, who swallowed it, and who no longer placed the slightest obstacle in the way of Dr. Humes and the Rydberg drawings.

The second reconstruction

Arlen Specter had to sell his single-bullet theory to the doubting Commissioners during the second reconstruction that took place on May 24. During the reconstruction, a mark was made on the back of the JFK stand-in (Figure 47). Secret agent Kelley stated that the position of the back wound was based on the clothing and on the autopsy sketch.[484] These are two reasonably reliable sources. The mark was therefore chalked more or less in the correct position on the back of the stand-in. The position of the chalk mark proves that Specter, the man with the pointer on the photograph, was well aware of the fact that the location on the Rydberg drawing was eyewash, because he was wise enough not to use the drawing for his own investigation.

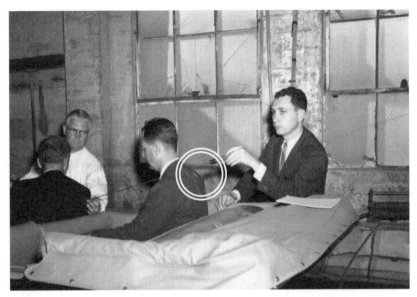

Figure 47 – Arlen Specter demonstrates the trajectory of the magic bullet during the second reconstruction.

The Warren Commission

The Warren Commission, on the other hand, deemed the Rydberg drawing suitable for public use, and also adjusted the text of its report to that
effect. The reason was clear: by raising the location of the back wound, the
conspiracy phantom could be kept at bay. The Commission had no intention of taking the hazardous path that could lead to any presumption of
a frontal shot. The reasoning was that a bullet being fired from the sixth
floor could only end up in the Adam's apple if the back wound was higher,
and therefore the wound *had* to be pictured higher than the actual location.
The fact that this was an intentional intellectual forgery on the part of the
Commission is clear from the manual corrections that were introduced to
the draft report by Commissioner Gerald Ford (Figure 48):

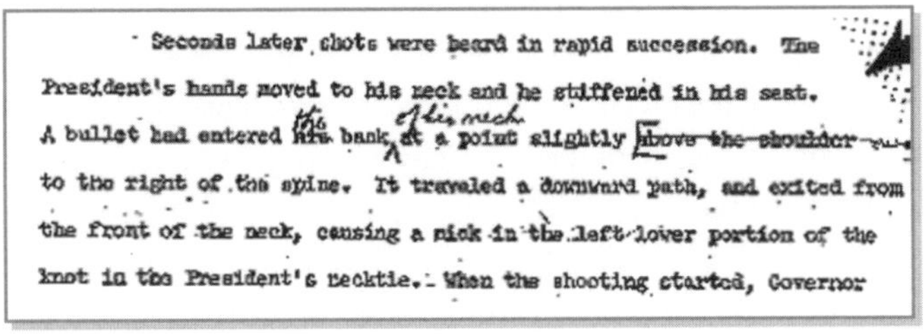

> Seconds later shots were heard in rapid succession. The
> President's hands moved to his neck and he stiffened in his seat.
> A bullet had entered the back at a point slightly above the shoulder
> to the right of the spine. It traveled a downward path, and exited from
> the front of the neck, causing a nick in the left lower portion of the
> knot in the President's necktie. When the shooting started, Governor

Figure 48 – Gerald Ford forged the final report of the Commission by changing 'back' to the 'back of his neck'.

Ford changed Kennedy's 'back' to 'back of his neck'. 'At a point slightly above the shoulder to the right of the spine' became 'At a point slightly above the shoulder to the right of the spine'. This is outright manipulation. Before Ford's editing, '*back*' meant 'back', and not 'back of the neck', while the word 'slightly' refers to 'above the shoulder' before the manipulation, and 'to the right of the spine' after his trick. The initial statement was correct and in agreement with the dossier. Ford's changes turned it into a lie. There were pages of corrections of this type. The word 'back' was taboo, and was systematically changed to 'back of the neck'.

The members of the Commission were not too worried about their credibility. Alan Dulles had already reassured them that nobody would read the report,[485] but a number of alert readers did apparently turn up. The Rydberg lie was so blatant that Specter's warning seemed to come true: the drawing threatened to affect the credibility of the entire report. To calm tempers, it seemed a good idea to appoint a commission of experts. Three years after the assassination, a forensic panel had to establish whether the photographs corresponded to the autopsy report and to the Rydberg drawing. The intention was obviously not to have a *critical* panel review the situation, and this was already clear from its composition: the choice fell on the three doctors who had signed the autopsy report, who had themselves instructed artist Rydberg, and who were the only doctors to have been interviewed regarding the autopsy by the Commission. These were the three experts who were now entitled to check themselves, and investigate whether or not they had blundered with regard to the task that was probably the most important job in their career.

The autopsy photos and x-rays

At the time the Warren Commission was in operation, Commissioner Rankin decided not to include the autopsy photographs as evidence for reasons of 'good taste'.[486] Under no circumstances were the members of the Warren Commission, the FBI[487] or even the doctors who had examined and carried out the autopsy on the naked president entitled to ever see the autopsy photos,[488] not even the x-rays. The autopsy doctors therefore only saw the autopsy photos for the first time on January 26, 1967,[489] in their capacity as members of the forensic panel. Humes transferred the report of this investigation, which took place in 1967, to the *Review Board* in 1996. On page two of the joint statement of the three doctors, we can read the following quote regarding the accuracy of the Rydberg drawing: 'Warren Commission Exhibits 385 and 386, which also depict the location of the neck wound, are accurate.'[490] The autopsy doctors persisted in their wrongdoing, and declared that the Rydberg drawing perfectly matched the autopsy photograph. The doctors were banking on the fact that the blatant lie would never be discovered, as they had undoubtedly been assured that the autopsy photographs would never be released. They were mistaken in this. The autopsy photographs have been disclosed and are available now. There is no doubt regarding the authenticity of the photos. The HSCA has thoroughly investigated this, and the photos certainly show Kennedy and have not been falsified.[491] We now know where Kennedy's back wound was really situated. The fear of sensational abuse of the photos proved totally unfounded. But the photographs did prove that the Rydberg drawing is manifestly incorrect.

Conclusions regarding Kennedy's back wound

The autopsy photograph of Kennedy's back wound (Figure 49) shows the hands of the doctors and a ruler with graduation marks of half a centimeter. [492] The ruler is only readable on the drawing the HSCA prepared.[493] We have indicated the location of the back wound according to the Rydberg drawing. The back wound on the photograph appears to be seven centimeters below the lower fold of the neck, but we cannot see the perspective in the photo. This distance of seven centimeters on the naked body should correspond to a distance of approximately ten centimeters in the case of tightly stretched clothing. This is evident from the autopsy photo with the side perspective (Figure 51 – see Chapter 25).

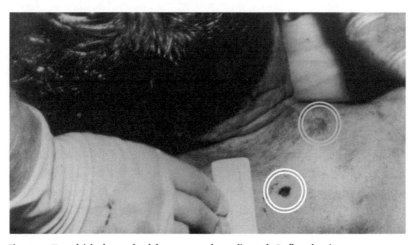

Figure 49 – Kennedy's back wound and the same wound according to the Rydberg drawing.

The bullet holes in the jacket and shirt are fifteen centimeters below the collar. The collar of a suit jacket is about three to five centimeters above the shoulder line. The wound should therefore be found at approximately ten to twelve centimeters below the shoulder line if the clothing is stretched tightly. The autopsy photo from the side perspective (Figure 51) shows that the wound was indeed situated about ten centimeters below the shoulder line, with tightly stretched clothing. This means that Kennedy's jacket and shirt could not have moved more than two centimeters upwards. If the wound was situated ten centimeters below the shoulder line, there is no reason whatsoever to call this location the 'neck' or the 'base of the neck'. All the semantic games in this context were inappropriate.

The Rydberg drawing is a blatant attempt at fraud. Not only is the wound drawn too high, but it is also placed too much to the right. This fraud is also intentional, which is clearly apparent from the conclusion of the forensic panel when the autopsy doctors finally had the opportunity to compare the drawing with the photos two years later. Instead of establishing that the Rydberg drawing was wrong, as any reasonable observer would have done, the doctors persisted in the lie. It follows that the Rydberg drawing was not a mistake caused by the fact that the photographs were not available in 1964, but was indeed intentional fraud. This did not prevent J. H. Stover, commanding officer of the US *Naval Medical School Bethesda*, from pulling out all the stops in a letter of thanks to Rydberg dated March 27, 1964, on the subject of his pictorial contribution to the history books:

> *This work was performed in an outstanding fashion, in a most expedient manner, and utilized for the most part off-duty hours. The illustrations thus produced most accurately depicted the situation required and immeasurably assisted the medical presentation.*

In mid-December, someone with a lot of power and influence was still assuming that the actual wound was situated too low for a passage wound going down into the throat. The Secret Service acted decisively to ensure that the autopsy report was modified in this area. From then onwards, there was no way back for the doctors, who were either accomplices or acting under marching orders. With the Rydberg drawing and their reaffirmation of the drawing in 1967, they continued on the disastrous path they had taken on November 23. Meanwhile, the Warren Commission had embarked on the same path, and therefore inevitably followed the autopsy doctors with regard to the back wound. The Commission was aware that what it was writing in its report was a lie. This is evident from the correct position of the back wound during the second reconstruction. The draft report of the Commission also described the correct location, until Gerald Ford deemed it necessary to make corrections, thereby brazenly falsifying history. We can learn a lot from all this. The persons who exerted heavy pressure on the doctors, and even the members of the Commission, did *not* themselves believe in the passage wound solution. Or, to say the least, they were not sufficiently sure to take the risk of thoroughly investigating the matter. If they had really believed in the passage wound, they would obviously not have situated the back wound higher, but would have looked for an explanation of the findings.

Who exerted pressure on the autopsy doctors on November 22? Who exerted pressure on the Parkland Hospital doctors on December 11? If there were 'men in suits' exerting pressure during the autopsy, these could only have been agents of the Secret Service. When the lost original of the autopsy report emerged, it turned out to have been in Rowley's drawer. The disappearance of the picture and sound material of Dr. Perry's press conference again pointed towards the Secret Service. It was agents of the Secret Service that took a hard line with the doctors in Parkland Hospital, and Kennedy's death certificate also fell under the responsibility of the Secret Service. It would therefore appear that it was above all the Secret Service that was involved in the manipulation of the autopsy data, the elimination to any allusion to a frontal throat wound and the destruction of the limousine as evidence. The Secret Service was under the direct command of President Johnson.

25. KENNEDY'S THROAT WOUND

The exit wound

A penetrating wound also needs an exit, of course. The location of this wound should be no problem: underneath the collar button of Kennedy's shirt. Doctor Carrico in Dallas described the wound as follows at 4:30 p.m. on Friday afternoon: 'one small penetrating wound at ant. neck in lower 1/3'.[494] In the final version of the autopsy report, we can read the following (underlining added):

> The wound <u>presumably of exit</u> was that described by Dr. Malcolm Perry of Dallas in the low anterior cervical region. When observed by Dr. Perry the wound measured 'a few millimeters in diameter', however it was extended as a tracheotomy incision and thus its character is distorted at the time of the autopsy.[495]

The autopsy doctors kept their options open in case the matter should still turn out differently. They only called the throat wound 'presumably of exit'. 'A few millimeters in diameter' also demonstrates selective interaction with the truth. On Saturday morning, Dr. Humes took some handwritten notes during his telephone conversation with Dr. Perry.[496] This shows that he knew exactly how large the throat wound was according to Dr. Perry (Figure 50): 'size 3 – 5 mm'. The reason why Humes did not include the dimensions reported by Perry in the autopsy report is that three to five millimeters is not large enough for an exit wound caused by a 6.5 mm bullet. Moreover, in this case the entrance wound, 7 by 4 mm, as already mentioned on page 3 of the autopsy report, would then be larger than the exit wound... That would cause raised eyebrows from anyone with any experience of bullet wounds. Humes therefore adapted the autopsy report to the desired report.

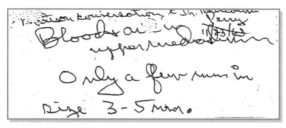

Figure 50 – Dr. Humes' notes of the telephone conversation with Dr. Perry.

But, despite all doubts, the passage wound seems on closer inspection to be the correct explanation for both wounds. During the autopsy, Kennedy's head was resting on a metal support, which resulted in the upper part of the spine being pushed upwards in a manner comparable to the position of a man sitting in a slightly bent-forward position (Figure 51). The bullet trajectory would have been horizontal if Kennedy had been sitting fully upright, but with a slight forward inclination, a descending trajectory is indeed possible. The manipulation of the back wound was therefore not only dishonest, but also not very smart. From a technical point of view, a downward trajectory from Kennedy's back to his Adam's apple was certainly possible.

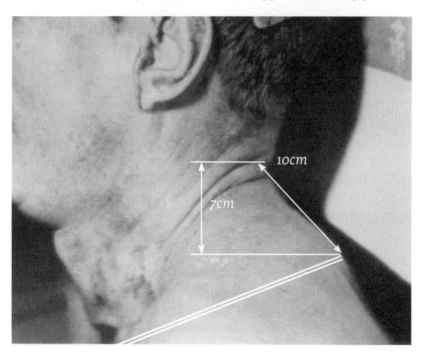

Figure 51 – From a point in the back fourteen centimeters below the mastoid process, or ten centimeters below the collar of tightly stretched clothing, a downward trajectory to the throat wound is possible if JFK was sitting in a slightly bent-forward position.

The tracheotomy

Surgeons normally perform a tracheotomy to save a patient's life. In the case of Kennedy, however, the result looked more like the work of a knife fighter in a dark alleyway than surgery (Figure 52). The incision in Kennedy's neck was 6.5 centimeters wide[497] according to the autopsy report. But this was also a half-lie. Dr. Humes, who had prepared and signed the autopsy report, himself mentioned seven to eight centimeters[498] in his testimony before the Commission: 'there was a recent surgical defect in the low anterior neck, which measured some 7 or 8 cm. in length.' That is three times the width of a normal tracheotomy. Nurse Diane Bowron removed the tracheal tube in Dallas,[499] but the Commission omitted to ask her about the original size of the incision. Neither Dr. Perry, who had made the incision, nor the other Parkland Hospital doctors were asked any questions on this subject.

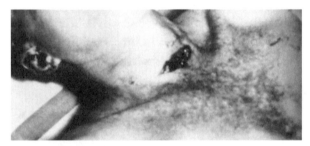

Figure 52 – A tracheotomy of 2 to 3.7 centimeters in Dallas had become seven to eight centimeters in Washington.

On November 11, 1966, Dr. Perry stated in an interview that the tracheotomy he had made measured two to three centimeters in length. Dr. Carrico stated the same size, and Dr. Baxter referred to *'roughly an inch and a half, or 3.7 centimeters.*[500] Dr. Crenshaw made the following statement regarding the difference between the wound in Dallas and on the autopsy photos:

> *The wound which I saw after Dr. Perry completed his work looked nothing like what I saw in the photographs taken at Bethesda. Dr Perry made a small and very neat transverse incision. I took it to be 1 to 1 1/2 inches in length. [...] When the body left Parkland there was no gaping, bloody defect in the front of the throat, just a small bullet hole and the thin line of Perry's incision.* [501]

In 1992, almost thirty years after the facts, the doctors drastically changed their opinion, and they suddenly could not remember anything abnormal about the tracheotomy. According to an article in the medical journal *JAMA* on May 27, 1992, the four Parkland Hospital doctors Perry, Jenkins, Baxter and Carrico declared that they had seen no difference between the autopsy photos and the tracheotomy incision in Dallas. This late denial in *JAMA* is certainly questionable, however. The *Journal of the American Medical Association* is strongly committed to the case of the believers, and even neglected its otherwise very strict quality standards in this context.[502] But the decisive argument justifying the doubts regarding the denial is that the tracheotomy on the autopsy photo looks anything but normal. Claiming the opposite would be equivalent to denying the light of the sun. Not a single surgeon would make an incision of seven to eight centimeters to insert a thin tube into the trachea. If any interventions had been made on Kennedy's body prior to the start of the autopsy, this would first and foremost have had to do with the throat wound, with a view to remove possible proof that this wound was, in fact, an entrance wound. Whether or not this is improbable, the tracheotomy wound on the autopsy photo in any case looks as if someone had been looking for a bullet in the wound with a finger.

Conclusion regarding the neck wound

If Kennedy had been sitting straight upright, the bullet trajectory would have been horizontal, perfectly parallel to the horizon. The HSCA analyzed this correctly. The trajectory through JFK says nothing about the angle at which the shots were fired. Everything depends on the angle at which Kennedy was bent forward (Figure 53). Dr. Braden explained to the HSCA that the bullet from Kennedy's back wound through to the throat wound could have followed a descending or an ascending trajectory, depending on the posture of the neck of the President. If the President leaned backwards, even an ascending trajectory was possible (Figure 53, on the right). We do not know exactly how Kennedy was sitting at the moment the magic bullet hit him, but a slightly hunched forward posture is not unlikely. According to the HSCA, the President was bending eleven to eighteen degrees forward. [503] To this, we should add three degrees for the slope of Elm Street. The lower back wound is therefore certainly possible. The only requirement is that Kennedy bends forward sufficiently. Whoever deemed the Rydberg maneuver necessary could have saved himself the trouble. The true location of the back wound presents no objection with regard to the passage wound option.

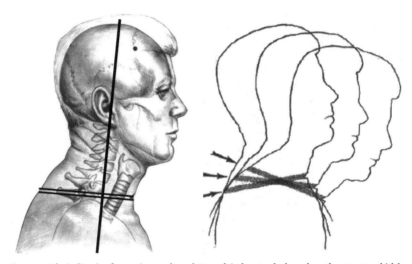

Figure 53 – The inclination for a trajectory through Kennedy's throat only depends on the extent to which he was bending forwards. [504 & 505]

26. KENNEDY'S HEAD WOUND

The Parkland Hospital doctors

On March 25, the Commission interviewed the Parkland Hospital doctors: the 28-year-old surgeon Dr. Carrico,[506] Dr. Perry,[507] obviously, and Drs. Clark[508] and McClelland. The four doctors declared unanimously that they had seen a large, gaping wound of five by seven centimeters at the back of Kennedy's head. The doctors also saw the damage to the cerebellum, situated below the brain. Dr. McClelland, who had closely examined the wound, phrased it as follows:

> *I was in such a position that I could very closely examine the head wound, and I noted that the right posterior portion of the skull had been extreme-ly blasted. [...] in such a way that you could actually look down into the skull cavity itself and see that probably a third or so, at least, of the brain tissue, posterior cerebral tissue and some of the cerebella tissue had been blasted out.*[509]

There are two disturbing elements in this statement: an exit wound is usu-ally larger than an entrance wound, and, the cerebellum, which is situat-ed at the lower part of the brain, was also damaged. Major damage to the posterior and the lower part of the head normally points towards a front-al shot. Two more professors were interviewed. Professor Dr. Baxter, the surgeon who headed the emergency department, stated: 'The right tem-poral and occipital bones were missing and the brain was lying on the ta-ble.' Professor Jenkins, the head of the anesthesia department of Parkland Hospital, confirmed this as follows:[510]

There was a great laceration on the right side of the head (temporal and occipital) [...] even to the extent that the cerebellum had protruded from the wound. I really think part of the cerebellum, as I recognized it, was herniated from the wound [...].

In brief, all Parkland Hospital doctors are unanimous that the wound was situated at the posterior part of the head and above the ear. We should therefore have no doubt that this was indeed the case. But conspiracists use the term 'occipital' in a sense that is too narrow. They depict the term 'occipital' as referring to a specific part of the skull that is situated in the lower posterior part of the head. This is not entirely correct. According to Dr. Grossman, a neurosurgeon at Parkland Hospital, doctors often use the term occipital for the posterior fifth of the head.[511] The assertion that the Parkland Hospital doctors really situated the head wound at the *base* of the posterior part of the skull is therefore incorrect.

The Bethesda Hospital doctors

The autopsy report[512], on the other hand, shifted the large defect of the skull too much to the front (underlining added):

There is a large irregular defect of the scalp and skull on the right involving chiefly the parietal bone but extending <u>somewhat into the temporal and occipital regions</u>. In this region there is an actual absence of scalp and bone producing a defect which measures approximately 13 cm. in greatest diameter.

The doctors in Dallas had situated the defect at the temple and the posterior portion of the skull, but, in Bethesda Hospital, the wound was situated 'somewhat' in this region. The gaping wound was mainly located at the parietal bone, i.e. to the side. For inexplicable reasons, the autopsy report also situated the entrance wound of the bullet ten centimeters too low. A comparison of the head wound in the Rydberg drawing (Figure 45) with the drawing of the HSCA (Figure 57) illustrates this incomprehensible discrepancy. The autopsy report did not mention the damage to the cerebellum, which had been seen by everyone in Parkland Hospital, nor did it mention the metal flake on the outside of Kennedy's skull. The President must also literally have had heavy worries in his head, because even with a gaping wound of one hundred square centimeters and the fact that part of his right brain was missing, his brain still weighed 1,500 grams according to the autopsy, the normal weight of a large and complete brain. The brain was also lost. Incredible as it may seem, nobody knows to this day where the President's brain went.

Rydberg also added in his two cents worth with regard to the location of the head wound. The entrance wound in the Rydberg drawing is much too low. The artist solved this problem by having Kennedy lean forward too far (Figure 54 – first illustration). Incredible though it may sound, the Warren Commission was about ten centimeters out with regard to the bullet wound in the back of Kennedy's head. Just look at the Rydberg drawing with Kennedy's head at the correct inclination (Figure 54 – third illustration) and imagine a bullet coming from a sixth floor entering at that spot. This bullet would have exited in the middle of the president's face. Which was not the case. The HSCA drawing had to place Kennedy's head wound 10 centimeters higher to obtain the desired exit with Kennedy's head at the right inclination.

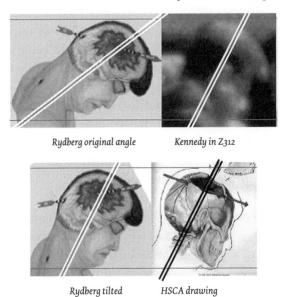

Rydberg original angle   Kennedy in Z312

Rydberg tilted   HSCA drawing

Figure 54 – With Kennedy's head in the correct angle just before the shot, the bullet trajectory is ascending.

Yet there are still believers who continue to defend the Bethesda autopsy. They do this against their own better judgment. The HSCA location is probably correct, although the scalp wound is not clearly visible in the autopsy picture. The corresponding drawing by Ida Dox in the HSCA Report (Figure 55) shows the supposed entrance wound more clearly.

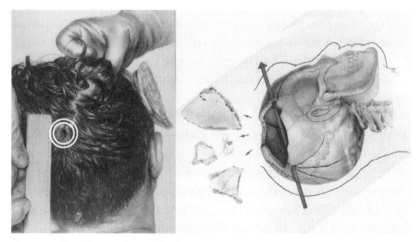

Figures 55 and 56 – The HSCA drawings by Ida Cox

In the conspiracy literature there is a lot to do about the absence in this picture of a gaping hole in the back of Kennedy's head. This gaping hole was mentioned by everyone who saw Kennedy lying on the gurney in Dallas, Parkland Hospital. It is an often cited mystery that can easily be solved: this picture shows the back of the head, the part of the head that was lying on the gurney in Dallas. If the deceased is lying on his back, as the Parkland doctors saw him (figure 56), the gaping wound above the right ear lies indeed 'at the back of the head'. But that does not change the fact that it is still above and not below or behind the ear.

Conclusion regarding the head wound

The Bethesda autopsy alone was responsible for the creation of a separate genre in the conspiracy literature. One can easily fill a large bookshelf with the ongoing discussion, but, in the end, the whole witch-hunt seems quite unnecessary. There seems to be a consensus that the drawing by Ida Dox (Figure 57) included in the HSCA report reflects the case reasonably correctly. In fact, the Commission could have saved itself all the tampering with the evidence. The reason that the exit wound is situated more to the posterior side of the skull than to the front has nothing to do with the direction of the shot. It is a logical consequence of the fact that the head was hit from the side. At time frame Z312, Kennedy was sitting with this part of his head directly in the line of fire from the sniper's nest.

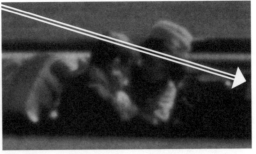

Figure 57 – Kennedy's head wound according to the HSCA investigation and situation in Z313

In Figures 55 and 56 we can see the mysterious metal flake located at the back of Kennedy's head, just above the hairline at the nape. It is therefore absolutely certain that the metal flake was there, and its size (6.5 mm) clearly indicates that it had something to do with the 6.5 mm bullets that hit the president. But what exactly? Bullets do not disintegrate before they hit, but afterwards.

There is another remarkable difference between the head wound that was established in Dallas and the head wound at Bethesda. On the autopsy table, Kennedy had a V-shaped incision (Figure 58 – on the right) at the level of the right temple. Nobody in Dallas had seen this wound. FBI agents Sibert and O'Neill reported[513] that 'surgery of the head area' had already taken place before the autopsy started. Maybe they were referring to the V-shaped incision, but they were never asked. Whatever the incision is, this surgery was in any case not carried out in Dallas, because there the emergency care providers only tried to resuscitate the president and keep his heart going. They did nothing to his head, and, even if they had done some surgery, it would obviously not have been to create an additional wound. Although the wound was certainly there when the body was laid out on the autopsy table at Bethesda, neither the autopsy report nor the Warren Commission ever mentioned a word about it.

But the V-incision seems to imply a link to the press conference held by Dr. Perry. During the press conference, Malcolm Kilduff (Figure 58 on the left), the press spokesman of the White House, stated that Kennedy had been hit in the forehead, and had pointed to his right temple when saying this. Similar to the tracheotomy that had been radically widened to conceal a possible entrance wound, the V-incision was also situated at a point where someone could have searched for possible proof of a frontal shot. No one knows what happened between Parkland and Bethesda, but it is a fact that the incision in the forehead was not noticed or made by anyone in Dallas, but was certainly there when Kennedy was laid on the autopsy table.

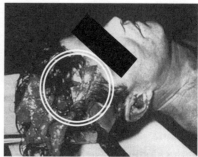

Figure 58 – In Parkland, Malcolm Kilduff points to the area where Kennedy was said to have been hit. On arrival at Bethesda, Kennedy's head showed an unexplainable V-shaped incision. The Commission does not say a word about this wound.

27. CONNALLY'S INJURIES

The Secret Service drawings

The wounds of Connally, who survived the attack, should never have really caused any problems. The Governor only had to take off his shirt, and the necessary observations could be made. In Volume XVII of the Hearings and Exhibits, we find the following drawings of his injuries[514] (Figure 59):

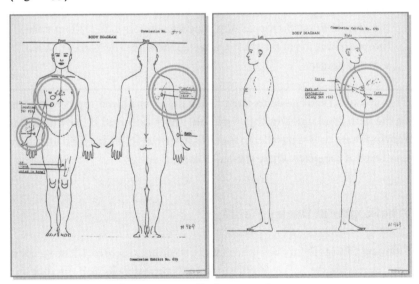

Figure 59– Drawing of Connally's injuries prepared by the Secret Service.

These drawings were not made by Dr. Shires, who was responsible for the care of the Governor. Dr. Shires said the following on this subject:

It was two individuals from the Secret Service [...] and they were given copies of our operative reports, statements [...], and then subsequently one of those same two men from Secret Service returned and charted the entrance and exit wounds which you have described previously, or we have looked at previously in these five diagrams.[515]

It appears that the Secret Service agents prepared the drawings. This should not be a problem, as long as they are correct. According to Dr. Shaw, the chief surgeon who treated Connally, the back wound was *'quite accurate'*,[516] but he could not agree with the chest wound and the shooting angle. He drew the location of the exit wound that was correct in his opinion above the inverted 'V' on the drawing, and added his initials R.R.S. The exit wound was now situated significantly higher, and the downward angle was much less steep. Dr. Shaw was also presented with CE680 (Figure 65 – on the right): the side view. The least he could say to this was the following:

I think the declination of this line is a little too sharply downward. I would place it about a 3rd off that line. [...] The reason I state this is that as they have shown this, it would place the wound of exit a little too far below the nipple. Also it would, since the bullet followed the line of declination of the 5th rib, it would make the ribs placed in a too slanting position.

This last observation seems useful. The bullet shattered ten centimeters of the fifth rib. Logically, this could only have occurred if the bullet was moving more or less parallel to the rib. Otherwise, the rib would only have shattered at the place where the bullet came through.

A helicopter at Dealey Plaza?

Drawing CE689 (Figure 60) is even more strikingly incorrect. The steepest line represents the Secret Service version. It almost looks as if the shot was fired from a helicopter. According to Dr. Shaw (R.R.S.), the Secret Service indicated the exit wound correctly in the chest, but the wound in the back had to be placed quite a bit further down. The wound in the thigh should also be moved significantly towards the knee in this drawing.

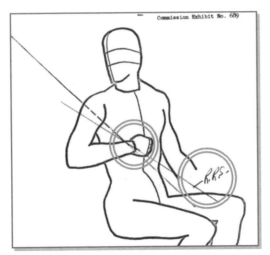

Figure 60 – Connally seems to have been shot from a helicopter according to the drawing of the Warren Commission.

It is clear that, there was not yet any mention of the magic bullet at the time the drawing was made. According to this drawing, Kennedy would have been sitting almost five feet higher than Connally if the magic bullet had ended up in Connally's armpit via Kennedy. The backseat was higher than the jump seat, but almost five feet is more than a little excessive. Drawing CE689 clearly fits the second scenario: one transit bullet for Kennedy, one separate bullet for Connally. In this scenario, Connally's bullet did not come through Kennedy's throat, but from the sixth floor. The Secret Service probably believed that the suitable declination could be a little steeper that what appeared from the wounds.

Dr. Gregory, who treated the Governor's wrist, was also presented with the artistic drawing of the Secret Service[517] and immediately pointed out another significant error. The wounds in the hand had been marked incorrectly. Where 'entrance' was marked, on the palm side of the hand, it should say 'exit', and vice versa. The bullet first hit the back of the hand, and then the palm.[516] The back of the right hand therefore had to be turned towards the chest. Connally's right hand should therefore situated in the vicinity of the exit wound in his chest at the time the magic bullet struck. It's not easy to turn your right hand with its back towards a point situated ten centimeters below the right nipple. The Secret Service's simple solution was to turn Connally's hand round, contrary to the medical file, to enhance the credibility of this position.

The white hat

Connally's hat was another problem. The Governor was holding his inseparable Stetson in his right hand. We know this because, at moment Z231 (Figure 61), he is still moving the immaculate hat above the side of the limousine, even though his wrist had allegedly already broken by the bullet that went through his hand. To the day of his death, Connally remained convinced that he had been hit by a separate bullet between Z231 and Z234. He did not believe in the hypothesis of a delayed response to the bullet, as he had clearly felt the impact of the bullet: 'as if someone doubled his fist and came up behind you and just with about a 12-inch blow hit you right in the back right below the shoulder blade.'[519]

Figure 61 – Kennedy has already been injured in Z230, but Connally is moving his hat, which doesn't seem to be spattered with blood, although his wrist and hand that should already be shattered at this point according to the single-bullet theory.

One argument in favor of the assumption that the Governor was only injured around frame Z230 is the fact that, according to the later findings of the doctors, Connally's hand at that moment (Figure 61) was more or less in the right position to be hit at that moment. More or less, because, from Zapruder's perspective, we can see the bottom of the hat. This means that the ball of the thumb was turned towards the exit wound, not the palm. But at time point Z224 (Figure 62), the last moment at which the magic bullet is possible, the hand was not even in the correct position. How could the bullet that exited Connally's chest ten centimeter below the nipple enter his right wrist when it was not there? Moreover, if the bullet continued from the wrist into his thigh, the hat would also have been damaged. The hat was never examined, and disappeared without a trace. There can only be one explanation for this: it was undamaged. If the hat had been covered in blood and damaged, it would certainly have been included in the evidence. It is only somewhat conceivable that nobody paid further attention to it if it was lying around somewhere intact. If Connally was holding his hat in his hand, with the palm of his hand towards his chest, according to the official doctrine, the magic bullet would first have to go through the hat before it could reach Connally's thigh. In this case, the bullet hole or holes in the hat would have been very important for the determination of the bullet's direction. The Warren Commission had no problem whatsoever with the disappearance of the hat. (Connally's clothes were never evidence in the case, they were returned to his wife, who decided to have them dry-cleaned before any examination took place).

Figure 62 – Zapruder frame Z224. Kennedy has already been hit, and his left arm is moving towards his throat with his fist clenched. Connally's hand is not where it should be.

In Z272 (Figure 63), three seconds after his hand and wrist were allegedly already badly injured, Connally is still holding his hat in his hand. There is no blood on the cuff of his shirt sleeve, and the same applies to his hat. Is it credible that Connally's wrist bone had already been shattered, and that the bullet had already moved straight through his hand and hat?

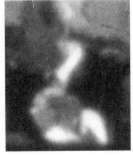

Figure 63 – Connally in Z272, three seconds after his hand and wrist were allegedly shattered; his cuff is still snow-white, and the hat in his hand is still immaculate.

At Z312 you can see Connally's cuff, still white, in the direct line of a bullet fragment exiting Kennedy's head.

The lapel flap

If Z223 is compared to Z224, it seems that Connally's suit jacket suddenly changes shape. In the literature, this is referred to as the *lapel flap*. Believers such as Dale Myers, who has based an impressive computer simulation on this aspect, sees the *lapel flap* being caused by a passing bullet. What is also visible in Z224 (Figure 62) is the approximate place of Connally's nipple. This is not where his hand is, and Kennedy has already brought up his left arm to his throat with his fist clenched. This is not a normal posture for a president during a parade. Kennedy could also not have moved his arm faster than sound. Therefore, if there was a magic bullet, it was fired before Z224. We do not know what makes Connally's lapel move in Z224, but, if it was a bullet, it was certainly not the magic bullet.

Conclusion regarding Connally's injuries

The pantomime with the injuries is one more blemish on the investigation. The picture that emerges from it is that the investigation couldn't care less about the truth. Whether or not Kennedy was assassinated by an international conspiracy of Cuban origin, or by the vindictive mafia, or by a coup d'état, no longer had the least importance. He was dead. Oswald had to be the sole perpetrator, at whatever cost. Anything that could create any doubt in this respect was *inconvenient truth*. There is no other explanation whatsoever for the continuous errors in the locations of the injuries. These errors are by no means random, because they all show a clear unity of purpose.

Fortunately, the HSCA did provide a reliable location of Connally's armpit injury (Figure 64) fifteen years later. With this we can make progress. We will address the problems with the timing, the hand and the hat later. According to this sketch, Connally's torso, including his arms, is approximately sixty centimeters wide, or 23.6 inch, the chest itself is about forty centimeters, or 15.8 inch, wide. According to the HSCA drawing, the bullet hit Connally very much to the right. The point where the bullet entered the body is actually situated in the armpit, 20 centimeters (7.9 inch) from the centerline of Connally's upper body.

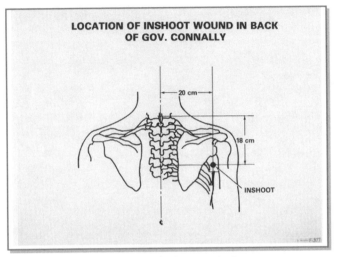

Figure 64 – Connally's armpit wound according to the HSCA investigation

PART 6

BALLISTIC INVESTIGATION

28. BREAKDOWN OF THE PROBLEM OF THE MAGIC BULLET

The single-bullet theory has become well-known in the meantime: the bullet went through Kennedy's back, left his body on the left below his Adam's apple and continued on to Connally, first hitting his right armpit and then his chest, wrist, hand and thigh, and then, by its own power, moved under the mattress of the gurney. It should be no surprise that the single-bullet theory is also one of the most controversial aspects of the investigation. There is so much that is incomprehensible in this case, but the conspiracists feel that this beats everything.

The most famous example of this criticism is contained in the closing argument of Jim Garrison, who was played by Kevin Costner in the *JFK* film by Oliver Stone. He demonstrates with a pointer how the bullet would have moved in the space between JFK and Connally. It's convincing at first glance, but is misleading on closer examination.

It does indeed sound suspicious that a bullet from an Adam's apple coming in a line from right to left could hit the person sitting in front in the right armpit. The presentation of the problem has become a classic. Images such as those in Figure 65 can be found everywhere on the Internet.

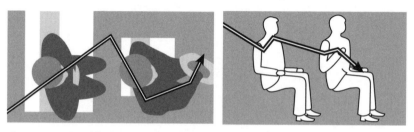

Figure 65 – Top view of the classic magic bullet drawing – Side view of the classic magic bullet drawing

A problem also arises in the vertical plane. Can a bullet from a back wound at the height of the shoulder blade reach the Adam's apple in a downward trajectory? The (im)possibility of the magic bullet is the central issue for every Kennedy researcher. In all fairness, it has to be said that it appears that the conspiracists have a point here. In any case, it's true that the believers have never really excelled in clearly proving that they are right in this area. There have indeed been numerous computer simulations, drawings and reconstructions. They are very interesting, but all contain conspicuous errors. How could we prove conclusively, once and for all, whether or not the magic bullet was possible?

It is impossible to clarify a three-dimensional problem in a two-dimensional picture, but this fact is not insurmountable. We just have to work in steps, and divide the three-dimensional problem into two two-dimensional sub-problems, in a horizontal and a vertical plane. We can then put the partial solutions together again. Every architect does this with a front view and a floor plan, and every construction worker knows what the architect intended and whether it is possible to realize the structure in three dimensions. The existing attempts to prove the (im)possibility of the magic bullet on paper make yet another important mistake. The distance from the sniper's nest to Kennedy's back wound was in the critical phase fifty two to fifty seven yards (47 to 52 *meters*). But, to produce the three injuries, the bullet would have had to cover another three feet (less than *one meter*) in the following phase. It is therefore necessary to work with a separate drawing for these two aspects and at a scale suitable for the drawing. A drawing at the scale of the Dealey Plaza is never accurate enough for the situation in the limousine. A drawing that is accurate enough to properly determine the position of the wounds would be much too large if you needed to include the sniper's nest as well.

Method

The magic bullet met insufficient obstruction to change its direction on its path through the back and neck of Kennedy.[520] Therefore the muzzle and all the injuries lay in a straight line. There are, in fact, four points in a straight line: Kennedy's back wound, Kennedy's throat wound and Connally's armpit wound in the limousine, and, outside the limousine, the rifle barrel in the sniper's nest. The limousine and the wounds were moving together.

Kennedy and Connally could have been sitting somewhat more to the left or to the right, and the location of their wounds may have been slightly higher or lower. This results in a bandwidth of possibilities. But the location of the wounds in the limousine does not change very much in the short period of time within which the magic bullet could have been fired. There are only 1.5 seconds between Zapruder *frames* Z196 and Z224. Outside the limousine, the 'shooting angle' from the sniper's nest certainly depends on the time of the shot. The limousine was moving, so there was a specific angle from the sniper's nest to Kennedy's back at every moment in time. We need to look at the four aspects (inside and outside the limousine, horizontal and vertical plane) separately, and then join them together again.

29. THE LANDING STRIP
OF THE MAGIC BULLET

We can best visualize the first aspect, the horizontal pane in the limousine, as a landing strip. The part outside the limousine, the trajectory of the bullet, is then the aircraft (Figure 66). The width of the landing strip is determined by the possible left or right variation of Kennedy's back wound and Connally's armpit wound.

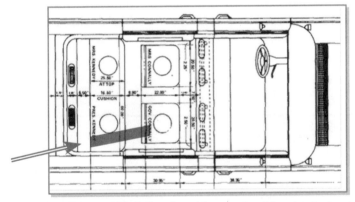

Figure 66– The landing strip within the limousine and the approach path from the sniper's nest

Three wounds

There are three relevant wounds for the magic bullet: Kennedy's back and throat wound and Connally's armpit wound. They must lie exactly in a straight line, as they were all caused by the same bullet. Everyone assumes that the problem lies in the line from Kennedy to Connally. The president and the governor were sitting one behind the other. The TSBD was on the right-hand side behind the limousine. How then could a bullet that hit Kennedy close to his backbone, and that moved from right to left, hit Connally in the right armpit? The first surprising finding of our study is that the problem does not lie there. Strangely enough, it is much harder to hit Kennedy in the back and in the center of this throat at the same time. Up to today, nobody has paid enough attention to this because the discussion is traditionally overshadowed by the second part of the trajectory from Kennedy to Connally. But this finding has very far-reaching consequences.

KENNEDY'S WOUNDS IN THE HORIZONTAL PLANE

According to the HSCA investigation, the wound in the president's neck was 0.1 inches (*0.25 centimeters*) to the left of JFK's center line (Figure 67). The back wound was located 1.8 inches (*4.5 centimeters*) to the right of the center line (Figure 68).[521] The autopsy photos confirm this. The HSCA also determined that the distance between the throat and the back wound, the trajectory that the bullet traveled through Kennedy, was five and a half inches (*fourteen centimeters*) long.[522] Kennedy's neck had a circumference of 15.5 inches (*39.4 centimeters*).[523] You can easily measure the distance that the bullet traveled through Kennedy, five and a half inches (*fourteen centimeters*) with a flexible piece of metal wire by pressing the ends against the shoulder blade and the Adam's apple of a man with a shirt size compared to Kennedy's. This test confirms the distance of five and a half inches (*fourteen centimeters*).

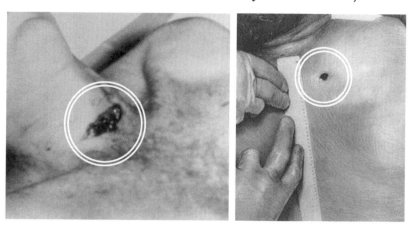

Figure 67 - Kennedy's throat wound, 0.1 inch (0.25 centimeters) to the left of his center line.
Figure 68 - The back wound, 1.8 inches (4.5 centimeters) to the right of the center line.

In a trajectory of only five and a half inches (*14 centimeters*), the bullet has to move 1.9 inches (1.8 + 0.1 inches) (*4.75 centimeters (4.5 + 0.25 centimeters)*) to the left. That's a lot. The bullet has to go through Kennedy at an angle of twenty degrees to his shoulder line. There is a zero tolerance for this condition: only an angle of twenty degrees can achieve sufficient deflection to the left.[524] The limousine drove up Elm Street in the direction of the passage under the railway. The rear of the automobile was thereby almost directly facing the TSBD. If someone was aiming at Kennedy's back from the sniper's nest, the angle at which Kennedy was hit was much smaller than twenty degrees. Starting from Kennedy's back wound, a bullet at a smaller angle with regard to Kennedy's shoulder line would cause an exit wound to the right, and not to the left of the Adam's apple. But there is yet another variable. What if Kennedy was not sitting up against the back of the rear seat, but was turned to the right, towards the public? A smaller shooting angle to the limousine would then be sufficient to hit Kennedy's back and throat at the determined locations (Figure 69). In fact, the sum of the angle at which the bullet cut the limousine and the angle by which Kennedy sat turned towards the public in the limousine is exactly and in any case twenty degrees. Then, and only then, could the bullet have moved from 1.8 inches (*4.5 centimeters*) to the right of Kennedy's backbone to 0.1 inches (*0.25 centimeters*) left of his Adam's apple.

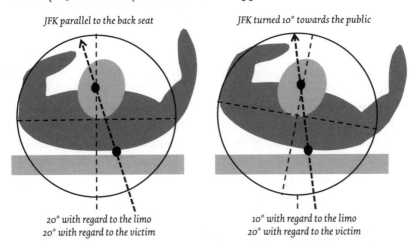

JFK parallel to the back seat   JFK turned 10° towards the public

20° with regard to the limo   10° with regard to the limo
20° with regard to the victim   20° with regard to the victim

Figure 69 – *If Kennedy sat with his back against the rear seat, the bullet would have had to come from 20 degrees to the right of the limousine in order to hit Kennedy in the back 1.8 inches (4.5 centimeters) to the right of the center line and 0.1 inches (0.25 centimeters) to the left of the center line. If Kennedy sat turned 10 degrees towards the public, an angle of only 10 degrees is required.*

The question of how far Kennedy was turned to the audience is therefore important. There are a lot of photos of the passage of Kennedy through Dallas, and the findings are relatively consistent. We are, of course, above all interested in photos immediately before the crucial moment. Less than

3.5 seconds before the back-shot, Earl Croft took a photo on which we can clearly see whether Kennedy sat turned towards the public (Figure 70). Here, Kennedy's shoulder is almost parallel with the back seat.

Figure 70 – The Croft photo just before the magic bullet. Kennedy is sitting parallel, with his back against the rear seat.

There is also a typical story attached to this picture. Earl Croft was a 20-year-old missionary from the Church of the Latter Day Saints based in Salt Lake City. He was only passing through Dallas purely by chance. He took four photos in Dealey Plaza, of which Figure 70 was the third. He then took a fourth photo, according to him simultaneously with the shot that killed the president. Croft was alone in Dallas, knew nobody and left the city shortly after the assassination without talking to anyone. A few blocks further, in the *Union Railway Station*, he took the train to Denver, Colorado. He left the square at the moment the limousine disappeared under the tunnel and jogged to the station in order to just catch his train. He could not recall having spoken to anyone in Dallas. He had certainly not contacted the FBI. Croft stayed in Denver at a place that was not his official address. Nevertheless, at 10 a.m. the next morning, two FBI agents stood at his door and subjected him to a difficult and exhausting interrogation. The agents took the undeveloped film with them. The FBI claimed afterwards that the fourth photo, the crucial photo taken at the moment of the fatal shot, unfortunately did not come out properly during the development. Never once does the name Croft appear in the whole range of Warren volumes. The photo in Figure 70 is also mentioned nowhere.[525] Croft still does not know today – and it doesn't appear anywhere in the file – how the FBI managed to locate him so quickly. The HSCA only followed up on the photo fifteen years later. Contrary to the Warren commission's opinion they saw great importance in it.

Kennedy barely changed his sitting position in the few seconds after this photo was taken.[526] The Croft photo therefore helps the investigation to find an answer to the question as to whether Kennedy was turned to the right at the moment the shot hit his back. There are good reasons to believe this. The president had not come to Dallas to stare at Connally's back immediately in front of him. The public had shown up en masse to see the Kennedy's, and they had the right to get what they had come for. Kennedy himself certainly deliberately looked at the bystanders on his side of the car. This would entail a slight inclination to the right. Finally, we can also look at the analysis made by NASA engineer Thomas Canning. Canning was a *cum laude* graduate aeronautics expert and holder of a *NASA Medal for Exceptional Scientific Achievement*. The HSCA commissioned him with the investigation into the trajectory of the bullet. Canning was clearly a man who knew what he was talking about. He investigated the issue thoroughly and scientifically, and confirmed that Kennedy was sitting upright, or at the most *slightly* turned to the right:[527] 'The angular position of his torso was very slightly to the right or forward, perhaps straightforward.' Kennedy was certainly not seated more than ten degrees turned to the right with respect to the backrest of the rear seat. An angle of ten degrees from the backrest of the rear seat (Figure 69 – right) is a slight inclination to the right and is consistent with many photos of the parade. A slightly smaller rotation is also possible. In principal, all angles between six and ten degrees are therefore possible for Kennedy's rotation in the direction of the public. In order to hit Kennedy at an angle of exactly twenty degrees, only those bullets can be considered that cut the limousine at an angle of ten to fourteen degrees. Only then does the sum of the rotation of JFK and the shooting angle come to twenty degrees, so that a bullet can hit Kennedy in the two wounds that have been documented.

POSITION OF THE PASSENGERS

After passing through Kennedy, the magic bullet has to move right to Connally's armpit. In order to calculate the angle of the connecting line with respect to the limousine, we need to know the positions of Kennedy and Connally. They are well documented. There are hundreds of photos of the motorcade. Kennedy sat very close to the right side of the limousine the whole time. Connally sat against the backrest of the jump seat.

Kennedy had his right arm on the edge of the limousine most of the time. He had good reasons for this. As a true politician, he knew that every inch that he was closer to the people was important. Kennedy also realized how important it was to adopt a natural posture. We also should not forget that Kennedy was also strapped into a corset to support his painful back (Figure 71). As someone suffering from a bad back, Kennedy more than likely also looked for support for his elbow during the long period of waving.

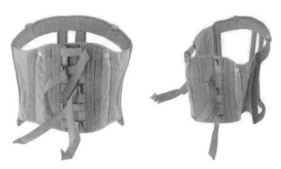

Figure 71 - Kennedy's corset prevented him from falling to the side after the shot.

There is another important constant in the photos of the parade. On all the photos, Kennedy and Connally each remain on their own side of an imaginary diagonal in the limousine. Connally's shoulder is to the left of this line, and Kennedy's shoulder to the right. That did not change during the entire ride. The photo that spectator Davis took (Figure 72), is a classic in the genre.

Figure 72 - The imaginary diagonal from the handle of the side window.

The photo that Dave Powers took from the Secret Service car following Kennedy's car (Figure 73), shows from a unique perspective how Kennedy sat behind Connally (ruler and perspective lines added).

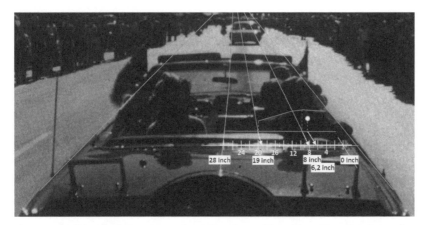

Figure 73 – The photo taken by Dave Powers gives the best picture of the positions of Kennedy and Connally, one behind the other.

POSITION OF KENNEDY AND CONNALLY IN THE LIMOUSINE

Based on this analysis, we have a pretty good idea of where Kennedy and Connally were sitting at the moment of the magic shot. They could have been sitting a little more or less to the left or right compared to the positions in Figure 73. As Kennedy sat somewhat more to the left and Connally reasonably to the right, we obtain the smallest possible angle that a connecting line between the wounds can form with respect to the limousine (Figure 74). The angle is only 3.1 degrees.[528] If Kennedy sat on the far left and Connally more towards the center, we obtain the greatest possible angle with respect to the limousine (Figure 75). The angle is then 14.3 degrees.[529] A bullet can hit both Kennedy's back and Connally's armpit in an angle with respect to the limousine that can vary from 3.1 to 14.3 degrees.

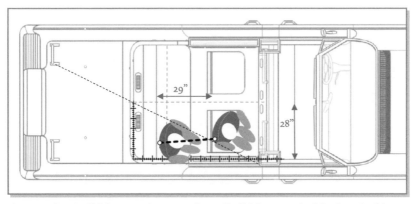

Figure 74 – If JFK sits slightly more to the center and Connally slightly more to the right, the angle of the magic bullet with respect to the limousine is 3.1 degrees.

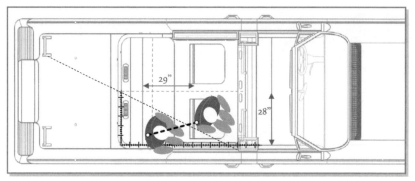

Figure 75 – IF JFK sits to the extreme right and Connally more towards the center, the angle of the magic bullet with respect to the limousine is 14.3 degrees.

The ten to fourteen degrees limitation in order to pass through Kennedy's back and throat is thereby a strict requirement in both directions. A bullet that can hit Kennedy's back and throat can also *always* reach Connally's armpit. For every bullet that cuts the line of the limousine at an angle of between ten and fourteen degrees, the three wounds can be aligned in a single line in the horizontal plane. This is an important conclusion. It means that a magic bullet is only possible if the line of the limousine is cut at an angle that lies between ten and fourteen degrees with respect to the axis of the car. As an initial test, we can now extrapolate the angle between ten and fourteen degrees backwards, to a point where Kennedy is approximately halfway on his passage behind the road sign. This gives a first impression of the feasibility of the magic bullet (Figure 76). We come very close to the sniper's nest, but just a little too far to the left. As the car continues driving, its rear turns even more to the left, away from the sniper's nest. This seems to indicate that there is a time before Z212 at which the magic bullet is possible in the horizontal plane.

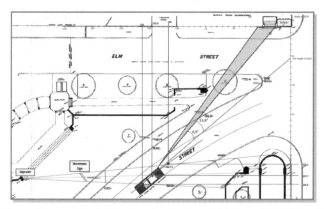

Figure 76 – First rough extrapolation backwards at time Z212. A magic bullet must be fired before this moment.

30. THE FLIGHT PATH

In the next phase, we move to the investigation using the Dealey Plaza scale. Our landing strip allows the three intermediate stations (Kennedy's back, Kennedy's throat and Connally's armpit) to be met with a flight path between ten and fourteen degrees. In which Zapruder frames does the angle of the shot from the sniper's nest to Kennedy's back lie within the limits? In the crucial period when, from Zapruder's position, Kennedy was behind the Stemmons road sign. But we can still see a part of Kennedy's head above the road sign for a slightly longer time. This allows the road sign to be used as a reference point to determine Kennedy's position on the map of the Plaza at each point in time (Figure 77).

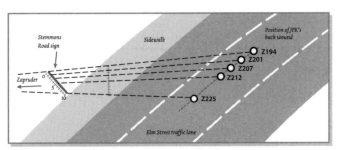

Figure 77 – The position of Kennedy's head measured on the basis of the position with respect to the road sign in the relevant frames of the Zapruder film

We know the coordinates on our map for each of these points, and for the sniper's nest (Figure 78). Using basic trigonometry, the angle of the sniper's nest with regard to Kennedy's back wound can then be determined for each Zapruder time frame. The coordinates (Column a and b-c in table Figure 85) are, in fact, the sides of a right-angle triangle. The hypotenuse is calculated as the square root of the sum of the squares of the other two sides (Column d in table Figure 85). This hypotenuse is the length of the shot to reach Kennedy. By dividing the hypotenuse by the horizontal side, you obtain the cosine, which can then be converted into the angle from the sniper's nest to Kennedy's back wound (Column e in table Figure 85).[530]

Angle of the limousine with regard to the sniper

It is not the angle with regard to the façade of the TSBD that is important for the investigation of the possibility of the magic bullet here, but the angle with regard to the axis of the limousine. So we must also consider the orientation of the limousine. The limousine gradually turned to the left in the direction of the tunnel, and thereby turned its back towards the sniper. You can calculate the angle on the basis of the coordinates of the limousine at time Z196 and Z225, and this can be checked on the basis of the extrapolation of the edge of the limousine on the Y-axis (Column f in table Figure 85). At Z196, the limousine has an inclination of 35.39 degrees with regard to the TSDB.[531] At Z225, the limousine has an inclination of 41.42 degrees with regard to the TSDB.[532] The rotation is evenly distributed over the Zapruder frames in between.

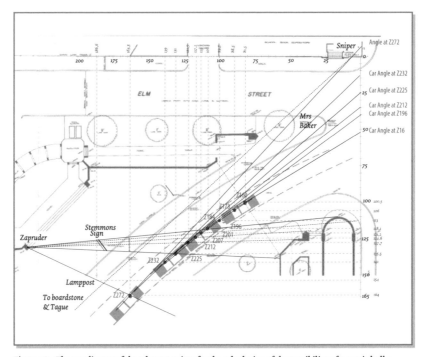

Figure 78 – The coordinates of the relevant points for the calculation of the possibility of a magic bullet.

The angle of the shot with respect to the limousine

It is now possible to calculate the angle of a shot from the TSBD against the axis of the limousine by deducting the two angles from each other (the angle of the shot with respect to the façade of the TSBD and the angle of the direction of travel of the car with respect to the façade). From the table (Figure 79), it appears that a shot that intersects the limousine between ten and fourteen degrees is possible in the short period between Z197 and Z211. In the horizontal plane, a single bullet could cause the three wounds in this short period of 0.76 seconds of time, because one Zapruder frame corresponds to 1/18.3 seconds.

	Zapruder-frame	Perpen-dicular distance to Elm Street.	Perp. distance to Houston Street.	Distance from weap-on to TSBD corner	Distance from weap-on to back wound	Angle of shot wrt TSBD façade	Angle of limo wrt Elm axis	Angle of shot wrt limo
	Z	a	b	c	d *	e **	f	g = e-f
1	196	118,10	108,00	-7,50	155,07	49,60	35,39	14,21
2	197	118,72	109,00	-7,50	156,19	49,47	35,60	13,87
3	198	119,34	110,00	-7,50	157,32	49,34	35,81	13,54
4	199	119,96	111,00	-7,50	158,44	49,21	36,01	13,20
5	200	120,58	112,00	-7,50	159,56	49,09	36,22	12,86
6	201	121,20	113,00	-7,50	160,69	48,96	36,43	12,53
7	202	121,77	113,70	-7,50	161,57	48,91	36,64	12,27
8	203	122,33	114,40	-7,50	162,46	48,85	36,85	12,01
9	204	122,90	115,10	-7,50	163,35	48,80	37,05	11,74
10	205	123,47	115,80	-7,50	164,23	48,74	37,26	11,48
11	206	124,03	116,50	-7,50	165,12	48,69	37,47	11,22
12	207	124,60	117,20	-7,50	166,01	48,64	37,68	10,96
13	208	125,22	118,06	-7,50	167,04	48,56	37,89	10,67
14	209	125,84	118,92	-7,50	168,08	48,48	38,09	10,38
15	210	126,46	119,78	-7,50	169,11	48,40	38,30	10,10
16	211	127,08	120,64	-7,50	170,15	48,32	38,51	9,81
17	212	127,70	121,50	-7,50	171,18	48,24	38,72	9,53
18	213	127,87	121,77	-7,50	171,48	48,21	38,93	9,29
19	214	128,03	122,03	-7,50	171,79	48,19	39,13	9,05
20	215	128,20	122,30	-7,50	172,09	48,16	39,34	8,81
21	216	128,37	122,57	-7,50	172,39	48,13	39,55	8,58
22	217	128,53	122,83	-7,50	172,69	48,10	39,76	8,34
23	218	128,70	123,10	-7,50	172,99	48,07	39,97	8,10
24	219	129,67	124,23	-7,50	174,47	48,01	40,18	7,83
25	220	130,64	125,36	-7,50	175,95	47,95	40,38	7,56
26	221	131,61	126,49	-7,50	177,43	47,88	40,59	7,29
27	222	132,59	127,61	-7,50	178,90	47,83	40,80	7,03
28	223	133,56	128,74	-7,50	180,38	47,77	41,01	6,76
29	224	134,53	129,87	-7,50	181,86	47,71	41,22	6,49
30	225	135,50	131,00	-7,50	183,34	47,65	41,42	6,23

* $d = SQRT(a^2+(b-c)^2)$ ** $e = degrees(ACOS(a/d))$

Figure 79 - The calculation of the angle of the shot (through the three wounds) with respect to the limousine for each Zapruder frame.

For each of these possible points in time, Kennedy must have a specific inclination to the right. If Kennedy sat turned six degrees to the right, a magic bullet could take place at time point Z197; if Kennedy sat turned through ten degrees, only a shot in Z211 could cause the three injuries. This is an easy test to check the reliability of magic bullet drawings. If a researcher claims Kennedy is hit at Z224, and his drawing does not show a Kennedy-figure in the limousine turned 13,5° degrees to the right, the whole argument is proven incorrect.

Conclusions regarding the horizontal plane

On the basis of the positions of the victims in the car, the angle of the limousine with respect to the sniper's nest and the working hypothesis that Kennedy sat turned to the right between six and ten degrees, a magic bullet is possible for the times between Z197 and Z211. A bullet that wounded Kennedy in the back and to the left of the Adam's apple would also certainly have hit Connally in its further trajectory.

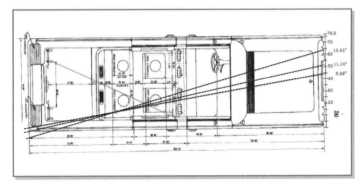

Figure 80 – Three theoretically possible magic bullets in the horizontal plane. Z211 is the most likely moment.

31. THE DOWNWARD LANDING TUNNEL

We know that a magic bullet is possible in the horizontal plane in the 0.76 seconds between Z197 and Z211. We can now look at the situation again, but in a side view this time. Can a bullet that descends from the sniper's nest in the corresponding time period (Z197-Z211) cause the three wounds?

The first question once again concerns the situation in the limousine. Can the three wounds lie in a downward straight line inside the car? The next question (in the Dealey Plaza scale) is then, of course, whether that line can be extrapolated backwards to arrive at the exact height of the sniper's nest. We require two elements in order to investigate the first question: the height dimensions of the limousine and the vertical location of Kennedy's back wound and Connally's armpit wound. The throat wound is a special case, because its vertical location is very dependent on the extent to which Kennedy was bending forward (see Figure 53). On the basis of the analysis of the Croft photo and the sharpest Zapruder frames, HSCA expert Canning stated the following: 'I concluded that he was hunched forward somewhere between 11 and 18 degrees forward of vertical, in the upper torso.' Moreover, in view of the fact that Elm Street slopes 3 degrees downhill, all shots between 14 and 21 degrees could have traveled from Kennedy's back to his throat. While the throat wound was so spectacularly important for the horizontal plane, it hardly plays a role here. That is a very surprising conclusion, because the conspiracists – and with them the Warren Commission, the Secret Service and the autopsy doctors in the early stage – considered this transit particularly insurmountable. The Secret Service and the autopsy doctors even went through all the fuss of moving the back wound up in order to mask their own disbelief about the descending trajectory from Kennedy's back wound to the throat. But reaching the throat wound on a downward path from the shoulder blade does not present any problem at all in the vertical plane. As a consequence, the descending trajectory in the limousine only depends on two relatively easily measurable points, one in the back of each victim.

The height dimensions of the limousine

A floor plan of the limousine can be found in both the annexes of the Warren Commission and those of the HSCA, but a diagram of the side view of the limousine is nowhere to be found. Although it seems obvious, nobody seems to have had the idea to also record the height dimensions of the limousine. The one page from the report of the Warren Commission devoted to the limousine makes us none the wiser. The top of Kennedy's head would have been located at 52.78 inches (1.34 meters) above the level of the road. The Commission even took the tire pressure of the limousine into account here. In the whole file, you will only find a side view of the limousine on three under-exposed black-and-white photos that the FBI took on Saturday morning, November 23, and a number of color photos that the Secret Service took on Saturday afternoon.[533] Besides the 1963 dossier, there is very little information to be found about the height of the X-100 in general. According to the Ford Motor Company the height of the limousine was 1.55 meters (61 inches).[534] In the entire Internet, only one rudimentary side view can be found, to which we have ourselves added a ruler in the height and at the base (Figure 81).

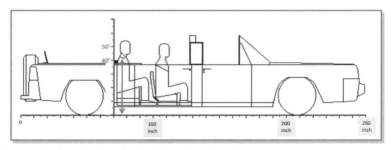

Figure 81 – Side view of the limousine (with ruler added in both dimensions).

On the basis of a detailed analysis of the FBI photos of November 23, 1963, we calculated the following height dimensions:
- Base of the vehicle   9 inches
- **Seat height of jump seat**   **17 inches**
- **Seat height of back of rear seat**   **21 inches**

- Seat height of front of rear seat   24 inches
- Top edge of jump seat   36 inches
- Top edge of door Connally   40 inches
- Top edge of limousine Kennedy   42 inches
- Top edge of rear seat   44 inches

Only the heights of the two seats and of the sloping seat cushion on the rear seat where Kennedy was sitting are actually important for our investigation. The height difference is limited to four inches (21-17) or 10.16 centimeters in our measurement, and to three inches or 7.62 centimeters according to Secret Agent Inspector Kelley,[535] but he did not state where the height difference was measured at the front or back of the cushion. Both seat cushions were sloping to the rear, but the jump seat to a much lesser extent than the rear seat. It is therefore important where Kelley measured the height difference.

The importance of the strongly rearward sloping rear seat is not to be underestimated. Believers rightly point to the significant height difference between the jump seat and the rear seat, but the seat cushion on the rear seat also slopes back by 3.94 inches (ten centimeters). Kennedy's back starts at the lowest point. This already accounts for half of the difference. Of course, from a three dimensional view, Kennedy did not sit completely at the very lowest part of the cushion. But it is his coccyx, the point where his spine starts, that will determine the additional height with regard to the limousine. It is also not impossible that the thick cushion on the rear seat gave way much more under his weight than the rather thin cushion of the jump seat. In the end, we have a 3.5 inch or 9 centimeter height difference between the seats of Connally on the jump seat and Kennedy on the rear seat. Given the lack of an adequate investigation at the time that this was still possible, a reasonable estimate is the best alternative.

The height difference between the wounds

With this difference between the seats, we must now add the difference between the heights of the injuries. If we put the top of the shoulder blades of Kennedy and Connally at the same level (Figure 82), there is a height difference between the back wounds of 11.5 centimeters. Connally is approximately five centimeters smaller than Kennedy.[536] If half of this difference is in the length of the legs and half in the trunk, Connally's armpit would therefore be possibly 2.5 centimeters lower. There is therefore a height difference between the back wounds of Kennedy and Connally of approximately 11.5 to 14 centimeters. Connally sat nine centimeters lower than Kennedy on the jump seat. Connally's armpit wound lay physically 11.5 to 14 centimeters lower than Kennedy's back wound. The back of Kennedy was about 69 centimeters from Connally's back. In order to drop a distance of between 20.5 centimeters (9 +11.5 centimeters) to 23 centimeters (9 +14 centimeters) over a distance of 69 centimeters, the downward angle must be between 16.5 and 18.4 degrees.[537]

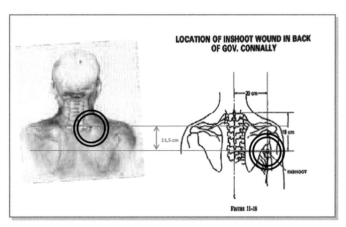

Figure 82 – The height difference between the back wound of Kennedy and the armpit wound of Connally

We can also calculate the height difference in another way by considering the upper edge of the seats. The height difference between the upper edge of the jump seat and that of the rear seat was 8 inches or 20.32 centimeters. If Kennedy's back wound and Connally's armpit wound were situated at the same height above the edge of their respective seat backs, the difference in height is 8 inches. Somewhat more upward variation is now possible, as opposed to downward variation. This results in an estimate of the height difference between the wounds between 7.5 inches (19 centimeters) and 9 inches (23 centimeters), or a downward angle between 15.4[538] and 18.4 degrees.

Conclusion regarding the downward angle in the limousine

If the estimated height difference between Kennedy's back and throat wound is about 7.5 to 9 inches, the downward angle of the shot at the limousine varies between 15.4 and 18.4 degrees.

32. THE DOWNWARD ANGLE OF THE SHOT

After the investigation of the horizontal plane of the limousine with the Dealey Plaza scale and the investigation of the vertical plane of the limousine, the next question is if and when the angle of the downward line that connects the three wounds agrees with the shooting angle from the sniper's nest. That is now the final question. The magic bullet was theoretically possible in the horizontal plane in the time frame from Z197 to Z211. We must now consider whether the downward shooting angle in this period was between 15.4 and 18.4 degrees. If so, it is then mathematically proven that the magic bullet was possible. In order to calculate the shooting angle, we need to know the difference in level between Kennedy's back wound and the weapon. We therefore need certain information:

1. The height of the window sill at the sniper's nest;
2. The height of the rifle above the window sill;
3. The difference in height between the sidewalk at the TSBD and the position of JFK for each of the points from Z196 to Z225;
4. The height of Kennedy's wound above street level.

The window sill of the sixth floor of the TSBD is at 60.4 feet (18.41 meters) above street level. According to the Commission, the distance between the weapon and the window sill was approximately 0.8 feet or 24 centimeters.[539] CE1310[540] (Figure 83) shows that the barrel of the rifle was 1.8 feet (55 centimeters) above the floor level at the time of the measurement and that the window sill had a height of 1.1 feet (33 centimeters) (Figure 84). The weapon was therefore 0.7 feet (21.3 centimeters) above the window sill.

Figure 83 - The very low window sill of the sniper's nest.   *Figure 84 - The measurement stick in inches.*

Kennedy's armpit rested on the side of the limousine at a height of 42 inches (1.11 meters) above the ground. The difference in height between the wound and the armpit is 4.5 inches (11.43 centimeters). Together, that makes 46.5 inches or 1.18 meters above Elm Street. Elm Street slopes significantly downwards. *Commission Exhibit 882,*[541] the ground plan of Dealey Plaza that was prepared on May 31, 1964, contains a table that shows the height of the limousine above sea level at different times (Figure 85). According to this plan, the height of the window sill of the sniper's nest was 490.9 feet (149.63 meters) above sea level. The descent is not equally steep at all points of Elm Street. On the topographical chart, the height from the street level is given as 50 feet (15.24 meters). We are particularly interested in the situation between Z197 and Z221. From Z186 to Z207, Elm Street slopes down by 2.90 degrees,[542] and by 3.46 degrees from Z207 to Z225.[543] On the basis of this information, you can draw up a table for the downward angle to Kennedy's back wound per Z-frame.

FRAME NO.	STATION NO.	ELEV.	RIFLE IN WINDOW		TOP BRIDGE HANDRAIL	
			ANGLE TO HORIZON R=K-H	LINE OF SIGHT DIST. K=R	ANGLE TO HORIZON B=K-H	LINE OF SIGHT DIST. K=B
A		431.97	40°10'	91.6	-0°27'	447.0
161	3+29.2	429.25	26°58'	137.4	-0°07'	392.4
166	3+30.1	429.20	26°52'	138.2	-0°07'	391.5
185	3+49.3	428.13	24°14'	154.9	+0°03'	372.5
186	3+50.8	428.05	24°03'	156.3	+0°03'	371.7
207	3+71.1	427.02	21°50'	174.3	+0°12'	350.9
210	3+73.4	426.80	21°34'	176.5	+0°22'	348.8
222	3+85.9	426.11	20°23'	188.6	+0°24'	336.4
225	3+88.3	425.98	20°11'	190.8	+0°26'	334.0
231	3+93.5	425.69	19°47'	196.0	+0°28'	329.0
235	3+96.8	425.52	19°26'	199.0	+0°30'	326.8
240	4+02.3	425.21	19°01'	204.3	+0°34'	320.4
249	4+10.0	424.79	18°32'	211.9	+0°40'	313.1
255	4+16.4	424.46	18°03'	218.0	+0°44'	307.1
313	4+65.3	421.75	15°21'	265.3	+1°28'	260.6

COMMISSION EXHIBIT 884

Figure 85 - The table for map CE882 with the elevation of Elm Street per Z-frame.

Landing in the tunnel

In Figure 86, we calculated the downward shooting angle for the period between Z196 and Z225. From 207, the descending angle is below 18.3 degrees. That remains the case until Z211, the last time point at which the magic bullet is possible in the horizontal plane. The downward angle at this point in time is still 17.36 degrees. If you also take into account a gradient of 3.46 degrees in Elm Street, you can calculate that Kennedy was bent forward by approximately fourteen degrees.

	Zapruder frame	Distance base TSBD to wound	Height difference muzzle/ wound in feet	Muzzle above window sill	Window sill level 6th floor	Street level Elm Street	Height wound above ground	Distance in feet Muzzle to wound	Cosine	Downward angle shot to horizon	Decline Elm Street	Angle in respect to limo
	Zap	a	b*	c	d	e	f	g**	h***	i	j	k****
1	196	155,07	63,73	0,70	161,10	94,20	3,88	167,66	0,9249	22,34	2,9	19,44
2	197	156,19	63,79	0,70	161,10	94,13	3,88	168,72	0,9257	22,22	2,9	19,32
3	198	157,32	63,86	0,70	161,10	94,07	3,88	169,78	0,9265	22,09	2,9	19,19
4	199	158,44	63,92	0,70	161,10	94,00	3,88	170,85	0,9273	21,97	2,9	19,07
5	200	159,56	63,99	0,70	161,10	93,94	3,88	171,91	0,9281	21,85	2,9	18,95
6	201	160,69	64,05	0,70	161,10	93,87	3,88	172,98	0,9289	21,73	2,9	18,83
7	202	161,57	64,12	0,70	161,10	93,81	3,88	173,83	0,9294	21,65	2,9	18,75
8	203	162,46	64,18	0,70	161,10	93,74	3,88	174,68	0,9300	21,56	2,9	18,66
9	204	163,35	64,25	0,70	161,10	93,68	3,88	175,53	0,9306	21,47	2,9	18,57
10	205	164,23	64,31	0,70	161,10	93,61	3,88	176,38	0,9311	21,39	2,9	18,49
11	206	165,12	64,38	0,70	161,10	93,54	3,88	177,23	0,9316	21,30	2,9	18,40
12	207	166,01	64,45	0,70	161,10	93,48	3,88	178,08	0,9322	21,22	3,46	17,76
13	208	167,04	64,51	0,70	161,10	93,41	3,88	179,07	0,9328	21,12	3,46	17,66
14	209	168,08	64,58	0,70	161,10	93,35	3,88	180,06	0,9334	21,02	3,46	17,56
15	210	169,11	64,64	0,70	161,10	93,28	3,88	181,05	0,9340	20,92	3,46	17,46
16	211	170,15	64,71	0,70	161,10	93,22	3,88	182,04	0,9346	20,82	3,46	17,36
17	212	171,18	64,77	0,70	161,10	93,15	3,88	183,03	0,9352	20,73	3,46	17,27

$* b = c+d-e-f$ $** g = \sqrt{(a^2+b^2)}$ $*** h = a/g$ $**** k = i-j$

Figure 86 – In the horizontal plane, the magic bullet comes before Z211. In the vertical plane, the angle of decline can be a maximum of 18.4 degrees.

33   THE MAGIC BULLET: CONCLUSION

Our methodology was based on the observation that it is impossible to represent a four-dimensional situation, with three material dimensions and one time dimension, on paper in a single picture. The virtual attempts to credibly present the possibility of the magic bullet via a simulation in the stock of Kennedy literature have two major flaws. First and foremost, there is a large 'black box' content and, secondly, you have to choose one point in time. An additional problem is that all the calculations can be heavily influenced by the situation in the limousine. It's sufficient for Connally to move a few centimeters to shift the starting point of the shot by meters to the left or right.

We have broken down the situation into four sub-problems. We have worked with much greater accuracy in the limousine and have determined a horizontal and vertical bandwidth within which the three relevant wounds could lie in a straight line. We have linked the situation to the passage of time and to the scale of the Dealey Plaza. There is a specific shooting angle for each shot at Kennedy's back. It was then sufficient to check the Zapruder frames for which the shot would pass through all the required points, both in the horizontal and the vertical plane, as well as at the level of the limousine and, cumulatively, that of the Dealey Plaza. The points within the limousine are Kennedy's back and throat wounds and Connally's armpit wound. At the Dealey Plaza level, the points are the barrel of the rifle in the sniper's nest and Kennedy's back wound. In this way we were able to determine that a magic bullet was possible from Z207 to Z211, barely one fifth of a second.

The point in time that seems to be most eligible for the magic bullet is Z211. After all, we know that the foliage of a large oak tree limited the view of the car up to Z210. The sniper probably delayed his shot until Kennedy emerged from beneath the foliage of the large oak. The fact that the magic bullet is *possible* makes it very likely that this is also what happened. We have already soberly stated that the chance of such a remarkable bullet was small. It seemed unlikely that the three wounds would lie exactly in one line for that single moment at which the shot could have been fired, and, what's more, in a straight line that pointed directly to the sniper's nest. The reverse is also true: now that we know that such a moment actually existed, we can reasonably conclude that there was indeed a magic bullet on November 22.

According to our analysis, which we keep very concise for reasons of readability, this is what took place:

- It is certain that there was a shot at the limousine from the sniper's nest at time point Z211;
- Kennedy was thereby hit in the back, to the left of the tip of his shoulder blade, 4.5 centimeters to the right of the center line of his spine;
- At that moment, Kennedy sat turned approximately ten degrees to the right and bent forward about fourteen degrees;
- The shot exited from Kennedy's throat 0.25 centimeters left of the center line;
- The bullet tumbled and then penetrated Connally's left armpit. Connally's back wound was elongated, resembling a keyhole. This is a strong indication that the bullet that hit Connally had 'tumbled' and that, in turn, is an indication that the bullet had previously hit something else;
- The bullet scraped along Connally's fifth rib, causing a lateral flattening of the bullet. It lost energy, and exited Connally's chest below the right nipple without disintegrating;
- Connally's wrist was not near the exit wound at time point Z211 and was not hit by the magic bullet;
- After being diverted to the left by scraping along the rib, the bullet finally hit Connally's thigh backwards and came to a complete standstill there;
- While Connally's clothing was being removed, the bullet found its way unnoticed under the mattress. The gurney was placed in the elevator;
- As there was indeed a magic bullet, it would have certainly been lying on Connally's bed. Hospital assistant Tomlinson was therefore mistaken as to where he had placed the bed. He probably knew that, but didn't dare admit it.

The certainty of the sniper's nest as the origin

Some people claim that a shooter was observed in the south-west window of the sixth floor, completely in the other corner of the TSBD. But a magic bullet is impossible from the south-west angle of the sixth floor. The horizontal shooting angle with respect to the limousine is much too great from a west window of the TSBD during the whole of the crucial period from Z196 to Z225. A bullet that hit Kennedy under that angle would miss Connally. There can therefore not have been any shot at Kennedy from the other side of the TSBD in the crucial period.

We also know that the sinister Jim Braden was hanging around in the Dal-Tex building at the time of the shots. But one shot from the Dal-Tex building, even if this were possible from further back in the building, would have had an angle of 6.93 degrees with respect to the limousine in the horizontal plane at time point Z196, which would have been further reduced to only 2.58 degrees at time point Z225. The angles are much too small and, furthermore, would also imply that Kennedy would have been sitting turned to the right by thirteen to seventeen degrees, which was not the case. The shot would then also not have hit Connally at the required location.

Not only do the three wounds lie in one line with the sniper's nest in the south-east corner, they also do *not* lie in a line with other possible locations or points in time.

Consequences for the weapon

Four witnesses who had seen the magic bullet on November 22, refused to 'identify' the bullet. There is therefore considerable doubt that CE399 is the same bullet as the magic bullet that was found. The only explanation is that, for whatever reason, the FBI replaced the original magic bullet by another test bullet that had been fired with the Carcano. It seems absurd to replace one bullet that was shot with the Carcano by another bullet that was also shot by the Carcano, but nothing surprises us anymore by now. Perhaps the FBI damaged the original bullet, or lost it. Or maybe the bullets were switched by mistake, and nobody dared to admit it later? Or was there another problem with the bullet that did not bear publication? Perhaps the four witnesses only meant that they could never be *completely* sure that the shown bullet was the same one that was found in November? We will probably never find out, but the matter is, in fact, of little importance, because we are sure that, even if CE399 was exchanged, the magic bullet and the main shot were fired with the same weapon.

How can we be sure of this? We know that the magic bullet was fired from the sniper's nest. There are also witnesses who saw the gun barrel sticking out of the window on the sixth floor at the time of the fatal shot: not only Brennan, who was sitting on the wall in front of the TSBD, but also Bob Jackson, a reliable journalist who was in the media car that was part of the motorcade and who shouted to his colleagues: 'There is the weapon! [...] It came from that window!' He thereby pointed towards the southeast window of the sixth floor of the TSBD.[544] Once we are sure that the magic bullet as well as the shot that killed Kennedy were shot from the sniper's nest, it is inconceivable that the weapon was exchanged in the 5.5 seconds between Z2111 and Z313. Consequently, we know that both bullets were fired with the same weapon. If the bullet fragments from the head shot bear the marks of the Carcano, the original magic bullet must have shown the same marks. Once we accept this, there cannot have been a reason to replace the bullet found on the Parkland stretcher by another bullet.

Connally's wrist

Dr. Olivier, *Wound Ballistic Expert* with the U.S. Army,[545] clarified that Connally's wrist fracture was not caused by a separate bullet, because if a bullet had hit the wrist directly, it would have caused a lot more damage than the doctors had established. Dr. Gregory, who treated Connally, also testified that the wrist fracture seemed more the result of a bullet that had already spent a great deal of its energy.[546] He kept the possibility open that a fragment of the head shot could have hit Connally in the wrist. This seems like a purely theoretical idea at first sight, but it doesn't seem so impossible if we have a close look at Z311.

Figure 87 – Did a fragment of the head-shot hit Connally's wrist?

At that moment, Connally was already leaning against his spouse, and his torso therefore did not form an obstacle for a bullet fragment from the bullet that hit Kennedy's head. Such a fragment could have certainly injured Connally's wrist. In Z312 (Figure 87) you can still see the untainted white sleeve, Connally's hand and the undamaged rim of the hat in his hand. The wrist lies right in the line of a bullet fragment from the head shot. The bullet that hit Kennedy's head disintegrated as a result of the contact with the skull. In our firm opinion, a fragment of the bullet that hit Kennedy's head caused Connally's wrist fracture. The fragments from the head bullet still had a high kinetic energy. This can be confirmed on the basis of the substantial dent such a fragment made in the chrome strip above the windshield of the limousine. The assumption that Connally's wrist and hand were not hit by the magic bullet, but by a fragment of the bullet that hit the head, solves many problems: the problem of the movement with the hat from Z230 up to and including Z272, the problem of the *pristine condition* of CE399 and the problem of the weight of the fragments that remained in the wrist. It seems so logical that a fragment of the head bullet caused the wrist fracture that it is amazing that nobody except for Dr. Gregory took that possibility into account.

Connally shows a seemingly late response to his severe injuries, but this impression partially arises from the fact that he was still sitting upright around Z230, and was moving the hand with which he was holding his hat. In the Zapruder film, Connally seems to be reacting later to the magic bullet than Kennedy. The FBI, the conspiracists, but also Nellie Connally and the Governor himself, were therefore convinced that the victims could not have been hit by the same bullet. But if we could disregard the movement with the hat, there is a lot less evidence for Connally's reaction being delayed. The hypothesis that Connally's wrist fracture was caused by a fragment of the bullet that hit Kennedy's head also solves a major problem in this context.

34. THE FIRST SHOT

Our finding that the magic bullet was fired from the sniper's nest around Z211 has important implications for the shot that preceded it. Believer Bugliosi situated the first shot with great certainty at time frame Z160. The limousine had then just turned into Elm Street. This is somewhat problematic, because only few people responded at that time. The trained secret agents, for example, were still unaware of any harm. Frazier, the weapon expert of the Commission, said that someone with 'considerable practice' required 2.3 seconds to reload the Carcano and shoot again.[547] This would correspond to 42 Zapruder frames before another shot could be fired, after aiming very fast. If another shot was fired at the limousine with the Mannlicher Carcano before Z211, when the magic bullet hit, then it must have been fired at the latest around Z169 – or earlier, of course.

It is reasonably sure that the limousine was shot at around Z160, and this can be derived from the statements made by Jacqueline Kennedy[548] and Governor Connally. The limousine turned into Elm Street past the TSBD. Shortly afterwards, the president's wife heard Mrs. Connally exclaim: 'Oh No No No!' She then turned her head away from the spectators on her side of the limousine. Jacqueline Kennedy's head turns to the right from Z171 onwards. Connally stated the following:

We had just made the turn, well, when I heard what I thought was a shot. I heard this noise which I immediately took to be a rifle shot. I instinctively turned to my right because the sound appeared to come from over my right shoulder...

From Z164, Connally turns his head sharply to the right. It only takes four frames, i.e., just over two tenths of a second, to turn his head by a quarter. Connally was not able to see the president over his right shoulder, so he then turned to the left to look at the president over his other shoulder. In Z204, Connally turned to the left in a position that was slightly orientated towards the left, which was in accordance with his statement. The magic bullet was fired shortly afterwards.

The reactions of Governor Connally and Jacqueline Kennedy in the Zapruder film are unmistakable. It is remarkable that nobody – including the Secret Service agents – appeared to have heard the first shot, except for Connally, motorcycle officer Baker and perhaps Rosemary Willis, the girl in the red dress who stopped running to look round, and Mrs. Baker-Rachley. Mrs. Baker-Rachley[549] – not related to Officer Baker – was standing immediately in front of the TSBD entrance, on the triangular traffic island at the edge of Elm Street, and saw the impact of a bullet on the asphalt, shortly after Kennedy had driven through the bend into Elm Street.

Motorcycle officer Baker and his meeting with Oswald

One person who certainly heard the first shot was motorcycle officer Baker. We can determine when this shot was fired by checking where he was situated at that moment. The Zapruder film can be compared to the hands of a secure clock, which recorded the events at Dealey Plaza accurately to five hundredths of a second. This allows for the synchronization of all other events with this clock. Between the foliage and the spectators, we can see a yellow Chevrolet Impala with press people drive by in the background of the film, the sixth car behind the president, known as 'Camera Car #1'. The next car is 'Camera Car #2'.[550] Officer Baker is driving to the right and behind this car, on his motorcycle. Another amateur filmmaker, spectator Hughes, filmed the motorcade from a different angle. The entire press motorcade drove ahead of him in Houston Street, straight in the direction of the TSBD. Researcher Dale Myers has very accurately calculated that Hughes frame 649 corresponds to Zapruder 154.[551] This is how we know that Baker was situated at the center of the courthouse, past the corner of Main Street, at time frame Z154. In his hearing before the Commission,[552] Baker confirmed that he was more or less at the center of the courthouse when he heard the first shot. We can therefore conclude that Baker indeed heard a shot around Z160.

Connally and agent Baker were the only ones to immediately recognize the sound of a shot in the first bang. Jackie Kennedy only reacted to Connally's exclamation. The Secret Agents, who should have been focused and ready for this kind of incident, did not hear anything. Perhaps this could be explained by the fact that Baker had just returned from a deer hunt, and recognized the sound better. He also happened to look straight ahead and up, which means that the TSBD, where he saw pigeons flying up from the roof, was directly in his line of vision. He therefore immediately assumed that the shot had been fired from there. It is tragic that none of the president's security staff heard the first shot and responded in an alert manner. If the driver of the limousine had given full throttle at Z160, it would have been very unlikely that the president would have been hit a second time. As the Secret Service did not hear anything, the car continued for another nine seconds at a snail's pace in the line of fire, with the fatal result we all know. Yet these events were not followed by any sanction or reproof.

As soon as he had heard the first shot, Baker accelerated his Harley Davidson. He drove up to the curb on Elm Street, parked his motorbike and rushed inside the TSBD. Truly, the building superintendent, pointed out the way to the staircase at the back of the building. Together, they ran to the second floor, where they met Oswald. During the investigation, Baker repeated this complete route twice. The first time, he needed 90 seconds to reach the place where he met Oswald, the second time 75 seconds. After the first shot, Oswald needed another 153 frames, or 8.4 seconds, to fire twice. Then he reloaded the rifle again, because an unused bullet was found in the weapon. This took him at least an additional two seconds. Oswald therefore started making his way down to the cafeteria about eleven seconds after Baker started his rush to the TSBD, and he had to arrive at least a few seconds earlier. The question is whether Oswald managed to reach the cafeteria on the second floor in less than 64 (75 less 11) to 79 (90 less 11) seconds. Moreover, he was not supposed to meet Vickie Adams and her friend on the staircase during his descent. What if Oswald did not have enough time for all this? What if it is certain that Adams was on the staircase at the time that Oswald should also have been there in order to reach the second floor in time? In both cases, Oswald would have had an alibi for the time of the assassination.

35. THE LAST SHOT

The time of the last shot is not a problem. In frame 313 of the Zapruder film, we can see how the head of the president is hit. A spray of blood and brain tissue spreads in a red cloud over the limousine. We also know reasonably accurately where Kennedy's head was positioned at that time because another spectator, Orville Nix, filmed the attack from the opposite direction. The shooting angle against the façade is[553] 46 degrees, and the driving direction of the limousine[554] is 39.5 degrees against the façade of the TSBD. Consequently, the trajectory of the bullet against the limousine in Z313 is 6.5 degrees. The rear of the limousine is already turning away from the sniper's nest towards the right (Figure 88).

There is no doubt that the back of Kennedy's head was hit, because there are marks of a bullet impact on the inside of the limousine in the windshield and in the chrome strip above the window. These can only be caused by bullet fragments that were projected from the back to the front. We are also assuming that Connally's wrist injury was caused by a fragment of the Z313 bullet. The logic of this is clear from a top view of the limousine (Figure 91). In the vertical plane, Connally was already leaning fully against his wife at that moment, which is why the bullet fragment did not hit him in the back.

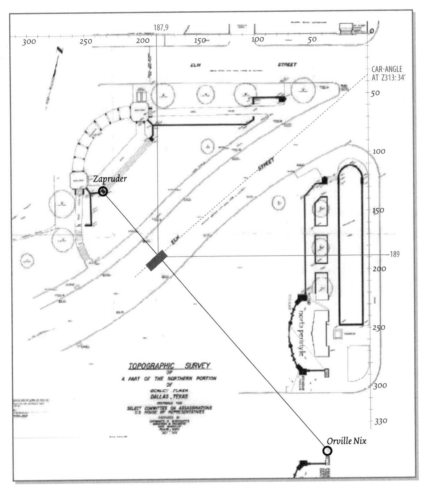

Figure 88 – The position of the limousine at the time of the fatal shot.

36. JAMES TAGUE,
THE 'FORGOTTEN' VICTIM

James Tague was a 27-year-old used-car salesman. He passed through Dallas quite by accident, and parked his car at Dealey Plaza in order to see the president drive by in the distance. He took up post on the opposite side of Main Street, near the Triple Underpass. That is more than a football field away from the TSBD. Almost immediately after the attack, Tague told Deputy Sheriff Eddy Walthers that he had noticed a bullet impact on the concrete. Walthers pointed out to Tague that he was bleeding. It appears that something, perhaps a shard of concrete or the ricochet of a bullet fragment, had hit his chin. They did indeed find a 'very fresh'[555] scar impact at the south curb of Main Street. Patrol Officer L.L. Hill subsequently recorded everything accurately. He also reported the fact over his police radio[556] at 12:40, ten minutes after the assassination. Press photographer Tom Dillard took a photograph of the curb, which made it to the headlines the next day.

In a murder investigation, the reporting of a bullet impact is not a detail. Quite a few bullet impacts were, in fact, reported.[557] The Commission pushed all those witnesses aside with the assertion that no traces of a bullet impact could be found in the reported places. But in the case of Jim Tague, the situation was a little more complicated: no matter how minor his scratch was, he was a third victim of the attack, and this could not just be swept under the carpet. The fact that Tague had stood exactly in *that* position, and not a few inches to the left, seemed for some reason to be a minor (or major) disaster for the official version of the facts. The authorities therefore did not want to know about it. The further course of the investigation cannot be explained in any other way. There is not the slightest doubt that the FBI was aware of Tague's injury. The police report, the radio communication, the press articles, the photograph of the curb stone could not simply be ignored. But James Tague was not mentioned at all in the five volumes of the FBI summary report for the Commission! There was not a trace of a stray bullet fragment or a third victim with a scratched chin. It is clear why Tague's account was not popular with the FBI: if you are aiming to conclude an investigation quickly and without much ado, complications like this are highly inconvenient. Hoover decided on the easiest explanation of three shots and three hits, and was not inclined to smile at subordinates who believed they could entertain an opinion that clashed with that of the director. The three available bullets were already reserved for Kennedy's back, Connally's back and Kennedy's head. There was no bullet left for Tague. The FBI agents knew what to do, and therefore did what they could to ignore the entire business. That is bizarre. If the FBI was so sure of its case and firmly believed that there was only one gunman on Dealey Plaza, it would naturally have been in their own interest to thoroughly investigate the matter and come up with an explanation for Tague's wound. The FBI should then immediately have secured the damaged curb as important evidence. There is no doubt that they deliberately pursued the opposite.[558] Hoover's solution with the three bullets that hit the target eventually ended up in the trash can anyway, because separate bullets for Kennedy and Connally would have been inevitable proof of a conspiracy. But even afterwards, when the FBI scenario had already been abandoned, the investigation remained terrified of the consequences of a third victim. And even when there seemed to be a bullet to spare, Tague was consistently ignored.

The young car salesman was very frustrated by this state of affairs, especially because he was considered to be a stargazer when he told his story. But James Tague was not a show-off. There is no flaw in his story. He stood where he claimed he stood near the Triple Underpass when he heard the shots. A deputy sheriff had indeed pointed out his injury to him. The motorcycle officer had reported a possible victim with a minor injury via the radio. Tague had made a statement at the homicide department of the Dallas Police. There was a fresh chip in the concrete south curb of Main Street, and a report had been prepared about it. James Underwood of the local TV station KRLD had been involved, and photographer Dillard of the *Dallas Morning News* had taken photographs of the curb (Figure 90). One of these photographs even appeared in the newspaper of November 23, with the caption 'Concrete scar' and the short text:

A detective points to a chip in the curb... A bullet from the rifle that took President Kennedy's life apparently caused the hole.[559]

In the end, Tague phoned the FBI himself. Only then did the federal agents became somewhat interested in his statement, albeit rather reluctantly. First and foremost, they were interested in his reply to the question whether or not he knew Jack Ruby. This was apparently more important than determining if, where and when one of the three bullets hit. There was subsequently a deafening silence once again, but Tague was confident that the FBI would continue its work after this initial sign of attention. But then he learned through the media that the Warren Commission was about to finalize the investigation, and that the FBI had been right all the time: three shots, three hits. Tague's unrest flared up again. He feared for his credibility and did not want to have the reputation of a braggart among everyone he had told his story for the rest of his days,[560] and he told his story often. Jim Lehrer of the *Dallas Times Herald* happened to hear his account by accident. He sensed an exclusive story, and called Tague the very same day. Tague agreed to an interview, but asked Lehrer not to disclose his name. Barely an hour later, Lehrer had to phone him back to let him know that the anonymity was unsustainable: 'he called back and said, "Jim, I put this on the wire service and they're calling me from all over the country. Matter of fact I've had to give them your name."' The publication in the newspaper followed, and the FBI and the Warren Commission could not ignore the account again.

Six months after the assassination, Jim Tague briefly went to take some photographs of the curb stone in question again. It was still in the same condition as on the day of the attack. He then departed with his family to visit his parents in Indianapolis. When Tague was finally heard on July 23, 1964, in the Commission's injury time so to speak,[561] he learned to his dismay that the Commission was aware of his private visit to Dealey Plaza on a completely random day:

> Mr. LIEBELER. *That was about the time that you felt yourself struck?*
> Mr. TAGUE. *I just glanced. I mean I just stopped, got out of my car, and here came the motorcade. I just happened upon the scene.*
> Mr. LIEBELER. *Now I understand that you went back there subsequently and took some pictures of the area, isn't that right?*
> Mr. TAGUE. *Pardon?*
> Mr. LIEBELER. *I understand that you went back subsequently and took some pictures of the area.*
> Mr. TAGUE. *Yes; about a month ago.*
> Mr. LIEBELER. *With a motion picture camera?*
> Mr. TAGUE. *Yes; I didn't know anybody knew about that.*

This is a very disturbing fact. It demonstrates that the Commission, presumably through the FBI, was perfectly aware of the position of the damaged curb stone that contained essential evidence. Moreover, someone with direct access to the members of the Commission apparently had an unhealthy interest in what Tague did in his private time. The fact that the Commission was still embarrassed with regard to Tague's injury, even after the theory of the three bullets that hit the target had been abandoned, is apparent from its final report. In the report, Tague is mentioned in one single paragraph, as a 'trivial item' on page 116.

A third victim, however, remains a very serious matter. The crucial question in the entire dossier is whether there were more bullets, and whether one gunman was able to fire all these bullets within the available time. A fragment of a bullet, however minimal, is the hard proof that someone fired an entire bullet from a specific place, at a specific time and with a specific weapon. Any objective investigation should therefore have a razor-sharp focus on the fragment that hit the concrete curb in front of Tague's feet. The FBI only showed some interest in the curb stone after James Tague had taken the initiative *himself*. When the curb stone was finally examined, it appeared that the scar consisted of lead and antimony, the unmistakable signature of the impacting core of a bullet. As there was no copper trace to be found in the scar, the impact of a full bullet, i.e. a direct shot, could be excluded. All this is also outlined in the beginning and at the end of this single paragraph in the Warren Report. But someone then deemed it necessary to switch to quotes in the middle of the paragraph (underlining added):

> According to Tague, 'There was a mark quite obviously that was a bullet and it was very fresh.' In Tague's opinion, it was the second shot which caused the mark, since he thinks he heard the third shot after he was hit in the face. This incident appears to have been recorded in the contemporaneous report of Dallas Patrolman L.L. Hill, who radioed in around 12:40 p.m. 'I have one guy that was possibly hit by a ricochet from the bullet off the concrete'.

The quotes as such add nothing to the facts. If a lead scar in the concrete can be established beyond doubt, then this scar is not there because Tague 'believes' it is there. If it was meanwhile one hundred percent certain that Tague was injured, then the initial radio message regarding 'one guy that was possibly hit' was outdated. This inevitably creates the impression that the Commission only used quotes here in order to evoke five associations with uncertainty in three sentences. Then, the Commission added a round on the house:

The mark on the curb <u>could have</u> originated from the lead core of a bullet.

What other lead objects were flying around at the speed of sound at 12:30 in Dealey Plaza? The Commission not only covered the matter much too lightly, it was also intellectually dishonest. The Commission was well aware that there was a bullet impact. It had presented numerous questionable statements, shaky evidence and arguable facts, whether relevant or not, as unshakable certainties, but in the case of Tague they had a clear and certain fact. When they could no longer disregard the evidence, the Commission did everything it could to trivialize this simple and clear fact, and to describe it as doubtful.

Which shot injured Tague?

The impact on the curb stone does not originate from a direct shot, or from a shot between the magic bullet and the head shot. There are many reasons for this, but the simple explanation is that there is no bullet left for an additional shot. The lack of copper in the lead trace of the impact scar made by the core of the bullet also points to the fact that it was not a full bullet. The impact could also not be a detached fragment of the magic bullet, because this was found in pristine condition. In the first shot, at Z160, the declining angle is too sharp to project a fragment over a long distance a couple of centimeters above the ground without hitting anything. An overhanging traffic light is situated at the very beginning of Elm Street, in front of the doors of the TSBD. A shot that ricocheted off the traffic lights would have occurred around Z113 if Oswald was aiming more or less for the limousine, but we can also rule out this possibility because the first shot only fell at time frame Z160. In the end, only Z313, the head shot, remains as the source for the fragment that hit Tague.[562]

A fragment that started from Kennedy's head and moved in the direction of the curb flew at an angle of 37.23 degrees[563] with regard to the façade. At time frame Z313, the longitudinal axis of the limousine with regard to the TSBD front façade formed an angle of 39.7 degrees.[564] The angle of Kennedy's head in the direction of the curb is therefore *smaller* than the angle of the limousine against the façade of the TSBD. Against all intuitive expectations, the bullet fragment that flew towards Tague moved from left to right in the limousine at an angle of -2.5 degrees (37.23 – 39.7) with regard to the axis of the limousine, i.e. from Kennedy's head to the right side of the car, and not to the left as what could normally be expected. Connally, meanwhile, was lying with his head in his wife's lap, but there was another Secret Service agent on the front seat, next to the driver, and the windshield had not been damaged on the right side. On the basis of these calculations, it could at first sight be expected that Z313 could be excluded as the source for the Tague fragment. If you analyze the problem from the vertical plane, the fragment from Kennedy's head would move towards the curb with a declining curve of 3.9 degrees.[565] This also seems like bad news, because, if the detached fragment moves in a declining curve from Kennedy's head, it seems more logical that it would hit the back of Secret Agent Kellerman on the front seat. The fact that there was a hard impact in the chrome strip implies, however, that a fragment was possible just above the heads of the car occupants. The relatively strong slope the limousine followed towards the tunnel must also be taken into account.

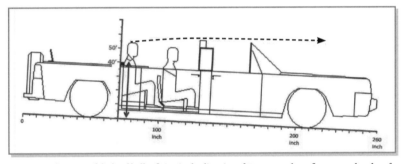

Figure 89 – A fragment of the head bullet flying in the direction of Tague must have flown over the edge of the windshield

In the vertical plane, we can demonstrate what presumably really happened (Figure 89). Elm Street slopes down by three degrees and the fragment could graze over the windshield in a curved trajectory and then continue its flight towards the curb stone, slightly descending with regard to the horizon. Eighty-five yards further, the fragment simply retained enough energy to break a shard of the concrete curb on impact. The bullet must have broken into at least four large fragments by then: one in the windshield, one in the chrome strip, one in Connally's wrist and the lead core that flew over the car in the direction of the Triple Underpass. As a fragment of the head bullet is the only possibility, we can conclude that Tague was injured in this way, and that the fragment must indeed have flown in a slight arc over the upper edge of the windshield.

37. OTHER BULLET IMPACTS

'Some evidence suggested that a third shot may have entirely missed and hit the turf of the street by the Triple Underpass', wrote the Commission in its report.[566] The passage refers to a shot that spectators saw hitting the grass near a manhole cover. The Commission reported that further investigation in the designated areas did *not* provide further indications of a bullet impact. But – once again - the euphemistic style of the Commission arouses suspicion. What does it mean if the evidence 'suggests' something?

Some digging into the unpublished *Commission Documents* leads to an FBI report with the title *Lee Harvey Oswald – Internal Security – Russia – Cuba*. This seems to be some kind of 'thrash can' listing all sorts of information that was not investigated further. In between bits of marginal information, we discover the following sentence:

> *Wayne E. Hartman and wife, Edna, furnished information concerning gouged out hole in grass near TSDB observed by them on 11/22/63 after assassination, which they considered of possible significance. Described location of gouged out hole is in line with shot that struck President Kennedy in the head.*[567]

Mr. and Mrs. Hartman were not granted any interest by the Commission, and they therefore spontaneously reported to the FBI on August 10, 1964, during the final days of the Commission. They did this when they learned that additional investigation was being conducted into the incident with Tague. Wayne Hartman stated that he had seen a gouged-out hole with a diameter of three to four centimeters and a length of about 45 to 60 centimeters in the grass in the vicinity of a manhole cover. He could insert three fingers into the hole.[568] Mrs. Hartman confirmed the information.

On September 18, 1964, ten months after the attack, the FBI examined the area of the designated location with a metal detector. They only found the cap of a soda bottle and an aluminum plug, so there was nothing to worry about.

But three men had been standing together at the place that Hartman had indicated immediately after the assassination. This can be seen on the photograph in Figure 90. Two of them were Dallas police officers. The man in uniform was Agent Foster and the man in the civilian clothes was Deputy Sheriff Walthers. The third man on the photograph, a blond man in civilian dress, was not identified. According to the conspiracists, he clearly picks something up from the ground and puts it in his pocket.[569] Jim Garrison later started this rumor.[570] The FBI attempted to find out who the unknown man was, but did not succeed. The government authorities strongly denied that the man was a CIA or a Secret Service agent. Detective James Leavelle of the Dallas Police wrote to researcher Dennis Morisette that he had met the unknown man, but that the person in question unfortunately had refused to reveal his identity.[571] That was the end of it. The police had no problem with the fact that someone who refused to disclose his identity picked up evidence from a site where an assassination had just occurred.

Figure 90 – An unknown person picks up evidence

Agent Foster, the uniformed police officer, was heard by the Commission on April 9.[572] He stated that he had found a place where a shot had hit the ground.

No traces had been found on the street, but the manhole cover had been hit. To the surprise of the Commission, Foster explicitly confirmed that the manhole cover had been damaged. During his hearing, Foster was presented with a photograph on which the track was not visible, or not clearly visible. He also had not found a bullet. 'It ricocheted off it', he assumed. In addition, he stated that he immediately requested the police crime lab to take a photograph. This was rather an odd reaction if there had been nothing to see.

Despite Foster's testimony regarding a hole in the grass and a scar on the concrete of the manhole cover, the Commission continued to insist in its final report that there were no visible traces of a bullet impact, and that Agent Foster and spectator Skelton had made a mistake: 'Examination of this area, however, disclosed no indication that a bullet struck at the locations indicated by Skelton or Foster.'[573] The fact that Foster had seen the scar on the manhole cover was of no importance to the Commission. They also did not acknowledge the fact that a track in the grass was probably no longer visible when the site was examined later, and it didn't matter that several persons apparently noticed something interesting at this site immediately after the shots had been fired. Incidentally, who carried out the 'examination' the Commission refers to, and when did this examination take place? The Commission once again deceives us by being deliberately vague. Its report states the following: 'Dallas Patrolman J.W. Foster, who was also on the Triple Underpass, testified that a shot hit the turf.'[574] It sounds as if Foster saw something from atop the bridge. In reality, Foster was only on the bridge at the moment of the shot itself. From his testimony, it's clear that he went to the site of the bullet impact after the shot, and that he saw the tracks at the site and on the manhole cover with his own eyes, and not from the bridge.

The believers continually emphasize the fact that no bullet was found at the designated location, but they ignore the fact that there was a hole in the ground at the place where witnesses had reported a bullet impact. There are, moreover, also photos of the damage to the concrete around the manhole cover. Five witnesses are known by name. Agent Foster and Mr. and Mrs. Hartman confirmed that they had seen a hole in the grass that was 45 to 60 centimeters long and 3 centimeters wide, and this was never refuted or contradicted. Skelton saw a bullet hitting the turf in that area, and Deputy Sheriff Walthers had also seen the tracks, but was not interviewed about it. There are at least two other, unknown, witnesses, as well as the man who touched evidence and possibly even put it in his pocket. But a fourth man – a man with a checkered shirt – can also be distinguished on the photographs looking intensively at the grass. Finally, let us not forget that at least two press photographers came over to look. Whatever was there to be seen in the grass, it was interesting enough to keep them intensively occupied – while they were making the most important photographs of their lives.

There is no doubt that there was a track in the grass field. We should now explore where and when this track could have been created. On our topographic map, the line that links the place the witnesses refer to with the sniper's nest forms an angle of 46 degrees against the façade of the TSBD. At time frame Z313, the angle of the bullet was also exactly 46 degrees. The head injury and the damage to the grass or concrete around the manhole cover are therefore on one line with the head shot in the direction of the sniper's nest. The logical conclusion is that the damage around the manhole cover also originated from a detached fragment of the bullet that hit Kennedy's head. This fragment must also have flown over the windshield, similar to the fragment that flew in Tague's direction. Another aspect that points in this direction is a part of Kennedy's skull that was found slightly further on in the grass field, in the same line with regard to the sniper's nest.

We are now already looking at five potential fragments of the head shot, as well as a small piece of Kennedy's skull. Let us also not forget the three small fragments that were found under the jump seat of Mrs. Connally. Together, this provides the following, coherent picture of the fragmentation of the head shot (Figure 91).

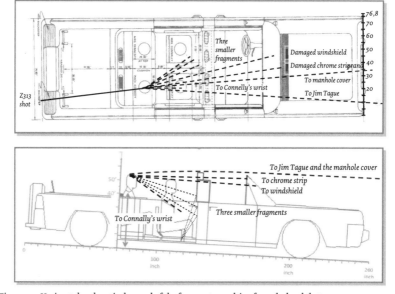

Figure 91 – Horizontal and vertical spread of the fragments resulting from the head shot.

38. *BADGE MAN ON THE GRASSY KNOLL*

Most conspiracy theories assume a frontal shot at the limousine from the bushes behind the colonnade where Zapruder was situated. The perpetrators would then allegedly have fled through the parking lot situated behind them. The major argument in favor of this scenario is the initial reaction of the spectators, who rushed towards the *Grassy Knoll* after the shot.

Witnesses of a frontal shot

Spectator Mary Moorman took a controversial Polaroid photograph at the time of the fatal shot allegedly showing a man with a rifle in the foliage. The most creative detectives even recognized a police badge on the shirt of the gunman, which earned him the nickname *Badge Man*[*]. Discovery Channel made a reconstruction of Moorman's photo, together with the author Gary Mack, and came to the conclusion that a man situated where Badge Man was situated would indeed be in the perfect position to aim a frontal shot at Kennedy.[575] But the possibility of a shot does not mean that there was effectively a gunman. The human shape on the Moorman photograph is probably the product of our imagination. The effect of seeing human figures in random shapes is scientifically known as 'pareidolia'. The oldest and most charming example of this phenomenon is the man in the moon. Our brain is amazingly efficient in recognizing thousands of different faces. A human shape is a template that is deeply engraved in our mind, and

---

[*] *Badge* refers to a police badge.

we therefore often believe we distinguish it, where in reality there are just clouds, or moon craters or – in this case – tree foliage.

The statements of the witnesses who point out the *Grassy Knoll* as the origin of a gunshot are not really conclusive because of the fact that Dealey Plaza is a real echo chamber. Yet a number of witnesses deserve more attention than they were given by the Warren Commission. Railway Supervisor Holland saw a puff of smoke exactly at the place where Badge Man allegedly stood. He ran to the spot immediately, but did not find anyone there.[576] Holland also later stated that the spot showed fresh footprints, and that there were several fresh cigarette butts. It had rained that morning, and the butts were dry.[577] But in his affidavit of the day itself, he had not mentioned a word about cigarette butts or footprints. The footprints emerged in his statement before the Warren Commission as an additional memory, but they were situated at the parking lot, not behind the *picket fence*.[578] His testimony improved and became more spectacular with time, and that is highly suspicious. The same applies to witness J. C. Price. On November 22, 1963, he stated to the Dallas Police on his own initiative that he had seen a man running from behind the *picket fence* to the parking lot.[579] Strangely enough, the FBI reported on November 24 that Price had not witnessed anything special.[580] In an interview with conspiracy author Mark Lane two years after the facts, Price added a rifle to his memory. When researcher Barry Ernest contacted him, Price was willing to testify if the researcher brought his checkbook along to the meeting.[581] He therefore seems hardly a reliable witness, but the fact remains that Price had already stated on November 22 that he had seen a man running away behind the fence. These are the best witnesses. On closer inspection, the evidence for the presence of a gunman on the grassy knoll behind Zapruder is rather thin and/or highly unreliable. Zapruder himself also mentioned that he heard shots behind him, but as he was turned towards Elm Street, the TSBD was also situated (on the left) behind him.

The backward movement

It is an undeniable fact that Kennedy moved abruptly backwards after the head shot. This is often seen as evidence for a frontal shot. That is also shown in the movie *JFK*, in which Jim Garrison (Kevin Costner) repeats several times: 'back and to the left, back and to the left, back and to the left.' The reasoning that a human body should move in the direction of the bullet in the case of a gunshot wound is based on the false premise that a bullet has enough kinetic energy to drastically move a human body. However, this only happens in movies, with the aim of increasing the dramatic effect. The kinetic energy of a bullet can be calculated by multiplying half of its mass by the square of its velocity in meters per second. This means that a small bullet with a high velocity can indeed have a large amount of kinetic energy, but this is largely lost. The kinetic energy is transferred into the impact on the skull, the fragmentation of the bullet and the projection of the fragments. There is also a massive *blast out* of brain tissue and blood. (In the case of Kennedy, 35 percent of the content of the right cerebral hemisphere and large sections of the skull were projected and sprayed out at high velocity.) Such an explosion not only absorbs kinetic energy, it also causes a backwards momentum. In addition, the impact time of the bullet is very brief, and immediately after the backwards momentum of the explosion, gravity takes over. The contraction of Kennedy's back muscles explains the further backwards movement. Professor Kenneth A. Rahn calculated scientifically and in detail how this happened on the *Academic JFK Assassination Site*.[582]

Small children are sometimes told a white lie in order not to complicate matters needlessly. The Commission was guilty of shamelessly using this type of simplicity. It was deemed useful, for example, to include the Zapruder frames in the reverse sequence in the evidence. As a result, it appeared to the original viewers who had never seen the Zapruder film that the movement of the head was forward. Now we know the correct sequence of the frames, this illustrates, once again, the extent of falsification the Commission was prepared to include. Believers claim that this was an innocent printing error, but in the context of the many demonstrable manipulations, we can no longer grant the Commission the benefit of the doubt.

Acoustic evidence

When we mention the 'official version', we never, of course, refer to a frontal shot, because a frontal shot points towards a conspiracy. It is therefore highly surprising to almost everyone that, according to the most recent official version of the assassination, there was a frontal shot after all, albeit allegedly a shot that completely missed the limousine. The HSCA arrived at this stunning conclusion in 1978, on the basis of a scientifically-based, acoustic analysis:

The acoustics analysis indicates that four shots were fired at the Presidential limousine with the first, second, and fourth shots coming from the Texas School Book Depository and the third from the grassy knoll.[583]

The finding of the HSCA was based on newly discovered evidence. A motorcycle officer had apparently left his microphone switched on during the transit through Dealey Plaza. Conspiracist Penn Jones discovered this fact, and immediately assumed that an accomplice officer had in this way intentionally blocked the radio traffic during the assassination. Researcher Gary Mack, curator and archivist of the *Sixth Floor Museum* and blessed with a slightly stronger sense of realism, subsequently asked himself a pertinent question: was it possible that shots could be heard on this recording? Apparently, nobody had thought of this possibility. Thanks to historian Mary Ferrell, who fanatically archived all evidence of the assassination, Mack got hold of a recording of the radio traffic on the police channel. With this, he approached two recording studios. No less than seven shots were counted. This was too much of a good thing, but the interest of the HSCA had been aroused.

The HSCA hired Bolt, Berenak & Newman (BBN), a specialized agency that had previously examined the missing eighteen minutes of the Nixon tapes on the Watergate scandal. BBN organized an extensive investigation at Dealey Plaza. They situated the open microphone at 39 yards behind the presidential limousine. That was the supposed position of the motorcycle officer with the open mike. According to the BBN expert, the sounds of their reconstruction demonstrated that three shots had been fired from the sniper's nest, and one from the grassy knoll. The expert stated happily that there was a fifty percent chance that his findings reflected the reality correctly. But fifty percent does not sound very convincing for an expert, and the HSCA was therefore forced to appoint other experts to further investigate the matter. The new panel mathematically sophisticated the model of the first investigation. They focused thereby exclusively on the one shot from the grassy knoll. The second investigation confirmed a frontal shot with 95 percent certainty, according to the experts. Meanwhile, a HSCA researcher had also found the motorcycle officer and identified him as Officer McLain. Like Officer Baker, he was driving next to Camera Car #3, but on the other side. He allegedly was the man with the open microphone. This immediately seriously shakes the high certainty of the experts. In the investigation into the first shot, we have already established where Baker was situated when he accelerated in the direction of the TSBD. This point was situated about 66 yards from the bend on Elm Street, and, at this moment, Kennedy had already past the bend. Baker and McLain were therefore not driving 39 yards behind the limousine, but at least double this distance. The HSCA, however, had to close the investigation immediately after being informed of the findings of the second expertise. The special inquiry commission made its decision on December 31, 1978, its final session, after a heated debate behind closed doors. A majority of the members backed the conclusion that a fourth shot had been fired from behind the *Picket Fence*. This is how the existence of a frontal shot that didn't hit anybody or anything became an item in the most recent official version of the events on Dealey Plaza.

The credibility of this decision was confined to a very short life span. Four days after the HCSA had published its decisions, Officer McLain heard the recording in question for the first time. He immediately was aware that this could not have been his microphone. He was not familiar with the conversation on *Channel 1* that was recorded on the tape, he had used *Channel 2*. Moreover, McLain was certain that he had used his siren, and this sound was not registered by the open microphone. He also noted that the motorbike in the recording was driving too fast, and could therefore not have been part of the motorcade. With some goodwill, the conspiracists could perhaps maintain that the officer perhaps made a mistake, but this illusion was also taken from them. *Gallery Magazine* added a plastic record with the recording in question as a supplement to a special edition about the assassination. An attentive listener noticed something strange that had escaped all the experts. They had apparently concentrated too much on the gunshots, and had overlooked all other noises. But the reader of *Gallery Magazine* heard that somebody in the recording says: 'hold everything secure!' This sentence was, of course, only said after the assassination. Two scientific studies proved afterwards that the reader was right. The tape contained sounds from *after* and not during the attack. It is therefore impossible to hear any shots on it. The acoustic proof that had been declared 95 percent certain by experts therefore fell completely by the wayside. But this was still recorded as truth in the final report of the HSCA.

No *Badge Man*

From a purely theoretical point of view, it is still possible that someone shot at the limousine from the *Grassy Knoll* around Z313. It is, however, one hundred percent sure that someone shot from a position situated *behind* the limousine at that moment. The damage caused by the bullet impacts on the inside of the windshield and on the chrome strip shows this clearly. Eight bullet fragments and a fraction of Kennedy's skull were propelled forward in a fan-like movement, pointing without any doubt to a shot from the direction of the TSBD.

We must apply Ockham 's razor* here. There is sufficient explanation for the head wound and the bullet impacts; it is therefore not necessary to consider a frontal shot. An additional, unproven hypothesis of a second, perfectly simultaneous frontal shot is out of the question. There were no other gunmen than those in the TSBD and, anyway, nobody has any idea where the frontal bullet could have disappeared to afterwards.

A shot after Zapruder frame 313

It is not impossible that a fourth shot was fired after Z313. Witness Charles Brehm was standing on the grass field between Elm and Main Street with his young son. On November 24,[584] he stated to the FBI that another shot followed after the president had already been hit in the head. Brehm, a former military man, had experience with gun shots and he stated that the shots came from the direction of the TSBD. The Commission nevertheless preferred to ignore what he had to say, because a shot after Z313 would imply that four shots were fired, and this was not negotiable.

The Commission's worries were, once again, unfounded. A shot after Z313 was, in fact, so unlikely, that it could be excluded, even if a witness believed to have heard differently. The marksman must certainly have seen that his Z313 shot was a direct hit. If the Carcano was indeed the weapon of the assassination, he even had to reload first, giving him two seconds to take in the result of his previous shot. For him, as for anyone who saw the impact of the head shot, it must have been clear that an additional shot was

---

* Epistemology coined by the English Franciscan friar William van Ockham (1288-1347). He stated that one should not assume the existence of something if an experience could be explained in another way. If several hypotheses are possible to explain something, one should opt for the hypothesis with the simplest explanation. You 'shave off' all unnecessary complications in order to end up with the simplest explanation.

no longer necessary. The fact that witness Brehm heard an additional shot has a technical explanation. The sound of the gun came from the correct direction, the TSBD, and reached the witness with a velocity of 245 meters per second. The bullet, however, reached a speed of 670 meters per second. As the bullet passed by the spectator with a speed exceeding the speed of sound this caused a bang, similar to a plane breaking through the sound barrier. This bang is heard slightly before the actual sound of the gun. In this case, Brehm had the convincing impression of two gunshots in quick succession. The first bang came from the place where the bullet was situated at the moment it broke through the sound barrier, the second one from the place from where the bullet was fired.[585] As a matter of fact, many witnesses reported to have heard two shots in quick succession.

The many contradictions and the confusion regarding the number of bullets and the direction from which the shots came simply arose from a physical and perfectly explainable phenomenon: a supersonic bullet can be heard twice from two directions.

39. CONCLUSION OF
THE BALLISTIC ANALYSIS

In his section, we have analyzed on a step-by-step basis whether the magic bullet was a figment of Arlen Specter's imagination, a desperate attempt to keep up the lone-nut hypothesis, or whether it could have been a real possibility. Our calculations demonstrated that the latter was, in fact, the case. This caused much amazement, because we were very critical of the careless drawings the believers often came up with, and because, on closer inspection, the known evidence for the single-bullet theory was found to be incorrect in several areas. The magic bullet was theoretically possible during a very short time frame between Z207 and Z211. The first frames of this time frame can be excluded because, at that moment, Kennedy was not visible for the sniper due to the foliage of a large oak tree. The fact that four points (three injuries and the barrel of the gun) were perfectly aligned in the four examined planes (the horizontal and vertical plane of both the limousine and Dealey Plaza) at the correct time frame, Z211, leaves no doubt that a magic bullet really was fired. Governor Connally's wrist did not fit into the picture, as the position of his wrist was not in line with the trajectory of the magic bullet. Moreover, Connally was still moving his uninjured hand and his snow-white cuff and Stetson above the edge of the limousine in Z230 and Z272.

There is no doubt that a shot was fired before the magic bullet. Connally was certain that he had heard a shot before he was hit. On the basis of the head movement of Jackie Kennedy and the Governor, we can confirm that this shot must have occurred around Z160. An analysis of the statements of motorcycle officer Baker and his position at the moment he heard the shot pointed in the same direction. This first shot missed the limousine. Mrs. Baker-Rachley witnessed the impact of the shot on the turf, and nobody in the limousine responded to an injury around Z160. It is unimaginable that the Secret Service did not notice this first shot, but this, unfortunately, remains a fact. Perhaps something somehow went wrong with the first bullet, which could also explain the much lower sound of the shot. The Carcano was notorious for its many misfires. The third shot, fired at time frame Z313, was the fatal shot for Kennedy. This bullet also originated from the sniper's nest. The bullet fragments originate from the Carcano that was found on the sixth floor, to the exclusion of all other weapons. Or, to be more accurate, the fragments originate from a bullet that was *at some point in time* shot through the barrel of this Carcano. The radius in which the fragments spread out after the bullet had exploded points towards a shot that came from the sniper's nest. There is no reason whatsoever to assume that a frontal shot was fired. The testimonies in this connection are presumably due to the sound effect of the bullet that was passing by the witness at a speed faster than sound, which caused the impression that two shots were fired in quick succession and from opposite directions.

According to our analysis, eight fragments from the head bullet were projected forward. A fragment of the skull was also projected over the windshield in the direction of a manhole cover at the south side of Elm Street. There is no doubt that the head shot was fired from behind the limousine. One of these fragments presumably hit Connally's wrist. The chemical analysis indicated that the fragment from Connally's wrist originated from the 'pristine' bullet CE399. This analysis gave rise to technical questions, however. The NAA test was invalid for the Carcano bullets with full metal jackets. While Connally was sitting down, he could also never have held the back of his wrist in a position that was near the exit wound in his chest. Moreover, Connally's hat must have been visible above the edge of the limousine, after the car emerged again from behind the Stemmons freeway sign. In addition, Connally was still moving three seconds after the magic bullet with an uninjured wrist and a pristine hat. It is technically possible to fire three bullets with a Mannlicher Carcano in the limited time frame. Oswald was a very mediocre marksman, and the rifle was highly unreliable, but the inaccuracy of the weapon was (deliberately or accidentally) to the advantage of the shooter. In the specific situation of Dealey Plaza, the inaccuracy of the Carcano resulted in a *favorable* deviation.

CE399 is quite flattened at the bottom, and therefore less *pristine* than is often claimed. If we disregard the wrist fracture, this minimal damage can be explained. The bullet passed through Kennedy's body without touching any hard body parts. The speed of the bullet thereby decreased sufficiently to make the projectile turn round. The bullet then entered Connally's armpit backwards and shattered his fifth rib by sliding with its bottom sidelong across it. Finally, the bullet, with barely any speed left, ended in Connally's thigh.

A whole series of riddles now appear to be solved, and they largely seem to tip the balance in favor of the believers. But there are also a number of new insights:

1. The magic bullet was fired at time frame Z211;
2. The wrist injury was incurred at time frame Z313 and was not caused by the magic bullet;
3. The wrist injury at a later point in time explains why Connally seems to be reacting late to the magic bullet in the Zapruder film;
4. It is curious that the exit wound in Kennedy's throat is smaller than the entrance wound in his back; normally, this would be the other way round. The counter-pressure of the clothing and tie could be a reasonable explanation for this;
5. The damage to the manhole cover and the surrounding grass have been clarified;
6. A plausible explanation for Jim Tague's wound has been found;
7. The relatively pristine condition of bullet CE399 is much more acceptable;
8. Many witnesses are certain that the second and the third shot were much closer together than the first and second shot. This could be explained by the sound effect of the supersonic bullet;
9. A fourth shot after the head shot, or between the head shot and the magic bullet seems impossible, despite the testimonies in this respect.

We are nevertheless still faced with a number of major problems:

1. There is still not the slightest explanation for the metal fragment on the outside of the base of Kennedy's skull;
2. There is no real explanation for the lapel flap of Connally's suit in frame Z224;
3. Could it really be a *coincidence* that a villain such as Jim Braden was in the ideal place to shoot Kennedy exactly at the time of the assassination?

As it is certain that there was a shot fired from behind the limousine at Z313, a simultaneous, frontal shot is not necessary to explain the facts. The acoustic investigation of the HSCA does not qualify as evidence. The basic hypothesis of the measurements (a motorcycle officer 39 yards behind the limousine) is not met, and it is proven that the recording was made after the assassination.

We can therefore state with a relatively high degree of certainty that three, and only three, shots were fired: one missed shot at time frame Z160, the magic bullet at time frame Z211 and the head shot at time frame Z313.

Our evidence schedule now looks as follows:

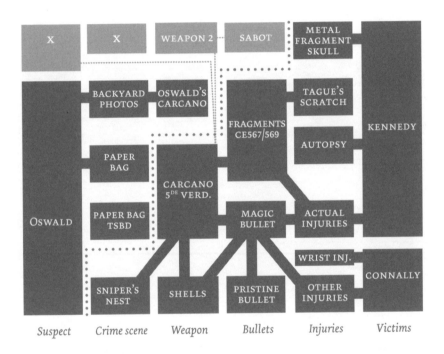

If we could link Oswald to the sniper's nest, we would still have a fairly con-clusive chain of evidence, despite its many problems. But what happens if we cannot place Oswald with sufficient certainty at the scene of the crime, or, even stronger, what if he had an alibi for the time of the assassination, and we could therefore state with certainty that he was *not* in the sniper's nest? Would he have been just a *patsy*, a fall guy, as he himself said? In the next part, we will fully focus on the ultimate question in any crime story: Who did it? *Whodunit?*

PART 7

WHODUNIT

40. OSWALD'S *WHEREABOUTS*

Oswald just before 12:00 noon

We now know that President Kennedy's assassin fired from the sixth floor of the TSBD. But was Oswald there at the time? Everyone who worked in the TSBD was enjoying the autumn sunshine on Dealey Plaza on that Friday afternoon, while watching the corner of Main Street with great anticipation. Everyone except Oswald. He preferred his own company, reading an old newspaper in the sparsely furnished staff room. Bearing in mind that he didn't bring his lunch with him, he couldn't even look forward to the luxury of a quiet meal, unless, of course, 'curtain rails' were on the menu that day. Oswald's absence from the Plaza is impossible to understand. He was a political fanatic. It is quite unthinkable that he would not be interested in Kennedy's motorcade. He maintained that he had seen two colleagues during his lunch, but they didn't remember seeing him. Oswald's entire statement on how he spent his time is therefore a complete lie. Even if Oswald had watched the parade, his behavior still doesn't make sense. Having just witnessed the assassination of the president, would anyone quietly return to the building and go and buy a Coke from the drinks' dispenser on the second floor?

There are strong indications of Oswald's guilt based on timing, but there are also some counter arguments. Oswald was not yet in the sniper's nest between 11:45 and 12:00 noon, that much is certain. He was still on the first floor at noon. His colleague Givens saw him there, reading a newspaper in the *domino room*, the staff room.[586] His immediate superior, William Shelley, also saw him on the ground floor. He was there at approximately 11:50 a.m., hanging about near a telephone.[587] Maintenance operator Piper saw him there at exactly 12:00 noon.[588] Mrs. Arnold, the secretary, even thought that she had seen Oswald on the ground floor just before 12:15, but she couldn't be sure.[589] In any case, Oswald was not in the sniper's nest at 12:00.[590]

Oswald after 12:00 noon

According to the Commission, Oswald was present on the crucial sixth floor afterwards, and there was a witness to this: Oswald's colleague Givens. Again according to the Commission, Givens saw Oswald near the sniper's nest on the sixth floor after 12:00 noon. Strange, because, as we mentioned above, in his original statement Givens maintained that he had seen Oswald on the first floor reading a paper at that time. This does not exclude the fact that Givens might have seen him shortly afterwards on the sixth floor, but why did the witness not mention this second significant fact on November 22? Maybe we could find out where Givens himself was at the time, and thereby determine which statement we should actually believe. According to his initial statement[591] – forensically the most reliable – Givens was on the sixth floor until 11.30 a.m. He then went downstairs to wash his hands. He decided to take his lunch break at 12:00, and saw Oswald with his newspaper.[592] Givens then left the building, stood on the sidewalk for a few minutes[593] and then collected a friend from the parking lot. Together, they walked to the corner of Main Street, where they watched the president drive by.

Oswald's and Givens' timelines can be summarized as follows in accordance with the initial statements:

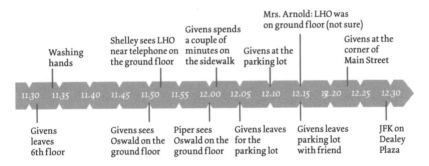

Givens was promoted to key witness after, and because, he deviated from this initial statement. He suddenly strenuously denied ever having mentioned that he had seen Oswald in the *domino room* reading the paper. The Commission was given a completely different account (underlining added):

> Well, it was <u>about a quarter till 12</u>, we were on our way downstairs, and we passed him, and he was standing at the gate on the fifth floor.
> I came downstairs, and I discovered I left my cigarettes in my jacket pocket upstairs, and <u>I took the elevator back upstairs to get my jacket with</u>

my cigarettes in it. When I got back upstairs, <u>he was on the sixth floor</u> in that vicinity, coming from that way.[593]

Oswald's and Givens' timelines suddenly look as follows:

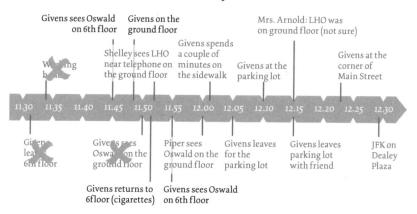

A witness who had seen Oswald on the sixth floor around 12:00... that was what the Commission wanted to hear. It accepted the cigarette story without protest, and only retained this witness account in its final report.[594] Givens' initial statement and other reliable witnesses were blatantly ignored. Did Givens deserve such a degree of blind faith? On February 13, the FBI noted the following about him:[595]

> Lieutenant Revill [...] stated that GIVENS had been previously handled by the Special Services Bureau on a marijuana charge and believes that GIVENS would change his story for money.

If believers still wanted to rely on this chief witness, regardless of the fact that he was susceptible to bribery, they are promptly faced with another problem: Bonnie Ray Williams. Williams was a young black TSBD worker who had arranged to watch the presidential parade from the sixth floor together with a few colleagues. That day, the lunch break was exceptionally brought forward to 11:50 a.m. Williams went downstairs, washed his hands, went back upstairs and installed himself by a window on the sixth floor just before 12:00, barely a couple of meters from the sniper's nest. While awaiting his colleagues, he quietly consumed his lunch, a chicken leg and a soft drink. Williams estimated that this would have taken approximately ten to fifteen minutes. Because no one turned up, he started to wonder whether he was at the right meeting place. He heard or saw no one on the sixth floor. If he had heard someone behind the sniper's nest barricade, he would obviously have checked to see if his friends were there.

Williams told the FBI that he arrived on the sixth floor just *after* 12.00 noon and that his lunch 'would take 5, 10 or 15 minutes'. On the basis of this, the FBI calculated that he would have left the sixth floor again by 12:05. According to the FBI's logic, arriving after 12:00, finding a suitable place to eat, lunching for five to fifteen minutes, leaving and descending the stairs can all be achieved *before* 12:05. The FBI apparently wanted to keep any problems associated with Oswald's absence on the sixth floor to an absolute minimum. But Williams was no pushover. In his statement to the Commission,[596] he wanted to 'dot the i's and cross the t's'. He was adamant that he had only finished his lunch around 12:15. In all that time he had neither seen nor heard Oswald on the sixth floor. Around 12:20 p.m., he joined his colleagues on the fifth floor. Together with his friends, Williams watched the president drive by from the window just below the sniper's nest. He was one of the black young men who were prominently visible in the open corner window on the fifth floor.

We can now complete the timeline as follows:

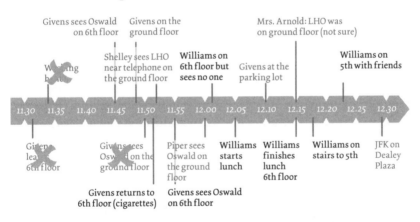

If Oswald had been on the sixth floor between 12:00 noon and 12:15, he must have been exceptionally quiet. He would not have been able to assemble the rifle in that time, which, according to the official version, had been dismantled and brought into the TSBD in a paper bag. But Oswald was still downstairs at 12:00 o'clock. He could not have arrived on the sixth floor *before* Williams. Oswald obviously could not have taken up his position in the sniper's nest while Williams was sitting alongside him, calmly munching his chicken leg. In view of the above, we now have to assume that Oswald didn't go to the sniper's nest until 12:20 p.m. (when the president would already have driven by), where he unpacked and assembled his weapon, fired three times and then reappeared in a flash on the second floor, totally unperturbed and not out of breath.

At any rate, it's safe to conclude that Oswald was not on the sixth floor *until* 12:20 p.m. That implies that Givens' second version, the cigarette story, was a lie and that there is no one left in the TSBD who would have seen Oswald on the sixth floor. Obviously, it is still possible that someone could have seen Oswald from the outside. In this respect, the Commission totally accepted the witness account of the 45-year-old construction worker Howard Brennan. He had to link Oswald to the sniper's nest. The Warren report includes the following statement:

> *Howard L. Brennan, a 45-year-old steam fitter, watched the motorcade from a concrete retaining wall at the southwest corner of Elm and Houston, where he had a clear view of the south side of the Depository Building. (See Commission Exhibit No. 477, page 62).*[597]

The Commission purposely put Brennan in the wrong position on the photographs in the evidence.[598] He was moved a considerable distance to a position from where he had a better view of the sniper's nest. This was a deliberate manipulation, because there was a film record of Brennan's true position, and the Commission must have been aware of the existence of this material. The top two photographs in Figure 92 show the actual situation at the time of the murder. The bottom two photographs reflect the Commission's version. During his cross-examination, Brennan twice confirmed the accuracy of the position in the reconstruction photographs.[599] Bearing in mind that images don't lie, we are left with only one possible liar. At best, Brennan is not an out-and-out liar, but is still a poor witness.

Figure 92 – The top photographs show where Brennan was really sitting. The bottom photographs reflect the Commission's version of his position.

The fact that Brennan was a poor witness is also corroborated by his first statement, made 25 minutes after the shooting.[600] Brennan looked up at the building when the second shot went off. He saw the perpetrator take aim and fire the third shot. The Warren report accepted the following statement from Brennan :[601]

> And I glanced up. And this man that I saw previous was aiming for his last shot. [...] Well, as it appeared to me he was standing up and resting against the left window sill, with gun shouldered to his right shoulder, holding the gun with his left hand and taking positive aim and fired his last shot.

This statement makes no sense at all. Brennan apparently assumed that the sniper was standing up and leaning with his right shoulder against the window on the left. The photograph of the window taken on the inside[602] Figure 93 shows that a man could never stand upright to fire through the dirty window, only the bottom section of which was open. Moreover, the man in CE1311 (Figure 93) is sitting much too close to the window. The position of the box on which the sniper took place in CE1311 (Figure 94) indicates much more accurately where the sniper was sitting.

Figure 93 – A shot fired from an upright position??   Figure 94 – The box on which it is claimed Oswald was sitting.

Even if Oswald bent over considerably to take aim, Brennan would at most have seen a section of the gun barrel and a head. He could never have known that the sniper was 178 cm high and weighed between 75 and 79 kg, facts which he included in his first statement to the police. Believers obstinately continue to recycle the fabrication that Oswald was standing up. Bill O'Reilly, anchor of the most popular talk show on Fox TV, published the popular bestseller *Killing Kennedy* in 2012. He also described Oswald as standing up against the left window sill in the crucial seconds on which his book is based.[603] Almost fifty years later, this sheer nonsense, based on Brennan's statement and the Commission's report, is still being peddled as the truth.

However, there is a better, almost never quoted, witness: Ronald Fischer, who looked up at the corner window on the sixth floor just before the shots were fired (underlining added):

I looked up and saw the man. I looked up at the window and I noticed that he seemed to be laying down there or in a funny position anyway, because all I could see was his head.[604]

Fischer was standing on the sidewalk, one and a half meters to the right of Brennan, and consequently saw Oswald from almost exactly the same angle. Fischer is obviously right in saying that only the sniper's head was visible, but the Commission needed Brennan's upright Oswald. After all, no other explanation was available for Oswald's description, which was distributed via police radio at 12.48 p.m.: 'W/M/30, slender build, 5 ft. 10 inches, 165 pounds'.[605] In turn, this vague description was the only possible explanation for the fact that Officer Tippit stopped Oswald. So Oswald had to be standing up, even if there was no open window to fire through at shoulder height. What's more, Brennan was subsequently unable to identify Oswald in the police line up.[606] He said later that he did recognize Oswald, but was afraid to identify him for fear of reprisals against his family. This seems a rather weak defense for someone who immediately put himself forward as a key witness, who pointed out the sniper's nest and dreamt up a personal description that would lead to an arrest.

Conclusion

There was one witness within the TSBD who allegedly saw Oswald on the sixth floor, but this witness was lying. On Dealey Plaza, Brennan noticed the gun barrel, but he was by no means the only one to do so. Journalist Bob Jackson and spectator Ronald Fischer, for example, also saw the gun barrel in the sniper's nest. We now know with certainty that shots were fired from the corner window on the sixth floor. The question is whether it is possible to prove that *Oswald* was the sniper. For some reason, the personal description provided by Brennan is a fabrication. As a matter of fact, Oswald weighed a lot less than the 75 to 79 kg indicated by Brennan.[607] There are no witnesses who could actually confirm that they saw Oswald on the sixth floor. That doesn't mean he wasn't there though, which isn't much help in our investigation. Maybe we could approach the matter from a different angle, and look for proof that Oswald was not in the sniper's nest. In other words, did Oswald have an alibi?

41. OSWALD'S ALIBI

We have reached a point in the investigation at which we need to bring together the pieces of the puzzle. One significant question remains, a question that should be part of any murder investigation: did the suspect have an alibi? Was Oswald actually on the sixth floor when the shots were fired?

Conspiracists favor seeing Oswald in the Altgens' photograph, which was taken after the second shot with the porch of the TSBD in the background of the limousine (Figure 36). Oswald is claimed to be one of the spectators standing on the entrance steps. This would obviously absolve him of the murder. But the man standing on the entrance steps of the TSBD was Billy Lovelady, not Oswald. He looked a lot like Oswald, but it was definitely Billy Lovelady . Oswald's defense also had another joker: if Oswald was the perpetrator, he would have had to descend the stairs after the assassination, moving like the wind, to arrive in the staff (lunch) room on the second floor just in time. This would have had to be accomplished before Officer Baker and Superintendent Truly arrived there. And there is another complication: Vickie Adams, a young office worker, and her friend, Sandra Styles, were also on the same stairs immediately after the third shot. If they didn't see or hear Oswald at a time when he should have been on the same stairs, we can only conclude that Oswald was not present on the sixth floor at the time of the assassination. In that case he has an alibi. The consequences would be highly significant, because if Oswald had an alibi he could obviously not have been the perpetrator. Furthermore, this would also prove the existence of both a conspiracy aimed at putting the blame on Oswald and a *cover-up*.

The commission failed to execute a reconstruction involving the three sides, i.e. Oswald, Ms Adams and Ms Styles, and finally Messrs. Truly and Baker. It appears that we will have to clarify this on the Commission's behalf. To this end, we will have to create a timeline for all three parties involved. None of those involved saw anyone from the other groups of stair users. Is that possible (figure 95)?

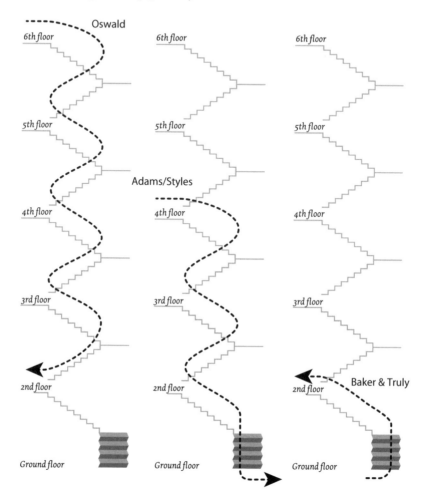

Figure 95 – Trajectories on the stairs

The sniper on the stairs

First, we allow Oswald to descend the stairs. He had to move from the sniper's nest to the lunch room on the second floor. How quickly could this be achieved? On March 20, 1964, the Warren Commission conducted two tests to define how long it would have taken Oswald to do this. Officer Baker acted as a stand-in for Oswald. The tests arrived at 78 and 74 seconds respectively.[23] They did not take into account the fact that Oswald had reloaded the weapon after the third shot, which would have taken at least 2 seconds. The minimum time Oswald would have needed to reach the staff room on the second floor would have been slightly more than the bare minimum of 74 seconds.[608]

However, the time for the overall trajectory tells us little about the exact time at which Oswald would have reached a specific point on the stairs. *Unsolved History*, a program aired by Discovery Channel, focused on this question. The advantage of a television program is that it gives us the opportunity to actually observe the proceedings. Discovery Channel filmed in a warehouse very similar to the TSBD. Gary Mack, the curator of the *Sixth Floor Museum*, also played a prominent part in the test. A man of Oswald's age and stature was kneeling at a window and would make his way to the second floor from there. The chronometers were ready. Less than a minute later 'Oswald' was downstairs. He had covered the distance in 48 seconds. Gary Mack was triumphant: 48 seconds was almost thirty seconds less than the Commission's test results. But this is a suspiciously low number of seconds.

We looked at Discovery Channel's approach in more detail. 'Our race will begin as the last shot is fired at the window,' the individual in charge of the test stated. But the documentary makers forgot that the sniper reloaded the weapon first. The sniper in the documentary was not hampered by book-boxes. He fired the shots from shoulder height whilst kneeling (Figure 96). The real sniper started from a position much lower down, and then had to squeeze through a very narrow opening in the wall of boxes. The sixth floor of the TSBD was disorganized and full of book boxes.

Figure 96 *The stand-in leaves without reloading. He straightens up from a kneeling position and is not hampered by book boxes.*

The stand-in takes 24.12 seconds (Figure 97) to reach the location where Oswald allegedly concealed the weapon. They're making it very easy for 'Oswald' to conceal the weapon. It is placed between two rows of boxes stacked barely one box high - despite the fact that Lieutenant Day made the following statement about the actual hiding place: 'It was hidden underneath and between several boxes. Scraps of paper covered up much of the remaining portions of the rifle.'[609] It appears that the test also doesn't include time for the removal of fingerprints either. The Discovery Channel stand-in reaches the stairwell within 27.02 seconds.

Figure 97 – The stand-in doesn't have to navigate through rubbish and book boxes without making a sound. The weapon is not placed between high stacks of boxes and covered with a box on top. The stand-in only has to put down the weapon during the test.

'Oswald' starts descending the stairs 27.52 seconds after his departure (Figure 98). Note the sign stating *6th floor*. The stand-in reaches the *4th floor* just 6.95 seconds later – the counter clocks up 34.47 seconds by then. The documentary does not show the passage through the *5th floor*. The stand-in reaches the next floor (*3rd floor*) after 39.57 seconds. He consequently took 5.10 seconds to walk from the fourth to the third floor. It is impossible, therefore, that the descent from the sixth to the fourth floor only required 6.95 seconds. The documentary mentions quite correctly that there are twice nine steps between each floor. The distances between floors are consequently equal. If all other floors require approximately 6 seconds each, the first two could not possibly be covered in 6.95 seconds. It seems incredible, but it appears that the documentary makers simply eliminated a floor.

Figure 98 – The stand-in descends from the sixth to the third floor in twelve seconds. The passage across the fifth floor is not shown.

The stand-in reached the second floor 45.30 seconds after the third shot (Figure 99). He took 5.33 seconds to descend from the third to the second floor. The documentary makers stop the clock at the entrance to the hallway. Again this is not correct. The real Oswald had to pass through another two doors in order to reach the cafeteria. Moreover, the door in the hallway closed automatically, however, and took three seconds to close completely. The door was fully closed when Officer Baker was able to see it from the stairs.

Figure 99 – It takes 5.33 seconds to move from the third to the second floor. The stand-in then takes a further three seconds or thereabouts to eventually reach the staff room on the second floor after 48.38 seconds.

The timeline in the Discovery Channel documentary can be illustrated as follows:

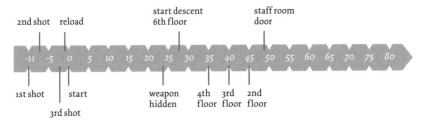

We feel it is necessary to adjust the timeline in the *Unsolved History* documentary to ensure that we know exactly where the sniper was during the descent. He obviously didn't leave until after the third shot, but officer Baker set off for the TSBD after the first shot. After the first shot, Oswald needed to reload, fire, reload and fire again (8.4 seconds). He also needed to reload again after the third shot (2 seconds). He then had to straighten up from a squatting position and start running (0.6 seconds). Before the sniper could leave, approximately eleven seconds would already have elapsed as far as Baker is concerned. We need to correct the timeline, apart from the eleven seconds at the start, with at least the following extra seconds:

1. Oswald has to leave the sniper's nest through the opening in the barricade (1 second) and avoid other boxes standing around the cluttered warehouse without making a sound throughout his entire passage across the sixth floor (1 second);
2. Oswald has to discard the clip (1 second);
3. Oswald has to conceal the weapon right down between two high stacks of boxes and place a box on top of the concealed weapon without leaving new fingerprints behind (4 seconds);
4. Discovery Channel skipped a floor in the test (6 seconds);
5. Oswald still has to pass through the hallway door (1 second) and this automatic door has to close completely (3 seconds).

According to our calculations, from his starting point to the stairs, Oswald required approximately seventeen seconds more than the time proposed in the television documentary. This implies that the descent would, in effect, have taken 65.38 seconds. The adjusted timeline now looks as follows:

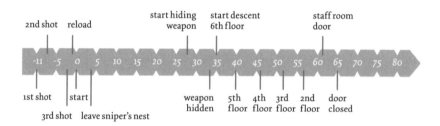

In the corrected version, the total time elapsed since the first shot amounts to approximately 76 (11+65) seconds. This agrees completely with the timing estimated by the Commission.

The officer on the motorcycle

We already looked at Baker's trajectory in more detail while discussing the initial shot. According to the tests conducted by the Warren Commission, he would have needed between 74 and 90 seconds to reach the location where he saw Oswald. Let's focus on this in more detail too.

There is no doubt concerning Baker's witness statement: he accelerated his motorcycle in the direction of the TSBD immediately after the first shot,[610] and drove approximately 61 m (200 feet) to Elm Street. At an average speed of 17 km/h, this distance would be covered in thirteen seconds. He parked his motorcycle at a distance of 13 m (45 feet) from the entrance to the TSBD.[611] The amateur recording made by spectator Couch clearly shows that Baker ran from his motorcycle to the door to the TSBD quite quickly (Figure 100). During later tests, the Commission claimed that Baker covered this distance in fifteen seconds. If the fifteen seconds relate solely to the 13 m Baker covered running, he would have been running at a speed of 3.1 km/h. However, this is not what the Couch film shows. We are, therefore, sticking to thirteen seconds to drive the motorcycle across a distance of 61 m, seven seconds to park the motorcycle and eight seconds to run. The film also shows that the spectators on Dealey Plaza are already moving in the direction of the grassy knoll.

Figure 100 – The film recorded by spectator Couch shows Officer Baker running at speed towards the hallway of the TSBD.

Baker encountered Superintendent Truly in the entrance to the TSBD, who immediately offered to follow him. Baker explained their further progress as follows:

> So we immediately went out through the second set of doors, and we ran into the swinging door [...]. [We] got through that little swinging door there and we kind of all ran, not real fast but, you know, a good trot, to the back of the building.

The distance from the hallway to beyond the third entrance door amounts to approximately 10 m (Figure 101). The time needed to enter the TSBD, including a brief conversation, cover the distance and pass three doors should be estimated at approximately fifteen seconds.

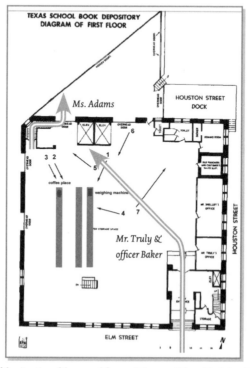

Figure 101 – Sketch of the situation of the ground floor and the route followed by Baker, Truly and Miss Adams.

Proceeding from the hallway in the southeast corner to the elevator in the northwest corner, Baker and Truly would have had to cover approximately 20 m 'at a steady pace'. At 7.2 km/h or 2 m per second they would have needed 10 seconds to reach the rear of the building (Figure 101). Baker and Truly then stood by the elevator and conferred as follows:

> I was following him [...] and we went across it to the northwest corner which is in the rear, back there. And he was trying to get that service elevator down there. [...] He hollered for it, said, 'Bring that elevator down here.' It seemed like he did it twice. I said 'Let's take the stairs'. He said, 'Okay' and so he immediately turned around, which the stairs is just to the, would be to the, well, the west of this elevator. And we went up them.

Merely reading the description aloud already takes more than twenty seconds. This must be about the minimum time that would have been required to carry out these activities: trying to get the elevator down (five seconds), calling for the elevator twice (eight seconds), and then conferring (four seconds) about the stairs. This would have amounted to about seventeen seconds. The distance to the stairs is then just a few meters (two seconds). Both men rushed up the stairs. Generally speaking, they would have taken less time per floor than the six seconds needed by the steadily proceeding stand-in in the Discovery Channel reconstruction. If Baker needed approximately four seconds to ascend a floor in a hurry, he would have been able to see the door of the hallway on the second floor after three seconds, before he had actually reached that floor. At that time, exactly 76 seconds had elapsed since the initial shot. Furthermore, the door was already fully closed. Exactly 76 seconds from the first shot is the minimum time, down to the last second, required by Oswald... This dossier is cursed.

The Baker timeline looks as follows:

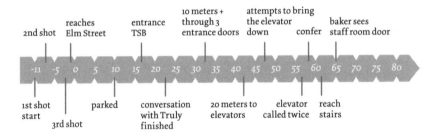

It is therefore possible that Oswald could have arrived on the second floor just before Truly and Baker. Oswald's presence on the second floor is consequently not a watertight alibi. According to the Commission, the time required by Baker and Truly could have been even as high as approximately ninety seconds, in which case Oswald would clearly have had even more time.

The women on the stairs

We still need to test whether Victoria (Vickie) Adams and her colleague Sandra Styles didn't cross Oswald's or Baker's paths. Both young ladies were enthusiastically watching the president, and the first lady in particular, from the fourth floor window. Soon after, Vickie Adams was on Dealey Plaza, where she still saw spectators running in the direction of the *Grassy Knoll*. The Couch film also shows all the spectators running in the direction of the grass verge, while Baker is running towards the hallway of the TSBD (Figure 100). If Adams and Styles were able to join this throng, they must have used the stairs very shortly after the assassination. Vicki Adams did not see or hear Oswald on the stairs. Conspiracists maintain that this proves that Oswald was not on the stairs; otherwise the women would have definitely seen or at least heard him. If Oswald was not on the stairs after the shooting, his presence on the second floor obviously acts as an alibi. Aware of that fact, the Commission decreed that Vicki Adams must have been mistaken and, contrary to all elements in the dossier, would not have descended the stairs until several minutes after the shots were fired. We need to establish whether the Commission had a sound case in this instance.

The first person who could have corroborated Miss Adams' account was obviously her friend Sandra Styles. After all, they descended the stairs together. The Commission did not cross-examine Sandra Styles, however. She did at some point make a statement, i.e. on March 19, 1964, and described the events as follows (underlining added):

> I saw people running and others lie down on the ground and realized something was happening but did not know exactly what was happening. VICTORIA ADAMS and I left the office at this time, went down the back stairs and left the building at the back door.[612]

This does not appear to have been several minutes after the shooting. Throughout the entire Warren Report, the name Sandra Styles is not even mentioned once.

Two other women, Elsie Dorman and office manager Dorothy Garner, also joined Victoria Adams at the fourth floor window. They made brief statements, but did not precisely define when Adams and Styles went down. And no one ever asked them for this information. Moreover, the Commission was not at all interested in what Dorman and Garner had to say. They were not cross-examined, and no mention of them was made, not even in a footnote to the report. There was, however, good reason to focus on Dorothy Garner in particular. Researcher Barry Ernest searched for decades for information on Vicki Adams. One late afternoon, he was scouring the umpteenth box of ultra-boring documents at the National

Archives . The box contained old documents that, for one reason or another, had been handed over to the Commission at some point. To his utter amazement, he found a remarkable letter (Figure 102) in which public prosecutor Martha Stroud reported to the Commission that Miss Adams' superior, the stern Mrs. Garner, observed Truly and Baker ascending the stairs *after* Miss Adams went down. Dorothy Garner is a highly reliable witness. She was Vicki Adams' exacting superior, and if she said that Vicki Adams descended the stairs before Officer Baker came upstairs, then it's highly likely that this is what happened. Oswald's alibi is suddenly much more credible. The Commission never saw this extremely significant letter from the public prosecutor. Someone obviously took the trouble to secrete this letter amongst other insignificant documentation. Only Barry Ernest's patience and tenacity ensured that we did get to see this document, albeit by coincidence and several decades later. Ernest also discovered the official death certificate of the president of the United States amongst other inconsequential documentation. Once again, the investigation was guilty of manipulating the evidence and scandalously rewriting history by ignoring a credible and highly significant statement that could have totally exonerated the accused, and shamelessly excluding it from the dossier and purposely misplacing it.

This is not the only time this has happened. The British Prime Minister, Tony Blair, apologized in a personal letter in June 2000 and publicly in 2005 for a judicial error committed by the government in the case of the *Guildford Four*. In 1974, the four men had been quickly arrested in connection with an IRA bomb attack. When it subsequently became clear that the suspects might have had an alibi at the time of the attack, the prosecutor fraudulently kept the documentation out of the dossier, and classified it in the folder marked 'not to be shown to the defense'. The Guildford Four, one of whom had already died whilst in prison, did not manage to clear their names until 1990. Having spent sixteen years in prison even though they were innocent, they were finally released. The decision to withhold Assistant Public Prosecutor Martha Stroud's letter is at least just as bad. In this case, however, no one took political responsibility, and there were no apologies. On the contrary, believers still unashamedly refer to the Warren investigation as the most in-depth and exemplary of all times.

Detective Leavelle of the Dallas police force was the officer who cross-examined Vickie Adams on February 17, 1964, when she made the following statement:

After the third shot, I went out the back door. I said, 'I think someone has been shot.' The elevator was not running and there was no one on the stairs. I went down to the first floor. I saw Mr. Shelley and another employee named Bill. The freight elevator had not moved, and I still did not see anyone on the stairs.

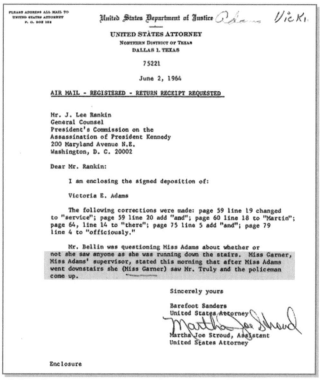

Figure 102 – *The letter from Assistant Prosecutor Martha Stroud purposely filed so as never to be found, which confirms that Vicki Adams descended before Officer Baker came up the stairs.*

If Vicki Adams went outside via the back door after the third shot, it doesn't sound as though many minutes had elapsed before she moved. There is another remarkable aspect to this account. In 2002, when Barry Ernest finally managed to track down Vicki Adams after 39 years of anonymity, she made the following statement about that February 17:

One time a detective from the Dallas police came to my apartment, showed his badge and asked to talk with me. I asked him why he needed to talk with me since I had already given my testimony to the Dallas Police. 'Oh' he responded, 'the records were all burned in a fire we had and we have to interview everyone again.'

There had been no fire at the Dallas police force. Why was the police detective lying? What happened to Miss Adams' earlier statements? She was cross-examined by 'several men' on November 22, 1963. What happened to the statements she made to the Secret Service and the CIA? Vicki Adams would declare in 2002 that she was embarrassed vis-à-vis her colleagues because all the attention in the investigations by 'several agencies' appeared to be focused on her: 'The people in my office were pretty chagrined that the secret police and CIA and all those others were interested in me.'[613] There is no trace of this focus on Miss Adams in the dossier, nor of the statements she made. Vicki Adams always maintained that she had written a six page letter about the events immediately after she got home on November 22, and sent it to the editor of *The Monitor*, a catholic newspaper based in San Francisco. Her foster father was the paper's advertising executive. The letter never arrived on the editor's desk, and was subsequently never found.

Once again we are faced with yet another recurring phenomenon. Detective Leavelle appeared on Vicki Adams' doorstep on February 17, the day on which she had moved to a new address. The apartment had been rented in her flat mate's name. Miss Adams hadn't notified anyone of the new address yet, not even her boss, colleagues or the post office.[614] But she suddenly came face to face with Detective Leavelle in his white cowboy hat (Leavelle was the tall man standing to the left of Oswald when he was shot). If you hear an account such as this one just once you might shrug your shoulders, but this happens all too often in the Kennedy dossier. We mentioned Tague earlier, who found out that the Commission knew that he had been on Dealey Plaza early one morning months after the assassination; or Croft, who received a visit from the FBI on November 23 at an address two thousand miles away from Dallas that was known to no-one.

In the end, Commission Attorney David Belin did question Vicki Adams, but it was a cross-examination conducted by a staff member rather than by the Commission members themselves. Belin intimidated Miss Adams with transparent posturing, and tried to convince her that she was wrong. Miss Adams stuck to her story, however,[615] 'And after the third shot, following that, the third shot, I went to the back of the building down the back stairs.' Despite the fact that she was wearing 8 cm high heels, Vicki Adams ran down the stairs together with Sandra Styles. They didn't see anyone on the stairs and didn't hear anyone call for the elevator. The elevator was not moving. They didn't stop on the way and then reached the first floor.

> Mr. BELIN - When you got to the bottom of the first floor, did you see any-
> one there as you entered the first floor from the stairway?
> Miss ADAMS - Yes, sir.
> Mr. BELIN - Who did you see?
> Miss ADAMS - Mr. Bill Shelley and Billy Lovelady.

Belin suddenly became interested when Vicki Adams related that she had met her colleagues, Shelley and Lovelady on the ground floor. He immediately conducted a thorough investigation into the activities of the men Vicki Adams had referred to. The Commission rubbed its hands. Shelley[616] and Lovelady[617] were not in the TSBD immediately after the shots, so if Miss Adams had encountered them as soon as she got downstairs, she must have descended the stairs much later – quite a lot later actually, because Shelley and Lovelady had initially participated in the search outside, and only then re-entered the building.

Did Vicki Adams make a mistake about the timing or... about the meeting itself? After all, Shelley and Lovelady were both adamant that they had *not* seen Ms Adams and Ms Styles, neither immediately after the shooting nor upon their return. Lovelady had seen one girl, but 'couldn't swear that it was Vicki'. Encountering someone is a reciprocal act. If the men didn't encounter Vicki, she would not have seen them either. Perhaps Vicki Adams came across Shelley and Lovelady at the railroad yard, and consequently made a mistake about the location of the encounter. In any case, the error apparently relates to the actual encounter and not the timing of her departure from the fourth floor.

When researcher Barry Ernest finally found Vicki Adams in 2002, the 22-year-old girl had matured into a charming 61-year-old woman. She had totally lost her faith in the government back in 1963.

> I saw what I saw, and my testimony apparently didn't fit what the gov-
> ernment wanted. That is too bad. Repeatedly I asked that my testimony be
> confirmed by another witness who was with me part of the time, but I was
> basically blown off.[618]

Vicki Adams was a highly reliable witness with great integrity, as demonstrated by her earlier life. When she was eleven years old, her parents suddenly abandoned her, and she grew up in orphanages. Upon completing her secondary education, she joined the Ursuline Sisters as a novice.

In 1962, whilst she was teaching sixth-grade pupils, she started to doubt her faith. She decided to leave her safe existence, because she didn't want to teach children something she no longer believed in herself. Mid-1963 she got a job at the *Texas School Book Depository*, which would change her life for ever. However, following her negative experiences with the official approach to the dossier, she never talked about the traumatic event again, and henceforth banished it from her life. She did not follow the polemics about the murder because she was not interested in other people's opinions on what happened on Dealey Plaza. She was there. In 2002, she finally decided to recount again that this, and only this, is what happened on November 22, 1963: when the presidential motorcade approached, she was in the company of other girls working in the office when they opened a window on the fourth floor. Her colleague and friend Sandra Styles was standing alongside her. The limousine passed by and she heard one shot.

> *I saw that something was wrong and watched as Mrs. Kennedy appeared to be climbing out of the car. I saw a Secret Service man jump in and the car began speeding up toward the triple underpass. Before it reached that I turned to Sandra and I said, 'I want to see what is going on.' We ran to the back of the office and down the stairs.*
>
> *We ran down the stairs. We were both in high heels. No one was there. We would have heard other steps. The noise on those steps is very obvious. And remember, the elevator cables were not moving. It was quiet.*
>
> *We ran outside and noticed a lot of people running toward the railroad tracks. The railroad yard behind the grassy knoll was quite a distance away. I could not see anything other than people running toward the railroad cars and I tried to run that way, too. But a policeman stopped us. I didn't get very far – maybe 10 or 20 feet from the depository building. So we turned back to Houston and to the front of the building.*[619]

The Commission's view

The Commission didn't want Miss Adams on the stairs so soon after the assassination, however. It consequently limited itself to the sections in the statements made by Adams, Shelley and Lovelady that it considered useful to create its feeble logic. The Commission proceeded on the basis of the following elements:

Vickie Adams had made two statements:
- **A.** Together with Sandra Styles, she had gone down immediately after the third shot;
- **B.** She remembered having met Shelley and Lovelady on the ground floor.

The facts of the case show:
1. Sandra Styles had confirmed that they ran down immediately.
   Which confirms premise A.
2. Adams was part of the recognizable throng running in the direction of the Grassy Knoll, which occurred immediately after the assassination.
   Which confirms premise A.
3. Dorothy Garner confirmed that Vicki Adams went downstairs before Baker came up the stairs.
   Which confirms premise A.
4. Neither Shelley nor Lovelady remembered an encounter with Ms Adams.
   Premise B is consequently a mistake.

Nevertheless, the Commission concluded as follows: premise A is incorrect because premise B is correct! This is what the Commission distilled from all this as the evangelical truth[620] (underlining added):

> *Victoria Adams, who worked on the fourth floor of the Depository Building, <u>claimed</u> that within <u>about 1 minute</u> following the shots she ran from a window on the south side of the fourth floor down the rear stairs to the first floor, where she encountered two Depository employees--William Shelley and Billy Lovelady.*

Vickie Adams made only a 'claim' about her timing. However, as soon as her encounter with Shelley and Lovelady is mentioned, she is no longer making claims but stating the plain truth: 'where she encountered'. The fact that, upon closer inspection, the encounter didn't appear to have taken place did not affect the Commission's decision-making at all. Vicki Adams stated that she left 'after the third shot'. The Commission decided to turn this into 'within about 1 minute' of the shots. But one minute's difference is of vital importance with respect to the situation in the stairwell immediately after the assassination. The Commission also concluded that Adams must have been mistaken *because* she didn't hear Oswald. The fact that Oswald might not have been on the stairs at all wasn't even a hypothetical possibility as far as the Commission was concerned. The Commission also concluded that she was mistaken about the timing on the basis of the fact that Vicki Adams did not encounter Officer Baker and Mr. Truly. We will now verify whether this was correct.

For the Commission, the encounter with Shelley and Lovelady was absolutely necessary to delay Vicki Adams' departure by a few minutes. In order to substantiate the precarious encounter a little more, the Commission even had the audacity to write the following: 'On entering, Lovelady saw a girl on the first floor <u>who he believes was Victoria Adams</u>'. However, what Lovelady really said to the commission is as follows (underlining added):[621]

> *Mr. BALL - Who did you see in the first floor?*
> *Mr. LOVELADY - I saw a girl but <u>I wouldn't swear to it it's Vicki</u>*

Including this distortion of Lovelady's words, the Commission devoted no more than two paragraphs to the uncomfortable witness Adams. Bugliosi's 1,518-page report did not refer much to Victoria Adams either. She was only mentioned once in a mocking way:

> *So if it wasn't Oswald who shot Kennedy from the sixth-floor window [...]*
> *it must have been some other Book Depository employee right? But who?*
> *Charles Givens? James Jarman? Victoria Adams? (Why not? Women can*
> *pull a trigger too, you know.)*[622]

It was probably meant to be funny. With all due respect to Bugliosi's painstaking efforts, this sneering remark is the last thing Vicki Adams deserved. She was a gentle, honest young woman, who was ignored as a witness and intimidated in an unacceptable manner. It is unbelievable that the grand master does not breathe a word about this witness in all other respects.

Oswald's alibi

It is a sad state of affairs, but ultimately it may have less relevance to the investigation. In the end, the only really important issue is the actual facts, the time it took Victoria Adams to complete the trajectory. What are the bare facts?

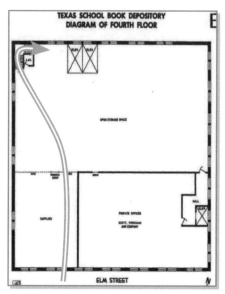

Figure 103- The fourth floor and the route to the stairs covered by Vicki Adams and Sandra Styles.

Adams and Styles were standing at the second window, starting from the left, on the fourth floor (Figure 103). They could reach the stairs in almost a straight line and cover the thirty meters in fifteen seconds. The Discovery Channel simulation demonstrated that a floor could be easily crossed in 5.5 seconds, which implies that three floors would require approximately seventeen seconds. If Adams left five seconds after the fatal shot, she would have been at the bottom of the stairs on the ground floor 37 seconds later, right by the back door of the TSBD. The stairs end right by the back door (Figure 101). Oswald was not yet on the stairs at that time, and Baker and Truly were not in the main hall on the ground floor.

Victoria Adams' timing consequently does not give Oswald a sound alibi. It *is possible* that Miss Adams did not see or hear Oswald if she left so quickly. She could also have been standing outside without coming across Baker and Truly . The timeline looks as follows:

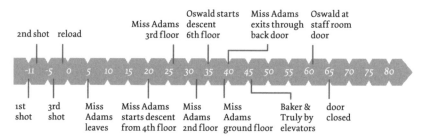

Once again the Commission could have saved itself from lies and manipulation. The choice between a departure five seconds or five minutes after the assassination makes no difference. Oswald is not exonerated in either case. Adams and Styles were already outside after forty seconds. Baker and Truly were walking towards the elevator at that time. Oswald had just started his descent, for which he would need just over twenty seconds, the time lost by Baker and Truly by the elevator. When they walked up the stairs, Oswald had just arrived in the staff room (Figure 104).

Would Victoria Adams give Oswald an alibi if we assume that she hadn't left until, for example, twenty seconds had elapsed, and she didn't hear or see Oswald? No, because then she would definitely have encountered Baker and Truly. Oswald is still the hapless person he always was.

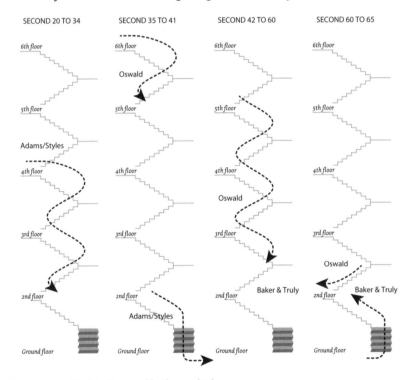

Figure 104- Combined timeline Oswald, Adams and Baker

The final joker does not exonerate Oswald. Miss Adams' presence on the stairs, immediately after the shooting, is possible without her seeing or hearing Oswald. And it is equally possible that she would not encounter Baker and Truly during her journey. Finally, Oswald's presence on the second floor does not exclude him from still being in the sniper's nest 76 seconds earlier. That's why Oswald does not have an alibi at the time of the assassination. We have now investigated everything we need to know about the crime. It has been an arduous journey through a highly complex dossier. Time to formulate our conclusions.

42. DILEMMA

Oswald is guilty

We are faced with a dilemma: there is no proof that Oswald was in the sniper's nest, but equally no proof that he wasn't there. Based on the data in the dossier, it's not unreasonable to assume that he was in the sniper's nest. If he was indeed the shooter we can also reasonably assume that the Carcano that was found belonged to him. The official injuries inflicted upon the victims can be explained on the basis of three shots and one sniper. After the last shot, Oswald could have arrived on the second floor just in time to encounter Truly and Officer Baker and later, murder Tippit while on the run.

On the basis of this hypothesis, our chain of evidence looks as follows:

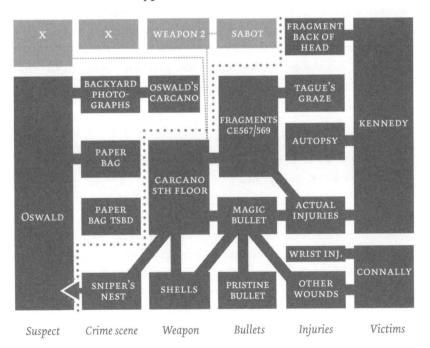

| Suspect | Crime scene | Weapon | Bullets | Injuries | Victims |

The problems associated with the shells and paper bag in the sniper's nest are in all probability due to the extremely clumsy approach of the police in Dallas. The non-identification of the pristine bullet by four witnesses remains a mystery, but, the question as to whether the bullet in the dossier is the same bullet that was picked up at the Parkland Hospital ultimately does not affect the relationship between the victims and the perpetrators. The problems associated with the autopsy report and Rydberg's drawing seem to be the result of political intervention, intended paradoxically to counter conspiracy rumors.

In addition, quite a few improbabilities would be required to maintain the hypothesis. Once Williams had finished his lunch, Oswald would have had little time to prepare for the assassination, but it is not impossible. Oswald was a bad shot and the weapon was unreliable and poorly adjusted. But it is not totally impossible that it could have been used to carry out the shooting. Neither is it totally impossible that the second floor could have been reached within the proposed time limit. The fact that the weapon showed very few fingerprints isn't totally impossible either. It is also not completely impossible that Oswald was in possession of four, and only four, Carcano bullets. It isn't completely impossible that Frazier and his sister were wrong (by 30 cm) about the length of the paper bag that Oswald brought with him in the morning. It isn't completely impossible that Oswald's was driven by a need for self assertion but that he continued to deny any responsibility at the same time following his arrest. Moreover, all the above improbabilities would have to occur simultaneously. Contrary to accepted judicial principles, let us interpret any doubts to the suspect's disadvantage. This still leaves two extremely disturbing questions unanswered:

- Is the Carcano in the backyard different from the Carcano in the TSBD?
- How do we explain the mysterious, additional external wound on the back of Kennedy's head?

Maybe we shouldn't believe our own eyes after all, and the Carcano found at the crime scene is the same weapon as the one in the backyard photographs. The HSCA experts reached the same conclusion. Perhaps it is not always possible to clarify *everything*, and the metal fragment at the back of Kennedy's head is one of these mysteries that cannot be solved. Reality is sometimes more bizarre than our imagination, or can even defy logic altogether. The official version does not mention a conspiracy. If we pursue that option, we also have to add the presence of Jim Braden on Dealey Plaza and Ruby in the role of a second disturbed loner to the long list of improbabilities in a single weekend.

What if we were to join the conspiracists? In that case, we would have to accept the existence of a plot that would have entrusted Oswald with the execution of the crime of the century. A conspiracy that would choose Oswald as the sniper appears highly unlikely. It is immediately obvious though that the role of *patsy*, the born loser, appears to match Oswald's personality to perfection. Could the conspiracists be right after all?

Is Oswald merely a fall guy

Let us now reconsider the case from this improbable angle. No one can prove that Oswald was present in the sniper's nest, which raises the possibility, at least theoretically, that he was *not* there. In this hypothesis, the real culprit must have hidden an old Carcano with an identical serial number to Oswald's museum piece on the sixth floor. The assassination was executed by an experienced sniper using a sound weapon with bullets that had been prepared in advance with the above-mentioned Carcano. In that case, the unexplained wound on the back of Kennedy's head might have been inflicted by a *sabot* fragment. A bullet does not fragment before impact, but a piece of sabot travelling with it could explain Kennedy's minor additional injury.

The scapegoat hypothesis also explains the difference between the Carcano in the backyard photographs and the Carcano in the evidence. It makes the absence of fingerprints on the weapon acceptable and does away with the question as to why Oswald hadn't adjusted his gun sight in order to be able to fire more accurately and accommodate right-handed use. Another advantage is that this hypothesis explains why Oswald never bought or possessed bullets.

Assuming Oswald was a fall guy, the palm print taken from the weapon constitutes fabricated evidence. Because no fingerprints were discovered on the weapon at the crime scene, the 'planted' fingerprint had to be applied in an improbable position, underneath the gun barrel. If the palm print on the Carcano was falsified, there must have been an accomplice within the police force. We are now entering the dangerous territory of speculation, but it has become apparent more than once in this dossier that falsified evidence is not just a figment of the conspiracists' imagination.

Moreover, not a single believer has ever been able to provide a rational explanation for the unnecessary, post-mortem fourth set of Oswald's fingerprints taken at night. Ruby also received at least passive support from within the police force, and there is a long list of unanswered questions with respect to Officer Tippit. The involvement of certain members of the police force in the events following the assassination is speculation, but by no means a totally unreasonable assumption.

The *patsy* hypothesis also offers a possible solution to the mystery of the exchanged pristine bullet. It cannot be ruled out that the bullet could have been exchanged in the course of the investigation; Four consecutive reliable witnesses were adamant in this respect. There is no doubt they were put under considerable pressure to change their statement, but they stood by what they said, i.e. that the bullet in the evidence was not the same as the bullet they had seen on November 22. It is unthinkable that the FBI could have made a genuine mistake, or would have lost the bullet that was fired at the president. If the bullet was exchanged, it was as a result of a conscious intervention. If we accept that the FBI exchanged the bullet for a reason, we are faced with the question: why on earth? No valid reason can be found if the Carcano was indeed used for the shooting. The situation is different in the fall-guy hypothesis. Maybe the bullet showed signs of the use of a sabot or perhaps, for one reason or another, the necessary traces pointing to the Carcano were missing?

A paper bag of only 60 cm is not an insurmountable problem in the fall-guy hypothesis, in which Oswald would no longer have to carry in a Carcano. It remains unclear what he actually carried into the building, and why he lied about it to the police, but a 60 cm package could definitely not accommodate a Carcano. The official version does not provide a credible explanation as to how the weapon got into the TSBD.

The fall-guy hypothesis also solves another awkward problem. If Oswald's had merely been driven by a need to assert himself, he would have had no reason to persistently deny that he had carried out the assassination. If Oswald was a (in some form or other collaborating) fall guy, his attitude following his arrest suddenly seems much more logical.

If Oswald was not the perpetrator, we would be rid of a list of burning problems, but other questions would arise at the same time. Why were Oswald's fingerprints on the book boxes? Why was he the only one not in the vicinity of anyone else at the time the president passed by? Why did he flee, and feel an urgent need to collect a weapon from his rented accommodation? If not a weapon, what was in the paper bag he took into the TSBD that morning? The only sane comment we can make here is that Oswald did not necessarily have to pull the trigger to be an accomplice. Maybe he was allocated a completely different role in the scenario, which would in some way explain his absence from Dealey Plaza, his flight and his taking the paper bag into the building.

What would our diagram look like if we assumed that the sniper was someone else, not Oswald ?

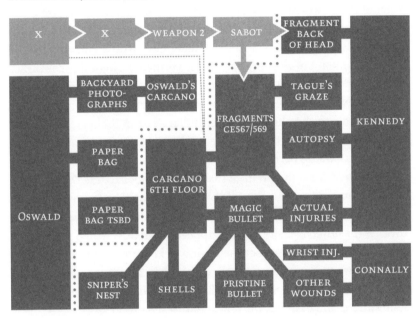

There are two major sticking points. The first is the need of a second sniper and a second weapon. These problems can be solved, however. The sniper could have hidden in the TSBD or on the roof in the night from Thursday to Friday. He could have left the building after the shooting, dressed in a police uniform for example, and taken advantage of both the general confusion and lack of adequate quick sealing of the crime scene. According to the police radio logbook, the TSBD wasn't completely secured until 1.35 p.m.,[623] more than an hour after the assassination! At least three witnesses, Terry Wood, John Puddington[624] and James Worrell[625] saw how a man ran away through the back door of the TSBD soon after the attack. The second sticking point is Oswald himself. One way or another, our hypothetical conspiracists had to prevent Oswald, the fall guy, from becoming the focus of attention anywhere but at the sniper's nest. Which means that we haven't quite closed the loop with the conspiracy hypothesis either.

A difficult choice

A dilemma is by definition an impossible choice. The truth is that everything depends upon whether we believe that the Carcano in the TSBD was different from Oswald's Carcano in the backyard photographs and that the metal fragment on the back of Kennedy's head is relevant and inexplicable on the basis of the official shots with the Carcano. If the answer to either of those two questions is positive, there was another weapon in the TSBD. In that case, Oswald was the *patsy* he maintained he was, someone who was involved in the plot from the sidelines without knowing the full story. The amount of evidence against him is then the logical consequence of the efforts made by the conspiracists to point the finger of suspicion entirely at him. They presumably also intended to eliminate him before he would be able to shed light on his subsidiary role in the plot. This would also put the Tippit murder in a different light. Maybe it was an act of self defense on Oswald's part?

We started from the premise that if we cannot exclude Oswald from being the one and only sniper, this hypothesis would be given preference. At least we know that both Oswald and the Carcano were present in the TSBD. If the official version were to appear possible, it would presuppose fewer extra elements. We proposed using Ockham's razor as our guiding principle: when several hypotheses can explain an event in equal measure, preference will be given to the hypothesis that comprises the fewest assumptions and assumes the fewest entities. As soon as we were able to confirm the single-bullet theory and that Oswald did not have an alibi, his guilt appeared to be a fact. The lone nut theory was the most difficult one, with the ballistic possibility of a magic bullet. Once we arrived at this point, the remaining pieces of the puzzle would fall into place automatically. However, after this initial increase in certainty, our confidence gradually diminished again. After all, the second starting point of our investigation was that we needed to find an explanation for *all* relevant findings, and that's where the lone nut theory becomes problematic. Looking at it sensibly and objectively, there are too many unsolved problems and we have constantly had to support the working hypothesis with the most implausible assumptions.

Ockham's razor enables us to make the right choice between two similar hypotheses. The question is, however, whether both hypotheses explain the events in equal measure.

Score card

The logical approach in order to weigh up the quality of the various hypotheses is to list the different problems. If there is no problem, the item can be ticked off. Illogical or implausible situations can be indicated with a question mark. Serious and unsolved problems can be crossed. This produces the following results:

	Problems	lone nut	conspiracist sniper	conspiracist patsy	total patsy
1	Oswald's suitability as a conspiracist	✔	✘	✔	✔
2	Oswald's lack of interest in the JFK motorcade	✔	✔	?	✘
3	Origin of the four bullets?	?	?	✔	✔
4	Paper bag on arrival at TSBD	✘	✘	?	✘
5	Bringing second sniper into TSBD	✔	✔	?	?
6	Presence of sniper in Sniper's Nest	?	?	?	?
7	When did Osward assemble the weapon?	?	?	✔	✔
8	Oswald's shooting skills	?	?	✔	✔
9	Suitability of the weapon	?	?	✔	✔
10	Absence of fingerprints on the Carcano	?	?	✔	✔
11	Presence of fingerprints in the Sniper's Nest	✔	✔	✔	✘
12	Oswald early presence on the 2nd floor	?	?	✔	✔
13	Taking second sniper out of the TSBD	✔	✔	✘	✘
14	Fragment on the back of Kennedy's head	✘	✘	✔	✔
15	Presence of Jim Braden	✘	✔	✔	✔
16	Oswald's attitude after the arrest	✘	✔	✔	✘
17	Palm print on the weapon	✔	✔	?	?
18	Apparent difference with the backyard photographs	✘	✘	✔	✔
19	Jack Ruby's motive	?	✔	✔	✔
20	Reason for exchange of pristine bullet	?	?	✔	✔

On the basis of this systematic analysis, it is clear that the hypotheses are *not* of equal value. We can all make individual evaluations of each specific problem, and allocate a degree of seriousness to them. But, irrespective of these evaluations, there appears to be a major difference between the lone nut hypothesis and the conspiracy/fall-guy hypothesis.

The hypothesis based on Oswald being a lone nut who committed the assassination leaves five unexplained questions of major importance:

- How did the weapon get into the TSBD in a bag measuring just 60 cm long?
- What caused the minor injury on the back of Kennedy's head?
- What was Jim Braden doing in the Dal-Tex building?
- Why didn't Oswald just admit that he had murdered Kennedy if his only motive was a drive to assert himself?

- Why is the Carcano in the evidence different from the Carcano in the backyard photographs?

Perhaps it was his Carcano that was found in theTSBD after all. Despite the striking difference with regard to the tab at the bottom, we also see strong similarities between the backyard Carcano and the TSBD-Carcano when we look at the end of the barrel of the weapon (Figure 21).

But then we are still faced with the following illogical or implausible situations:

- Where did Oswald get four, and only four, bullets from?
- There is no proof that Oswald was in the sniper's nest.
- Where and how did Oswald manage to assemble the weapon, without a screwdriver and with Bonnie Ray Williams hanging around the sniper's nest until 12:20 p.m.?
- Oswald was at best a marksman with average skills, who fired two perfect shots within five seconds.
- The weapon was totally unreliable, and the gun sight poorly adjusted.
- The weapon contained no fingerprints on the sections that the sniper would have had to touch in order to fire.
- Oswald managed to reach the second floor just in time, down to the second. This remains an unbelievable coincidence, and the time for various time-consuming aspects, such as the cleaning of the weapon and concealment of the cartridge clip and weapon, is cut very short.
- Ruby didn't have a single motive for Oswald's murder.
- Why did four witnesses refuse to identify the pristine bullet?

This means that the official doctrine is relying on five major problems and nine implausibilities.

However, if we consider the hypothesis in which Oswald is part of a conspiracy in which he is unwittingly used as a fall guy, only one unexplained and significant question remains:

- How did the real sniper manage to leave the building after the shooting without being seen?

And we are left with five illogical, unanswered or implausible situations:

- Did the Dallas Police plant Oswald's palm print on the Carcano?
- How were the conspirators able to prevent Oswald from watching the motorcade?

- What did Oswald carry into the TSBD in a paper bag in the morning if it wasn't his Carcano?
- How did the sniper manage to enter the TSBD?
- How did the sniper manage to enter the sniper's nest if Bonnie Ray Williams was in the vicinity until 12:20 p.m.? This problem is of lesser significance, as the real sniper used *sabots* and another weapon, which was probably already assembled.

Each hypothesis has its sticking points, but some are more significant than others. It depends on the degree of uncertainty you are prepared to accept. In any case, we cannot merely rely on Ockham's razor. The hypotheses that we are comparing are not of equal value.

INTRINSICALLY UNSOLVABLE

It becomes clear why the dossier remains so intrinsically unsolvable. Accepting the official story means you answer 'yes' to ALL the following questions, without any exception:

1. The shots are technically possible with a poorly adjusted Carcano.
2. Oswald has the technical ability to fire the two mastershots.
3. The found Carcano is indeed Oswald's Carcano, in spite of the differences noticed in the backyard photos.
4. There is a reasonable explanation for Oswald possessing only four bullets.
5. Oswald brought the Carcano into the TSBD in the paper bag he carried on Friday morning.
6. Oswald remained on the first floor while JFK was supposed to drive past any minute. He arrived at the 6th floor around 12.20 p.m., re-assembled the rifle and shot the president at 12.30.
7. It is possible not to leave any fingerprints on the weapon, the shells and the clip.
8. There is an explanation for Kennedy's second head injury at the outside of his skull, or this is considered irrelevant.
9. The presence of Jim Braden in the Dal-Tex Building and his contacts with Marcello, Hunt and Ruby are pure coincidence.
10. Oswald's behavior after the assassination (not boasting, denying, not confessing on his deathbed...) are compatible with his alleged motive (killing the president to become important).

11. Ferrie's trip tot Texas and his strange behavior in the aftermath of the assault are in no way connected to the murder.
12. Ruby killed Oswald without any motive and without any interference of third parties.

If the answer to one of these questions is 'No', then the possibility of a conspiracy that used Oswald as a fall guy is the only reasonable alternative. Decisive here is whether you can answer, without any exception, 'Yes' to the following six questions:

1. People with strong motives to kill Kennedy were desperate or reckless enough to take the risk in attempting an assault. They decided to use a leftist patsy to deflect the attention from the real perpetrators.
2. Oswald could be talked into a certain form of complicity in the assault.
3. Firing a prepared Carcano bullet with another rifle is technically possible.
4. Another sniper entered the TSBD without being noticed and brought a second weapon into the TSBD.
5. Kennedy's second head wound, at the outside of his skull, can be explained by a sabot.
6. The sniper left the TSBD unobserved with the second weapon after the shooting.

In the final analysis we can disregard some problems. We can accept for instance that if Oswald was a nutcase after all, his behavior after the shooting does not have to fit into normal logic. Or we can state the fact that, once we accept a conspiracy, the question whether the paper bag contained the Carcano or not becomes irrelevant. Both answers are compatible with the hypothesis of a conspiracy using Oswald as a scapegoat. Also other important questions, e.g. whether Kennedy's body was altered before the autopsy, are not decisive here. If the alteration happened, it was part of a cover-up. That could as well take place in the hypothesis of a lone nut as in the hypothesis of a conspiracy. It suffices that Johnson believed that there was a conspiracy (which he did) to explain his potential interference with the procedure.

Kennedy was shot on 22 November 1963, so one of the two lists must be accepted with only affirmative answers. But which one? For now, we will reserve judgment on the final conclusion and turn to another key question: if he had lived, would Lee Harvey Oswald have been convicted of the assassination of John Fitzgerald Kennedy?

43. GUILTY AS CHARGED?

We are now quite familiar with the believers' mantra that there is irrefutable proof against Oswald, and that he would have been found guilty across the board in a court of law. According to Bugliosi, Oswald would still have been found guilty, even if 80% of the evidence had been thrown out. Being a former public prosecutor, Bugliosi knew what he was talking about. In the documentary trial on the BBC *On Trial: Lee Harvey Oswald*[627], he did indeed manage to persuade the jury to find Oswald guilty. In his opening plea during the fictitious court case, he stated the following:

> *The evidence will show that Oswald's rifle, to the exclusion of all other weapons, was determined by fire-arms experts to be the rifle that fired the two bullets and struck down President Kennedy. [...] Ladies and Gentlemen of the Jury, I have every confidence that after you folks fairly objectively evaluated all of the evidence in this case, that you will find that Lee Harvey Oswald, and Lee Harvey Oswald alone was responsible for the assassination of President John F. Kennedy. Thank You Ladies and Gentlemen.*

Perhaps Oswald would indeed have been convicted quickly and without any problem in the Dallas of 1964. Enormous political interests were at stake at that time. Adding to this a good dose of populism, Oswald would not have stood a chance. But the real question is whether he would have been convicted without a hitch in an *impartial* court case. Whether or not he really was guilty is another question. It is a fact of life that historic and judicial truths are not always identical. Ruby, for example, who committed the murder that was watched by millions of people, was never convicted. His was given a trial, but it resulted in a *mistrial*. A new trial was set to follow, but Ruby died before it could take place. From a legal point of view, he was consequently never convicted of Oswald's murder. So, would a jury still be able to convict Oswald 'beyond reasonable doubt' today, distanced and freed from the 1964 context?

Basic principles

Criminal law is based on strict rules. Citizens learnt their lesson from centuries of experience with all-powerful rulers; only the strictest, rigorously applied criteria provided the necessary protection from abuse of power. Judgments merely legitimized by the decision-maker's divinity were no longer accepted. Free citizens no longer took their ruler's word for it. A sovereign who wanted to incarcerate an unruly knight or condemn him to death for high treason was no longer at liberty to exercise jurisdiction at random. The accused was given the right to speak and defend himself. The accuser had to submit plausible evidence. Following on from this, separation of powers became a generally accepted principle. The power to exercise jurisdiction became strictly separated from the proclamation and the implementation of the law. A number of basic principles associated with a fair trial have now become acquired rights. For example, a conviction must always be based on a pre-existing law, the final verdict in a trial can never be decided in advance, the judge and party must always be different personae, there must always be a presumption of innocence – meaning that the prosecutor has to provide proof of guilt rather than the accused proving his innocence - and the accused has the right to defend himself. In Oswald's case all these elementary judicial principles were manifestly flouted.

From a legal point of view, the murder of the president in 1963 was no different from any other murder. It was not a federal crime, and consequently a purely a Texan issue. By taking the president's body and by opposing the Texan authorities at gunpoint, the Secret Service committed a crime. This in itself already put the legality of the entire further procedure in jeopardy. It shouldn't come as a surprise, however, that the law was suspended. Where necessary, even the laws of nature were temporarily put on hold in this dossier. As is usual in these cases, government bodies used national security as an excuse to justify any deviations. Putting principles on hold for practical reasons is not acceptable, however – that is exactly where the essence of a principle lies.

The Warren Commission was a political entity with its own logic. There was no critical cross-examination of the defendant by a counsel. There was no separation of powers. On the contrary, there was just an inextricable tangle. Earl Warren, Chief Justice of the Supreme Court, represented the judiciary. Four members of Congress represented the legislature, and the Commission reported on behalf of the president, the executive. There was no disclosure of evidence and not continuous management of the evidence on the basis of a secure custody chain. President Johnson, who installed the Commission, was both judge and party. The investigators (the FBI, Secret Service, CIA and Dallas Police force) were party. The illustrious names of the judges were also a bad omen. In principle, a judge should be anonymous. Too much emphasis on a judge's importance and prominence detracts from what he has to say. The law stipulates that a verdict should be reached by a jury of voluntary independent citizens, rather than a jury of dignitaries.

Maybe the Warren Commission was right in many ways about the basics, but the fact that it was not trusted is the result of its own approach, rather than being due to its critics. It brazenly violated all the painstakingly acquired rules that were needed in order to reach a communal verdict. This cannot be done with impunity. This had a major impact on the credibility of the final verdict. It would be unjust to hold the Warren Commission responsible for the fact that Oswald did not get a fair and public trial. It was not the Commission's task, but that is why we should give Oswald a chance posthumously.

The question is, therefore, whether Oswald met the criteria for a conviction *from a legal point of view*. Even if you did consider Oswald guilty, an acquittal could still be unavoidable on the basis of the absolute necessity for legal certainty in criminal cases. The disadvantage of a guilty party being exonerated was, and remains, preferable by far to the danger of convicting an innocent party on the basis of procedural errors and manipulated evidence. Manipulated evidence is totally unacceptable, and considered non-existing in jurisdiction. In principle, evidence without a custody chain should also be avoided. Certainty that the accused is *innocent* is not required, but certainty of guilt is an absolute necessity. Reasonable doubt is enough to exonerate the accused. Oswald consequently does not need to prove that he is innocent. The jury needs to establish whether there is sufficient evidence to convict him.

Conspiracy

Oswald cannot be convicted for conspiracy for the simple reason that he was never prosecuted for this. That in itself is significant. Waggoner Carr, the Texan Attorney General, was asked to call the White House urgently on the night of the assassination. Washington wanted to prevent the inclusion of the crime of 'conspiracy' in the charge sheet at all costs.[628] President Johnson's immediate entourage once again actively intervened in the procedure in order to nip any allusion to an international conspiracy in the bud. As a result, Oswald cannot be convicted of conspiracy.

Inadmissible evidence

It is now abundantly clear that the investigation into the murder of the 35th President of the United States was conducted in a disgraceful way. Excuses for the bulkiness of the dossier as replacement evidence for the thoroughness of the investigation are no longer needed. Below, we summarize the Top Ten items of evidence that should be considered inadmissible in fair and legal proceedings against Oswald.

1. **Magic bullet**: there is no certainty that this is the same bullet as the one found in Dallas. No less than four witnesses refused to identify the bullet. The custody chain is incomplete. It appears that investigators made false declarations with respect to the applied identification.

2. **The shells** in the TSBD: once again, the custody chain is insufficiently documented. It is clear that the investigators later made false declarations with respect to the identification of the evidence.

3. **The paper bag** allegedly used to bring the weapon into the TSBD: the crime scene was not photographed in its original state. The first people to arrive on the scene did not see the striking paper bag. There is doubt about the origins of the bag, which was apparently made on the day of the assassination. The original bag was badly damaged by the investigators. The bag is of a different format than that remembered by witnesses. There are no traces to link the bag to the weapon. Fibers originating from a blanket were left behind by the investigators themselves when they placed the blanket on top of the opening of the bag.

4. **The weapon**: this weapon does not appear to be the weapon that Oswald was holding in the notorious backyard photographs. There are, for whatever reason, confusing witness statements about the discovery of a Mauser. The palm print was allegedly discovered in Dallas, but the impression of it was withheld when the FBI took over the dossier. The palm print could not be found in Washington. Ultimately, a letter from Hoover in the dossier provides the proof that links the print to the weapon. Hoover has no credibility at all in this issue, however.

5. **The two large bullet fragments** found in the limousine: the fragments were added to the evidence, but not as part of the investigation. Secret agents who had unlawfully removed the vehicle from Dallas had access to it without any kind of supervision for a number of hours, and continually contaminated the crime scene whilst they were in charge of it. Prior to the actual investigation, secret agents who did not have the authority to deal with the dossier allegedly proceeded to collect evidence in a very rough manner (by swiping their hand across the seats). The limousine is then made unsuitable for further investigation, which constitutes a deliberate obstruction of the judicial process. No report was written of the investigation that did take place. Moreover, the fragments do not contain any biological material that might provide evidence that the bullets went through Kennedy's body.

6. **The autopsy report**: the date on this document has been falsified. The original notes were burnt and the dossier was subsequently fabricated on the basis of assumptions. Some of the findings that were recorded could not have been investigated during the autopsy. It is clear that doctors made false declarations relating to a very misleading drawing that was presented as evidence. The findings in the autopsy report are at odds with the findings of the doctors who treated the president in Dallas. No matter how implausible it may sound, we cannot exclude the possibility that the president's body was 'fixed' before the autopsy. There is, for instance, an undisputable document that the president arrived in Bethesda in a different coffin than the one mentioned in the official version. In any case, the autopsy report would be unacceptable in criminal proceedings in Texas, because the law stipulates that the autopsy should have been carried out in Texas.

7. **The witness statements** made by Givens and Brennan: Givens is a manifestly unreliable witness, who initially made a statement completely at odds with his later accusatory witness statement against Oswald. He was known as a witness who would say anything in exchange for money. Brennan could not have seen what he claimed to have seen. The witness was also lying, or made a mistake, when he indicated the position he was at when he allegedly saw Oswald. And, whatever his reasons were, he didn't recognize Oswald in the police line-up.

8. **Oswald's interrogation**: despite repeated requests for legal representation Oswald was not provided with a lawyer. There are no regular minutes of the interrogations, not even a simple transcript or tape recording. Everything Oswald was subsequently *claimed* to have said is inadmissible evidence.

9. **Evidence found during the search of Mrs. Paine's house**: serious questions also remain about the legality of the search of Mrs. Paine's house. For example, Mrs. Paine granted approval for the house search without a search warrant, even though she neither owned nor rented the premises. Technically she was a third party, who could not have granted such authorization. The police also stated that the house search took place as part of an investigation into a crime of which Oswald had not yet been accused at that time. According to some sources, the second house search took place while the involved parties were not present. Evidence such as the all important backyard photographs is subsequently found in the (private) possession of police officers. The police were evidently not just investigating Mrs. Paine, but also hunting for souvenirs. The house search inventory was falsified. For example, a mini camera that appeared to invoke too many CIA suggestions was described as an exposure meter. The 'exposure meter' had, however, been used to produce photographs that were part of the dossier.

10. **All incriminating statements by Marina Oswald**: Marina Oswald should not have been able to supply incriminating evidence or witness statements in a procedure against her husband. Marina provided a series of incriminating elements against Lee. For instance, Lee had left his wedding ring behind in a teacup on that fatal morning. Marina's statement about the abandoned wedding ring would consequently have had a significant psychological effect on a people's jury. The dossier also has to totally rely on Marina's statements with respect to the backyard photographs, which she allegedly took.

The implication that Oswald could have been the possible perpetrator of the attack on General Walker is also based solely on Marina's statements. With her background of a totalitarian regime, the FBI also knew that, Marina was susceptible to subtle persuasion to say what was expected of her. It is therefore not impossible that Marina had words put in her mouth, or that her statements were presented differently from what she intended. There was also a language barrier. To put it in a nutshell, we need to steer clear of all Marina's statements in the dossier. Incriminating statements originating from a spouse are inadmissible in a court of law.

The question with this inadmissible evidence is not whether you believe it or not, or whether Oswald is guilty or not. We are dealing with a fundamental legal principle here, i.e. evidence has to be collated and presented correctly.

In addition to the errors in the investigation that would lead to the above-mentioned evidence being rejected, there is also the unmistakable conclusion that evidence *for the defense* was withheld and destroyed. The investigation into avenues pointing in the direction of other potential suspects was vigorously obstructed.

We cannot revert to a society in which an investigation provides proof of dubious origin, and evidence that does not fit into the proposed hypothesis is allowed to become lost, or is ignored or amended. Our society does not accept evidence that has clearly been tampered with. A police officer cannot merely send a citizen to the electric chair solely because he, or his superiors, has a grievance against this person. Consequently, the Oswald dossier has to continue without the prosecutors even alluding to the above-mentioned evidence. This inadmissible evidence should in no way still be part of the dossier. The question now remains as to whether anything useful is left for a public prosecutor from a legal point of view.

Reasonable doubt

Reasonable doubt is grave doubt based on reasoning and common sense after having considered the evidence or lack of evidence carefully and without prejudice. Absolute certainty is not a prerequisite, but in order to raise the evidence above reasonable doubt, it should be convincing in the sense 'that you would be willing to rely and act upon it without hesitation in the most important of your own affairs.'

What evidence remains in this dossier after having removed the inadmissible elements? Kennedy was fired at. Oswald worked in the TSBD and did not have an alibi for the time of the assassination. There are photographs of the autopsy and X-rays and there is also the Zapruder film. Theoretically, you could prove on the basis of this that a magic bullet was fired at Z211 – which we did in Part 6. Due to the lack of any witnesses who saw Oswald on the sixth floor, we have to rely on the conclusion that the last time he was seen before the shooting was on the ground floor, around 12:00 noon. He was seen again for the first time after the assassination on the second floor. No one encountered him on the stairs. There is no link between Oswald and a weapon, because the weapon has been excluded from the evidence. A jury would consequently have to assume that, from a legal point of view, no weapon was ever found. The paraffin test of Oswald's cheek was negative, which would point to him not having fired a rifle on that fateful day. To put it in the words of the Dallas police chief Curry, the only legal representative for the investigation:[629]

> We don't have any proof that Oswald fired the rifle, and never did. Nobody's yet been able to put him in that building with a gun in his hand.

Insofar as it is still necessary in this already seriously flawed dossier, there is sufficient reason for reasonable doubt: Oswald's lack of skill as a marksman, the presence of Jim Braden in the Dal-Tex building… Many elements can apparently be explained by including the presence of a second (better) marksman with a (better) weapon and the use of *sabots* in the account. Criminal proceedings do not require certainty that this is what really happened: all that's needed is doubt about Oswald being the actual perpetrator.

Finally, a jury also has to consider the following elements:

1. Oswald did not have a single motive for the murder;
2. He maintained his innocence right up till the end;
3. The entire investigation dossier bears witness to a genuinely shocking bias against the accused;
4. An investigation into other people who did have a clear motive was never implemented.

Irrespective of whether you believe in Oswald's innocence or not, an honorable jury member should refuse to convict him of the Kennedy murder. Obviously not all jury members would agree, in which case they would have to take a vote. The jury has to come to a unanimous decision that guilt is beyond reasonable doubt; otherwise Oswald would escape the electric chair.[630] In order to exonerate Oswald completely, three of the twelve jury members would have to have doubts, as ten votes were sufficient to find him guilty in Dallas in 1963.

Bugliosi was wrong when he maintained that 80% of the evidence could be ditched. He knew full well that a lack of reasonable doubt does not depend upon the quantity, but on the quality of the evidence. This quality has to be satisfactory in all its essential elements. He knew very well that a conviction by the Commission, and even by a television court, did not offer the guarantees required with respect to a fair trial. The television trial, 'On Trial: Lee Harvey Oswald', involving Bugliosi as the public prosecutor and the actual witnesses in the witness box, only took five hours, and was consequently preposterous. The actual trial would have taken many weeks.

Walt Brown's book *The People versus Lee Harvey Oswald* contains 632 pages and, even though it is obviously a fictional account, is extremely well documented.[631] Brown starts from the premise that they should have declared the case inadmissible halfway through because of the lack of a *prima facie case* – a case at first sight. In the book, Oswald's lawyer trashes the witnesses called by the public prosecutor and other evidence. The lawyers and the judge mutually decide to continue the trial in the interest of both the truth and the accused Oswald, who would be better off with an acquittal rather than a case interrupted halfway through. Because the judge decides on the basis legality and the jury only on facts, the judge in Brown's book arrives at a 'directed verdict' of 'not guilty'. The jury doesn't even have to come to a decision because, according to the judge, from a legal point of view there is insufficient incriminating evidence on the basis of which the jury could make a *factual* judgment. In *The People versus Lee Harvey Oswald*, Oswald walks away a free man. Based on the research in this book, we can only in all honesty corroborate Walt Brown's vision. Any self-respecting constitutional state should recognize that this dossier is too tainted to act as a basis for a conviction beyond all reasonable doubt. Oswald is therefore acquitted of the murder of President Kennedy.

The Tippit case is associated with highly contradictory witness statements. Once again we are faced with a serious ballistics problem. The discovered shells did not match the bullets found in Tippit's body. It is also doubtful whether Oswald could have been present at the crime scene at the time of the murder. In all probability, however, Oswald would have ended up in the electric chair for this murder.

44. FINAL CONCLUSIONS

We have now reached the final stage of our research into the fascinating Kennedy assassination dossier. The findings, both individual and as a whole, are disappointing and shocking as far as the FBI, the Secret Service, the Dallas Police and the Warren Commission are concerned. According to Bugliosi this is not a complex dossier. It has merely been made unnecessarily complex by relentless critics and conspiracy theorists[632]. We have to disagree with this, as the matter was not made needlessly complicated by the critics, but by the circumstances, the Warren Commission and the FBI. The investigation was prejudiced from the start. Evidence was manipulated or even manufactured where necessary. It was riddled with lies, and information was withheld, destroyed and falsified. Respect for the fundamental principles of a correct criminal investigation was sorely lacking. Data important *for the defense* was removed from the investigation. Exonerating evidence purposely disappeared into a bureaucratic black hole. Witnesses were intimidated or blatantly ignored. The judiciary and main investigation authority were prejudiced, and the right to a defense and the presumption of innocence were not respected.

The list of serious breaches of even the most elementary principles is staggering. The special circumstances are no justification for this; on the contrary, the murder of the president, the potential consequences of a conspiracy and the importance of public perception should have resulted in a particularly scrupulous and thorough investigation. The mistakes are of such a general nature, and recur with such regularity that there is definitely a pattern, or even better a number of patterns that reinforce each other. The commission of politically appointed heavyweights was too faint-hearted. It allowed itself to be hoodwinked too easily. The FBI nervously observed the instructions of its autocratic director.

Too many avenues were simply taboo for the investigation. Under no circumstances did President Johnson want to hear the word 'conspiracy' in connection with the assassination. The Dallas police force apparently relied on its own routine to tackle murder cases efficiently, and wasn't too bothered about the odd procedural mistake here and there. The end result was a monstrous mixture of failings produced by their many creators. Any self-respecting constitutional state should take the honorable way out. In a civilized society, you cannot judge a citizen on the basis of such a biased dossier, bulging with infringements of the law of evidence. That does not mean that Oswald is innocent, however.

Because the magic bullet is so implausible but possible, we must assume that this is what actually happened. Three injuries and a sniper's nest cannot be perfectly aligned in four dimensions, i.e. from left to right, from front to back, from bottom to top and in time, for no reason. We consequently know that, at point Z211 in time, a shot was fired at the limousine from the corner window on the sixth floor of the Texas School Book Depository. That is the key information. The fatal bullet that shattered Kennedy's skull five seconds later, also definitely originated from the sniper's nest. Witnesses saw the barrel of the gun protruding from the corner window. The limousine had already been shot at, at point Z160 in time, before the magic bullet. This shot completely missed its target, but was heard by Governor Connally who reacted to it, and officer Baker who quickly made his way to the TSBD on his motorcycle. The impression that more than three shots were heard from different directions is an acoustic phenomenon that can be attributed to the bowl-like shape of Dealey Plaza. In some locations, a supersonic bullet is heard twice, i.e. when the bullet passes through the sound barrier, followed soon after by the sound of the shot. The third bullet fragmented upon impact with Kennedy's skull. One fragment hit the front windshield and another fragment damaged the chrome edge at the top of the windshield. A third fragment flew over the top of the front windshield, together with a fragment of Kennedy's skull, scratched a sewer cover and made a hole in the grass on the edge of Elm Street. The fourth fragment flew in the direction of Connally's wrist when he was already lying in his wife's lap. The fifth fragment flew across the front windshield and ended up 80 m down the road against an edging stone. A concrete fragment was thrown up and injured the spectator, Tague. Three smaller fragments flew across the governor, who had collapsed sideways, and eventually ended up underneath Mrs. Connally's jump seat.

Oswald's weapon, or in any case a similar Mannlicher Carcano, was found at the crime scene. It is unclear how he could have brought in the weapon. According to two witnesses who saw him that morning, the paper bag in which he had allegedly concealed the weapon was too short to contain a dismantled Carcano. His palm print was found on the weapon, however, albeit under abnormal circumstances. His finger prints were also found on the barricade in the sniper's nest. The cheap gun sight on a Carcano is geared to left handed use, and the weapon is not very accurate. Under these circumstances, the two accurate shots within a short interval were highly improbable. However, unlikely events are not impossible. Oswald could also have arrived on the first floor just in time without having encountered Vicki Adams and Sandra Styles. Officer Baker and superintendent Truly could also have reached the first floor without passing the women who were descending the stairs. Whilst on the run, Oswald murdered officer Tippit and was in possession of the murder weapon when he was arrested. Oswald lied during his interrogation, which also weighs against him.

The main prosecution argument is that Oswald did not have an alibi for the time of the murder, a moment in time that everyone spent in the proximity of others. After all, it isn't every day that a popular president drives past in an open-top limousine. It seems implausible that Oswald would not have gone to watch the parade. Another important fact is that no other suspect was present in the TSBD. Oswald's historic guilt consequently seems to be a reality, providing we can disregard two significant elements: (1) it is not certain that the weapon found in the TSBD was Oswald's Carcano and (2) there was an additional minor injury on the back of Kennedy's head that cannot be explained.

The alternative hypothesis with Oswald as a patsy appears improbable at first sight, but, upon closer inspection, it has the advantage that a whole series of mysteries vanish like frost under the morning sun. The slight injury to the back of Kennedy's head may have been caused by the bullet being accompanied by a *sabot*, a bullet shell which makes it possible to fire the bullet from a larger caliber weapon. The *sabot* hypothesis suddenly appears to offer a solution to the problems surrounding the Carcano: the difference from the weapon in the backyard photos, the absence of fingerprints, the weapon's unreliability... The disadvantage, of course, is that this hypothesis requires a second sniper and a second weapon, for which there is not a single direct piece of evidence in the dossier.

The sets of questions on page 372 illustrate the extent to which the final answer remains a dilemma. It is not enough to simply state that a conspiracy is improbable or unproven, because you then end up with a series of lone nut questions and have to accept even more improbabilities arising from that hypothesis. Jumping back and forth between the two hypotheses, where one is even more improbable than the other, makes you intellectually seasick in the end. But wandering around endlessly in the labyrinth is also not an option. Kennedy was murdered, so one of the unproven hypotheses must be the right one.

I finally made my choice. One good reason for my final preference was the principle of cautiousness. If Oswald was a lone nut, the story ends there. But if there was, after all, a conspiracy that wasn't unmasked, the consequences would be very discomforting. Ethically speaking, we must then aim for the most unfavorable hypothesis. Fifteen years ago, there was also no conclusive proof that human activity was responsible for climate change. In that debate also, powerful lobby groups promoted their predetermined opinions. They kept pushing ahead with explanations that anyone who looked at the facts could see were incorrect. In the mean time, we now see the consequences of this deliberate ignorance and lack of precaution. The correct functioning of our democratic constitutional state is a similar major worry. The Kennedy dossier contains enough incriminating material to consider the possibility that the murder was, in fact, an assault on democracy. If that possibility had been taken seriously in 1963, history would have gone through another loop. And that conclusion is still valid today. But this reflection in itself is not enough to make a decision about a murder case. There are many other reasons that determined my final choice in this dilemma. I don't believe that Ruby was an enraged and incensed patriot. I don't believe in two direct hits by Oswald with a defective, unadjusted Carcano. I don't believe that Oswald would keep denying everything if he was the sole perpetrator. And what must you think about a murderer who only had only four bullets in his possession? Four bullets whose origin is a complete mystery. But the overriding reason was that, unlike the official version, this hypothesis meets the minimum requirement, i.e. it accords significance to *all* essential elements in the dossier, not just the ones that fit the hypothesis. In view of the fact that there are not that many possibilities for incorporating all the information into a single logical context, I am convinced that the account below is very close to what actually happened.

Balanced account

We are applying the principle of 'tabula rasa', or even better *'fabula* rasa', to the different fables that are in circulation concerning the Kennedy assassination. We have now evaluated all the elements, and have eliminated a lot of incorrect data claimed by both believers and conspiracists. Using the remaining material, we are left with a series of facts that should combine into a coherent totality. What really happened on Dealey Plaza on November 22, 1963? Which scenario fits all the pieces of the puzzle and how can we fill in the missing pieces? This is what I believe happened:

1. John F. Kennedy was the victim of a conspiracy. The conspirators could be found amongst the higher echelons of the oil industry and the mafia, and certain elements within the CIA were also actively involved. All these groups had a powerful motive to eliminate Kennedy. They had established specific partnerships, for example, as part of the ongoing sabotage activities in Cuba. The CIA was familiar with secret operations in which it used appearance and reality, manipulation and force to compel easily-influenced people to act in a way in which they would never act under normal circumstances. This frequently involved a coup d'état or the assassination of a head of state. It definitely had the necessary know-how in this respect.

2. Oswald probably carried out the attack on the ultra-right-wing General Walker. His CIA guardian angel, Baron de Mörenschildt, was aware of this. Maybe the baron passed on this message to his CIA bosses in November, pointing out that Oswald worked in the TSBD and represented a potential threat to the safety of the president. Thus, in one way or another, Oswald attracted the conspirators' attention. A shot from the TSBD, where they could lure Oswald into a trap to act as a patsy, seemed to be a perfect opportunity. Oswald was an ideal candidate for a fall guy. His earlier record as a pro-Castro agitator, communist militant and Soviet defector made it easy to divert attention in those directions following the murder.

3. The conspirators approached Oswald and skillfully fed him what he wanted to hear. They explained that he could make a significant contribution by giving the sniper access to the TSBD and helping him to prepare the sniper's nest. Unlike the sniper, Oswald was free to move around the sixth floor inconspicuously because of his job.

Prior to the murder, he had to watch the stairs and prevent anyone from entering the sixth floor at the crucial moment. That's why Oswald did not have an alibi at the time of the assassination. He had probably been tempted with a large sum of money and escape route abroad. He would leave behind his Russian wife, Marina, who had jilted him the day before. He was ready to start a new, affluent life on distant shores.

4. The conspirators knew that Oswald had bought a Carcano. Bullets had been prepared in advance using this weapon, or a similar one, to ensure that, after the assassination, the trail pointed to the discovered Carcano. Oswald was instructed to carry something into the building in a paper bag, which he had been provided with earlier, on the morning of November 22, 1963. Maybe the package was presented to Oswald as a signal to the conspirators to confirm that he was involved in the plot. The sniper entered the building during the night on Thursday and hid either in the building or on the roof.

The conspirators relied on the fact that they would have no problem in swaying President Johnson and FBI Director Hoover after the assassination. Believers emphasize the implausibility of a plot by placing the conspirators in the smoky back room of a gambling joint. Human communication is much more subtle, however. Silence and omitting to act are often more efficient forms of complicity. There were huge interests at stake, and the protagonists were certainly no choirboys.

5. At around 12.30 p.m. on November 22, 1963, the sniper fired three shots at the president using the prepared Carcano bullets, *sabots* and a weapon with a caliber in excess of 6.5 mm. He hit the president twice. All the bullet impacts can be explained on the basis of three shots.

6. Immediately after the shots, Vicki Adams and her friend ran downstairs. They were at the back door of the TSBD barely forty seconds later. Motorcycle officer Baker and superintendent Truly passed the third door of the TSBD entrance at exactly the same time. They consequently did not see Adams and her friend running out of the building. Oswald descended the stairs after the women and, because he did not have to cover the distance across the sixth floor and did not have to clean or conceal a weapon, arrived comfortably on the first floor before officer Baker and superintendent Truly. Baker and Truly came across the chillingly calm Oswald and left him alone.

They continued to run up the stairs and encountered Dorothy Garner, Vicki Adams' boss. On the roof, they could merely establish that no shots had been fired from there.

7. The sniper was hiding in anticipation of a suitable moment to leave the building. He had plenty of time to do so because, initially, all attention was focused on the *Grassy Knoll* and none of the many exits from the building were monitored. He may well have worn a police uniform.

8. The limousine had meanwhile arrived at Parkland Hospital. Kennedy was taken to *Emergency Room One* on a stretcher. He remained on the stretcher throughout the fruitless attempts by doctors to save him. Governor Connally was undressed in *Emergency Room Two* and taken to the operating theatre on the first floor, where he was moved onto an operating table. His stretcher was put in the lift, and was later put in the corridor on the ground floor by technician Tomlinson. Some time later, he discovered a bullet on this bed. Maintenance technician Tomlinson made a mistake concerning the location where the bullet was found.

9. At Dealey Plaza, the police established that Jim Braden had no good reason for being in the Dal-Tex building. He could only explain his presence with transparent lies. In reality, Braden was there to keep Oswald under control. The conspirators obviously did not intend Oswald to survive either a successful or unsuccessful assassination. Braden was probably instructed to follow Oswald and take him to a location indicated by the conspirators. Perhaps the unexpected, brief arrest of Jim Braden was the stumbling block. Officer Tippit was probably the innocent victim of this combination of events, a man in the wrong place at the wrong time.

10. The moment Kennedy had been put in his casket, the presidential entourage wanted to leave Texas as quickly as possible with the deceased president, his spouse Jacqueline and the new President Lyndon Johnson. From an emotional point of view, it was unthinkable for the Secret Service and the widow to leave Kennedy's remains in Dallas. Johnson agreed for political reasons, because the presence of Jacqueline Kennedy at his side provided him with greater legitimacy.

11. Admiral Burkley, the president's personal physician, realized that an autopsy could be highly detrimental to the president's reputation, and convinced the first lady to opt for Bethesda Naval Hospital.

12. In the TSBD, the Dallas police force conducted a chaotic search based on an accumulation of procedural faults. The police discovered a Carcano, a weapon of a similar type to the one with which Oswald posed in his backyard earlier, but with a few striking differences.

13. Oswald, who couldn't find his contact Braden at the agreed location, wandered around Dallas like a headless chicken and collected a pistol from his rented digs. From there, he continued his flight and encountered Officer Tippit in unexplained circumstances. In a panic, he murdered the officer. Oswald was subsequently arrested in the *Texas Theatre*. He shouted out loud that he was no longer resisting so that he was able to get away alive from there as well.

14. The fact that Oswald had been arrested forced the conspirators to implement a risky crisis measure. A live Oswald represented an unacceptable risk as far as they were concerned. They knew the loud-mouthed nightclub operator Ruby, who was in financial constraints, and were aware that he had free access to the police building. Another advantage was the fact that Ruby and Oswald did not know one another and that Ruby was not *au fait* with the other details of the conspiracy. Ruby did not act when he first approached Oswald on Friday night.

15. In view of the fact that Oswald might make certain confessions as long as he was alive, a number of conspirators considered it necessary to provide for an escape route. To this end, stunt pilot David Ferrie drove all the way from New Orleans to Galveston under some grandiose pretext, and was paid the impressive sum of 7,000 dollars. If necessary, he had to fly to Mexico with a number of people for whom the place had become too hot. In Galveston, Ruby Breck Wall, the chairman of AGVA, an organization that acted as a cover for the mafia. Hij bevestigde that there was no reason to panic, and that he daags nadien en met hulp van binnen het politiekorps would do what was asked of him.

16. President Johnson realized early on that the president's body had to be checked for signs of a shot from the front. Johnson had a sharp political insight, and was paranoid by nature. He assumed that Kennedy had without doubt been the victim of a conspiracy. Initial information about Oswald pointed to the fact that the real culprits wanted to place the blame on Cuba and the Soviet Union.
Kennedy was Believer Number 1, because he realized that any fool with a gun could assassinate him. Johnson was Conspiracist Number 1.

For political and geopolitical reasons, it was highly undesirable and extremely dangerous if the conspiracy, which Johnson was certain existed, should be brought to light.

17. If the president arrived at Bethesda in a shipping casket, it was Johnson who arranged for the president's body to be removed from the original casket and be taken away by helicopter from the rear of Air Force One, the presidential plane, upon landing in Washington. In any way, the president's body was examined for signs of a shot fired from the front, which would need to be removed. As a result the small incision for the tracheotomy was nevertheless turned into a gaping, jagged opening of more than seven centimeters. The contents of the skull were also examined for traces of a frontal bullet. This also created a V-shaped wound in the forehead, which FBI agents Sibert and O'Neill described in their report as a surgical intervention prior to the autopsy. There were no traces of a frontal shot, as it never happened. The entire operation consequently had the reverse effect and would even intensify the rumors of a conspiracy. This was obviously not the original intention of the intervention. Paradoxically, the fact that Johnson took action in order to eliminate any possible traces of a shot from the front points to him not being involved in the conspiracy. If he had been aware of the conspiracy, he would have known that the only shots that were fired came from the TSBD.

18. The new president put the entire investigation into the hands of his old friend J. Edgar Hoover, the director of the FBI. He thought he could trust Hoover without fail, but the old satrap was no longer smart enough to keep the dossier properly under control. In many ways he even had a counterproductive effect, and would eventually also become one of the main causes of subsequent, never-ending conspiracy theories. As a reward, Hoover received the lifelong appointment for which he had hungered for a long time.

19. Following a bad start, the Dallas police force was not given the opportunity to score or at least conceal its mistakes and was not happy. The dossier was, therefore, handed over in unfortunate circumstances, which again led to a lot of trouble later on.

20. The inexperienced autopsy physicians in the Bethesda Navy Hospital in Washington were under military command and were told they had to follow instructions in order to avoid a nuclear war. They obeyed, and were prepared to adapt and antedate their report until it more or

less reflected the official version of the facts. And these facts were partly manufactured. This version predated the one bullet theory.

A number of photographs from the autopsy, X-rays and even the president's brain were removed from the dossier, because they were incorrectly assumed to be in conflict with the official version. The physicians purposely asked an illustrator to create a completely inaccurate representation of Kennedy's injuries. The head wound was placed ten centimeters too low and the back injury ten centimeters too high and too far to the right. Using a rough estimate, the investigators thought that the adapted locations would better match a shot from a window on the sixth floor. During a later investigation, the physicians made the manifestly untrue statement that the drawing matched the autopsy photographs. Johnson's Secret Service was always nearby when problems arose concerning medical findings.

21. On Sunday morning, Ruby made a second attempt to carry out his orders, and succeeded in murdering Oswald. As soon as he heard the news, David Ferrie in Galveston could do a U-turn in the direction of New Orleans. The threat had been lifted, and there was no longer any need to expatriate anybody.

22. The FBI knew what to do, and managed the investigation in accordance with its ruthless director's wishes. Because he could no longer handle the complexity of the matter, or had become too headstrong and arrogant, any intervention by Hoover only made the case more suspect than necessary. The fear running through his department resulted in a series of unnecessary errors and blatant manipulations of the dossier.

23. Fearing that the limousine might contain potential proof pointing in the direction of a conspiracy, President Johnson decided that this evidence also had to be destroyed immediately.

24. Johnson prevented a series of overlapping and contradictory investigations and commissions from seeing the light of day. He appointed his own political commission, consisting of seven heavyweights whom he considered capable of organizing a problem-free cover-up. He urged the members of the commission to seriously consider the fact that they had a historic responsibility to avoid a nuclear war. Despite the social importance of its members, the Warren Commission was overtaken by events. It was provided with the facts by the FBI, the CIA and the Secret Service. All these organizations had manipulated and filtered their dossiers for their own benefit.

And it was intended to be like that. The commission merely had to corroborate the FBI reports, the conclusion of which had been decided in advance.

25. For safety reasons, the conspirators eliminated or intimidated a number of troublesome witnesses.

26. Robert Kennedy was well aware that Johnson and Hoover could ruin the deceased president's reputation. His own reputation and his chances of a further political career were also at stake. He had no choice but to accede to the decisions of Hoover and Johnson regarding the course of the investigation.

27. Because tailor Zapruder had produced a staggeringly clear film documenting the assassination, and quite cleverly made sure that he was fireproof, the authorities could no longer maintain the initial incorrect but simple official version of the facts (three shots, all three hitting their target). Counsel Arlen Specter of the Warren Commission appeared to be the first to understand what probably happened on Dealey Plaza, but that conclusion came far too late, as a result of which the correct analysis gave the impression that it was a far-fetched attempt at a cover-up. During previous attempts at documenting an explanation without a magic bullet, a lot of documentation and other evidence had been put into circulation or totally ignored. The commission could no longer conjure away these manipulations in the advanced stage that its investigation had reached at that time. The dossier is consequently awash with contradictions.

28. The commission also made another strategic error. It opted to go over the top and made its report and appendices too cumbersome, on the assumption that this intimidation would work. But times were changing in the sixties, and people no longer took for granted that what they were told by the authorities was actually true. Critics read the 27 volumes, with their red pens poised, and reeled from one surprise to another. Fifty years on, the controversy has still not been brought to a close.

The ostensible insolvability of the dossier is mainly due to the highly heterogeneous nature of both the assassination and the plot, with a successful attempt to put the investigation on the wrong track via a patsy, compounded by the total confusion that reigned at the time, the many, stupid mistakes made by the investigators, and, finally, the cover-up. Although he was not part of the conspiracy, Johnson used his authority over the Secret Service to drastically intervene and destroy evidence about the plot that he suspected existed. His intention was not to make himself complicit after the facts, but to avoid a geopolitical crisis. Together with Hoover, he cooperated in the cover-up. Hoover maintained close contacts with mafia bosses and oil billionaires, and had therefore his own reasons to prevent an investigation in this direction.The Dallas police force made many mistakes in the belief that they would finalize the case quickly and efficiently following Oswald's arrest. Moreover, the proposed solution that governed the commission's early activities had, out of necessity, been replaced halfway through by a totally different account. Once again, this had a seriously detrimental effect on the general impression created by the dossier.

There are in fact three criminal initiative-takers: the conspirators, Oswald, who agreed to take on a subsidiary role in the assassination plot, and President Johnson, who directed a cover-up. The overall explanation only becomes clear when these persons are scrutinized both jointly and individually. Because of the specific allied circumstances surrounding the dossier, such as the initial confusion, the shameful lack of respect for procedural rules by the Dallas police force, the dysfunctional director of the FBI and assignment of the investigation to a politically appointed commission, the case was compromised to a far greater extent than could have been foreseen or prevented. It is this tangled web of accounts that makes the dossier so complex, not the justified criticism.

John Fitzgerald Kennedy was a president with too many qualities. He was dynamic, intelligent and optimistic. He was young, had style and charisma, was educated, broad minded, charitable, visionary, progressive and courageous. Kennedy's charm, charisma and disarmingly boyish appeal kept his popularity intact, even when he got it wrong. He openly accepted his responsibility and learnt from his mistakes. He was also rich enough not to be susceptible to bribery. This also had a downside, however. He was reckless, and his amorous escapades made him vulnerable to blackmail. He loved politics because it was a contact sport but, in keeping with the family tradition, he always wanted to win. This meant that he did not display enough fear, respect or deference to the growing group of powerful opponents whom he antagonized with his bravado and policies. His brother took it another step, or more than one step, further – possibly too far. Being different from John Kennedy, Robert was not able, or did not want to sufficiently disguise his dislike of his opponents. No doubt the Kennedys had too much faith in their own myth, and acted with too much haste.

Their father had never told them that those who want it all are often left with nothing. Kennedy disliked hypocritical narrow-mindedness and aggressive ignorance. He detested liars, complainers, jingoists, hypocrites and egotists. The extent to which, and the manner in which he let them know who was the boss became untenable for his reactionary opponents. For the first time, political, criminal, bureaucratic and military firebrands were faced with a president they could not manipulate. It was a totally new situation that breached all the existing rules of the game. It culminated in a coalition of covetous and false opponents who came to hate him more with each new humiliation. To make matters even worse for his adversaries, John Kennedy would probably have been re-elected. He already had too many measures in store for his second and final term of office – a term of office that would cement his place in history. His opponents knew what to expect. He would dump Vice-President Johnson, appoint a new FBI director, curtail the CIA, and continue the fight against organized crime and the fiscal loopholes valued by the oil industry. He would leave Cuba for what it was, a small island. He wanted to stop the escalation of the war in Vietnam, promote a civil rights agenda and enter into a dialogue across the Iron Curtain. Cynical hardliners considered this to be a combination of subversive and naïve illusions.

The assassination of John F. Kennedy tells the age-old tale of the alpha male who always gets the best of everything with complete impunity, and the frustrated beta males who chafe inwardly until they mutely perceive that the coalition has become strong enough, or until they've had enough, whatever the consequences. *Chimpanzee politics*. We have only just left the savannah and are being measured up for suits. If a specific frustration threshold is breached within a group of social animals, the irresistible and instinctive reaction is to take the only action that our genes tell us will produce a result: a cruel, bloody murder.

Flip de Mey
Dallas, November 8, 2012
Antwerp, May 2, 2013

EPILOG

In an extremely polarized dossier, there is always a strong temptation to select and interpret the facts in accordance with the chosen side of the over-
heated debate. The aspiration of this book was not to fall into this trap. We
aimed to first look at the facts objectively, and only then to draw conclusions. The arguments of both the believers and the conspiracists therefore
had to be subjected to an equally critical analysis. My conclusive decision
in favor of a conspiracy hypothesis was only made at the very last moment.
Contrary to most books on the assassination of Kennedy, however, the arguments of the believers were incorporated. Our investigation therefore
confirms a whole series of essential elements in their case:

- The magical bullet is technically possible, and it is indeed more
  than likely that the second shot could have injured both Kennedy
  and Connally at the same time with a single bullet.
- There was no frontal shot.
- All shots were fired from the sniper's nest in the TSBD.
- There were only three shots, at time Z160, around Z211 and at mo-
  ment Z313 of the Zapruder timeline.
- The presence of Vickie Adams on the staircase soon after the attack
  does not provide Oswald with an alibi.
- Oswald did indeed have the time to reach the second floor, where he
  met Officer Baker less than ninety seconds after the attack.
- Jim Tague had not been hit by a separate bullet; he was injured by
  the third shot from the TSBD.
- Oswald killed officer J.D. Tippit.
- Whatever went wrong during the autopsy is irrelevant. This also
  applies to the destruction of the limo as evidence, and many other
  manipulations. These irregularities may fit into both the official account and a conspiracy theory.

- Johnson and Hoover were not part of the conspiracy.
- Many peculiarities that were blown up to represent evidence of a conspiracy can be logically explained on the basis of the long series of special and unique conditions that made any normal investigation impossible.

All in all, no fact has surfaced that *conclusively* contradicts the official theory. All hypotheses contain highly unlikely elements that have never been explained. Nevertheless, one of these improbable and improvable hypotheses must be the right one. This book provides the explanation for this bizarre situation. The weight of the cover-up operation was crushing. The driving forces behind this sabotage dared not or could not take the risk of examining the case down to the bone. As a result, all traces that could have pointed towards a conspiracy were ignored, manipulated or destroyed. But inevitably much evidence that could have enhanced the plausibility of the official account was thereby also destroyed.

The believers can therefore find plenty of confirmation of their point of view in this book. But they must finally acknowledge that the investigation is fraught with negligence, fraudulent manipulation and incorrect statements. If they continue to believe the official account beyond any doubt, they may, in fact, be the greatest victims of an embarrassingly poor and incomplete investigation, and the massive cover-up operation that followed.

Flip de Mey

END NOTES

1. (Warren Commission Hearings and Exhibits Vol. I, 1964) p.68.

2. (Mallon, 2002) p.86: Marina received $ 70,000 in donations, an amount that, in terms of purchasing power, should be compared to the hourly wage of her husband: 1.25 dollars.

3. (Mallon, 2002) p.79 to 82. 'I have not understood this to this day', says Mrs. Paine about the sudden rejection by Marina.

4. (Warren Commission Hearings and Exhibits Vol. VI, 1964) p. 445.

5. (George, 2013) p. 22. A CBS poll in 1960 showed that 4 million Americans made their choice after the televised debates between the candidates Nixon and Kennedy, 78% of them decided in favor of JFK. In the end, Kennedy only beat his opponent by 112,827 votes, from a total of more than 68 million votes cast.

6. (Warren Commission Hearings and Exhibits Vol. I, 1964) p. 51 Marina Oswald Testimony.

7. (Warren Commission Hearings and Exhibits Vol. XVII, 1964) p. 210 CE496. There are a number of white lies on the form: his previous job, his honorable discharge from the Navy (which had been amended to dishonorable discharge after he had defected to the USSR) and the mention that he was not living in rented rooms, but in Irving, at the address of Mrs. Paine, where, in reality, only his wife Marina lived.

8. (Warren Commission Hearings and Exhibits Vol. I, 1964) p.65.

9. (Warren Commission Hearings and Exhibits Vol. VI, 1964) p. 293.

10. (Warren Commission Hearings and Exhibits Vol. V, 1964) p. 451, for the time: Waldron p. 739.

11. Fetzer p. 18, Crenshaw p. 30, Robertson p. 72, Livingstone p. 170.

12. Livingston p. 12; Fetzer p. 18.

13. (Hill, 2012) p. 280.

14. (Lifton, 1980) p. 121.

15. (Ernest, 2010) p. 120, statement of Mrs. Adams to Dallas police officer Leavelle dated February 17, 1964.

16. (Becker, 2011) p. 182.

17. (Warren Commission Report, 1964) p. 160. Three agents from the FBI and the Secret Service walked this distance in an average time of 6.5 minutes.

18. (Kelin, 2007) p. 85.

19. (Warren Commission Hearings and Exhibits Vol. XXII, 1964) p. 86, CE1119.

20. (Warren Commission Hearings and Exhibits Vol. VI, 1964) p. 444 testimony of taxi driver Whaley.

21. Dallas Police Department, Radio Recording, Channels 1&2, November 22, 1963. The recording can be heard on www.jftippit.com/html/timetable_nov.htm.

22. CD4, FBI report Agent Clements, p.11.

23. When it comes to where Jack Ruby was, and the Warren Commission aims to demonstrate that he could not have been at Parkland Hospital, despite the iron-clad testimony in this context by a star journalist who spoke to Ruby there, the Commission suddenly has a reason to assume that the dramatic events would inevitably have caused traffic delays.

24. Bugliosi makes a sarcastic remark about the low tip that Oswald gave the driver, whereas Oswald simply rounded up to the next dollar. Incidentally, the trip had a lucrative ending: the taxi, which, unlike the presidential limousine, was not hastily converted, was sold for 35,750 dollars in 2010.

25. (Bugliosi, 2007) p. 960.

26. (Bugliosi, 2007) p. 71.

27. (Crenshaw, 2001) p. 72.

28. (Bugliosi, 2007) p. 71.

29. (Crenshaw, 2001) p. 76.

30. (Warren Commission Hearings and Exhibits Vol. XXIII, 1964) p. 833 CE 1974.

31. (Kurtz, 2006) p. 125 Gus Russo and Dale Myers.

32. Sergeant Jerry Hill during a radio interview (www.youtube.com/watch?v=cqkSV1TyYa0): Hill: 'We got a message that he was in a library

at Marsalis and Jefferson.' Reporter: 'Where did those messages come from?' Hill: 'From people who had heard the description of the man.'

33 There are quite a few problems with regard to the color of the jacket, the size (medium, whereas Oswald's other clothing was small) and the presence of a laundry label (Oswald washed his clothes himself; the origin of the laundry label could not be determined). The time the jacket was found also causes some problems.

34 (Trask, National Nightmare, 2005) p. 116.

35 Historical CPI-U data from 1913 to the present index May 1978: 64,500, index May 2012: 229,815.

36 (Gibson, The Kennedy Assassination Cover-up, 2000) p. 36.

37 FBI document N° 105-569-94.

38 (O'Reilly, 2012) p. 126.

39 CIA memo see: www.scribd.com/doc/53847759/The-Marilyn-Monroe.

40 (O'Reilly, 2012) p. 147.

41 Dallas had approximately 650,000 inhabitants in 1964, and 133 homicides were committed in that year. In 2011, after seven consecutive years of improvement, the city still had a *crime index 5*, which means that the situation was worse in only five cities out of a hundred. (source: www.neighborhoodscout.com/tx/dallas/crime/).

42 The assassination of the president was not a federal offense at the time, and the legal authority was therefore determined by the place of the crime. Conspiracy, however, was a federal offense, but no charge was made in this context, either then or at a later point in time.

43 (O'Reilly, 2012) The Kennedy team was well aware that they were acting contrary to the law. Kenneth O'Donnell told the judge and the autopsy doctor who based their opposition on the law: 'We don't give a damn what these laws say, we're leaving now!'

44 Anthony Summers, *Not in your lifetime*, p. 8: 'Justice of the peace Theran Ward stated: 'As far as I am concerned, this is just a homicide case like any other.' 'Go f**k yourself!' replied Kenneth O'Donnell, special aid and personal friend of the president.' Summers continues: 'The Secret Agents pushed the doctor and the judge against the wall at gunpoint, and rushed out of the hospital, taking the body of the president with them.'

45 Invalid source specified. Loc. 1448-50.

46 Invalid source specified. Loc 1461-62.

47 The court case of District Attorney and notorious troublemaker Jim Garrison against Clay Shaw in New Orleans only confused matters even more. In 1986, a pseudo court case was staged for the 21-hour television documentary *On Trial* with Vincent Bugliosi as the prosecutor and Gerry Spence as Oswald's defender. The jury found Oswald guilty.

48 (Sneed, 1998) p. 241.

49 Warren Commission Executive Session of Dec 5, 1963 p. 8.

50 Warren Commission Executive Session of Jan 22, 1964 p. 11-13.

51 In the transcript of the executive session, the astonishment of the commission members stands in sharp contrast with their public and solemn oaths to ensure independence and an in-depth investigation in order to find the whole truth. The record literally states the following: 'The FBI is very explicit that Oswald is the assassin, or was the assassin, and they are very explicit that there was no conspiracy, and they are also saying in the same place that they are continuing their investigation. [...] But they are concluding that there can't be a conspiracy without those [leads] being run out. Now that is not from my experience with the FBI. [...] Why are they so eager to make both of those conclusions, both in the original report and their experimental report, which is such a departure.'

52 Warren Commission, Executive Session of Jan 27, 1964, p. 20 (p. 153).

53 Bugliosi, p. xxix, in fact, openly admits this: 'Yes, the Commission was biased against Oswald, but only *after* it became obvious to any sensible, reasonable person that he had murdered Kennedy. Actually, that fact was clearly evident within hours of the assassination.' In other words, because the guilt of Oswald was already established mere hours after the attack, the independent body that had to judge his guilt was entitled to be biased, according to Bugliosi. 'Only after it became obvious' therefore means a few hours after the murder, not after the objective judgment of the evidence during the activities of the Warren Commission.

54 Warren Commission, Executive Session January 27, 1964, p. 153: Dulles would commit perjury to protect the identity of CIA agents.

55 Warren Commission, Executive Session of Jan. 27, 1964, p. 15.

56 Invalid source specified. loc 250.

57 Invalid source specified. loc 423.

58 (Nelson, 2011) p. 140.

59 www.time.com/time/magazine/article/0,9171,
    879566,00.html.

60 (Bugliosi, 2007) p. 952.

61 (Bugliosi, 2007) p. 952. Bugliosi has an efficient
    way to dismiss the less obvious aspects of the
    dossier: 'If there is one, and only one, contribu-
    tion to the assassination debate I would want to
    make, over and beyond the substance of this
    book, it's the obvious notion that once you prove
    the positive or negative of a matter in dispute, all
    other questions about the correctness of the con-
    clusion become irrelevant.' Bugliosi continues:
    'What the Warren Commission Critics and con-
    spiracy theorists seem incapable of seeing is that
    the answers to their countless questions are ir-
    relevant since Oswald's guilt has already been
    conclusively established by other evidence.'

62 (Bugliosi, 2007) p. 832.

63 (Aaronovitch) p. 123.

64 CIA Document #1035-960 dd. 1/4/1967.

65 (Warren Commission Report, 1964) p. 178.

66 (Bugliosi, 2007) p. 952.

67 (Warren Commission Hearings and Exhibits
    Vol. V, 1964) p. 98.

68 (Bugliosi, 2007) p. xxi.

69 Savage's uncle Rusty adds an interesting detail
    here: 'Coincidentally or not, Howard was stand-
    ing near Ruby and witnessed the shooting of
    Oswald.' Savage goes one step further: 'Rusty
    told me that Tom Howard was known to hit the
    bottle frequently'. ((Savage, 1993) p. 225). I leave
    the statement regarding Howard's presence in
    the basement and the latter's drinking habits to
    be accounted for by Savage.

70 (HSCA Report, 1978) p. 158.

71 (Twyman, *Bloody Treason. The Assassination of
    John F. Kennedy*, 1997 E-book) Location 6579.

72 (HSCA Vol. IX, 1978) p. 183.

73 (Warren Commission Hearings and Exhibits
    Vol. XV, 1964) p. 228. The dancer Jada, whose act
    was considered too explicit by Ruby, was berated
    and later dismissed because she did not adapt the
    act sufficiently to meet Ruby's standards. On the
    other hand, (CD4 – p. 519 FBI report of the inter-
    view of Elaine Rogers dd. 28.11.63) Ruby courted
    Ms Rogers over the phone, initially by reading
    her poetry, but the conversations gradually be-
    came more suggestive, and finally '*completely ob-
    scene, and Miss Rogers felt that Ruby obtained some
    sexual gratification from the conversations had over
    the Phone. Ruby began each obscene conversation*

*with furnishing Miss Rogers a detailed description of
his privates [...]. Ruby would then describe in minute
detail how he would have sexual intercourse with her
and describe in great detail the pleasure she would de-
rive from this act.*'

74 (Warren Commission Hearings and Exhibits
    Vol. XIV, 1964) p. 642, Carousel stripper Kathy
    Kay Coleman had a relationship with Dallas po-
    lice officer Harry Olsen.

75 (Warren Commission Report, 1964) p. 347.

76 See, e.g. CD4 p. 515 – FBI report of the interview
    of Mrs. Weston.

77 See, e.g. CD4 p. 514 – FBI report of the interview
    of Mrs. Weston.

78 CD4, p. 511, 24/11/63 interview of Nancy Powell,
    striptease dancer at the Carousel: '*She felt that the
    club was solvent financially.*'

79 (Warren Commission Hearings and Exhibits
    Vol. XXIII, 1964) p. 270 to p. 339 in Vol. XXIII relate
    to documents regarding Ruby's persistent tax
    problems. In October 1961, Ruby's tax arrears
    amounted to 20,826 dollars.

80 (Warren Commission Report, 1964) p. 334: on
    November 21, he phoned, among other people,
    his lawyer Graham Koch to discuss his persistent
    tax problems. CE 2251 (CD84 p. 203).

81 (Warren Commission Hearings and Exhibits
    Vol. XXIII, 1964) p. 118.

82 Dallas Municipal Archives, JFK Collection, Box 7,
    folder 3 item 2.

83 Vectorsite.net, 19.3. Ruby's 1959 trip to Cuba.
    Zoppi, entertainment columnist for The Dallas
    Morning News expresses it as follows: '*He was a
    born loser, a real low-level loser. He didn't have twen-
    ty cents to his name [...] he was a hanger-on who was
    very impressed by famous people, impressed by 'class'
    and with anybody that he thought had it [...]. But the
    people that knew him knew Ruby was a zero [...]. He
    would announce: "Hi, I'm Jack Ruby." -- like that was
    supposed to mean something.*'

84 (Warren Commission Hearings and Exhibits
    Vol. XXVI, 1964) p. 470.

85 CD4 p. 509: FBI Report 44-1639, John Anderson,
    trumpet player at the Carousel, in my opinion
    adequately summarizes how Ruby's surround-
    ings feel about him: '*Ruby is a man with a big heart
    and also can show extreme emotion of friendship and
    kindness. He stated that in spite of Ruby's temper, and
    strong emotions, he could not consider him to be the
    type who would resort to murder.*'

86 (Meagher, 1967) p. 391.

87 (HSCA Vol. IX, 1978) p. 588, marginal reference 1113.

88 (Warren Commission Hearings and Exhibits Vol. XXVI, 1964) p. 651.

89 (HSCA Vol. IX, 1978) marginal reference 737: 'These records, along with Ruby's safety deposit box records and SA Flynn's reports of his visits with Ruby, indicate Ruby made at least three trips to Cuba in August and September of 1959.'

90 (HSCA Vol. IX, 1978) p. 189.

91 (HSCA Report, 1978) p. 156 : The HSCA nevertheless observes that the activities of the AGVA, the American Guild of scantily dressed Variety Artists, are very difficult to separate: 'The committee's difficulties in separating Ruby's AGVA contacts from his organized crime connections was, in large degree, based on the dual roles that many of his associated played.'

92 (HSCA Vol. IX, 1978) p. 196 marginal reference 834.

93 Taniment Library & Robert F. Wagner Labor Archives, Preliminary Inventory for the American Guild of Variety Artists Records WAG.095: 'In 1962 the Senate Committee on Government Operations chaired by Senator John McClellan started investigations into possible AGVA links with organized crime.'

94 (HSCA Report, 1978) p. 156.

95 (Meagher, 1967) p. 392.

96 Ruby had been identified at the Parkland Hospital by the widely respected journalist Seth Kantor, who knew Ruby. (Warren Commission Report, 1964) p. 336).

97 Donald A., Purdy, G., Jack Ruby Chronologies, jfkassassination.net/russ/jfkinfo/jfk9/hscv9g.htm. Ruby was, for example, seen by Ferdinand Kaufman, Associated Press photographer, on the fourth floor of the police station between 4 and 4:30 p.m.; in the late evening until the early hours of November 23, Ruby was spotted by Jeremiah O'Leary, Ike Pappas, Samuel Mack Pate and Jerry Lee Kunkel. By the deadline time of The Dallas Morning News, around 4 a.m., Ruby is hanging about there in the lay-out room. Ruby is also repeatedly seen at the police station on Saturday.

98 (Warren Commission Hearings, Vol. XXV, 1964) p. 143 CE2243.

99 (Warren Commission Hearings, Vol. XXV, 1964) p. 208 CE 2284.

100 (Warren Commission Hearings, Vol. XXV, 1964) p. 208 CE 2284 p. 3.

101 (Warren Commission Report, 1964) p. 337.

102 (HSCA Vol. IX, 1978) p. 439.

103 (Warren Commission Hearings, Vol. XXV, 1964) p. 143 CE2243.

104 (Sloan B. , 1993-2012) loc 2404-17.

105 (Bugliosi, 2007) p. 1016.

106 CD4 contains a large number of reports on the questioning of everyone who knew the Carousel professionally, and no one ever saw Oswald there.

107 (Warren Commission Report, 1964) p. 373.

108 E.g., (HSCA Vol. IX, 1978) p. 427 'Dolan could not conceive of Ruby being connected to the mob, as he was too erratic and closely associated with policemen all the time.'

109 CD4 – p. CD4 p. 514 – FBI report of the interview of Mrs. Weston, wife of Wally Weston, a friend ('perhaps his closest friend at the time'): Her first impression after the murder of Oswald was 'that his act was occasioned by an intense desire on the part of Ruby to make a name for himself and obtain nation-wide publicity'. Others have also confirmed this view, e.g. Ms Rogers (CD4 p. 520): 'Miss Rogers does not think Ruby shot Oswald because of any feeling of patriotic duty but feels that it is merely another attempt on the part of Ruby to be a big man'.

110 (Bugliosi, 2007) p. 985.

111 (HSCA Vol. IX, 1978) p. 21.

112 (HSCA Vol. IX, 1978) p. 65 referring to Bill Davidson, 'New Orleans: Cosa Nostra's Wall Street', The Saturday Evening Post, Feb. 29, 1964.

113 (HSCA Vol. IX, 1978) p. 65 referring to Ramsey Clark, Crime In America (New York: Pocket Books, 1971), pp. 56-57.

114 (HSCA Vol. IX, 1978) p. 74.

115 (HSCA Vol. IX, 1978) p. 75.

116 (HSCA Vol. IX, 1978) p. 83.

117 (Reid, 1969) pp. 158-159.

118 (Twyman, Bloody Treason. The Assassination of John F. Kennedy, 1997 E-book) loc. 6846.

119 (HSCA Vol. IX, 1978) p. 96.

120 (HSCA Report, 1978) p. 170.

121 (HSCA Vol. IX, 1978) p. 99.

122 (HSCA Report, 1978) p. 170.

123 FBI Files – New Orleans Field Office, part 1, p. 63: G. Wray Gill, his lawyer and employer, for example, states: 'Ferrie is brilliant, but mentally unstable.'

124 FBI Files – New Orleans Field Office, part 1, p. 50. Report of Ferrie's questioning dd. 28/11/63 (Mary Ferrell Foundation, www.maryferrell.org/mff-web/archive/viewer/showDoc.do) and (HSCA Appendix Vol. X, 1978) p. 112.

125 (HSCA Appendix Vol. X, 1978) p. 112 Including the cooperation with Marcello associates in a flying taxi company. Further indications:

126 Reitzes, David 'David Ferrie: Presumed Guilty - Garrison's Villain and Hollywood's clown', www.jfk-online.com/ferriepre.html.

127 Ibid. He had *only a Bachelor's Degree from a fifth rate college, called Baldwin-Wallace in Bera, Ohio, and a bogus Ph.D. from "Phoenix University" in Bari, Italy'*.

128 (HSCA Appendix Vol. X, 1978) p. 116 footnote 36. John Stanley, *Archbishop of the Metropolitan Eastern Province. American Orthodox Catholic Church* consecrated Ferrie to the office of bishop in June 1961, but following his dismissal from Eastern Airlines, and in view of the underlying reasons, he was deprived of his title.

129 CD75 – FBI DeBrueys Report of 02/12/1963, FBI interview Ferrie dd. 27/11/1963.

130 ibid.

131 (HSCA Appendix Vol. X, 1978) XII, marginal reference 441 and further. Ferrie, for example, allegedly supported Marcello's escape from Guatemala in his capacity as pilot after the latter's first deportation.

132 (Mellen, 2005) p. 35: John J. Martin was CIA employee under the name Jack Martin until June 1958, when he left on 'sick leave', presumably because of his alcohol problem; he did not return to the CIA afterwards.

133 (Lambert, 1998) p. 24;

134 (Lambert, 1998) p. 25.

135 CD75 FBI DeBrueys Report p. 218.

136 John S. Craid, *The Mystery of David Ferrie*, (www.acorn.net/jfkplace/09/fp.back_issues/05th_Issue/ferrie.html): Banister's secretary Delphine Roberts allegedly told Anthony Summers that Oswald and Ferrie had visited a training camp for Cuban exiles together at least once for target practice.

137 CD75 FBI DeBrueys Report p. 218.

138 CD75 FBI DeBrueys Report p. 219 FBI report of the interview of G. Wray Gill, on November 27, 1963.

139 CD75 FBI DeBrueys Report p. 220 FBI report of the interview of G. Wray Gill, on November 27, 1963.

140 (HSCA Vol. IX, 1978) p. 74, marginal reference 364

141 See footnote above: Patricia Lambert believed that the 7,000 dollars related to severance pay, not to the remuneration for assistance in the trial.

142 CPI index November 1963: 30800, CPI May 2012: 229.815.

143 (HSCA Appendix Vol. X, 1978) p. 113 marginal reference 451: 'to celebrate Marcello's victory in the *Royal Orleans'*. Even Ruby closed his *Carousel* in Dallas to avoid unseemly situations, but in New Orleans a party was apparently not inappropriate.

144 (HSCA Appendix Vol. X, 1978) marginal reference 451 with reference to FBI teletype, Nov. 26, 1963, to Director from SAC New Orleans, p. 13; FBI interview of G. Wray Gill, Nov. 27, 1963.

145 FBI Files – New Orleans Field Office, part 1, p. 51.

146 (Lambert, 1998) p. 44 on the basis of the interview with Beauboeuf.

147 John S. Craig, *The mystery of David Ferrie*; www.acorn.net/jfkplace/09/fp.back_issues/05th_Issue/ferrie.html.

148 FBI Files – New Orleans Field Office, part 1, p. 51.

149 (Summers, *Not in your lifetime*, 1998) p. 3510.

150 FBI report, No.62-109060-2143, Dec. 18, 1963, p. 1, interview with Chuck Rolland: 'Ferrie called in advance on November 22, 1963, arrived on November 23, 1963, between 3:30 and 5:30 p.m., but he did not discuss the operation of the ice rink as Ferrie had suggested he would do.'

151 (HSCA Appendix Vol. X, 1978) marginal reference 455.

152 FBI Files – New Orleans Field Office, part 1, p. 53.

153 mcadams.posc.mu.edu/weberman/nodule24.htm: *'Gaeton Fonzi discovered that the check-in and check-out times for the Alamotel Motel and Driftwood Motel conflicted. Alamotel Motel records indicated that David Ferrie and friends checked into the motel early Saturday, November 23, 1963, and did not leave until 8:00 or 9:00 p.m., Sunday, November 24, 1963. Yet the registration records and witnesses at Driftwood Motel in Galveston showed that the three men registered late Saturday, November 23, 1963, and checked out at 10:00 a.m. Sunday, November 24, 1963. The significance of this was unclear.'*

154 See Google Maps.

155 HSCA Segregated CIA Collection, Box 42, FERRIE, DAVID WILLIAM - OS/SAG FILES FOR HSCA STAFF MEMBERS p. 15. NARA Record Number: 1993.07.20.14:07:44:370280.

156 (Lambert, 1998) p. 27.

157 (Lambert, 1998) p. 60, David Ferrie, Autopsy protocol, Feb. 22, 1967, Orleans Parish Coroner's office, Dr. Nicholas J. Chetta Orleans Parish Coroner and Ronald A. Welsh, pathologist.

158 (Warren Commission Hearings and Exhibits Vol. XIV, 1964) Vol. XIV, p. 600.

159 (Bugliosi, 2007) p. 413. Bugliosi does not waste many words on Ferrie and Galveston. Galveston is only casually mentioned twice. On p. 413, we learn that the doctors of the Parkland Hospital were attending a medical conference in Galveston. Bugliosi does find the time and place, however, to sarcastically add here that the conspiracists overlooked an argument, i.e., the possibility that the doctors attended the congress on purpose that weekend, to ensure that the president would not receive the best possible treatment, thereby reducing the chance that he would survive. It is not quite clear what exactly Bugliosi aims to achieve with such attempts to ridicule the dossier. It is excessive, and the conspiracy theorists manage to produce enough foolish arguments on their own behalf.

160 (Warren Commission Hearings and Exhibits Vol. XIV, 1964) p. 605.

161 (Warren Commission Report, 1964) p. 358.

162 House Select Committee *Hearings*, Vol. IX , 905-7; Warren Commission *Report*, 334; see also FBI Report of interview with Jean Aase, December 3, 1963, Commission Exhibit No. 2266 (Warren Commission *Hearings*, Vol. XXV, 190); Special Agents George H. Parfet and Richard B. Lee; see also FBI Report of interview with Lawrence Meyers, December 3, 1963, Special Agents George H. Parfet and Richard B. Lee, Commission Exhibit No. 2267 (Warren Commission *Hearings*, Vol. XXV, 191-2).

163 (Warren Commission Hearings, Vol. XXV, 1964) p. 191 CE 2267.

164 (HSCA Appendix Vol. X, 1978) marginal reference 1187, Dec. 12, 1963 FBI interview of Meyers (JFK Document 004531).

165 (Warren Commission Hearings and Exhibits Vol. XXVI, 1964) p. 343, CE 2888.

166 Marquis W. Childs, Washington correspondent, on October 10, 1963 in Washington Calling.

167 In 1961, Dr. Albert E. Burke attended a meeting at the home of H. L. Hunt in Dallas. He gave the following account of his harrowing experience afterwards: '*I have listened to communists and other groups that can only be called enemies, accuse us of the worst intentions, the most inhuman ways of doing things, as the most dangerous people on earth, to be stopped and destroyed at all costs... But nothing I have heard in or from those places around us compared with the experience I had in the Dallas home of an American, whose hate for this country's leaders, and the way our institutions worked, was the most vicious, venomous and dangerous I have known in my life. No communist ever heard, no enemy of this*

nation has ever done a better job of degrading or belittling this country. That American was one of this nation's richest and most powerful men! It was a very special performance by a pillar of the American community, who influences things in his community. It was a very special performance because in that living room during his performance - in which he said things had reached the point where there seemed to be "no way left to get those traitors out of our government except by shooting them out" during that performance, there were four teenagers in that room to be influenced.' Source: www.spartacus.schoolnet. co.uk/JFKSinvestOil.htm.

168 Thomas G. Buchanan, *Who Killed Kennedy* (1964).

169 www.spartacus.schoolnet.co.uk/ JFKoildepletion.htm.

170 (Livingstone) p. 65.

171 (Warren Commission Hearings and Exhibits Vol. XXIII, 1964) p. 363.

172 (Warren Commission Hearings and Exhibits Vol. XXIII, 1964) p. 363.

173 David Talbot, *The Mother of all Cover-Ups*. The account is as follows: '*The summer after the assassination, Hoover was relaxing at the Del Charro resort in California, which was owned by his friend, right-wing Texas oil tycoon Clint Murchison. Another Texas oil crony of Hoover's, Billy Byars Sr. -- the only man Hoover had called on the afternoon of November 22, 1963 besides Robert Kennedy and the head of the Secret Service -- also was there. At one point, according to Anthony Summers, the invaluable prober of the dark side of American power, Byars' teenage son, Billy Jr. got up his nerve to ask Hoover the question, 'Do you think Lee Harvey Oswald did it?' According to Byars, Hoover 'stopped and looked at me for quite a long time. Then he said, "If I told you what I really know, it would be very dangerous to this country. Our whole political system could be disrupted."'*

174 (Nelson, 2011) p. 184.

175 (Moldea, 1978) p. 160.

176 Braden afterwards turned up in Houston. In the interview with his probation officer there he never mentioned his brief arrest after the assassination of Kennedy.

177 Invalid source specified. loc 1743.

178 See, e.g., FBI Memorandum dd. 5/7/69 L.A.F.O N° 56-156 (Ser. 2851-3001) on, among others, Jim Braden.

179 Braden filed a lawsuit against Noyes for defamation and libel. His lawyer Ken Trombly stated that Braden was an honorable citizen; Braden won the case and had Noyes remove the book from the market.

180 (Noyes, 1973) p. 157.

181 (Garrison, 1988) According to Garrison, it was easy to establish which numbers had been called by Ferrie: 'Gill instructed his secretary to draw a penciled line through every call made by the office,' Garrison writes, 'leaving exposed the calls made by Ferrie' (Garrison, 127). "They're easy to pick out," he quotes Gill as saying. "Those cities there didn't have a damned things [sic] to do with this office. You know better than anyone about ninety percent of my business is right here in New Orleans.'" Be that as it may, there are a number of calls to such exotic lands as Guatemala, to where Gill's most valuable client, Carlos Marcello, had been threatened with deportation in 1963, and where the office had reason to call numerous times.

182 (Warren Commission Hearings, Vol. XXV, 1964) p. 335.

183 (HSCA Vol. IX, 1978) p. 419.

184 www.lotuseaters.org/jfkdad.shtml.

185 (HSCA Vol. IX, 1978) p. 422 marginal reference 955.

186 (Warren Commission Hearings and Exhibits Vol. XXII, 1964) p. 894.

187 (Ernest, 2010) p. 231.

188 (Beschloss, 1997) p. 559.

189 David Talbot, *The Mother of All Cover-Ups*.

190 news.bbc.co.uk/2/hi/americas/1848157.stm, BBC1, Friday, March 1, 2002, 09:50 GMT, Kevin Anderson. 'Referring to the report by the Warren Commission, "it was the greatest hoax that has ever been perpetuated," Nixon said. He did not elaborate why he questioned the report.' But the full quotation reads as follows: "They pinned the assassination of Kennedy on the right wing, the Birchers. It was done by a Communist and it was the greatest hoax that has ever been perpetuated". Nixon, in fact, claims that the left wing inspired authors (such as Mark Lane) accused the John Birch Society, and that was the 'hoax'. According to Nixon, the assassination was carried out by a communist, i.e., Oswald.

191 www.crimemagazine.com/08/fordadmits,0109-8.htm.

192 educationforum.ipbhost.com/index.php?showtopic=5774 John Simkin.

193 *Reagan in his Own Voice* CD 5 Track 13.

194 Memo by FBI Special Agent Graham Kitchel in Texas, regarding 'GHW Bush of Zapata Off-Shore Drilling Company' received 75 minutes after the assassination.

195 (O'Neill, 1987) p. 184.

196 (Warren Commission Hearings and Exhibits Vol. IX, 1964) p. 169 and p. 175.

197 George Bush has the somewhat strange tendency of being in the wrong place at historic moments in time. The code name for the failed Bay of Pigs operation was 'Zapata', which just happened to be the name of Bush's oil company. The ships the insurgents used to go ashore were called the 'Barbara' and the 'Houston'. George lived in Houston with his wife Barbara. Bush also happened to be in Dallas on November 22, 1963, denounced (when it was too late) potential conspirators to the CIA, and was also good friends with de Mohrenschildt, who in turn was Oswald's only friend.
In 1981, when Bush was Vice-President, John Hinckley Jr. shot President Ronald Reagan. Bush knew the Hinckley family very well; in fact, he had a dinner appointment with the brother of the perpetrator down in his diary for the day after the attack. When the attacks of September 11, 2001 occurred, Bush, again, was well in with the Bin Laden family, and had even shared a table with a Bin Laden in the context of the Carlyle Group on that day.

198 (Fonzi, 1993) p. 190.

199 en.wikipedia.org/wiki/George_de_Mohrenschildt, footnote 45.

200 CIA Exec Reg. # 76,51571 9.28.76.

201 (Epstein E. J., *The Assassination Chronicles: Inquest, Counterplot and Legend*, 1992), p. 559.

202 Invalid source specified. p. 300.

203 CD 75 FBI DeBrueys Report of 02 Dec 1963 re: Oswald/Russia p. 573.

204 (HSCA Report, 1978) p. 218.

205 (HSCA Report, 1978) p. 219.

206 NARA Record Number: 104-10135-10019.

207 (Nelson, 2011) p. 70.

208 'CIA: Maker of Policy or Tool? Survey finds widely feared agency is tightly controlled.' *New York Times*, April 25, 1966.

209 (Douglas, 2008) p. 332.

210 (Douglas, 2008) p. 333.

211 *The Pentagon Papers*, Gravel Edition, Volume 2, pp. 769-770Dit.

212 (North, 2011) p. 163.

213 Congressional record – Senate 7/10/62, p. 13047.

214 (North, 2011) p. 168.

215 (North, 2011) p. 185.

216 (North, 2011) p. 206.

217 New York Times 10/11/1962.

218 Caro, Master of the Senate, p. 116.

219 (Krusch, 2012) loc. 2714.

220 (Krusch, 2012) loc. 2837.

221 (Warren Commission Hearings and Exhibits Vol. III, 1964) p. 429.

222 (Warren Commission Hearings and Exhibits Vol. VI, 1964) p. 128.

223 (Warren Commission Hearings and Exhibits Vol. IX XXIV, 1964) p. 412 FBI Report: 'O.P. Wright: [...] Tomlinson, a member of the staff, called him and pointed to a bullet that was lying on a hospital gurney at this place.'

224 (Warren Commission Report, 1964) p. 57.

225 (Bugliosi, 2007) p. 83.

226 (Warren Commission Hearings and Exhibits Vol. XVIII, 1964) p. 811 Memo from Rowley, Chief of the Secret Service.

227 CD 1095. This document contains 86 pages of explanations given by the various members of the Secret Service on November 27.

228 FBI Memorandum 11/23/63, Devons to Conrad.

229 www.parklandhospital.com/whoweare/kennedy.html.

230 (Warren Commission Hearings and Exhibits Vol. VI, 1964) p. 43.

231 (Warren Commission Hearings and Exhibits Vol. XI, 1964) p. 81.

232 (Warren Commission Report, 1964) p. 81.

233 Laboratory Report, by an unknown author. FBI laboratory report concerning firearms, fingerprints, bullets and other evidence taken from the Dallas Police Department, City of Dallas Archive – Box 1 Folder 8.

234 (McKnight, 2005) p. 182.

235 (Warren Commission Hearings and Exhibits Vol. V, 1964) Wound ballistic expert US Army Dr. Olivier p. 82 and 86. (Warren Commission Hearings and Exhibits Vol. VI, 1964) p. 111: Dr. Shires testified that a fragment was visible on Connally's chest x-rays. (Warren Commission Hearings and Exhibits Vol. IV, 1964) p. 124 Dr. Gregory removed two fragments from the wrist, but there were still large fragments left behind in the wrist. The femur still contained at least one fragment.

236 (Warren Commission Hearings and Exhibits, Vol. II, 1964) p. 376.

237 (Warren Commission Hearings and Exhibits, Vol. II, 1964) p. 38.

238 (Warren Commission Hearings and Exhibits Vol. IV, 1964) p. 113.

239 (Warren Commission Hearings and Exhibits Vol. XVII, 1964) p. 849 CE 853.

240 (Warren Commission Report, 1964) p. 95.

241 CD7 p. 288 FBI report Memorandum Todd. Dd. 26/11/63.

242 (Warren Commission Hearings and Exhibits Vol. IX XXIV, 1964) p. 412.

243 www.jfklancer.com/hunt/phantom.htm.

244 The FBI reports in question can be consulted on History-matters.com: www.historymatters.com/ essays/frameup/EvenMoreMagical/images/ Slide6.GIF and Slide5.GIF.

245 (Warren Commission Hearings and Exhibits Vol. II, 1964) p. 347.

246 (Warren Commission Hearings and Exhibits Vol. V, 1964) p. 449 ff.

247 (Warren Commission Hearings and Exhibits Vol. III, 1964) p. 428-486.

248 (Warren Commission Hearings and Exhibits Vol. III, 1964) p. 432 for CE567 and p. 435 for CE569.

249 (HSCA Appendix VII) p. 369.

250 http://ares.jsc.nasa.gov/Education/websites/craters/GunlabTour.htm#sabot.

251 (Warren Commission Report, 1964) p. 85.

252 (HSCA Appendix Vol. I, 1978) p. 494.

253 http://history-matters.com/archive/contents/ other/contents_fragment-tests.htm.

254 (Warren Commission Report, 1964) p. 559. Firearms Expert Cunningham (Warren Commission Hearings and Exhibits Vol. III, 1964) p. 451 and the following, also excludes that Oswald 'reloaded' the bullets on used shells. The only possibility is that there was an empty shell in Oswald's revolver, but then, after four shots had been fired and the fours shells were thrown away, an empty shell should have been left in Oswald's revolver, which was not the case. Oswald could also have fired five shots, one of which missed, but this seems improbable at such close range. It remains a mystery how it is possible that the brand of the bullets did not agree with the brand of the shells. Here also, the three bullets that were found in Tippit's body remained in Dallas for four months before they went to the FBI laboratory. There is also no certainty that the bullets in Tippit's body came from Oswald's revolver. The .38 Special was slightly smaller, and wobbled in the barrel of Oswald's revolver.

255 Dallas Municipal Archives, Box 9, Folder 4, Item 31. A 'CSS' is a type of report on the examination of the scene of a crime.

256 (Krusch, 2012) The photo was shown in the electronic book *Impossible, the Case Against Lee Harvey Oswald*. The photo is said to have come from the FBI Dallas Field Office File 89-43, RG 65, JFK Collection, National Archives, RIF 124-10063-10042, the photo can also be seen in Noel Twyman's *Bloody Treason*, p. 110.

257 C.D.5 p. 169.

258 (Warren Commission Hearings and Exhibits Vol. IX XXIV, 1964) p. 262, CE2003.

259 (Warren Commission Hearings and Exhibits Vol. IX XXIV, 1964) p. 252 and 332.

260 (Warren Commission Hearings and Exhibits Vol. IX XXIV, 1964) p. 330.

261 (Warren Commission Hearings and Exhibits Vol. XVII, 1964) p. 512. A clearer version of the photo can be found in Jesse Curry's own book *JFK Assassination File*.

262 (Bugliosi, 2007) End notes p. 419.

263 (Warren Commission Hearings and Exhibits Vol. XV, 1964) p. 146.

264 (Warren Commission Hearings and Exhibits Vol. IX XXIV, 1964) p. 260, CE2003.

265 (Shaw, 1976) p. 159.

266 I could not find this document in the *Dallas Municipal Archives* and Krush does not provide a clear source. The boxes of the Municipal Archives contain 4,153 documents, so it's not easy to find a document here if it is not referenced to the correct box and folder.

267 (Warren Commission Hearings and Exhibits Vol. IV, 1964) p. 250.

268 (Warren Commission Hearings and Exhibits Vol. IV, 1964) p. 258.

269 (Warren Commission Hearings and Exhibits Vol. IV, 1964).

270 CD735 p. 71.

271 (Krusch, 2012) loc. 3699 and the Dallas Municipal Archives, www.jfk.ci.dallas.tx.us/25/2595-001.gif.

272 (Warren Commission Hearings and Exhibits Vol. VII, 1964) p. 401.

273 Wikipedia (en.wikipedia.org/wiki/John_F._Kennedy_assassination_rifle) suggests that the name 'Mannlicher-Carcano' for the weapon with which Kennedy was said to have been shot is incorrect, and that it is, in fact, a 'Carcano', as the addition of Mannlicher only refers to the ammo clip.

274 (Warren Commission Hearings and Exhibits Vol. III, 1964) Frazier Testimony p. 394.

275 (Warren Commission Hearings and Exhibits Vol. III, 1964) Frazier Testimony: 'a very cheap Japanese telescopic sight.'

276 Tom Whalen, WBAP television reporter, said in a report at 2:13 p.m. that the weapon was a British 303. The he source is not specified, but, according to Gary Mack, archivist of the 6th Floor Museum, was 'someone who actively participated in the research in the TSBD' (posted on July 16 on alt.assassination.jfk.alt.conspiracy.jfk). In Groden's *The Search for Lee Harvey Oswald*, there is a photo on p. 117 of a group of people on the steps of the TSBD, in which the Enfield can be seen.

277 (Brown, The People v. Lee Harvey Oswald, 1992) p. 327.

278 (Warren Commission Hearings and Exhibits Vol. IV, 1964) p. 261.

279 (Warren Commission Hearings and Exhibits Vol. XVII, 1964) p. 290 CE 637.

280 (HSCA Appendix Vol. IV, 1978) p. 261.

281 (Warren Commission Hearings and Exhibits Vol. IV, 1964) p. 23.

282 www.kenrahn.com/jfk/the_critics/griffith/Planted_palm_print.html, Michael T. Griffith: Was Oswald's palm print applied to the so-called murder weapon?

283 www.youtube.com/watch?v=P2W_-ID8RMI.

284 (Savage, 1993).

285 The weapon was back in Dallas at the moment of Oswald's death, so that the weapon itself could also have been used to apply the palm print in the morgue.

286 (Warren Commission Hearings and Exhibits Vol. XXVI, 1964) p. 828.

287 (Warren Commission Hearings and Exhibits Vol. III, 1964) p. 394.

288 (Warren Commission Hearings and Exhibits Vol. III, 1964) p. 494.

289 (Warren Commission Hearings and Exhibits Vol. III, 1964) p. 492.

290 (Warren Commission Hearings, Vol. XXV, 1964) p. 799.

291 (Weisberg, Whitewash, 1966).

292 (Brown, Treachery in Dallas) p. 26.

293 (Bugliosi, 2007) p. xxviii.

294 (Bugliosi, 2007) p. xxviii.

295 (Warren Commission Hearings and Exhibits Vol. III, 1964) p. 442.

296 (Warren Commission Hearings and Exhibits Vol. III, 1964) p. 450.

297 (Warren Commission Hearings and Exhibits Vol. III, 1964) p. 450.

298 (Warren Commission Hearings and Exhibits Vol. XI, 1964) p. 314.

299 (Warren Commission Hearings and Exhibits Vol. XI, 1964) p. 315.

300 (Warren Commission Report, 1964) p. 120.

301 (Warren Commission Report, 1964) p. 119.

302 www.giljesus.com/jfk/rifle.htm.

303 educationforum.ipbhost.com/index.php? showtopic=4781&st=15 Jack White.

304 Photo of the serial number *Life Photo, courtesy to Jerry McLeer* (jfkresearch.freehomepage.com/c2766.html).

305 (Warren Commission Hearings and Exhibits Vol. XVII, 1964) p. 238.

306 (HSCA Appendix Vol. VI) p. 146;

307 Photo Courtesy to Gil Jesus.

308 (Warren Commission Hearings and Exhibits Vol. XVI, 1964) p. 510.

309 (HSCA Appendix Vol. VI) p. 89.

310 (HSCA Appendix Vol. VI) p. 88, marginal number 230.

311 (HSCA Appendix Vol. VI) p. 88, Figure III-8 (JFK Exhibit F206).

312 (HSCA Appendix Vol. VI) p. 145.

313 (Warren Commission Hearings, Vol. XXV, 1964) p. 899.

314 (Warren Commission Hearings and Exhibits Vol. XVI, 1964) p. 513.

315 (Warren Commission Hearings and Exhibits Vol. XVI, 1964) p. 960.

316 (Warren Commission Hearings and Exhibits Vol. IV, 1964) p. 197.

317 (Warren Commission Hearings and Exhibits Vol. II, 1964) p. 226.

318 CD87 p. 288 Affidavit 22/11/63 Buell Wesley Frazier.

319 Texas File # DL 89-43 by Special Agent JAMES W. BOOKHOUT/cah/tjd.

320 Zabell, Sany, 'Fingerprint Evidence', *Journal of Law and Policy*: 'latent prints usually present an "inevitable source of error in making comparisons," as they generally "contain less clarity, less content, and less undistorted information than a fingerprint taken under controlled conditions, and much, much less detail compared to the actual patterns of ridges and grooves of a finger."'

321 (Brown, The People v. Lee Harvey Oswald, 1992) p. 304.

322 See, for example, PAT A. WERTHEIM, C.L.P.E., 'Scientific Comparison and Identification of Fingerprint Evidence', July 2000 issue of *Fingerprint World*).

323 Anthony Summers, *The Kennedy Conspiracy*, 2002.

324 (Warren Commission Hearings and Exhibits Vol. VI, 1964) p. 360: TSBD shipping clerk Mr. West: 'No sir, I have never seen him in the vicinity.'

325 CD 5 – Gemberling Report November 30, 1963, p. 129.

326 FBI file 105-82555, sec 39, p. 7.

327 FBI 105-82555 Oswald HQ File, Section 6, p. 13.

328 (Warren Commission Report, 1964) Appendix X p. 579.

329 (Warren Commission Hearings and Exhibits Vol. IV, 1964) p. 90-94.

330 (Warren Commission Hearings and Exhibits Vol. VI, 1964) p. 96.

331 Commission Document 897 - FBI Gemberling Report of 04 Apr 1964 re: Oswald - Russia/Cuba p. 163.

332 Commission Document 897 - FBI Gemberling Report of 04 Apr 1964 re: Oswald - Russia/Cuba p. 167.

333 Commission Document 897 - FBI Gemberling Report of 04 Apr 1964 re: Oswald - Russia/Cuba p. 163.

334 www.giljesus.com/index.htm Gil Jesus, *Was Lee Harvey Oswald REALLY Guilty?*

335 (Kritzberg) p. 39-46;

336 Sheriff's report, 23/11/1963, Deputy Sheriff Luke Mooney.

337 (Warren Commission Hearings and Exhibits Vol. III, 1964) p. 284;

338 (Kritzberg).

339 (Kritzberg).

340 *www.jfk-online.com/alyea.html*, website with David Reitzes as webmaster. Bugliosi refers to him in his end notes as (p. 540) „one of the best researchers in the field'.

341 (Warren Commission Hearings and Exhibits Vol. XVII, 1964) p. 220 CE508.

342 (Warren Commission Hearings and Exhibits Vol. XVII, 1964) p. 510 CE734.

343 (Warren Commission Hearings and Exhibits Vol. IV, 1964) p. 269 with specific indication that "in that sense CE733 shows a RECONSTRUCTION" of the book boxes below the window.

344 (Warren Commission Hearings and Exhibits Vol. VII, 1964) p. 147.

345 Dallas Municipal Archives, Box 12a Folder 51 item 1.

346 (Warren Commission Hearings and Exhibits Vol. III, 1964) p. 286.

347 Dallas police report 23/11/1963 Officer Roger Craig, Dallas County Deputy Sheriff.

348 (Warren Commission Hearings and Exhibits Vol. VI, 1964) p. 260.

349 (Ernest, 2010) p. 151.

350 (Warren Commission Hearings and Exhibits Vol. VI, 1964) p. 300.

351 (Warren Commission Hearings and Exhibits Vol. VII, 1964) p. 142.

352 (Warren Commission Hearings and Exhibits Vol. VII, 1964) p. 103.

353 (Warren Commission Hearings and Exhibits Vol. VII, 1964) p. 98.

354 (Warren Commission Hearings and Exhibits Vol. VII, 1964) p. 122.

355 (Warren Commission Hearings and Exhibits Vol. VII, 1964) p. 162.

356 (Warren Commission Hearings and Exhibits Vol. VII, 1964) p. 96.

357 (Warren Commission Hearings and Exhibits Vol. VII, 1964) p. 102.

358 (Warren Commission Hearings and Exhibits Vol. III, 1964) p. 286.

359 (Ernest, 2010) p. 151.

360 (Warren Commission Hearings and Exhibits Vol. IV, 1964) p. 205.

361 (Warren Commission Hearings and Exhibits Vol. VII, 1964) p. 107.

362 (Warren Commission Hearings and Exhibits Vol. III, 1964) p. 291.

363 (Warren Commission Hearings and Exhibits Vol. IV, 1964) p. 258.

364 Dallas Municipal Archives, JFK Collection, Box 2, folder 1.

365 (Warren Commission Hearings and Exhibits Vol. IV, 1964) p. 206.

366 (Warren Commission Hearings and Exhibits Vol. XVII, 1964) p. 215.

367 (Warren Commission Hearings and Exhibits Vol. XVII, 1964) p. 501.

368 Dallas Municipal Archives, Box 12, folder 5.

369 Warren Commission Hearings and Exhibits Vol IV, 1964, p. 251.

370 Dallas Municipal Archives – JFK Collection Box 1 folder 15 'Cross-examination, by unknown author. Typed rudimentary draft version with handwritten corrections concerning the interrogation of Lee Harvey Oswald, (Original), date unknown.'

371 (Trask, Pictures of the pain, 1994) p. 435.

372 *HSCA on assassinations plan.* Passengers are incorrectly assumed to be sitting in the centre of the seats.

373 American University in Washington. Commencement Address, June 10, 1963: 'And if we cannot end now our differences, at least we can help make the world safe for diversity. For, in the final analysis, our most basic common link is that we all inhabit this small planet. We all breathe the same air. We all cherish our childre's futures. And we are all mortal.'

374 (Trask, *Pictures of the pain*, 1994) p. 41.

375 (Warren Commission Hearings and Exhibits Vol. XVIII, 1964) Hickey p. 765 and Kinney p. 732.

376 vincepalamara.com/2012/02/23/chiefs-directors-jfk-limousine/ On November 23, 1963 Tom Wicker commented in an article in the *New York Times*: 'A bucket of water stood by the car, suggesting that the back seat had been scrubbed out.' In his book *On Press*, Wicker would subsequently explain that it was 'a bucket of bloody water'. Hugh Sidey of *Time Magazine* mentioned 'A young man, I assume he was a Secret service man, with a sponge and a bucket of red water, and he was trying to wipe up the blood and what looked like flakes of flesh and brains in the back seat.' Charles Roberts of *Newsweek* confirmed Wicker's and Sidey's reports that Secret Service agents were busy 'mopping up the back seat.'

377 CD80 Letter James J. Rowley to Rankin, dated 6/1/64, p. 1.

378 CD80 Letter James J. Rowley to Rankin, dated 6/1/64, p. 14, report by SAIC Geiglein and SA Taylor on the guarding of the limousine.

379 CD80 p. 12.

380 CD80 Letter James J. Rowley to Rankin, dated 6/1/64, p. 2. Some sources claim that, after having spoken to Greer at the entrance to the White House, Nick Prencipe went to the garage, where he did not see anyone, neither guards nor any other activity around the limousine. Prencipe then allegedly inspected the limousine and discovered an opening at the lower end of the windshield on the passenger side. This account seems rather implausible.

381 (Warren Commission Hearings and Exhibits Vol. V, 1964) p. 67.

382 The five FBI agents included Orrin Bartlett, Charles Killian, Cortlandt Cunningham, Robert Frazier and Walter Thomas. CD80 p. 13.

383 CD80 Memorandum from Charles Taylor, White House, Protective Research Section, 11/27/63.

384 CD80 Letter James J. Rowley to Rankin, p. 4.

385 Anthony Marsh, *Best Witness: JFK's Limousine.* 2nd Annual COPA Conference, October 22, 1995. Marsh is the first to report, on the basis of an enlargement of photograph CE350, a possible *dent* at the back of the rear view mirror.

386 The three agent names appear to be Frazier, Killian, and Cunningham.

387 CD80 Exhibit 3, mentioned in letter James J. Rowley p. 4 §3.

388 FBI Memorandum 11/23/63, Devons to Conrad.

389 (Warren Commission Hearings and Exhibits Vol. XVII, 1964) p. 867, CE872.

390 CD80 Memorandum from Charles Taylor, White House, Protective Research Section, 11/27/63 p. 3.

391 See e.g. CD80 Memorandum from Charles Taylor, White House, Protective Research Section, 11/27/63 56 CD80 p. 5.

392 CD80 p. 5.

393 www.automotiverestorations.com/press/press_019.html: Another chance for the Kennedy Lincoln Kevin N. McDonald.

394 (Fetzer, Murder in Dealey Plaza, 2000) p. 134, Douglas Weldon J.D. The Kennedy limousine: Dallas 1963.

395 (Fetzer, Murder in Dealey Plaza, 2000) p. 146, Douglas Weldon J.D. The Kennedy limousine: Dallas 1963.

396 www.thehenryford.org/research/kennedyLimousine.aspx.

397 (Warren Commission Report, 1964) p. 76.

398 CD3, Secret Service Report p. 30: 'approximately 120 degrees'.

399 Degrees (ACOS (SQRT (4962 – 212) / 4962)).

400 (Warren Commission Report, 1964) p. 217.

401 CE585, CE882, CE883 and finally Shaneyfelt Exhibit #25. There is also table CE884, with data that remained invisible even under a microscope.

402 (Warren CommissionHearings and Exhibits Vol XX, 1964) p. 92-155.

403 (Warren Commission Hearings and Exhibits Vol. XVII, 1964) p. 330 CE672.

404 (Cutler, The flight of CE399, 1969) p. 40: Cutler concludes: 'To erase, or cause the professional surveyor to erase, any one of these inlets is so unethical, so clumsy, so puerile that it immediately becomes suspect. Granted, the stormsewer theory is speculation; it has more verisimilitude than the Commission's elimination of physical facts on the basic plot of the scene of the crime in attempted confirmation of the Single Bullet Theory.'

405 (Warren Commission Hearings and Exhibits Vol. XVII, 1964) p. 262.

406 (Warren Commission Hearings and Exhibits Vol. XVII, 1964) p. 901.

407 (Warren Commission Hearings and Exhibits Vol. XVII, 1964) p. 899. The photographs of the various setups are included in Commission Document CD295.

408 (McKnight, 2005) p. 97.

409 The model is now exhibited in the *Sixth Floor Museum* on Dealey Plaza, and its perfect finish is still surprising today. The caption merely states: 'Data for the model was collated on December 2, 3 and 4, 1963.'

410 (McKnight, 2005) p.46 'Leaking the conclusions was part of the FBI's campaign to put the Commission in a box and force it to endorse the FBI's findings.'

411 Warren Commission, Report Executive Session December 5, 1963, p. 1.

412 Executive Session December 5, p. 11.

413 (Warren Commission Hearings and Exhibits Vol. XVII, 1964) p. 901.

414 In the same Vol XVII, p. 211, the signature of H.S. Aiken – a single signature – is allocated an illustration of 272 cm2 (16.5 x 13 cm), but the site plan of Dealey Plaza has to be condensed to 100 cm2 (8 x 13 cm).

415 Allen Dulles: 'But nobody reads. Don't believe people read in this country. There will be a few professors who will read the record [...] the public will read very little.' Document related to: National Archives, *Transcript of a meeting with the Warren Commission Staff at which General Counsel J. Lee Rankin, other members of the staff, and John J. McCloy and Allen W. Dulles, members of the Commission, were present. Includes a general discussion with personal points of view set forth.*

416 (Warren Commission Hearings and Exhibits Vol. XVII, 1964) p. 928.

417 (HSCA Report, Vol. II, 1978) JFK Exhibit F-133, Vol III. p. 148.

418 Dallas Municipal Archives, Box 12a, folder 27, item 1.

419 (Cutler, The flight of CE399, 1969) p. 66.

420 (Horne, Inside the Assassination Records Review Board Vol. I, 2009) Appendix 39.

421 MD 177 - ARRB Call Report Summarizing 2/14/97 Telephonic Interview of Dennis David. www.history-matters.com/archive/jfk/arrb/master_med_set/md177/html/md177_0003a.htm.

422 (Lifton, 1980) p. 674.

423 (Lifton, 1980) p. 576.

424 (Horne, Inside the Assassination Records Review Board Vol. V, 2009) Appendix 61: ARRB staff report of its interview of former Navy hospital corpsman Dennis David p. 360-365.

425 (Horne, Inside the Assassination Records Review Board Vol. I, 2009) Appendix 52 p. 269.

426 Lifton, 1980) p. 695.

427 Lifton, 1980) p. 708.

428 Horne, Inside the Assassination Records Review Board Vol. I, 2009) fig. 68 Boyajian confirmed the 1963 statement to the ARRB: MD 236 - ARRB Call Report of September 5, 1997 Telephone Interview of Roger Boyajian (former NCOIC of Marine Security Detail at Autopsy of President Kennedy).

429 (Lifton, 1980) see, for example, interview Douglas Mayfield p. 408.

430 Time, February 16, 1981, p. 4.

431 The Associated Press, January 23, 1981, AM Cycle.

432 (Brown, The Warren Omission, 1996) p. 100.

433 'I remember how Curtis LeMay was sitting there [among the spectators of the JFK autopsy] with a large cigar in his hand.' - Paul O'Connor, quoted in William Law, Eye of History.

434 (HSCA Appendix VII) p. 193.

435 ARRB Testimony of Jerrol Francis Custer, 28 Oct 1997 p. 8.

436 ARRB Testimony of Jerrol Francis Custer, 28 Oct 1997.

437 (Horne, Inside the ARRB, Vol. II, 2009) p. 474.

438 FBI Report 11/22/63, date dictated 11/26/63 Commission part of Document CD7 p. 281-287.

439 Commission document CD7 p. 5.

440 Commission document CD7 p. 3.

441 Hill is not mentioned in the list of 28 attendees prepared by Sibert and O'Neill, but his presence at certain points in time is confirmed by the testimony of William Greer, among others (Vol. II, p. 112 ff.) and by Hill personally (Hill, 2012) p. 305.

442 (Hill, 2012) p. 305.

443 (Warren Commission Hearings and Exhibits Vol. II, 1964) Vol. II. p. 143.

444 (Warren Commission Hearings and Exhibits Vol. II, 1964) Vol. II. p. 112.

445 (Lifton, 1980) p. 441.

446 (Horne, Inside the Assassination Records Review Board Vol. V, 2009) p. 646.

447 (Horne, Inside the Assassination Records Review Board Vol. V, 2009) Vol. V. p. 645.

448 (Warren Commission Hearings and Exhibits Vol. VI, 1964).

449 www.history-matters.com/archive/jfk/arrb/master_med_set/md41/html/Image0.htm ARRB MD41.

450 (Lifton, 1980) p. 711.

451 (Lifton, 1980) p. 714.

452 Testimony Jerrol Francis Custer before the ARRB Staff on October 28, 1997.

453 (Warren Commission Hearings and Exhibits Vol. XVI, 1964) p. 978.

454 ARRB MD 44 - Sibert and O'Neill Report on the Autopsy (11/26/63)—'Gemberling Version'.

455 (Lifton, 1980) p. 347 Article on the front page of the New York Times of November 26, 1966.

456 (Fetzer, Murder in Dealey Plaza, 2000) Mantik p. 272. I was unable to find an additional report dated December 9 in which this is reported.

457 (Epstein E. J., Inquest, 1966) p. 41.

458 Commission document CD107 p. 2.

459 (Epstein E. J., Inquest, 1966) p. 41 Epstein refers to several other newspaper quotations along the same line.

460 Warren Commission, Executive Session January 27, 1964, p. 35 (p. 174).

461 (Horne, Inside the Assassination Records Review Board Vol. V, 2009) p. 654.

462 HSCA Numbered files NARA Record Number: 180-10086-10438 p. 22.

463 HSCA Numbered files NARA Record Number: 180-10086-10438 p. 23.

464 CD77 with the Autopsy Report attached, also known as CE391.

465 Horne, Douglas. Inside the ARRB, Appendix 35.

466 (Warren Commission Hearings and Exhibits Vol. VI, 1964) p. 14.

467 Documents transferred by James J. Humes to the ARRB on February 13, 1996 on the occasion of his statement before the ARRB, p. 1697-1700, letter to D.A. Arlen Specter dated December 11, 1967.

468 (HSCA Appendix VII) p. 192 no. 534.

469 HSCA Vol. I. p. 330.

470 Warren Commission Hearings, Vol. II, p. 373.

471 ARRB MD 74 (D) - DOCUMENT: Affidavit of Leonard D. Saslaw, Ph.D. (dated May 15, 1996).

472 (Warren Commission Hearings and Exhibits Vol. XVII, 1964) p. 45 CE397.

473 CD 107 FBI Supplemental Report p. 2.

474 Warren Commission Hearings and Exhibits Vol. XVII, 1964, p. 23-24 CE393. This is not the photograph that is included in the evidence, because the bullet hole on that photograph cannot be distinguished at all. This photograph is Exhibit 59, included on p. 69 of the FBI Supplementary Report (CD107).

475 Shirt (Warren Commission Hearings and Exhibits Vol. XVII, 1964, p. 25 CE394).

476 ARRB MD6 White House Death Certificate.

477 (Ernest, 2010) p. 188.

478 Commission Document 77 - Secret Service Memorandum of Dec. 20, 1963 re: Clinical Autopsy Records p. 3;

479 (Warren Commission Hearings and Exhibits Vol. II, 1964) p. 361.

480 (Warren Commission Hearings and Exhibits Vol. II, 1964) p. 93.

481 (Warren Commission Hearings and Exhibits Vol. II, 1964) Vol. II p. 350.

482 (HSCA Vol. IX, 1978) p. 93.

483 (Warren Commission Hearings and Exhibits Vol. VII, 1964) p. 366-366.

484 (Warren Commission Hearings and Exhibits Vol. V, 1964) p. 133.

485 Dixit Allen Dulles. Document related to: National Archives, Transcript of a meeting with the Warren Commission Staff at which General Counsel J. Lee Rankin, other members of the staff, and John J. McCloy and Allen W. Dulles, members of the Commission, were present. Also (Brown, The Warren Omission, 1996) p. 4.

486 (Epstein E. J., Inquest, 1966) p. 182 note 33.

487 Sibert & O'Neill report 26/11/63 p. 5.

488 HSCA Appendix 1, p. 327, here, Humes states that he first saw the photographs on November 1, 1966 following the request to catalogue and authenticate the photographs in the National Archives. In January 1967, the doctors saw the photographs again 'when we went to the archives again and made some summaries of our findings.'

489 Papers of James J. Humes turned over to ARRB on February 13, 1996 at his ARRB Deposition.

490 MD221p. 001693, History Matters Archive, Papers of James J. Humes turned over to ARRB on February 13, 1996.

491 (HSCA Appendix Vol. VI) p.225.

492 (HSCA Appendix Vol. I) p. 186 testimony of Dr. Baden: 'This particular drawing shows the back of the president and the head [...], and a perforation of the skin at the right side of the upper back with a ruler in centimeters next to it.'

493 (HSCA Appendix Vol. I) p.186.

494 (Warren Commission Report, 1964) p. 519 CE392.

495 (Warren Commission Hearings and Exhibits Vol. XVI, 1964) p. 981.

496 (Warren Commission Hearings and Exhibits Vol. XVII, 1964) p. 29 CE397.

497 (Warren Commission Report, 1964) p. 540 CE387.

498 (Warren Commission Hearings and Exhibits Vol. II, 1964) p. 361.

499 (Warren Commission Hearings and Exhibits Vol. VI, 1964) p. 137.

500 (Fetzer, Assassination Science, 1998) Dr. Charles Crenshaw replies p. 54 and p. 59 note 69. Dr. Crenshaw does not mention who the researcher was who made the 'recorded interview'.

501 (Fetzer, Assassination Science, 1998) Dr. Crenshaw replies p. 54.

502 (Fetzer, Assassination Science, 1998) p. 19 The dispute between Dr. Crenshaw and *JAMA* ended with an extrajudicial settlement whereby Dr. Crenshaw received 213,000 dollars of compensation.

503 (HSCA Report, Vol. II, 1978) p. 43.

504 HSCA Hearings, 1978, Hearings Vol. I, p. 231. Dr. Baden: *'This is a drawing prepared by Miss Dox with the medical panel [...]. Each of these trajectories could produce the autopsy findings as depicted on the left and cause a similar track within the body itself. We cannot on the basis of the autopsy findings alone, in this instance, determine from whence the bullet came.'*

505 The HSCA calculated the distance between Kennedy's back and throat wound as 14 centimeters.

506 (Warren Commission Hearings and Exhibits Vol. VI, 1964) p. 1.

507 (Warren Commission Hearings and Exhibits Vol. VI, 1964) p. 9.

508 (Warren Commission Hearings and Exhibits Vol. VI, 1964) p. 20.

509 (Warren Commission Hearings and Exhibits Vol. IV, 1964) p. 33.

510 (Warren Commission Hearings and Exhibits Vol. VI, 1964) p. 48.

511 *Boston Sunday Globe*, June 21, 1981, quoted in mcadams.posc.mu.edu/occipital.htm

512 (Warren Commission Hearings and Exhibits Vol. XVI, 1964) p. 980, CE387.

513 CD7 Report O'Neill and Sibert dated 26/11/63 p. 3

514 (Warren Commission Hearings and Exhibits Vol. XVII, 1964) p. 336 p. 337 - CE679-CE680.

515 (Warren Commission Hearings and Exhibits Vol. VI, 1964) Vol. VI, p. 112.

516 (Warren Commission Hearings and Exhibits Vol. IV, 1964) p. 104-105.

517 (Warren Commission Hearings and Exhibits Vol. IV, 1964) p. 126.

518 (Warren Commission Hearings and Exhibits Vol. II, 1964) p. 374 Dr. Humes.

519 (Warren Commission Hearings and Exhibits Vol. IV, 1964) p. 131.

520 (Mason, 2002) Mason p. 13: 'An accelerating bullet will follow a straight line if no force is applied to it.'

521 HSCA report, p. 43 figure II-13.

522 HSCA report, p. 43 figure II-13.

523 www.jfklibrary.org/Research/Ready-Reference/JFK-Miscellaneous-Information.aspx

524 $(=degrees(ACOS(SQRT(14^2 - (4,75)^2) / 14))) = 19.83$ degrees.

525 (Trask, Pictures of the pain, 1994) p. 224.

526 HSCA Hearings Vol.2 p. 176.

527 HSCA Hearings Vol.2 p 175.

528 The distance from JFK's back wound to Connally's armpit wound is here $=SQRT(9,5-8)^2 +(42-14)^2) = 28.04$ inch. The angle can then be calculated as follows $=DEGREES(ACOS((42-14)/28,04))) = 3.07$ degrees.

529 The distance from JFK's back wound to Connally's armpit wound is here $=SQRT(12-5)^2 +(41,5-14)^2) = 28.38$ inch. The angle can then be calculated as follows $=DEGREES(ACOS((41,5-14)/28,38)))$ $=14.28$ degrees.

530 E.g., at Z196 JFK's entry wound has coordinates 108 on the Elm Street axis and 118 on the Houston Street axis. The muzzle is situated 7.5 feet from the corner of the TSBD. The distance between Kennedy's back wound and the muzzle can be calculated as the square root of $(118^2+(108-7.5)^2)$ or in an electronic worksheet: $=SQRT(1182+(108-7.5)^2)$, which is 15.07. The formula to calculate the angle with regard to the façade at this point with coordinates 100.5 and 118 in an electronic worksheet would then be $= Degrees (ACOS(100.5/15.07)) = 49.6°$.

531 $=degrees(ACOS((117,0 - 98,7) /SQRT((117 - 98,7)^2 + (131 - 118)^2)) = 35.39$ degrees.

532 $=degrees(ACOS((140,0 - 123) /SQRT((140 - 123)^2 + (151 - 136)^2)) = 41.42$ degrees.

533 The FBI took a number of black-white photographs. Three of those were included in the appendices as CE344-345-346, and are also knows as *Commission Document CD3*. The Secret Service took color photographs of the limousine; two of them were (in black-white) included in the appendix as CE 352 and CE 353.

534 (Fetzer, Murder in Dealey Plaza, 2000) p. 158 Ford Motor Company, internal document.

535 The back seat of the presidential limousine could be raised 26.7 centimeters (10.5 inches), but was mounted at the lowest position on November 23.

536 Inspector Kelley mentions in his interview that Connally was two inches shorter than Kennedy.

537 Calculated in centimeters: $=Degrees(ACOS(69/ SQRT(20,5^2+69^2))$ $= 16.5$ degrees and $=Degrees(ACOS(69/SQRT(23^2+69^2)) = 18.4$ degrees.

538 Calculated in centimeters: $=Degrees(ACOS(69/ SQRT(19^2+69^2)) = 15.4$ degrees.

539 (Warren Commission Hearings and Exhibits Vol. XXII, 1964) p. 479.

540 (Warren Commission Hearings and Exhibits Vol. XXII, 1964) p. 484.

541 (Warren Commission Hearings and Exhibits Vol. XVII, 1964) p. 901.

542 $=DEGREES(ACOS(20.3 / SQRT(1.03^2 + 20.3^2) = 2.9$ degrees or shorter on the basis of the percentage of the slope, which corresponds to the radial: $=DEGREES(1.04/17.2) = 3.46$ degrees.

543 =DEGREES(ACOS(17.2 / SQRT(1.04^2 + 17.2^2)) = 3.46 degrees or shorter on the basis of the percentage of the slope, which corresponds to the radial: =DEGREES(1.04/17.2) = 3.46 degrees.

544 (Bugliosi, 2007) p. 43.

545 (Warren Commission Hearings and Exhibits Vol. V, 1964) p. 74.

546 (Warren Commission Hearings and Exhibits Vol. IV, 1964) p. 128.

547 (Warren Commission Hearings and Exhibits Vol. III, 1964) p. 394. According to the HSCA, it would technically even be possible to reload the Carcano in 1.7 seconds, but in this case without aiming and working with stationary targets. There is, however, a problem with the test of the HSCA team. They used the metal target at the end of the barrel of the rifle, and not the telescopic sight that was used by the Dealey Plaza gunman. Blakey mentions in his report to the HSCA that it is indeed possible to shoot quicker without the telescopic sight: 'The weapon can be fired quicker with open iron sights, and with reasonable accuracy, than was demonstrated by the FBI test in 1963, during which telescopic sights were used.' Anyone who has ever used binoculars can confirm this. It takes a while before you can find the desired object in the sight again. (HSCA Appendix Volumes VIII, 1978) p. 183.

548 (Warren Commission Hearings and Exhibits Vol. V, 1964) p. 178.

549 Vol. VII, p. 510.

550 (Trask, Pictures of the pain, 1994) p. 424.

551 (Myers, 2007) p.142.

552 (Warren Commission Hearings and Exhibits Vol. III, 1964) p. 242.

553 Degrees(ACOS(187.9-7.5)/261.3) = 46.33 degrees.

554 Degrees(ACOS((187.9)/(SQRT(187.9^2+(189-34)^2)) = 39.52 degrees.

555 (Warren Commission Report, 1964) p. 117.

556 (Warren Commission Hearings and Exhibits Vol. XXIII, 1964) p. 914, Police radio log CE1974 p. 166.

557 Royce G. Skelton, who was on the bridge across the tunnel, saw a bullet strike the concrete in front and to the left of the limousine. Agent J.W. Foster testified that there was a bullet impact near a manhole cover in the vicinity of the tunnel. At least one passenger of the front car of the motorcade, in which Dallas Police Chief Curry was also seated, saw a bullet strike near the limousine. A secret agent in the vice-presidential car behind the president also claims to have seen a bullet impact behind the car in which he was seated, according to the statement he made in an interview with Vince Palamara. Finally, Mrs. Baker-Rachley stated formally that she had seen a bullet impact at the level of the first traffic sign, in the center of the leftmost lane, behind the limousine.

558 See, for example, (Hurt, 1985) p. 132 'On their guard as ever, for whatever reason, Hoover's agents did not undertake any steps to investigate the Tague shot, as far as known.'

559 (McKnight, 2005) p. 98.

560 (Sneed, 1998) p. 112.

561 (Warren Commission Hearings and Exhibits Vol. VII, 1964) p. 552.

562 (Warren Commission Hearings and Exhibits Vol. XXI, 1964) p. 475, Shaneyfelt Exhibit 27. The Tague bullet impact is situated exactly 23 feet, 4 inches removed from the Triple Underpass, according to Hoover. According to our calculations, that point is 384 ft removed from Houston Street and 338 ft from the TSBD façade. Kennedy's head at that point is 187.9 ft removed from Houston Street and 189 ft from the TSBD façade.

563 =Degrees(ACOS((384-187.9)/SQRT((338-189)^2 + (384-187.9)^2)) = 37.228 degrees.

564 =degrees(ACOS(SQRT((189-34)^2+187^2)/)187) = 39.65 degrees.

565 Starting from Kennedy's head, 52 inches (4.3 feet) above street level (418.6 ft above sea level on Z313), to the level of the curb at 406 ft, the bullet fragment must descend 16.9 ft, over a distance of 246 ft (=SQRT((384-187)^2 + (337-189)^2) = 246). This results in a descent of =degrees(ACOS(246/SQRT(246^2+16.9^2)) = 3.929 degrees.

566 (Warren Commission Report, 1964) p. 115.

567 C.D. 1518 p. 2.

568 FBI file 8/6/64 DL 100-10461. By Special Agents Switzer and Barret.

569 FBI 124-10052-10212.

570 (Garrison, 1988) p. 209.

571 www.jfkassassinationfiles.com/documents.

572 (Warren Commission Hearings and Exhibits Vol. VI, 1964) p. 252.

573 (Warren Commission Report, 1964) p. 116.

574 (Warren Commission Report, 1964) p. 116.

575 (Discovery Communications DVD, 2011).

576 (Warren Commission Hearings and Exhibits Vol XX, 1964) p. 163.

577 (Ernest, 2010) p. 80.

578 (Warren Commission Hearings and Exhibits Vol. VI, 1964) p. 239.

579 Voluntary statement Sheriff's department J.C. Price 22/11/1963.

580 CD5 Gemberling Report p. 65 'saw nothing relevant'.

581 (Ernest, 2010) p. 158.

582 http://karws.gso.uri.edu/jfk/scientific_topics/Physics_of_head_shot/8-Plausibility.html.

583 (HSCA Appendix Vol I, 1978) p. 58.

584 CD5 Gemberling Report p. 28.

585 (Rem, 1992) p. 30.

586 CD5 p. 329.

587 (Warren Commission Hearings and Exhibits Vol. VII, 1964) p. 390.

588 (Warren Commission Hearings and Exhibits Vol. VI, 1964) p. 383.

589 CD5 p. 41.

590 CD 87 Secret Service Report 8 January 1964 p. 292.

591 CD 5 Gemberling Report FBI – p. 329.

592 CD 5 Gemberling Report FBI – p. 329.

593 (Warren Commission Hearings and Exhibits Vol. VI, 1964) p. 349.

594 (Warren Commission Report, 1964) p. 143.

595 CD 735 p. 295.

596 (Warren Commission Hearings and Exhibits Vol. III, 1964) p. 161-184.

597 (Warren Commission Report, 1964) p. 63.

598 (Warren Commission Hearings and Exhibits Vol. XVII, 1964) p. 197.

599 (Warren Commission Hearings and Exhibits Vol. III, 1964) p. 140.

600 (Warren Commission Hearings and Exhibits Vol. VII, 1964) p. 349.

601 (Warren Commission Report, 1964) p. 62.

602 (Warren Commission Hearings and Exhibits Vol. XXII, 1964) p. 491 CE1301.

603 (O'Reilly, 2012) p. 264.

604 (Warren Commission Hearings and Exhibits Vol IX XXIV, 1964) p. 208.

605 (Warren Commission Hearings and Exhibits Vol. XVII, 1964) p. 398.

606 (Warren Commission Hearings and Exhibits Vol. III, 1964) p. 147.

607 (Warren Commission Hearings and Exhibits Vol. XVII, 1964) p. 308.

608 (Warren Commission Hearings and Exhibits Vol. III, 1964) p. 254.

609 (Ernest, 2010) p. 304.

610 Bugliosi maintains that Baker 'Revved up' after the third shot (Bugliosi, 2007) endnote 839. Belin does ask him: : 'Well, I revved that motorcycle up'. However, this by no means implies that, as Bugliosi maintains, Baker only reacted after the third shot. After all, Baker clearly refers to the distance from the start of the time he spent: '180 to 200 ft from the point where we had first stated, you know, heard the shots.' Belin indicates clearly that he timed it together with Baker with 'we paced off from the point where you heard the first shot'. The '55 to 61 meters' only match the first shot in Z160.

611 (Warren Commission Hearings and Exhibits Vol. III, 1964) p. 247.

612 (Warren Commission Hearings and Exhibits Vol. XXII, 1964) p. 676, CE 1381.

613 (Ernest, 2010) p. 332.

614 (Ernest, 2010) p. 333.

615 (Warren Commission Hearings and Exhibits Vol. VI, 1964) p. 388.

616 (Warren Commission Hearings and Exhibits Vol. VI, 1964) p. 330.

617 (Warren Commission Hearings and Exhibits Vol. VI, 1964) p. 340.

618 (Ernest, 2010) p. 325.

619 (Ernest, 2010) p. 329.

620 (Warren Commission Report, 1964) p. 154.

621 (Warren Commission Hearings and Exhibits Vol. VI, 1964) p. 340.

622 (Bugliosi, 2007) p. 832.

623 (Warren Commission Hearings and Exhibits Vol. XXII, 1964) p. 470.

624 Ciccone, 2012, p. 67.

625 Warren Commission Hearings and Exhibits Vol II, 1964, p. 2.

626 Mcgrayne, 2011, p. 67.

627 In the 1986 docu-trial, which took 21 hours, Bugliosi was the public prosecutor and Spence, a well known criminal lawyer, took on Oswald's defence. It was a 5 hour broadcast with a real jury, presiding judge and actual opening statements. The witnesses were not actors but (where possible) the authentic witnesses.

628 (Warren Commission Hearings and Exhibits Vol. V, 1964) p. 259.

629 Interview with Jesse Curry, *Dallas Morning News*,
     6 Nov 1969. Article by Tom Johnson.

630 CODE OF CRIMINAL PROCEDURE, Chapter 37,
     Art. 37.071. Procedure in Capital Case, Seconden.
     3, Subsection d.1.

631 (Brown, The People v. Lee Harvey Oswald, 1992).

632 Bugliosi, 2007, p. xxvi.

LIST OF PEOPLE MENTIONED

Aase, Jean: female companion of Gruber, a childhood friend who visited Jack Ruby in Dallas. At some point in time, received a telephone call from the office where David Ferrie was employed by lawyer Gill.

Adams, Victoria (Vickie): young employee at the TSBD, ex-novice of the Ursuline order. Watched the motorcade drive past from the fourth floor together with Sandra Styles. Descended the staircase immediately after the attack, but did not meet either Oswald or Officer Baker.

AGVA: American Guild of Variety Artists, which was infiltrated by the mafia. Appears everywhere as the explanation for contacts between various characters who are directly or indirectly involved in the case.

Altgens, James: American Press photographer who took a picture immediately after Kennedy reached for his throat. This photo shows the TSBD in the background, with a man in the doorway who strongly resembled Oswald, but turned out to be his colleague, Billy Lovelady.

Alyea, Tom: WFAA TV-station reporter. Was present when the sniper's nest was discovered and witnessed how Superintendent Fritz picked up the shells before any investigation had been carried out. His film disappeared later, but some fragments still exist.

Baker, Marion: motorcycle officer with the Dallas police force. Accelerated after the first shot and rushed into the TSBD where he met Oswald on the second floor. Did not meet Vickie Adams while rushing up the stairs.

Banister, Guy: ex-CIA detective in New Orleans, employer of Ferrie and Jack Martin. His office was situated at the same address as the address printed on the pamphlets of Oswald's pro-Cuba organization.

Beauboeuf, Alvin: Ferrie's boyfriend. Drove with him through stormy weather all the way from New Orleans to the seaside resort of Galveston in Texas on November 22 and 23, ostensibly to go ice skating.

Braden, Jim or Brading, Eugène: was arrested for his suspected presence in the Dal-Tex building at the time of the shooting. Had no reasonable explanation for his presence, but, because he had recently changed his name, the police did not realize that they were dealing with a convicted criminal and released him. Braden happened to be near Lamar Hunt, the son of oil billionaire Hunt, on the day preceding the assassination. Braden was staying in the same hotel as Jack Ruby the evening before the assassination, and he had had an office at the same address where David Ferrie was working. In 1968, Braden also happened to be present at the place where Bobby Kennedy was shot.

Brennan, Howard: construction worker who was sitting on a wall in front of the TSBD. Pointed out the sniper's nest immediately after the attack and provided a physical description of a man of 1.78 meter (5.8 feet) who was standing up. He was and remained a key witness for the Commission, because the description was an essential link to the murder of Officer Tippit, and because they could associate Oswald with the sniper's nest through Brennan.

Brown, Madeleine: Lyndon Johnson's mistress. Stated that Johnson was present at a private party at oil billionaire Murchison's estate the evening before the assassination. Johnson allegedly told her that he would be rid of 'those goddamn Kennedys' once and for all the next day.

Burkley, George: admiral and JFK's personal physician. Was the only person present at both Parkland Hospital and Bethesda Naval Hospital. Said to be the barrister-at-law for the autopsy in the closed environment of the military hospital. The personal physician issued a death certificate in which he situated the back wound at the level of the third thoracic vertebra. The death certificate was filed incorrectly during the investigation, and only re-appeared many years later purely by chance. The Commission did not deem it necessary to hear him as a witness.

Bush, George Herbert Walker: CIA informant in 1963. On November 22 and 23, he twice provided information regarding the attack, but still denies this. He was in Dallas on the day of the assassination. Developed his political career in Texas in the aftermath of the assassination. He was also a personal friend of George de Mörenschildt. Bush later became CIA Director, Vice President and President of the United States, but claimed that he could not even remember the name of the Commission that investigated the assassination. Was absolutely sure that the Commission had fully clarified the case.

Castro, Fidel: came to power in Cuba after a guerrilla war and confiscated American property, including the gambling casinos that were owned by the mafia. America was not very happy with a communist regime 90 miles off the coast of Florida. Reactionary forces tried to lure Kennedy into a trap through an ill-conceived invasion at the Bay of Pigs. They expected that the young President would provide air support when the invasion threatened to fail, but Kennedy refused. The Castro regime remained in power, and prepared to install Russian nuclear missiles. Russia did not have long-range nuclear missiles at that time, but the missiles in Cuba represented a loaded gun pointed at the head of the US. Kennedy was able to solve the crisis with diplomacy, much to the dismay of the more militant elements in the anti-Castro movement. The assassination of Kennedy appeared in every way to be an attempt at a double blow: Kennedy was eliminated and the assassination provided an ideal motive to invade the island. But President Johnson also did not take the bait, and did whatever he could to cover up the Castro connection in the Kennedy assassination. Castro would survive Kennedy by at least fifty years.

Connally, John: Governor of Texas. Was sitting in front of Kennedy in the limousine on a jump seat. He had five shot wounds, including a shattered wrist. He heard the first shot, to which he responded with the exclamation *Oh, no, no, no!'*, which caused Jackie Kennedy to turn her head. On the basis of this, it is possible to determine the first shot at around Z160 of the Zapruder film.

Connally, Nellie: wife of Governor John Connally. She was sitting next to him on the jump seat on the left. Pulled her husband into her lap after he had been hit. Had her husband's suit dry-cleaned later, thereby destroying irreplaceable forensic information. Nellie Connally remained

convinced for the rest of her life that her husband and the President had **not** been hit by one and the same bullet.

Crenshaw, Charles: Parkland Hospital doctor who insisted that Kennedy's injuries indicated a frontal shot. He was treated harshly by the *American Medical Association*, but eventually forced an amicable agreement.

Croft, Larry: missionary of the Latter-day Saints who took an exceptional good photograph in which the positions of the passengers in the limousine can be clearly seen immediately before the shooting. A photo that was taken by Croft at the moment of the third shot has disappeared. The FBI found Croft in Denver on the morning after the assassination, although nobody could have known his address there.

Curry, Jesse: Superintendent of the 1,075 officers of the Dallas Police. Instead of heading the investigation, he hung around at the Parkland Hospital, acted as driver for President Johnson and attended the inauguration of the new president. Left the phone off the hook in order not to be disturbed by alarming messages about a planned attack on Oswald. Became involved in a 'police war' with FBI Director J. Edgar Hoover because he openly expressed his displeasure when the police force had to transfer the dossier to the FBI.

Day, J.C.: Head of the Dallas Police crime laboratory. Made numerous procedural errors and made very contradictory statements in this context afterwards. Found a latent palm print on the Carcano, when nobody else was present, and removed it with cellophane tape. The FBI could not find this palm print later. As the card with the print was not handed over with the original evidence, a problem also arose regarding the authenticity of the print.

de Morenschildt, George, Baron: cosmopolitan who spoke six languages. Geologist in the oil industry. Became good friends with the unskilled worker Oswald, perhaps because the Baron originated from Minsk, and Oswald had lived there for a while. Was clearly also the CIA babysitter for Oswald. Committed suicide when the HCSA called him as a witness. He was also a personal friend of CIA Director and later President George H.W. Bush, and a childhood acquaintance of Jacqueline Kennedy.

Doughty/Dhority, C.N.: Dallas police officer who allegedly identified the third shell, but then denied it when it turned out that his initials were marked on the wrong shell.

Ferrie, David: pilot with a natural talent, but also an eccentric who had a sexual preference for boys. He suffered from a rare disease that caused him to lose all his body hair, and he had weird hobbies. Had extreme right sympathies. Assisted mafia godfather Carlos Marcello, used an office at the same address as Jim Braden and worked for Guy Banister at the address that was also printed on Oswald's Castro leaflets. There is also a photograph of a youth camp on which both Ferrie and Oswald can be seen together at a campfire. On the day of the assassination, Ferrie drove from New Orleans to Houston and then to Galveston. He returned to New Orleans after Oswald was murdered. He coincidentally died of a cerebral aneurysm when Jim Garrison wanted to call him as a witness. The name Ferrie is not mentioned anywhere in the entire Warren Commission report.

Fischer, Ronald: witness at Dealey Plaza. Stood slightly to the right of the place where Howard Brennan was sitting, and could see the barrel of the rifle, but only the head of the person in the sniper's nest, not the body.

Ford, Gerald: a Republican congressman who was appointed to the Warren Commission, where, according to many sources, he was an FBI informant. He rewrote crucial sections of the final report in order to situate Kennedy's back wound higher than the actual injury. He later became Nixon's Vice President, more or less by accident, and without ever having been elected to this office. When Nixon was forced to resign as a result of the Watergate scandal, the rather colorless Ford even unexpectedly made it to President.

Frazier, Buell Wesley: colleague of Oswald who lived in Irving, the Dallas suburb where Marina Oswald was staying, and where Oswald spent the weekends. Frazier gave Oswald a lift on the day of the assassination. According to Frazier, the elongated package that Oswald brought along that day was only 23.6 inches (60 centimeters) long, and was therefore shorter than the dismantled weapon.

Fritz, John Will: elderly Superintendent of the Dallas Police homicide squad. Allegedly contaminated the scene of the crime and later bent over backwards in order to deny the procedural errors made by the police.

Garrison, Jim: flamboyant New Orleans District Attorney. Questioned Ferrie on the Monday following the assassination, and then handed the suspect over to the FBI, where he was not questioned any further. Garrison reopened the case

in 1967. But, after Ferrie's death, he could only prosecute businessman Clay Shaw. This dossier was appallingly weak, and Shaw was acquitted. The JFK movie by Oliver Stone gives a highly romanticized account of this trial.

Gaudet, William: CIA agent who happened to obtain a travel visa for Mexico that was issued just before Oswald's visa (with one number difference). Wherever Oswald turned up in Mexico, Gaudet was never far away.

Gill, G. Wray: lawyer of Carlos Marcello and co-employer of David Ferrie. At some point, a telephone call was made from his office to Jean Aase, who happened to be at the same hotel as Jack Ruby and Jim Braden on the evening before the assassination.

Givens, Charles: key witness who allegedly saw Oswald on the sixth floor. His statement was obviously a lie, but the Commission acted as if nothing was amiss.

Greer, William: Secret Service agent who was driving the limousine and responded slowly at a time when his alertness could have saved the president.

Gruber, Alex: Childhood friend of Jack Ruby. Was together with him and Jean Aase at the Cabana Hotel on the night preceding the assassination, exactly at the time Jim Braden was also present there. After Oswald was arrested, he was the first person with whom Jack Ruby had a long-distance telephone conversation. Received death threats after Ruby had killed Oswald.

Hartman, Wayne and Edna: married couple who witnessed the impact of a bullet or bullet fragment in Elm Street, but who were mistaken according to the Commission.

Hill, Clint: Secret Agent assigned to Jacqueline Kennedy. Sprinted to the limousine after the head shot had been fired and pushed Jacky back into the car when she attempted to retrieve a piece of the president's skull. Hill clung to the back of the limousine, which drove to the hospital at full speed. He also provided a plausible explanation for the very late presence of the secret agents in a bar on the night before the assassination.

Hosty, James: FBI agent who had been assigned to keep Oswald under observation. When Oswald left a message for Hosty, FBI chief Shanklin ordered his agent to destroy this note in order to avoid the impression that the FBI had failed to point out that Oswald posed a safety risk with regard to the presidential visit.

Hoover, J. Edgar: FBI Director. Cynical potentate who considered any means permissible to help him perpetuate his position of power. He succeeded in this by keeping a secret file on every politician. He hated his new boss Robert Kennedy, who insulted him by putting a phone on his desk that enabled him to call him to order at any time. Hoover was pleased with the arrival of Lyndon Johnson in the White House, and with being given full authority on the investigation into the assassination of Kennedy. Hoover stuck so firmly to his original, unsubstantiated version of the attack that it became embarrassing, ultimately resulting in the Warren Commission taking the path of the magic bullet without the support of the FBI. The iron grip that Hoover had on his corps was so stifling that the otherwise highly efficient FBI had no choice but to provide contradictory and poor work in one of the most important investigations in the history of the U.S.

Humes, James: Commander in the U.S. Navy, and responsible for the autopsy at Bethesda Naval Hospital. Had no pathological experience, and this is a partial explanation for the many problems that arose from the autopsy.

Hunt, Lamar: son of billionaire Haroldson Hunt, possibly the wealthiest man in the world at that time. He was together with Jim Braden over lunch on the day before the assassination, and Jack Ruby also happened to be in the same building for an appointment with him. His father had his lawyer check out the security of the police building in Dallas on the day before Oswald was murdered there. One of the reasons why Haroldson Hunt hated Kennedy was that the latter intended to close tax loopholes of which the oil industry was the main beneficiary.

Johnsen, Richard: Secret Agent who absent-mindedly accepted a bullet from the Parkland Hospital staff and put it in his pocket while he was busy with the departure of the first lady, the new President and the casket with the remains of John F. Kennedy.

Johnson, Lyndon: Vice President of John F. Kennedy. Succeeded him after the assassination. Pure power politician. Was balancing on the edge of a political abyss on November 22, when, that very same day, his ultimate dream came true. Johnson was very apprehensive about geopolitical complications that could arise from the attack, and presumably undertook initiatives to preventatively eliminate any suspicion or proof of a frontal shot.

Kennedy, Jacqueline: wife of John F. Kennedy. Was seated next to the President at the time he was murdered. She refused to take off her blood-stained, pink suit: 'Let them see what they've done!'

Kennedy, John Fitzgerald: world record holder self-confidence. Thirty-fifth President of the United States of America following a narrow victory against the incumbent Vice President, Richard Nixon. JFK gradually presented himself as being more progressive in the field of equal civil rights and opted for diplomacy, rather than war, despite his status of heroic war veteran. He was the pacesetter of the NASA Apollo program that put the first men on the moon less than six years after his death. Kennedy could not leave his playboy ways behind him, despite his marriage and his office. His handsome appearance concealed his overall poor health condition. He had accepted Johnson as his running mate in 1960 for political reasons, but, in 1963, everything seemed to indicate that he would drop the Texan for the 1964 elections. At the start of the re-election campaign, he was assassinated by a sniper in Dallas on November 22, 1963.

Kennedy, Robert Francis: younger brother of the president, who took up a key position in John's cabinet on the compelling advice of their father Joe Kennedy. As Attorney General, the inexperienced lawyer found himself at the head of a giant administration. He increasingly showed himself to be the closest confidant of the president. His unconventional style was a thorn in the eye to Hoover. Bobby launched an open battle with organized crime, and also adopted a more fundamental approach towards civil rights than his pragmatic brother. Bob had a good marriage with his wife Ethel, with whom he had eleven children. After the death of his brother, he fell into a black hole, but threw himself into the battle again as Senator for the State of New York in 1968, and he was heading the Democratic nomination when he was also assassinated by a lone madman.

Khrushchev, Nikita: President of the U.S.S.R. in 1963.

Kilgallen, Dorothy: scandal journalist who claimed she had interviewed Jack Ruby in his prison cell. She was in any case in the possession of leaked Commission documents regarding Ruby. Her telephone was tapped by the FBI, which is how they became aware that John Kennedy allegedly had an affair with Marilyn Monroe, and that the diva threatened to publicize this. Both Kilgallen and Monroe died soon afterwards, both under suspicious circumstances.

Leavelle, James: member of the Dallas Police homicide squad. Was a surprised onlooker when Oswald was shot. Unexpectedly visited Vickie Adams with an incredible story about how her previous statements had been lost in a fire, and that she had to tell everything once again.

LeMay Curtis: General who may have been present at the autopsy. He hated Kennedy. Bit the dust with his attempt to escalate the Cuba missile crisis into a military conflict, and was not impressed with Kennedy's preference for ending the Cold War.

Lovelady, Billy: staff member of the TSBD who physically resembled Oswald, and was therefore confused with Oswald as the person standing in the porch of the TSBD at the time the shots were fired. Among others, Vickie Adams believed she had met Lovelady on the first floor of the TSBD after she had come down the staircase shortly after the assassination. Lovelady could not remember this meeting.

Marcello, Carlos: godfather of the oldest mafia family, which spread its tentacles over the entire southern region of the United States. Escaped deportation from the U.S. on the day of the assassination. Worked together with David Ferrie and lawyer Gill in this context. Paid Ferrie 7,000 dollars in cash for reasons that are not clear. Was also closely associated with Jim Braden and AGVA, and also with Jack Ruby through his minion Nofio Pecora.

Martin, Jack: staff member of Guy Banister's detective agency, where David Ferrie was also employed. Ex-FBI agent, but his drinking problem had caught up with him. His statements brought Jim Garrison onto David Ferrie's trail.

O'Neill, Francis: FBI agent who attended the autopsy together with his colleague James Sibert, and reported on this to FBI Director Hoover. From the FBI report, it appeared that the autopsy doctors had no knowledge of Kennedy's throat wound, and that they assumed that the bullet had remained in Kennedy's back until it was dislodged as a result of the cardiac massage at Parkland Hospital.

Oswald, Lee Harvey: headstrong worker with communist sympathies. Worked at the TSBD, and had bought an old rifle by mail order. Was a very mediocre marksman when he served in the U.S. Army. Was married to Marina Prusakova, a Russian citizen, but was living separated from his wife and children. He was seen on the first floor of the TSBD shortly before the assassination, and was seen on the second floor immediately after the assassination. It has not been proven where he was in the meantime. After the assassination, he wandered through Dallas and allegedly murdered Officer Tippit on the way. He was arrested in a movie theatre and was questioned for hours without legal assistance; no official report was made of the interrogation. Was shot in the basement of the police building by Jack Ruby.

Oswald, Marina: wife of Lee. He met her during his stay in Russia, and they married almost immediately afterwards. Their first daughter June was born while they were still living in the Soviet Union. Lee returned to the United States, but the marriage failed. Lee and Marina were separated at the time of the assassination. Precisely on the morning of November 22, Lee left his wedding ring behind in an empty cup on the breakfast table in the house of the Paine's.

Paine, Ruth: housewife living in Irving, a suburb of Dallas, who provided shelter to Marina Oswald. Lee Harvey Oswald stayed there on the weekends. On the day before the assassination, Oswald unexpectedly turned up in Irving. A blanket was found in Ruth Paine's garage in which the weapon had allegedly been previously wrapped up. Photographs showing Oswald with the weapon, the same weapon with which the assassination had allegedly been committed, were found during a second search of the house.

Randle, Linnie Mae: sister of Buell Frazier, who saw Oswald getting into her brother's car on the morning of the assassination. She was convinced that the bag Oswald was carrying was only 23.6 inches (60 centimeters) long and therefore too short for the dismantled weapon.

Rankin, J. Lee: general counsel for the Warren Commission. As the executive director of this Commission, he worked harder than anyone else.

Ruby, Jack: nightclub owner with mafia connections. Disaster tourist at the police station, who attended the press conference during which Oswald was pushed forward. He was noticed there because he corrected a police spokesman who mentioned Oswald's pro-Cuba organization using an incorrect name. Ruby was present in the same building as Lamar Hunt on the day before the assassination, and was later also in the same hotel as Jim Braden.

On the day after the assassination, he phoned Wall Breck in Galveston, a small coastal town where Ferrie was also staying at the very same moment. On the Sunday morning, Ruby appeared in the basement of the police building under mysterious circumstances and shot Oswald in full view of the assembled world press. The Warren Commission did everything possible to paint a decent picture of Ruby in its version of the facts. Ruby begged Earl Warren and Gerald Ford to transfer him to Washington, because he would never be able to tell the full truth in Dallas. But Warren and Ford did not respond to this, and Ruby died in prison without ever having given a conclusive explanation for his act or motive.

Rydberg, Harold: recruit with no experience in medical illustrations who was given two days to provide a drawing on the basis of the verbal instructions of the autopsy doctors, who, in turn, were not even allowed to see the photographs of the autopsy. The drawing was to become the only graphic representation of Kennedy's injuries in the entire report of the Warren Commission. The Commission was well aware that the drawing was completely incorrect, but nevertheless stubbornly denied this fact.

Shaw, Clay: businessman in New Orleans who was prosecuted by Jim Garrison on the grounds of complicity in a conspiracy to assassinate Kennedy. After Ferrie died, Shaw was Garrison's only remaining possibility to start his lawsuit. The case against the businessman was very weak, however, and he was acquitted. The trial is considered to be an all-time low in American legal history.

Sibert, James: FBI agent who attended the autopsy together with his colleague Francis O'Neill, and reported on this to FBI Director Hoover. From the FBI report, it appeared that the autopsy doctors had no knowledge of Kennedy's throat wound, and that they assumed that the bullet had remained in Kennedy's back until it was dislodged as a result of the cardiac massage at Parkland Hospital.

Specter Arlen: lawyer and Commission counsel who became the major defender of the single-bullet theory, the assumption that President Kennedy and Governor Connally had been hit by one single bullet. Specter later became Democratic Senator for Pennsylvania.

Stroud, Martha: assistant attorney in Dallas. Wrote a letter to the Warren Commission stating that Dorothy Garner, Vickie Adams' superior, had stated that Officer Baker had arrived on the fourth floor after Vickie Adams had left there. The letter was hushed op.

Tague James: spectator at Dealey Plaza who was slightly injured by a concrete shard when a bullet hit the curb. The Warren Commission did everything possible to ignore him.

Tippit, J.D.: Dallas police offer who addressed a man in East 10th Street from his patrol car for some unknown reason and was killed on the spot.

Tolson Clyde: Deputy Director of the FBI and Hoover's life partner.

Tomlinson, Darrell: hospital staff member who found a pristine bullet on a gurney in the corridor of Parkland Hospital.

Truly, Roy: Superintendent and caretaker of the TSBD. He employed Oswald at the TSBD in October 1963. Together with Officer Baker, he searched for the sniper in the building and thereby met Oswald. He told Baker that Oswald was an employee, and Oswald was then left alone.

Walker, Edwin: retired, ultra-right general. Oswald allegedly made a (failed) attempt on his life with the Carcano.

Wall, Breck: variety artist and chairman of AGVA. Was contacted by phone by Jack Ruby on the day after the assassination, when he was in Galveston, a few minutes after he had arrived there.

Warren, Earl: Chief Justice of the Supreme Court, and therefore the highest magistrate in the country. Was reluctantly put at the helm of the Commission that took his name. President Johnson left no doubt that Warren was expected to do his patriotic duty, and that the lives of tens of millions of Americans where thereby at stake. But the new President also ensured the Chief Justice that his mission merely involved the ratification of the investigation that was conducted by the FBI.

Williams, Bonnie Ray: TSBD colleague of Oswald. Had his lunch on the sixth floor, and did not hear or see anyone there until, at around a quarter past twelve, he left the floor from which the shots allegedly came.

Zapruder, Abraham: tailor who shot the most famous amateur film in world history, and whose sound business instincts prevented the film from disappearing, as lots of other evidence had.

BIBLIOGRAPHY

Aaronovitch, D. (2010). *Voodoo Histories. How conspiracy theory has shaped modern history*. London: Vintage Books.

Adams, D. (2012). *From an Office Building with a High Powered Rifle*. Waterville Or: Jody Miller / Kindle e-book.

Becker, D. (2011). *The JFK Assassination, a Researcher's Guide*. Bloomington: AuthorHouse.

Belin, D.W. (1988). *Final Disclosure*. New York: McMillan.

Benson, M. (1993). *Who's Who in the JFK Assassination*. New York: Citadel Press Group.

Bishop, J. (1968). *The Day Kennedy was Shot. An uncensored minute by minute account of November 1963*. New York: Funk & Wagnalls.

Blakey, G.R. (n.d.). *Fatal Hour*. New York: Berkley Books.

Brown, W. (1992). *The People v. Lee Harvey Oswald*. New York: Caroll & Graph Publishers.

Brown, W. (1996). *The Warren Omission*. Delmax: Delaware.

Brown, W. (1995). *Treachery in Dallas*. New York: Carroll & Graf Publishers.

Bugliosi, V. (2007). *Reclaiming History*. New York: W.W. Norton & Company Inc.

Buyer, R. (2009). *Why the JFK Assassination Still Matters*. Wheatmark: Tucson Arizona.

Caro, R.R. (1982). *The Years of Lyndon Johnson. Means of Ascent*. New York: The Power Broker.

Chambers, P.G. (2010). *Head Shot. The Science Behind the JFK Assassination*. New York: Amherst.

Christianson, S. (2006). *Bodies of Evidence, Forensic Science and Crime*. Guilford: The Lyons Press.

Ciccone, C. (2012). *Master List of Witnesses to the Assassination of President John F. Kennedy: Dealey Plaza, Dallas, Texas, 22 November 1963*. Privately published.

Connally, N. (2003). *From Love Field. Our Final Hours with President John F. Kennedy*. New York: Ruggedland.

Crenshaw, C. (2001). *Trauma Room One*. New York: Paraview Press.

Cutler, R. (1969). *The flight of CE399*. Manchester, Massachusetts: Omni-Print Beverly Mass.

Cutler, R. (1975). *Crossfire*. Danvers: Betts & Mirror Press.

David, J. (1968). *The Weight of the Evidence. The Warren Report and its Critics*. New York: Meredith Press.

De Bruyn, P. (1998). *8 Seconden in Dallas. Kennedy's Rendez-Vous met de Dood*. Antwerpen: Icarus.

Dicscovery Communications DVD. (2011). *Unsolved History: JFK Conspiracy Myths*.

Douglas, J. (2008). *JFK and the Unspeakable*. New York: Orbis Books Maryknoll.

Dugain, M. (2005). *La Malédiction d'Edgar*. Paris: Gallimar.

Epstein, E.J. (1966). *Inquest*. New York: The Viking Press.

Epstein, E.J. (1978, 2011). *Legend. The Secret World of Lee Harvey Oswald*. New York: EJE Pubication/ Kindle e-book.

Epstein, E.J. (1992). *The Assassination Chronicles: Inquest, Counterplot and Legend*. New York: Caroll & Graff.

Epstein, E.J. (2011). *The JFK Assassination Theories*. Kindle e-book.

Ernest, B. (2010). *The Girl on the Stairs, my search for a missing witness*. Kindle e-book.

Farrell, J.P. (2011). *LBJ and the Conspiracy to Kill Kennedy*. Kempton Illinois: Adventures Unlimited Press.

Fetzer, J.H. (1998). *Assassination Science*. Chicago: Catfeet Press.

Fetzer, J.H. (2000). *Murder in Dealey Plaza*. Chicago: Catfeet Press.

Fonzi, G. (1993). *The Last investigation*. Ipswich: Mary Ferrell Foundation Press.

Ford, G. (1966). *Portrait of The Assassin*. New York: Ballantine Books.

Garrison, J. (1988). *On the Trail of the Assassins.* New York: Sheridan Square Press.

Gibson, D. (2000). *The Kennedy Assassination Cover-up.* New York: Kroshka Books.

Gibson, D. (2005). *Kennedy Assassination Cover-up Revisited.* New York: Novinka Books.

Gilbride, R. (2009). *Matrix for Assassination. The JFK Conspiracy.* Trafford/Kindle e-book.

Gillon, S.M. (2009). *The Kennedy Assassination - 24 Hours After. Lyndon B. Johnson's Pivotal First Day as President.* New York: Basic Books.

Groden, R.J. (1995). *The Search for Lee Harvey Oswald.* New York: Penguin Studio Books.

Hancock, L. (2006). *Someone Would Have Talked.* Southlake Texas: JFK Lancer Productions & Publications.

Harold, W. (1967). *Photographic Whitewash.* Ipswich: Mary Ferrell Foundation Press

Hill, C. (2012). *Mrs. Kennedy and Me.* New York: Gallery Books.

Holland, M. (2004). *The Kennedy Assassination Tapes.* New York: Alfred A. Knopf.

Horne, D. (2009). *Inside the Assassination Records Review Board Vol I.*

Horne, D. (2009). *Inside the Assassination Records Review Board Vol II.*

Horne, D. (2009). *Inside the Assassination Records Review Board Vol V.*

Hosty, J.P. (1996). *Assignment: Oswald.* New York: Arcadia Publishing.

HSCA Appendix Vol I. (n.d.). Washington.

HSCA Appendix Vol I. (1978). Washington.

HSCA Appendix Vol IV. (1978). Washington.

HSCA Appendix Vol VI. (n.d.). Washington.

HSCA Appendix Vol VII. (n.d.). Washington.

HSCA Appendix Vol VIII. (1978). Washington.

HSCA Appendix Vol XI. (1978). Washington.

HSCA Appendix Vol X. (1978). Washington.

HSCA Hearings. (1978). Washington.

HSCA Report. (1978). Washington.

HSCA Report, Vol II. (1978). Washington.

HSCA Vol IX. (1978). *House Select Committee on Assassinations, Vol IX.* Washington.

http://whitehousetapes.net/tapes/johnson/telephone/convs/1963/LBJ_k6311_01a_04_hoover. (1963). *Presidential Recordings Program.* Miller Center of Public Affairs.

Hubbard-Burrell, J. (1992). *What Really Happened? JFK Five Hundred and One Questions & Answers.* Spring Branch Texas: Ponderosa Press.

Hurt, H. (1985). *Reasonable Doubt.* New York: Holt, Rinehart & Winston.

Kelin, J. (2007). *Praise from a Future Generation.* San Antonio Texas: Wings Press.

Kennedy-Bouvier, J. (2011). *Mijn leven met John F. Kennedy. Historische gesprekken met Arthur M. Schlesinger Jr.* Houten-Antwerpen: Spectrum.

Kritzberg, C. (1994). *JFK: Secrets from the Sixth Floor Window.* Tulsa Oklahoma: Consolidated Press International.

Krusch, B. (2012). *Impossible, the case against Lee Harvey Oswald (Vol 1) Location 3114.* Amazon.

Kurtz, M.L. (2006). *The JFK Assassination Debates.* Kansas: University Press.

La Fontaine, R.A. (1997). *Oswald Talked. The New Evidence in the JFK Assassination.* Gretna Louisiana: Pelican Publishing.

Lambert, P. (1998). *False Witness.* New York: M. Evans & Co.

Lane, M. (1966). *Rush to Judgment.* New York: Holt, Rinehart & Winston.

Lane, M. (2011). *My Indictment of the CIA in the Murder of JFK.* New York: Skyhorse Publishing.

Lane, M. (1968). *A Citizen's Dissent.* New York: Holt Rinehart & Winston.

Leaming, B. (2006). *Jack Kennedy. The Making of a President.* London: Orion Publishing Group.

Les Dossier des Grands Mystères de l'Histoire. (2003). *Le Mythe JFK. Commission Warren Le Rapport Truqué.*

Levine, R. (1993, 2001). *The Secret of the Century.* Smashwords Editions/Kindle e-book.

Life Magazine, 24 november 1966. (1966). 'A matter of Reasonable Doubt'. New York: Life, Time Inc.

Lifton, D. (1980). *Best Evidence.* Middlesex UK: Penguin Books.

Livingstone, H. (2006). *The Radical Right And The Murder Of John F. Kennedy.* Bloomington: Trafford Publishing.

Mallon, T. (2002). *Mrs. Paine's Garage.* New York: Pantheon books.

Manchester, W. (1967). *De Dood van een President.* Utrecht/Antwerpen: A.W. Bruna & Zoon.

Martin, O. (2010). *JFK Analysis of a Shooting. The Ultimate Ballistics Exposed.* Indianapolis: Dogear.

Mason, A.M. (2002). *The Magic Bullet: A Legal-Scientific Analysis of the Warren Commission's Single Bullet.* Saskatoon, Canada: Mason Andrew.

Matthews, C. (2012). *Jack Kennedy. Elusive Hero.* New York: Simon & Schuster/Kindle E-book.

May Ernest R. & Zelikow, P.D. (1997). *The Kennedy Tapes.* Cambridge Massachussetts: Belknap Press.

McAdams, J. (2011). *JFK Assassination Logic. How to Think About Claims of Conspiracy.* Dulles, Virginia: Potomac Books.

McClellan, B. (2003). *Blood, Money & Power.* New York: Hannover House.

McElwain-Brown, P. (2008). *Inside the Target Car.* Discovery Channel.

McKnight, G.D. (2005). *Breach of Trust.* Kansas: University Press of Kansas.

Meagher, S. (1967). *Accessories after the Fact.* Ipswich: Mary Ferrell Foundation Press.

Mellen, J. (2005). *A Farewell to Justice.* Washington D.C.: Potomac Books.

Menninger, B. (1992). *Mortal Error. The Shot that Killed Kennedy.* New York: St Martin's Press.

Moldea, D.E. (1978). *The Hoffa Wars.* New York: S.P.I. Books.

Moore, J. (1991). *Conspiracy of One.* Forth Worth Texas: The Summit Group.

Myers, D. (2007). *Secrets of a Homicide. Epipolar Geometric Analysis of Amateur Films Related to Acoustics Evidence in the John F. Kennedy Assassination.* www.jfkfiles.com.

Nelson, P.F. (2011). *LBJ The Mastermind of the JFK Assassination.* New York: Skyhorse Publishing.

North, M. (2011). *Act of Treason.* New York: Skyhorse Publishing.

Noyes, P. (1973). *Legacy of Doubt.* New York: Pinnacle.

O'Neill, T. (1987). *Man of The House.* New York: Random House.

O'Reilly, B. (2012). *Killing Kennedy.* New York: Henry Holt & Co.

Phillips, D.T. (2009). *A Deeper, Darker Truth. Tom Wilson's Journey into the Assassination of John F. Kennedy.* Illinois: DTP Companion Books.

Posner, G. (1993, 2003). *Case Closed.* New York: Anchor Books.

Prouty, F.L. (2011). *JFK. The CIA, Vietnam and the Plot to Assassinate John F. Kennedy.* New York: Skyhorse Publishing.

Reid, E. (1969). *The Grim Reapers.* Chicago: Henry Regnery.

Rem, E.P. (1992). *JFK Assassination Rifle Shots Phenomenon Exploded.* Washington: T.B.I. Publishing Co.

Rinnovatore, J.V. (2012). *Aftermath of the JFK Assassination Parkland Hospital to the Bethesda Morgue.* New York: Arje Books/Kindle e-book.

Russell, D. (2008). *On the Trail of the Assassins.* New York: Skyhorse Publishing.

Salandria, V. (1965). *The Warren Report?* Philadelphia: Liberation.

Salandria, V. (2004). *False Mystery. Essays on the Assassination of JFK.* Louisville Colorado: Square Deal Press.

Salandria, V. (1966). *The Impossible Tasks of One Assassination Bullet.* Philadelphia: Minority of one.

Savage, G. (1993). *JFK First Day Evidence.* Monroe Louisiana: The Shoppe Press.

Scheim, D.E. (1988). *The Maffia Killed President Kennedy.* London: W.H. Allen.

Shaw, G. (1976). *Cover Up.* Cleburne, TX: Privately published.

Shesol, J. (1997). *Mutual Contempt. Lyndon Johnson, Robert Kennedy and the Feud that Defined a Decade.* New York: W.W. Norton & Cy.

Sloan, B. (1993-2012). *Breaking The Silence (Revised 2012) The Kennedy Conspiracy: 12 Startling Revelations About the JFK Assassination.* Taylor Publishing/Kindle e-book.

Sloan, B.W. (1992). *JFK The Last Dissenting Witness.* Gretna: Pelican Publishing Co.

Smith, M.E. (1968). *Kennedy's 13 Great Mistakes in the White House.* New York: National Forum.

Sneed, L.A. (1998). *No More Silence.* Dallas: Three Forks Press.

Sturdivan, L. (2003). *The JFK Myths. The Evidence Speaks Loudly.* St Paul MN: Paragon House.

Summers, A. (1993). *Official and Confidential. The Secret Life of J. Edgar Hoover.* New York: G.P. Putnam's Sons.

Summers, A. (1998). *Not in Your Lifetime.* New York: Marlowe & Co.

Summers, A. (1980). *Conspiracy.* Columbus: McGraw-Hill.

Swearingen, M.W. (2008). *To Kill a President. Finally – an Ex-FBI Agent Rips Aside the Veil of Secrecy that Killed JFK.* Charleston: BookSurge.

Talbot, D. (2007). *Brothers. The Hidden History of the Kennedy Years.* New York: Free Press.

Trask, R.B. (1994). *Pictures of the Pain.* Danvers Massachusetts: Yeoman Press.

Trask, R.B. (2005). *National Nightmare.* Danvers, Massachussets: Yeoman Press.

Twyman, N. (1997 e-book). *Bloody Treason. The Assassination of John F. Kennedy.* New York: Laurel Publishing.

Twyman, N. (2000). *Illusion and Denial in the John F. Kennedy Assassination.* Laurel Mystery Books/Kindle e-book.

Twyman, N. (2010). *Bloody Treason. The Assassination of John F. Kennedy.* Laurel Mystery Books/Kindle e-book.

United Press International. (1964). *Four Days.* American Heritage Publishing Co.

Vermeulen, P. (2008). *Lee Harvey Oswald. Via Rotterdam naar Dallas. De Moord op JFK.* Eindhoven: de Boekenmakers.

Waldron, L. (2009). *Legacy of Secrecy. The Long Shadow of the JFK Assassination.* Berkeley: Counterpoint.

Warren Commission Hearings and Exhibits Vol I. (1964). Washington.

Warren Commission Hearings and Exhibits Vol II. (1964). Washington.

Warren Commission Hearings and Exhibits Vol III. (1964). Washington.

Warren Commission Hearings and Exhibits Vol IV. (1964). Washington.

Warren Commission Hearings and Exhibits Vol V. (1964). Washington.

Warren Commission Hearings and Exhibits Vol VI. (1964). Washington.

Warren Commission Hearings and Exhibits Vol VII. (1964). Washington.

Warren Commission Hearings and Exhibits Vol IX. (1964). Washington.

Warren Commission Hearings and Exhibits Vol X. (1964). Washington.

Warren Commission Hearings and Exhibits Vol XI. (1964). Washington.

Warren Commission Hearings and Exhibits Vol XIV. (1964). Washington.

Warren Commission Hearings and Exhibits Vol XV. (1964). Washington.

Warren Commission Hearings and Exhibits Vol XVI. (1964). Washington.

Warren Commission Hearings and Exhibits Vol XVII. (1964). Washington.

Warren Commission Hearings and Exhibits Vol XVIII. (1964). Washington.

Warren Commission Hearings and Exhibits Vol XIX. (1964). Washington.

Warren Commission Hearings and Exhibits Vol XX. (1964). Washington.

Warren Commission Hearings and Exhibits Vol XXI. (1964). Washington.

Warren Commission Hearings and Exhibits Vol XXII. (1964). Washington.

Warren Commission Hearings and Exhibits Vol XXIII. (1964). Washington.

Warren Commission Hearings and Exhibits Vol XXIV. (1964). Washington.

Warren Commission Hearings and Exhibits, Vol XXV. (1964). Washington.

Warren Commission Hearings and Exhibits Vol XXVI. (1964). Washington.

Warren Commission Report. (1964). Washington.

Weisberg, H. (1965). Whitewash. *The Report on the Warren Report.* Ipswich: Mary Ferrell Foundation.

Weisberg, H. (1966). Whitewash. Hyattstown, Md.: Privately published.

Weisberg, H. (1966). Whitewash II. Ipswich: Mary Ferrell Foundation Press.

Weisberg, H. (1969). Post Mortem. *JFK Assassination Cover-up Smashed.* Ipswich: Mary Ferrell Foundation.

Wills, C. (2009). Jack Kennedy, The IIlustrated Life of a President. Bellevu: Becker & Mayer.

Zirbel, C. (2010). *The Final Chapter on the JFK Assassination.* Kindle e-book.

INDEX

ACKNOWLEDGEMENT

I would like to thank the members of the reading committee: the very critical Fred Schalckens, Roger Delahaut, Benedicte Dirven – always *to the point*
– my sharp-witted neighbor Karin Van Acker, my good childhood friend
and language lover Flip Feyten, Louis Van Dievel, Wouter Verschelden and
above all, Fons Van den Maegdenbergh. The encouragement I received
from Fons –who works as author, cosmopolitan and photographer under
the name Fons Montevirgenes – was the decisive boost to start me off on
the tricky journey of this book. The advice of the reading committee was
taken to heart – and they were always right. Their suggestions made an important contribution to the final version of the book. Rien de Mey devoted
herself to the thankless task of proofreading the first version, following
which Ineke Vander Vekens of Linguine ensured the editing of the text.
Peter Frans Anthonissen was my indispensible advisor when it came to the
difficult transition of turning the manuscript into a book. Top photographers Annelies de Mey and Annemie Augustijns took care of the author's
photo. Maarten van Steenbergen and Judith Van Doorselaer were there for
me, from the first to the last minute, and kept the reputation of Lannoo
Publishers, the original Belgian publisher of this book, in high esteem.
Salika Tourlouse of Home Office orchestrated the translation of the book.

My special thanks goes to the Mary Ferrell Foundation (www.maryfer-
rell.org), which makes a huge amount of evidence and documentation online available on its excellent website, together with a very useful search
engine. I also owe thanks to acclaimed author and JFK expert Walt Brown.
He made the photographs available from the Fox dossier, which is his
property.

My family and relatives should, of course, not be forgotten - especially
the young generation Lotte, Maks, Philippe and Alynne, and my friends,
colleagues and partners who all showed a great deal of patience and understanding for my investment in this time-consuming project. Martine's
love and support was already mentioned in the dedication at the beginning
of this book. She was with me from the start to the finish, and, in this final
word, she gets an extra kiss.

Finally, I would like to thank Jack and Bobby Kennedy for their courage, their optimism, their vision and fighting spirit. Ted Kennedy was right: '*The work goes on, the cause endures, the hope still lives, and the dream shall never die.*' The victory of the assassins was, at best, a temporary one.

Flip de Mey

Illustration credits

Still images from the Zapruder film, illustrations 57, 61, 62, 63 and 87 are included with the consent of the copyright proprietor, The Sixth Floor Museum.

Illustrations 16 left, 22, 23, 24, 26, 27 left, 27 center, 27 right, 28 left, 28 right are the property of the Dallas Municipal Archives (http://texashistory.unt.edu/) and are included with the consent of the proprietor.

Illustrations 13, 15, 18, 21 left, 26 left, 32, 34, 36, 37, 43 left, 43 right, 45, 47, 60, 83, 84, 85, 93, 94, 101 and 103 are evidence that the Warren Commission added to its report in the Hearings and Exhibitions volumes, and are included with the consent of the NARA. Illustrations 16 right, 17, 33 left and 41 are part of the Warren Commission Documents, and are in the public domain.

Illustrations 5, 6, 19, 21 right, 35, 53 left, 53 right, 55 left, 55 right, 59 left, 59 right, 64 and 82 are evidence that the House Select Committee on Assassinations added to its report in the Appendix Volumes, and are included with the consent of the NARA.

Illustrations 39, 40, 42 and 50 are evidence from the ARRB dossier, and are included with the consent of the NARA.

Illustrations 3, 10, 11, 12, 22, 30, 31, 48, 73, 102 are documents that were created by persons in the public service in the performance of their duties. NARA informed us that documents created under those circumstances are part of the public domain and may be included in publications.

Illustration 2 is included courtesy of Google Maps.

Illustration 14 is included courtesy of the NASA Space Center.

Illustration 20 is included courtesy of Gil Jesus.

Illustration 29 is included courtesy of Ford Motor Company.

Illustration 70 is included courtesy of Robert Croft; illustration 90 is included courtesy of William Allen. For both photographs, our thanks go to Robin Unger's JFK Assassination Research Photo Galleries.

Illustration 92 is included courtesy of Marilyn Sitman.

Illustration 100 is included courtesy of Malcolm Couch.

We would like to thank all archives, foundations and institutes that have provided pictures for this book. The publisher and author have made every effort to trace all copyright holders of the illustrations printed in this book. If they have not fully succeeded in this, the proprietor of the image rights in question will be included in subsequent editions.

Design: Studio Lannoo

Inside: Wim De Dobbeleer

Translation: Home Office Translations

Cover image: © Bettmann/CORBIS

Published by: © Flip de Mey, 2013

D/2013/45/466 - NUR697/686

ISBN 978 94 014 1396 1